PUBLIC SERVANT, SECRET AGENT

Also by Paul Routledge

Scargill: The Unauthorised Biography
Madam Speaker: The life of Betty Boothroyd
John Hume: A Biography
Gordon Brown: The Biography
Mandy: The Unauthorised Biography of Peter Mandelson

PUBLIC SERVANT, SECRET AGENT

The Elusive Life and Violent Death

of Airey Neave

Paul Routledge

FOURTH ESTATE • *London*

First published in Great Britain in 2002 by
Fourth Estate
A Division of HarperCollins *Publishers*
77–85 Fulham Palace Road,
London w6 8jb
www.4thestate.com

Copyright © Paul Routledge 2002

10 9 8 7 6 5 4 3 2 1

The right of Paul Routledge to be identified as the author
of this work has been asserted by him in accordance with
the Copyright, Designs and Patents Act 1988.

A catalogue record for this book is available from
the British Library.

ISBN 1-84115-244-7

Typeset by Avon Dataset Ltd,
Bidford on Avon B50 4JH
Printed and bound in Great Britain by
Clays Ltd St. Ives plc

Contents

Preface

A gun lay unobtrusively on the settee beside my polite host, and the heavily-built man sitting on an armchair in the corner wore a tight-fitting black mask with tiny holes for his eyes and mouth. He was on edge and there was a tension in the room. I had come a long way, physically and in time, to see the killers of Airey Neave, and here I was, face to face. Not with the men who planted the bomb on 30 March 1979, almost twenty-two years ago to the day, but with 'someone connected with the Neave operation' who belonged to the small but highly dangerous Irish National Liberation Army.

The trail started five years earlier, when I was writing a biography of John Hume, leader of the SDLP, a shrewd nationalist and a rock for thirty years in the maelstrom of Irish – and British – politics. Hume crossed paths with Neave, the Conservatives' Shadow Northern Ireland Secretary, many times during the late 1970s. It was not a profitable relationship. Hume found Neave's traditional Tory attitudes towards Ulster Unionism and his militarist stance on the Troubles short-sighted and unsophisticated. Neave probably thought the former trainee priest slippery and threatening. He had, after all, engineered the short-lived exercise in political power-sharing that the Tory spokesman on Ulster utterly rejected.

Neave's impact on policy towards Northern Ireland during the four years he held the Shadow portfolio was limited, but his death at the hands of terrorist assassins in the precincts of the House of

Commons convulsed politics and prompted the question in my mind: 'Who was this man?' There was no biography of Airey Neave, yet he had lived an eventful life. Eton, Oxford and the Inns of Court were followed by capture in the siege of Calais, prison camps, escape from Colditz and service in military intelligence. He had served the indictments on Nazi war criminals in Nuremberg and entered Parliament at his third attempt in a by-election. A promising ministerial career was cut short by a heart attack, and he seemed destined to live out his political career in back-bench obscurity until the social upheavals of the 1970s propelled him into history as the man who gave us Margaret Thatcher.

It was a remarkable story, but no one had written it. I therefore resolved to do so and began collecting material. It was clear from the outset that Neave's family (his daughter Marigold and two sons, Patrick and William) were apprehensive about the project. Neave had not wanted a biography, beyond the books he had written about his life, nor did his widow, Diana, who died in 1992. Other approaches, I knew, had been rebuffed and I was hardly the writer of choice. Yet I persisted and the family finally agreed to cooperate, though not on a lavish scale.

Much more difficult was 'the other side' – the perpetrators of the murder. Over the years reporting from Ulster, through a republican contact I will not name, I had learned something of the Irish Republican Socialist Party, the political wing of INLA. After an initial social meeting in a Belfast bar, at which I outlined my intentions, I let the seeds germinate. Then, in the autumn of 2000, I approached the IRSP directly, and arranged to visit the party's headquarters in the Falls Road, the heart of republican Belfast. The taxi driver who took me there on 17 November advised against going into the pub opposite. 'Not with your accent [Yorkshire],' he grinned. Seamus Costello House, a large red-brick villa (allegedly bought with the proceeds of a bank robbery) is protected by steel mesh fortifications. A photographic tableau of the dead hunger strikers stands outside. Inside, the atmosphere is more homely, reminiscent of an old-fashioned trade union branch office, with people asking for advice and children playing about their mothers' knees. Banners and framed slogans decorate the walls. The furniture is utilitarian. Everyone smokes.

Paul Lyttle, the IRSP's spokesman, listened courteously to my pitch. It was clear from the first that my credentials had already been thoroughly checked. They knew who I was and where I was coming from before I opened my mouth. So, indeed, did the security services. This visit was known in London before I returned the following day. I told Lyttle that I wanted to write an account of Neave's death that was as authentic as possible. To that end, I wished to meet the killers, if possible; and if that could not be arranged, then to talk to INLA 'volunteers' involved in the operation. There had been many accounts of the assassination, mostly conflicting. Was it not now time for the truth?

The door seemed to be ajar. The IRSP man dwelt on the dangers that Neave presented to militant republicanism, being one of the few British politicians who (as an ex-POW) knew just how critical was the morale and organisation of 'the men behind the wire'. However, those men had virtually all been released under the Good Friday Agreement of 1998, and yes, the organisation might be willing to brief me. A decision would have to be taken by 'the executive', and this process would take some time. It was also plain that the IRSP/INLA felt that the assassinations of four of their top people in the aftermath of Neave's death should receive the same kind of public scrutiny currently being given by the Savile Enquiry to the killings on Bloody Sunday in Londonderry in January 1972. I said I had no difficulty in understanding their desire to get to the bottom of these high-profile murders, which were widely laid at the feet of the security services working through loyalist proxies. And I would say as much, though I fear the party's demands for a similar public enquiry will fall on deaf ears.

Weeks passed, and after Christmas I wrote again to the IRSP, pointing out my approaching deadline for completion of the book.

I also telephoned regularly, not a simple procedure. Seamus Costello House is not Millbank or Central Office. Finally, I was given a number to contact in the Irish Republic. It was a mobile, not reachable from London. Further frustrating delays followed before I got through to a man I will refer to as Eoin. He told me to go to Belfast on the weekend of 24 March, and get in touch again on Friday 23rd. On Thursday, I received a message to call him again, and was redirected to Cork, hundreds of miles to the south in the Republic. It was too late to book a direct flight, so I continued via Belfast on the 23rd. Foot and mouth disease had just broken out in County Louth, slowing the train journey to Dublin, but I reached Cork in the early evening.

My instructions were to book into the Silver Springs Hotel, a modern establishment a few miles south of the city, and to await a call the following day. It was a bright, clear morning and the telephone rang at 9.30 a.m. I was to take a taxi to a country pub about five miles away, where I would be met. I waited in the lobby, self-consciously British in a dark suit and university tie. Just after 10.00 a.m., two men entered and motioned me into the bar. One was young, in his twenties, powerfully-built and dressed in waxed jacket and jeans. The other was much older, with white hair. Waxed-jacket said: 'We will take you in the car. You will not look at the number plate. You will look down at the floor, not where we are going. Understand?' I did. He then asked if I had a mobile phone, and I fished mine from a travel bag thinking he wished to use it. He confiscated the instrument.

Outside, he stood guard so I could not see the number plate. The older man drove, through various country lanes. It was difficult to obey the injunction to stare at the floor, but since I had no idea where we were it seemed superfluous anyway. We stopped outside an isolated house, quite high up, with hills around. I was escorted into the front room, where the thick curtains were drawn. Eoin, now that I saw him, looked like a schoolteacher in his late thirties: neat, spare and casually but well dressed. He introduced the man in the mask as 'someone directly involved in the Neave operation'. I asked if I could take a shorthand note and he nodded. 'You're not wired?' he interjected suddenly. 'Open your shirt.' I unbuttoned my shirt to the waist to show there was no hidden microphone. He frisked me, arms, back, front and legs. The tension eased somewhat, though I then spotted the handgun next to him. Had I done anything silly, I think it would have been used.

However, coffee and biscuits were served, as though we were discussing details of the Easter holidays rather than the brutal murder of a British politician two decades earlier. We spoke for two and a half hours, a mixture of questions and volunteered statements. The man in the mask, who displayed a very detailed knowledge of bomb-making and the *modus operandi* of the assassination, occasionally tugged at his uncomfortable camouflage. Eoin, the more intellectual of the two, ranged across the whole subject of INLA, the armed struggle and prospects for the future. It was a fascinating, if eerie, dialogue. What follows in Chapter 18 is a distillation of that briefing. I believe it to be the most authentic account yet of the circumstances of Airey Neave's death. I expect that others may contest this assessment, but I am convinced that the IRSP/INLA deliberately gave this briefing to ensure that the truth is established, not least because they want the truth about the killing of their own.

At the close of the meeting, my mobile phone was returned, with the SIM card disabled so I could not be traced. The white-haired driver took me to a shopping centre, where I took a taxi back into Cork city to take the train to Dublin and Belfast. I drank a pint of Guinness at the station and pondered my experience. Instead of a reporter's elation at finding my quarry, I felt a curious unease, as though I had discovered something I would rather not have known. Yet there was no going back, and I turned for home with a determination to get all this out. I hope the succeeding pages will demonstrate the virtue of seeking the truth, unpalatable though it may be. The Irish Question is never going to be solved by meek acceptance of the official line.

It should be added that this biography is not authorised, nor did I seek authorisation. Neave had written much about his own life, but his widow Diana rejected writers' advances to sanction a biography of her husband. Patrick Cosgrave, a family friend, said she had asked him 'to spread the word among the writing classes that she would, in no circumstances, countenance such a project'. Plainly, we do not move among the same writing classes because no such word reached these quarters.

However, I was able to speak to Neave's children, Marigold, Patrick and William, for which I am grateful. I would also like to thank his cousin Julius Neave, of Mill Green House, Ingatestone. My gratitude also goes to Toni Luteyn, Neave's co-escaper from Colditz, still alive and well in The Hague; to Frau Lipmann, curator of Colditz Museum; to the dedicated staff at the unrivalled political history collection at the Linen Hall Library for their help and advice; to the librarians at Eton College and Merton College, Oxford; to my colleagues in Westminster, especially Desmond McCartan, formerly of the *Belfast Telegraph* and David Healy of Bloomberg Agency; to Colin Wallace, Brian Crozier, Gerald James, Michael Elliott, Kevin Cahill, Roger Bolton, Richard Dumbreck, Sir Edward du Cann, Sir William Shelton, Tam Dalyell, Lord Lawton, Lord Campbell of Alloway, Ken Lockwood of the Colditz Association, Steven Norris, Kevin Macnamara MP, and those in London and Belfast who would be embarrassed (or worse) if identified; to Clive Priddle, Mitzi Angel and Kate Balmforth at Fourth Estate for their patience, and Richard Collins for his professional copy-editing; to my agent Jane Bradish-Ellames and finally to my wife Lynne for living with a political murder for too many years.

Walworth, south London
November 2001

I

The Price of Liberty

At 2.58 p.m. on 30 March 1979 an enormous explosion shook New Palace Yard in the precincts of the Palace of Westminster. Seconds later, smoke was seen billowing from the wreckage of a saloon car on the ramp leading up from the MPs' car park into the cobbled courtyard just below Big Ben.

The blast was heard in the Commons chamber, where parliament was about to be dissolved for a General Election that would sweep Margaret Thatcher into Downing Street. Policemen and parliamentary journalists rushed to the scene and found an unidentifiable man, dressed in the black coat and striped trousers of an old-fashioned style still worn by Conservative MPs. David Healy, political correspondent of the Press Association news agency, was in the third-floor Press Gallery bar, whose back windows look down on New Palace Yard. A veteran reporter of the Irish Troubles, Healy recognised the familiar noise. 'I knew it was a bomb,' he said. 'I looked out of the window and saw smoke, and rushed downstairs. The car was burning, the windows all broken. And this guy was almost blown into a standing position behind the wheel. A cop shouted, "He's still alive! Clear the area!" I didn't think there was much life left in him. I couldn't tell who it was, though I had been having a drink with him only two nights earlier.'[1] Another Westminster lobby correspondent, Desmond McCartan of the *Belfast Telegraph*, who knew the victim well, wrote: 'The blackened, bleeding features amid the tangled wreckage of his

Vauxhall car concealed his identity, but the pain of his dying was clear.'[2]

Ambulancemen who arrived within minutes found the still unidentified figure slumped over the driving wheel, his face blackened, his hair and clothing charred from the blast. His right leg was blown off below the knee, and his left leg was almost completely severed. One ambulanceman, Brian Craggs, tried to give him oxygen: 'He was still breathing, but was very badly injured. He never regained consciousness.' A doctor and nurse also attended, before he was freed after half an hour of frantic effort by firefighters.

Others had also recognised the noise. In Margaret Thatcher's office, Chris Patten, a future Northern Ireland minister, exclaimed 'That was a bomb!' Thatcher's entourage witnessed the grim scene from an upstairs window and Guinevere Tilney, wife of a former Tory MP and adviser to the Conservative leader, was the first to discover the identity of the victim. In the car, dying, lay Airey Neave, Conservative MP for Abingdon, war hero and *habitué* of the murky world where the politics of democracy and the secret state intertwine, the man who had engineered Margaret Thatcher's rise to power. Mrs Tilney immediately went to the Neave family flat in Marsham Street to tell his wife Diana, and took her to Westminster Hospital where Neave was undergoing emergency surgery. The surgeons could do little. His heart stopped on the operating table and he died eight minutes after arriving at the hospital. His devoted wife was too late to see him alive.

It was a bloody end to a long career in public life, one marked in turn by disappointment and triumph ultimately crowned by Neave's brilliant campaign to secure the Conservative Party leadership for Margaret Thatcher, an event that would radically change British – and international – politics. For his key role in that crusade, Neave was rewarded with the Shadow Cabinet portfolio that he coveted: Northern Ireland. It was a strange post to covet. Ulster has traditionally been regarded by pundits as a graveyard for political ambition, and Neave was fifty-nine when he took on the job in February 1975, having hitherto shown no serious public interest in the issue.

Nor did Neave look the part. Usually described as a slightly-built, red-faced man, with thinning hair, sharp features and a broad smile that rarely gave way to laughter, he moved with an almost feline grace, seeming to drift along rather than walk. He listened much, said little and when he did speak, he did so quietly. At a party given by Alan Clark, Thatcherite minister and diarist, George Gardiner, a right-wing Tory MP of the 1974 intake, listened to Neave 'gently sounding out opinions in a voice you had to strain to hear'. Ian Aitken, political editor of the *Guardian*, found him 'slightly sinister'. He was not particularly clubbable at Westminster though he was a member of the Special Services Club, tucked away in a side street behind Harrods where former and serving 'spooks' debated the follies of the world over cocktails.

The Troubles had been in full spate for several years by the time of his appointment, and showed no sign of abating. Shootings and bombings in the province were commonplace, and by taking Shadow Cabinet responsibility for British government policy he placed himself in the front line. It was almost as if the decorated war hero was inviting the bomb that prematurely ended his life. He told the journalist Patrick Cosgrave: 'If they come for me, the one thing we can be sure of is that they will not face me. They're not soldier enough for that.'[3] His parliamentary agent Les Brown also claimed that Neave always knew he was on a death list, but realised it went with the territory. The writer Rebecca West had many years previously observed: 'It is, I think, against his principles to care much about danger.'

Margaret Thatcher had no doubt that Neave was the right man for the job. 'His intelligence contacts, proven physical courage and shrewdness amply qualified him for this testing and largely thankless task,' she calculated.[4] Her choice of priorities in this assessment is illuminating. She thought of him first as an expert in the field of military intelligence and only then as a man of nerve and astuteness. She did not immediately identify him as a politician with an agenda for bringing peace to the benighted province, where more than 247 people had died in the first year he was responsible for Opposition policy on Ulster. Her judgement was shared by Sir John Tilney, author of Neave's entry in *The Dictionary of National Biography*. Working from 'private information', Tilney pointedly describes Neave as an 'intelligence officer and politician'.

That Thatcher and Tilney should independently have come to the same conclusion should surprise no one, for Airey Neave was an intelligence officer who became a public servant. Like many who have trodden the same path, he did not slough off his first persona when he entered public life. The values of what has become known as 'the secret state', as well as the lessons of his wartime experiences, informed his outlook as a politician. He had many contacts among former security service officers and high-ranking army officers, and sympathised with the aims of the ultra-right groups that prepared for 'civil breakdown' in the 1970s. He was a public servant who never really stopped being a secret agent.

Neave's background helped. His was a conformist, upper middle-class upbringing – prep school, Eton and Oxford, with a career at the Bar beckoning as the Second World War broke out. The son of a prominent entomologist and scion of an Essex county family whose lineage stretched back several hundred years (and included a Governor of the Bank of England), it was only to be expected that he would possess a relatively orthodox outlook on life. In Neave's case, that sense of being British and right so endemic in his class was reinforced in his mid-teens when he was sent to Germany in 1933 to live with a local family and learn the language. He saw Fascism in practice, and formed a lifelong antipathy, amounting to an obsession, towards authoritarianism. Some of that feeling came from his pre-war and wartime adventures and filtered through a pessimistic fear of the spread of Communism that would harden during the Cold War and the civil unrest in Britain.

His initial links with the military were conventional enough, beginning when he enlisted in the Territorial Army as an undergraduate at Merton College. If Neave was swimming against the prevailing intellectual tide of leftism at university. His interest in the secretive world of Tory clubland politics also began at this period. He was a member of the Castlereagh Club, a political dining club that met in St James's, Piccadilly, usually once a fortnight, to hear the views of a Tory dignitary. Donald Hamilton-Hill, later second in command of Special Operations Executive (SOE), the wartime resistance organisation, was also a member. In pre-war days he was chairman of public relations and head of recruiting for the Young Conservatives' Union, and shared with Neave a predilection for the social contacts which ultimately led them into 'politically informative circles'. Confidentiality, if not mystery, was the order of the day. Hamilton-Hill recorded that members of the Castlereagh Club held 'off the record and interesting discussions – with no reporters present and members sworn to secrecy'. After a 'splendid dinner' they formed an easy and appreciative friendship over port, brandy and cigars.[5] For the young Neave, it was heady and exciting stuff, and plainly a taste for secrecy and subterfuge was being acquired early. One of their mentors was Ronnie Cartland, a Tory MP who would be killed at Dunkirk; Peter Wilkinson, who went on to General de Wiart's staff of the British Military Mission to Poland in 1939, was also a member. He later became Chief of Administration of the Diplomatic Service, and retired in 1976 as Coordinator of Intelligence and Security in the Cabinet Office. Val Duncan, subsequently knighted and chairman of the Rio Tinto Zinc Corporation, was also to be found at the Castlereagh table. In the late sixties, he would head an enquiry into the Foreign Office at Wilkinson's behest.

Quite why the enthusiastic diners chose an Irish grandee as the club's eponymous hero is unclear, but in Neave's case it was prophetic. Robert Stewart, Viscount Castlereagh, was born in Dublin in 1769 and became Tory MP for County Down at the end of the eighteenth century. He was appointed Irish Secretary in 1797 and his name became a byword for cruelty, although he was venerated as a great British statesman. In 'The Mask of Anarchy' of 1819, Shelley was prompted to write: 'I met Murder on the Way / He had a mask like Castlereagh'. Almost two hundred years later, his name was remembered in the British government's Castlereagh interrogation centre in Belfast, itself the subject of an enquiry into Royal Ulster Constabulary brutality during Neave's time as Shadow Northern Ireland Secretary. Thus was Neave drawn early on into the demi-monde of clubland, where politics meets the secret state. Security and intelligence expert Stephen Dorril argues its relevance: 'This is the key to the way these people operate. Their dining clubs go on for a long time. They are the networks of political power and advancement. They bring all the elements of the secret state together.'[6]

When the war rudely interrupted this agreeable scene, Neave was among the first to volunteer for active service. His experiences at Calais in 1940, his subsequent capture and imprisonment by the Germans, followed by escape from Colditz in 1942, brought him to the attention of British military intelligence on his arrival in neutral Switzerland, whence he was fast-tracked back to Britain and immediately recruited to MI9, the escape and evasion organisation for Allied servicemen. Nominally an independent section of the war effort, MI9 was in fact – and much to Neave's delight – a wholly-owned subsidiary of MI6, the Secret Intelligence Service.

Neave worked in this clandestine operation for three years, training agents to be sent into the escape 'ratlines' of Occupied Europe and debriefing escapers before following hard on the heels of the invading Allies in July 1944. His service also took him to forward engagement areas in France, Belgium and Holland, where he successfully spirited out remnants of Operation Market Garden, the abortive Arnhem raid. He ended the war a DSO and an MC. The closing stages of the war found Neave in Paris and Brussels in 1944 running British operations to grant awards and medals to MI9 agents who had helped

Allied servicemen to escape or evade the enemy. Such operations had a further, undisclosed objective: that of identifying agents who would continue to be valuable after the war in the context of a Cold War (or worse) between Western nations and the Soviet Union. The bureaux drew up lists of 'reliable' contacts who would be useful in the event of a Soviet invasion of Western Europe. It was sensitive work, not least because so many of the Resistance were Communists and at this stage still sympathetic to the Soviet Union.

This covert enterprise, known as Operation Gladio, brought together a wide range of skills, from those involving psychological warfare and sabotage to escape and evasion. Gladio's purpose was to set up 'stay-behind' units that would be active in a Europe threatened or even occupied by the USSR. Their existence has never been officially recognised, nor disclosed. Stephen Dorril argues: 'It appears that sections of MI6 were already thinking in terms of the next war, and part of that was a fear that the Red Army would continue from Berlin and go straight to the Channel coast. They wanted stay-behind units against the Red Army in the same way that they wanted them against the Germans. Some of these units put in place in 1944 were almost immediately being resurrected as anti-Communist units – ratlines for escape and evasion.'[7] SOE would take on the sabotage role, while Neave's old firm would carry on as before.

But in post-war austere Britain the climate was against such initiatives: money for secret operations was getting tight and it was difficult to sustain a continuity between wartime and post-war groups. The Labour Prime Minister Clement Attlee disapproved of such activities and the emphasis shifted from formal policy to the unofficial but well-connected world of former intelligence operatives. The thread continued in dining clubs, the Special Services Club and in the part-time Territorial Army. MI9 was reborn as Intelligence School 9 (TA) and Neave was commanding officer from 1949 to 1951, at a time when he was seeking to enter public life as a Conservative MP. IS9 later became

23 SAS Regiment, based in the Midlands, with a role to counter domestic subversion.

While his political career blossomed in the late 1950s, Neave's links with the secret state necessarily became more obscure. It is known that sometime in 1955, he approved the appointment of British spy Greville Wynne as the representative in Eastern Europe of the pressure-vessel manufacturers John Thompson, of which Neave was a director. Like Neave, Wynne had worked for MI6 during the war. He returned to spying in the mid fifties and used his business trips behind the Iron Curtain to recruit the Soviet spymaster Oleg Penkovsky, before being unmasked and jailed. He was freed in exchange for Russian agent Gordon Consdale. Wynne confessed that 'after a time, espionage is like a drug, you become to a greater or lesser extent addicted.' It is inconceivable that Neave was unaware of Wynne's MI6 role. Neave continued to meet with his old comrades, and to harbour fears of Communist subversion, but to the world at large he was a quiet, thoughtful man, assumed by commentators to be on the centre-left of his party. After his relatively brief, and not very glorious, ministerial career at the Transport and Air departments, he returned to the back benches in 1959. From there he campaigned successfully for compensation for British survivors of Sachsenhausen concentration camp, but unsuccessfully for the release from Spandau prison of Nazi war criminal Rudolf Hess, whose flight to Scotland in May 1941 had delivered him into British hands. He sought to assuage the suffering of refugees through his voluntary work for the UN High Commission for Refugees. In addition, he became a governor of Imperial College, London, and chairman of the Commons Select Committee on Science and Technology.

But behind the façade there still burned a sense of mission. He watched with apprehension the collectivist drift of Britain and the growing power of the trade unions. He believed the danger of expansionist Communism was both real and present and he believed fiercely in freedom. In the record of his wartime exploits, *They Have Their Exits*, he laid down his credo, 'No one who has not known the pain of imprisonment understands the meaning of liberty', a line that is engraved on the walls of the museum in Colditz castle as a testament to his dedication. The title of Neave's book was taken from *As You Like It*: 'All the world's a stage/And all the men and women merely players; / They have their exits and their entrances; / And one man in his time plays many parts.' No quotation more satisfyingly expresses the different sides of Airey Neave. He was a man who played many parts but the drama was discreet and informal. He played many roles behind the scene. Given the nature and scale of his involvement with the security services, it may also be argued that Neave valued his own freedom and that of those around him so much that he was prepared to countenance extreme measures to safeguard his concept of liberty. Roger Bolton, a television producer who knew him and put together a documentary on his assassination, argues the paradox that Neave was a moral man willing to do things that immoral people were not: 'If necessary, he took the gun out and there were difficult things to be done but for the most honourable of reasons.'[8]

Why did he imagine that he knew better than the rest? Neave was not a particularly gifted politician, and it seems unlikely that he would have risen to the ranks of a Conservative Cabinet in the ordinary way. And yet, of the Tory MPs of his generation, Neave left the most indelible mark on political history by riding an inner conviction that his grasp was somehow superior. He felt he should turn that comprehension to common advantage; he was a spook who believed he *knew*, and who acted on his beliefs and loyalties. He was not alone in such self-assurance, which is the stock in trade of the spy. Although he was not an orthodox MI6 officer, Neave shared the outlook of the security services and remained close to them. He may have been an elected politician in a democracy, but he shared the misgivings about the world around him expressed most cogently by George Kennedy Young, with whom Neave was actively acquainted.

While still deputy director of MI6, some time in the late 1950s, Young issued a circular to his staff on the role of the spy in the modern world. He noted scathingly the 'ceaseless talk' about the rule of law, civilised relations between nations, the spread of the democratic process, self-determination and national sovereignty, respect for the rights of man and human dignity to be found in the press, in Parliament, the United Nations and from the pulpit: 'The reality, we all know perfectly well, is quite the opposite, and consists of an ever-increasing spread of lawlessness, disregard of international contract, cruelty and corruption. The nuclear stalemate is matched by a moral stalemate.' Young further stated that ultimately it was the spy who was called upon to remedy situations created by the deficiencies of ministers, diplomats, generals and priests, and that the spy found himself 'the main guardian of intellectual integrity.'[9] Neave's nature is readily discernible here: the man who keeps himself to himself, but *knows*. The man who hates ostentation but goes about his dedicated business with a discreet energy, working for his Queen, country and traditions.

The Britain of the early 1970s, with its crippling strikes, inflation and civil war in all but name in Ulster, called forth men like him on a mission to save the country they loved. At least, that was the way they saw it. From the recesses of the security services, from the upper reaches of the City, from London's clubland, and from the right of the Conservative Party, came volunteers eager to fight the good fight, Neave among them. But if his greatest contribution to politics was to mastermind the coup that dethroned Edward Heath (employing the 'psy-ops' skills he had acquired in his intelligence years) and brought the leadership of the Tory Party to Margaret Thatcher, it did not rob him of a taste for the covert. Soon after Thatcher took over, amid nervousness in the City as inflation soared to 25 per cent and with the pound at little more than 70 per cent of its 1971 value, Neave attended a reception of Tory MPs given by George Kennedy Young, by now the ex-deputy director of MI6. General Walter Walker, former Commander-in-Chief of NATO's Northern Command, was also there. In 1973, at the height of industrial unrest, he had set up

Civil Assistance, a quasi-private army of 'apprehensive patriots' to give aid to the authorities.

It was never called upon to carry out this function but the theme did not lose its attractions. Neave became involved in Tory Action, a right-wing pressure group within the party, and the National Association for Freedom (NAFF), set up in late 1975 to counter 'Marxist subversion'. This organisation had more success than Civil Assistance, notably in the legal harrying of strikers. However, the most intriguing – and sinister – of Neave's operations came in 1976 when he became involved with Colin Wallace, an army intelligence officer working for Army Information Policy in Northern Ireland. Operation Clockwork Orange, initially created to undermine republican terrorists through a disinformation machine to the media, would spread its tentacles into the higher echelons of British politics to probe and exploit the weaknesses of key figures. Aware of Wallace's MI5 background and his disinformation programme, Neave would maintain his contacts with him when he was appointed Shadow Northern Ireland Secretary.

Neave's connections with the secret state, past and present, gave rise to speculation that he could also be given the task of liaising between the government and the intelligence services – a job similar to that undertaken by Colonel George Wigg, Paymaster-General in Harold Wilson's government.[10] Wigg, known in Parliament as 'the Bloodhound', certainly admired Neave, describing him as 'a smart operator who learned from me'. Plainly, the spooks' mutual admiration society crossed boundaries. It also influenced intelligence policy. Neave's high opinion of Maurice Oldfield was almost certainly instrumental in Thatcher's decision to appoint the former head of MI6 as Coordinator of Security and Intelligence in Northern Ireland in October 1979. Oldfield, in charge of MI6 from 1965 to 1977, had survived a bomb attack on his London flat in 1975.

In parliament, Neave gave full support to Roy Mason, the hard-line Labour Ulster Secretary, urging him to go further and 'pick off the gangsters' of the IRA. Neave's policy for Ireland, insofar as it was understood in London and Dublin, was a twin-track strategy of devolving some powers to local councils in Ulster, coupled with the toughest possible military crackdown on republican terrorism. He had no time for power-sharing between nationalists and Unionists, arguing that it had failed and should not be tried again. It was the agenda of a soldier rather than a politician who understood Ireland and the Irish. Nonetheless, his blood-curdling warnings of the wrath that was to come when the Conservatives took office made republicans sit up and take notice of him. They feared him. He believed he had a special insight into the guerrilla mind. 'I know how the IRA should be dealt with because I was a terrorist myself once,' he told an Irish journalist.[11]

Neave would have had the British army at his disposal. Indeed, he still thought of himself as 'one of them'. He believed that specially trained soldiers should be used to 'get the godfathers of the IRA' and rejected any suggestion of amnesty for convicted terrorists as part of a peace deal. It was quite clear that the price of liberty in Ulster could involve the annihilation of those engaged in violence for political ends. This Cromwellian solution was what Neave meant by liberty. The policy was to bring about his own death before it could be implemented.

Yet, for all the convulsions created by Neave's death, the secret state has left his assassination in a limbo of oblivion. Apart from an (officially) abortive police enquiry, which also involved the security services, there has been no attempt to investigate Neave's life and death. Sources as diverse as Enoch Powell and ex-collaborators with Neave believe that the authorities themselves may have had a hand in the bloody affair. Even his own daughter Marigold believes the facts have been suppressed. 'I think there was a cover-up,' she said across her kitchen table in deepest Worcestershire one cold January morning. 'They only say "he died a soldier's death".'[12]

2

Origins

Airey Neave was born at 24 De Vere Gardens, Knightsbridge, a stone's throw from Kensington Palace and just down the road from the Royal Albert Hall, on 23 January 1916. His father, Sheffield Airey Neave, continued an eccentric family tradition and burdened his son with family surnames, adding to his own that of his wife Dorothy Middleton. Thus, Neave was christened Airey Middleton Sheffield. As he grew up, Airey began to hate his whimsical collection of names, so much so that he rechristened himself Anthony during the war years and only reverted to Airey when he entered public life.

Airey must have quickly appreciated that his family was steeped in history. Of Flemish–Norman origin, the Neaves came to England in the wake of William the Conqueror and settled in Norfolk about 200 years before the earliest recorded member of the family, Robert le Neve, who lived in Tivetshall, Norfolk, in 1399. His forebears lived in villages around Norwich where they became landowners and sheep farmers. As they prospered in the wool trade, some le Neves struck out further afield, to Kent and Scotland, but they stayed chiefly in East Anglia, gaining social distinction. Sir William le Neve, a native of Norfolk, was Clarenceux King-of-Arms at the College of Heralds in London in 1660.

The failure of the wool trade in the mid-seventeenth century drove some enterprising members of the family to seek their fortunes in London, with mixed results. One generation was wiped out by the Black Death in the 1660s (the victims are reputedly buried under a church in Threadneedle Street) but Richard Neave, who lived from 1666 to 1741, fared better, establishing a prosperous business in London, with offices in the Minories. He made most of his wealth from the manufacture of soap, a new and very fashionable product for the period. He bought land east of London outside the city limits, where his sons began to establish what would become London docks. His business also expanded overseas, with estates in the West Indies, and he put his accumulated resources into his own bank in the City.

The business further prospered through judicious marriages and Richard's grandson, bearing the same name, bought the Dagnam estate in Essex, so beginning the family's long connection with the county which remains to this day. His grandson became Governor of the Bank of England in 1780 and a baronet in 1795. The family crest, a French fleur-de-lis, with a single lily growing out of a crown, long predates the adoption of the Neave motto, *Sola Proba Quae Honesta*, which translates literally as 'Right Things Only Are Honourable'. Speculation about possible royal connections linked to the appearance of a crown on the crest, admits Airey's cousin Julius Neave, has given rise to 'some fanciful but quite unsubstantiated theories' as to the family's origins.

However, the family's upward mobility was undeniable. Sheffield Neave, another Governor of the Bank of England (1857–9), gave his Christian name to succeeding generations (some noted for their longevity), one of whom was Airey's grandfather, Sheffield Henry Morier Neave (1853–1936), well-known in Essex for his eccentricity. He inherited a fortune while still at Eton, and went up to Balliol College, Oxford, where he acquired a degree but showed no inclination to pursue a profession thereafter. With plenty of money and no need to work, he indulged his passion for big game hunting, spending long periods in Africa, where he became convinced that control of the malarial tsetse fly was the only bar to great agricultural prosperity in sub-Saharan Africa. He returned to England and studied to become a doctor in middle age, eventually rising to become Physician of The Queen's Hospital.

At the age of twenty-five, Sheffield Neave married Gertrude Charlotte, daughter of Julius Talbot Airey. They lived at Mill Green Park, Ingatestone, which was to become the family seat, and it was to Mill Green that Neave would return after his incarceration in Colditz. He dreamed vividly of the house during his captivity, and lyrically described its chestnut trees, its May blossom and the white entrance gates in his first book, *They Have Their Exits.*

Sheffield Neave had his own Essex stag hounds and was a legend in the field. Ever the eccentric, the stags he hunted were not wild but carted to the meet in the same vehicle as the hounds: 'There was never any question of the hounds killing the stag, who was much too valuable to be lost in this way,' Julius Neave has explained.[1] 'They all came home to Mill Green at the end of the day and were stabled together.' Sheffield gave up stag-hunting at the turn of the nineteenth century, complaining that 'Essex is getting too built over', but he rode to hounds until nearly eighty, when he took up golf instead. Long after his death a particularly vicious jump over a ditch and stream was still known as 'Neave's leap'.

Gertrude Neave, the epitome of a Victorian lady, was an accomplished pianist and also composed music. She came from a distinguished family, one of her relations being General Lord Airey, chief of staff to Lord Raglan, Commander-in-Chief of the British army in the Crimean War. He was, reputedly, the 'someone who blundered' over confused orders which led to the Charge of the Light Brigade. Gertrude and Sheffield had two sons and two daughters. The elder son, Sheffield Airey, born in 1879, was Airey Neave's father; the younger, Richard, became a professional soldier and saw service in the Boer War, India and in Gallipoli in 1916. He also served in Ireland during the Troubles of 1920–22, and Airey may well have heard stories of 'the Fenians' from his uncle.

Airey's father went to prep school in Churchstoke, in the Welsh Marches, and then (as befits the grandson of a Governor of the Bank of England) on to Eton and Magdalen College, Oxford, to read natural sciences. He inherited his father's fascination with Africa and the diseases spread by insects. In the years before the Great War, he travelled in 1904–5 on the Naturalist Geodetic Survey of Northern Rhodesia, and to Katanga as entomologist to the Sleeping Sickness Commission of 1906–8. On his return from Africa, he served in a similar capacity on the Entomological Research Committee for four years before being appointed Assistant Director of the Imperial Institute of Entomology at the age of only thirty-four. He was to hold the post for thirty-three more years and then took over as director in 1942, the year Airey escaped from Colditz, before retiring in 1946.

A big, dominant man with a moustache, Sheffield Neave was a distant figure, immersed in his scientific work and given to a Victorian aloofness from his children. After Airey's birth, the family moved to a house in High Street, Beaconsfield, Buckinghamshire, where four more children were born: Averil, Rosamund and Viola, and then a second son, Digby. Dorothy Neave, descended from an Anglo-Irish family, played a traditional role in the family: she ran a comfortable if unostentatious household. There were servants and appearances to keep up but Dorothy was often unwell and died of cancer in 1943 when Airey was working for MI9. Airey's daughter Marigold says that he did not have a good relationship with his father. 'He was very much a scientist. Perhaps that is what made him not very easy to get on with. He was very remote, a very Victorian figure.'[2] If not physically robust, Airey's mother possessed a mental determination unusual in her position. 'Grandmother was quite forward-looking, quite progressive for those days. She was a liberal with a small "l",' recorded Marigold. 'His childhood was not very easy. His mother was very often ill. Officially, he looks very much like her, but he never talked about her. He talked about his father, but not in very glowing terms. He was a very strict character, powerful and good-looking: a strong face, very dark eyes. And physically he was very tough. It was a clash of personalities.' Group Captain Leonard Cheshire, the Dam Busters war hero, friend and contemporary at Merton, would come to a similar conclusion. Neave, he wrote, was highly independent and always ready to follow his inner convictions. 'No matter what the opposition, he would often do things that were a little wild, though always in rather a nice way and never unkindly.' This trait endeared him to school and university friends, 'but possibly had a different effect upon his father who one has the impression did not always give him the encouragement which inwardly he needed. Thus, at a very early age he learned to conceal his inner disappointments.'[3]

Airey Neave attended the Montessori School in Beaconsfield, a progressive school where his individuality was respected. In 1925, at the age of nine, he was sent to St Ronan's Preparatory School in Worthing, Sussex. The headmaster, Stanley Harris, was a remarkable man who had played football for England, and captained the Corinthians, the famous amateur team. The essence of his educational philosophy was captured in the school prayer, known as Harry's Prayer, which ran:

If perchance this school may be
A happier place because of me
Stronger for the strength I bring
Brighter for the songs I sing
Purer for the path I tread
Wiser for the light I shed
Then I can leave without a sigh
For in any event have I been I.

Set in several acres on the outskirts of Worthing, St Ronan's placed great emphasis on academic excellence, sport and self-development. In many ways an archetypal English prep school – numbering future air vice-marshals and an Asquith among its pupils – it was built in red brick and sat against the backdrop of the South Downs. Despite the usual rigours of such places, the school had a patriotic rather than militaristic air about it. There was no cadet corps but boys were taught shooting, and from time to time a former army sergeant – so old that he had been with Kitchener at Khartoum – came to the school to teach gymnastics and boxing. With their days filled, in the evenings boys were allowed to pursue their own interests. In Neave's time, some of them built a primitive radio – a crystal set with 'cat's whiskers' tuning. Others drew maps of imaginary countries, bestowing such nations with complex railway timetables. Essentially, they had to learn to make their own amusement, and learn to fend for themselves, all of which helped develop a form of independence.

In 1926 Stanley Harris died of cancer and his place was taken by his brother, Walter Bruce (Dick) Harris, then a housemaster at nearby Lancing College. If Airey was a better than average pupil he was not spectacularly so, and seems to have been suited to his first form which was 'composed mostly of boys with plenty of ability, one or two of whom however have no great idea of work'. In 1925, he won a combined subjects prize, but in class 1A in 1927 he was fourteenth. By the following year he had crept up to eleventh, then ninth and finally sixth, with 1,205 points. That autumn, he also won the Latin prize. The highest placing he received was third, but mostly he fluctuated around the lower end of the top ten. The boys were expected to take a full part in the life of the school. Airey played a waiter in the school play in 1928, and the St Ronan's magazine observed: 'A word must be given to Neave who by progressive stages became the perfect waiter.' Praise indeed.

One contemporary at St Ronan's recalls that Neave was a rather undistinguished small boy, neither games player nor leader nor scholar. He was teased mercilessly about his name. Others spoke warmly of him. Dick Harris described him as having been 'a gentle child'; echoing that sentiment, Lord Thorneycroft, a contemporary in parliament, would much later describe him as 'a very brave and yet gentle man'. His daughter Marigold insists that he hated prep school.

At the age of twelve, Airey went to his father's old school, Eton, one of three boys to go from St Ronan's in the Lent term of 1929. Eton's long-serving head, the Reverend Cyril Alington, retired later the same year and his place was taken by Claude Aurelius Elliott, a Fellow and Senior Tutor of Jesus College, Cambridge. Unlike at St Ronan's, at Eton the house system was everything. Neave's house tutor was John Foster Crace, a classics teacher who had been there since 1901 but had only become a housemaster in 1923. He was 'a reticent, reserved and inhibited bachelor with a reputation of being overfond of some of the boys'.[4] However, he was a good teacher and ventured out of his reserve to produce Shakespeare on the school stage.

At Eton the emphasis was not just on academic brilliance but on sport and other 'gentleman's pursuits' such as fencing and shooting. Scouting was also encouraged, including quasi-military activities such as signalling. As they grew older, boys joined the Officers' Training Corps. Eton boys shot at Bisley, beating teams from the Scots Guards and the Grenadier Guards. The school was also a forcing house for politicians. In June 1929, a month after the General Election that brought Ramsay MacDonald into power at the head of an all-Labour Cabinet, the *Eton College Chronicle* recorded that seventy-six Old Etonians sat at Westminster, more than sixty of them as MPs. Predictably enough, only four of the MPs were Labour, while two were Liberal. Three Old Etonians were ministers in the MacDonald administration, including a young Hugh Dalton making his mark as Parliamentary Under-Secretary at the Foreign Office.

Public figures of the highest rank, including the King and international figures such as Mahatma Gandhi, paid regular visits to Eton. The atmosphere was unashamedly elitist. In Neave's first year a particularly aggressive Etonian defined the expressive word 'oick' as 'anybody who hasn't been to Eton'. But when the school debating society considered whether 'This House would welcome the resignation of the Government', it was roundly defeated by forty-two votes to twenty, suggesting, perhaps, that the boys were more radical than their forebears.

The St Ronan's magazine recorded that Airey 'took remove at Eton, which is the highest form that a new boy who is not a scholar can go into', and throughout his five years at the school he was competent rather than brilliant. He usually finished among the top half-dozen in his class and on one occasion won a book prize for academic effort, having, as Eton had it, been 'sent up for good' three times in a single term. Although the records suggest that he was a good runner, he did not shine at the school's other traditional sports: cricket, racquets, fencing, soccer, rugby and rowing.

It might be thought that the momentous events away from the playing fields of Eton – the Wall Street Crash of 1929 and the Great Depression of the 1930s – would have passed him by. Indeed, the *Eton College Chronicle* of October 1930 suggested that the school was 'terrifyingly remote from the ordinary concerns of life', yet the same edition carried a spoof on a Communist takeover of the school, with references to 'Herr Hitler', and Old Etonians active in the higher reaches of politics would often return to talk to the school. In 1931, the fall of the Labour government amid economic collapse and the return of a national government under MacDonald greatly increased the number of Old Etonians at Westminster to 102, five of them in the Cabinet and nine more scattered in more junior ministerial jobs. It really did seem that being able to say one was an OE was a passport to power. Much has been said about the characteristics of an Old Etonian. A young OE might be considered arrogant, self-conscious, conceited, overconfident; the more mature species had become sober, active and intelligent, a leader of men; while in his dotage an OE might revert to arrogance and jingoism, but of a gentler kind. Neave was too reserved to fit the classic OE profile, but there was something of all those descriptions in him.

Before Neave left Eton he had an experience that few seventeen-year-old English boys of the period could expect to undergo. In September 1933 his parents sent him to Germany to brush up on the language. He was billeted with a family living in Nikolassee, west of Berlin, where he attended school with a boy of similar age who was a member of the Hitler *Jugend*. Adolf Hitler had become Chancellor of Germany on 30 January 1933, when President von Hindenburg asked him to form a government as the leader of the largest single party, the National Socialists. Public and political opinion in Britain was slow to catch up with the terrifying prospect opening up in Continental Europe. Winston Churchill expressed admiration for 'men who stood up for their country after defeat'. *The Times* asked sympathetically whether the street-orator would be an efficient ruler and the demagogue a statesman. They had their answer within weeks, when the Reichstag, the parliamentary building, was destroyed by fire. New decrees gave Hitler's private army, the SA (*Stürmabteilung*), the power to gaol Jews and dissidents without trial. The first concentration camp opened at Dachau and by July of that year German citizenship was allowed only to members of the Nazi Party. Forced sterilisation of 'inferior' Germans was ordered. The terror had begun, but many in Britain believed that war could be averted through the League of Nations. Hitler withdrew from the League, yet still Germany remained a favourite holiday destination and Nazism even found admirers at home, particularly in the upper reaches of British society.

As a foreigner, Airey was excused from giving the Nazi salute when the teacher came into his class, but he was made to sit at the back, where he cut a bizarre figure in a 'decadent' yellow (Eton) tie with black spots and longer hair than his classmates. He felt something approaching contempt for the growing nazification of the school. Dietrich, the elder brother of the boy with whom he attended school, was impressed by Airey's air of independence but warned that it was dangerous. On a railway platform at Nikolassee, Airey sniggered at a fat, brown-booted Nazi SA man. Years later, he recollected 'the bloodshot pig-eyes of the stormtrooper glaring towards us'. Dietrich hastily manoeuvred him out of sight.

Dietrich was not a party member but he did belong to a sports club in nearby Charlottenburg. Airey joined as an honorary member. With his indifferent performances at school in mind, he volunteered for the relay race. A Festival of Sport was declared in September and his club was 'advised' by the authorities to field a team. At this relatively early stage of the Nazi takeover, Hitler had not stolen all sporting events as his own and marching in the torchlight procession was regarded as light-hearted and theatrical. Airey's friend took him on the march in the face of official disapproval. He was dressed in 'civvies' and treated the occasion as something of a joke. His fellow marchers, however, did not: 'As we joined the uniformed Nazis with their band, our mood changed,' he recorded.[5] 'I felt as if I was being drawn into a vortex.' The march began at ten in the evening. Neave was in the centre, alongside Dietrich and directly behind a contingent of SA troopers in brown shirts and swastika armbands. Down each side of the procession, burning torches blazed. Initially, Neave admitted, he found the grandiose event thrilling. Crowds watched, their faces shining with excitement and pride.

Sportsmen who had been joking began singing; the mood became religious and the marchers expectant. On their parade from Lustgarten down Berlin's Unter den Linden, they passed the Royal Palace of Kaiser Wilhelm I and the Ministry of the Interior, home of Hermann Goering's newly established Gestapo. When Neave broke step with his fellow marchers, Dietrich rounded on him, but it happened again before they reached their festival site, the Brandenburg Gate. 'I found it difficult to keep in step,' he admitted. 'Something subconscious was drawing me away.'[6] The gate was floodlit and festooned with Nazi flags, resembling, he recalled, some gateway to Valhalla. As they marched towards the burned out ruins of the Reichstag, bands played the Horst Wessel song (the Nazi anthem) and Neave was caught up in the emotional turmoil that prompted cynical and doubting fellow marchers alike to give the Nazi salute. 'Some were on the verge of tears,' he said. 'Afterwards, I realised that they were lost forever to the Revolution of Destruction, whereas I would escape.'[7]

Massed bands prepared them for a half-hour speech by Reichssportkommissar von Tschammer und Osten. Airey, the product of a civilisation at odds with the hysteria of Fascism, was bored. The speech was tedious and hackneyed, 'a maddening anticlimax'. While he fretted, all around him the young intelligentsia listened to the brown-shirted thug with rapt attention, breaking into 'Deutschland über Alles' when the speech was over. Neave's reportage of these events has something of *ex post facto* reasoning about it. A British teenager, even one educated at Eton, pitchforked for the first time into a foreign country undergoing such convulsions, is unlikely to have come to such sophisticated conclusions. Recollecting these events twenty years later, Neave invested himself with a remarkably mature social and political intelligence, all of which certainly made for a better story. Had his liberal-minded mother known about the reality of Nazism, Airey mused, she would have recalled him instantly. Looking back, he realised that Hitler was preparing the young people of Germany for a war that he had always intended. His youthful eyes had been opened to the dangerous neurosis sweeping Germany but it would be seven more years before he was swept into the net of depravity. He returned to school for the remainder of his final year, to a Britain more perturbed about the controversial MCC bodyline tour of Australia than events in Berlin.

Eton in late 1933 must have seemed an anticlimax after the convulsions he had witnessed in Berlin. His school record shows flashes of distinction rather than consistency. After Eton, an orthodox journey through Oxford – he had chosen to go to Merton rather than follow his father to Magdalen – into the law seemed to beckon. Of good academic repute built initially on the classics, the Merton to which Neave went in the autumn of 1934 was still steeped in Victorian tradition. As the age of adulthood remained at twenty-one, the college stood *in loco parentis* to its undergraduates and took its responsibilities seriously. Discipline was officially strict, though the authorities turned a blind eye to certain misdemeanours. For the first year students lived in. They had agreeable but austere rooms. There were very few bathrooms: each set had a chamberpot, emptied by the college scout who acted as valet and housekeeper. A normal academic day began at 7.30 a.m. when the scout brought hot water for washing and shaving, and undergraduates then had to attend a roll-call at 8.00, 'properly dressed' in socks as well as gowns over their normal clothing. They signed their names in a register in a lecture room in Fellows' Quad, under the watchful gaze of the day's duty don. Attendance at matins in the college chapel was an acceptable alternative to roll-call.

After a day of lectures and tutorials, they were free for the evening. Drinking in Oxford's pubs was forbidden and the rules were enforced by bowler-hatted 'bulldogs' (university proctors' assistants) who toured the watering holes accosting suspects. College gates were closed at 9.00 p.m., and after that students had to 'knock up' the porter in his turreted fifteenth-century gatehouse to gain admission. They were fined sixpence after 10.30, and a shilling after 11.00. If an undergraduate had permission to stay out after midnight – rarely granted – he paid a fine of half a crown.

This was all quite expensive for the mid-thirties, when a young man at Oxford could live comfortably on £250 a year, so the curfew was regularly breached by climbing over the perimeter wall back into college. Indeed, it was one of Merton's traditional sports. Reputedly, twenty-eight break-in routes existed, the most popular being over the wall in Merton Street into the college gardens and then through the loosened bars of a ground-floor set of rooms, where it was customary to leave small change on the table of the hapless undergraduate who occupied the rooms. Dons discreetly allowed the bars to remain loose.

Neave was undoubtedly one of the climbers, an unconscious

rehearsal of his exploits at Colditz a few years later, and in captivity he must have mused on the irony of his position, where, for three years, he had perfected the art of breaking in rather than out. Once at Oxford, Neave quickly made his way to the worst company that Merton offered. He was elected to the exclusive Myrmidon Club, a group of undergraduates, never more than a dozen in number, who dedicated themselves to the good things of life. The club was founded in 1865, fancifully in emulation of George Bathmiteff, a Russian nobleman and Merton under-graduate who had dallied with a danseuse who wore a garter of purple and gold. Originally, its aims were to explore the Cherwell and other river systems, but with the advent of undergraduates like Lord Randolph Churchill in the 1870s the club soon became the haunt of young bloods. To perpetuate the memory of the danseuse, Myrmidons, named after the faithful followers of Achilles, wore purple dinner jackets faced with silver and white waistcoats edged with purple and gold. Their chief activities were eating and drinking, generally in each other's rooms but also formally every term in their own dining rooms above a tailor's shop in the High Street.

Within months of going up to Merton, Neave was inducted into the Myrmidons, at a meeting in the rooms of K.A. Merritt, a keen tennis player. Colin Sleeman, who was to become Captain of Boats and subsequently a distinguished lawyer and defence counsel at the Far East War Crimes Tribunal, was elected the same day. At that point the club numbered seven. They met regularly in Neave's rooms for the following year, and in June 1936 he was elected secretary. The minutes show him to have been a conscientious but terse recorder of events. On 20 October 1936, the Myrmidons met in Mr Logie's rooms, he wrote in a flowing (indeed, overflowing) Roman hand, and fixed the dates for lunch and dinner that term. It must have been a good meeting. Neave's account, in a trembling hand, is full of crossings-out and emendations. He signed himself with a flourish and then underneath wrote 'trouble', without further explanation. On 5

February 1937, he recorded that the Myrmidons met in Mr Wells's rooms and elected two new members. They organised lunch 'for a date now lost in the mists of obscurity', or perhaps the mists of Dom Perignon. The club now had nine members, and was 'full'. The minute books are the only formal history of the Myrmidons' activities, though they are still a legend for drinking and bad behaviour at Merton. Some idea of their academic application may be gained from the degrees posted in the college register. One got a fourth in geography, another a pass degree in mathematics; Merritt gained a third in history while Sleeman managed only a fourth in jurisprudence. The Myrmidons were capable of sottishness but were no more than undergraduate drunks. They invited Old Boys to their dinner, invariably held in London, where Neave had become a member of the Junior Carlton Club. They also aimed high in their guest invitations. As late as 1951, Winston Churchill, recently reinstalled as Prime Minister, wrote regretting that he could not attend their dinner because the pressure of affairs was 'considerable'.

The Myrmidons also gained an eccentric reputation for literary interests, chiefly through Max Beerbohm and his friends who had been members in the 1890s. The Myrmidons are assumed to be the model for the Junta in Beerbohm's gentle, witty Oxford novel *Zuleika Dobson*. In spite of being known as the 'most virile' of Merton's clubs, they also had a cultured side, which showed itself most strongly in amateur dramatics. The Myrmidons scorned OUDS – the self-esteeming Oxford University Dramatic Society – in favour of Merton Floats, the college's own theatre group, founded in 1929 by two undergraduates, Giles Playfair and E.K. Willing-Denton, the latter a 'prodigiously extravagant and generous' young man. This was, Playfair later recollected, a time of festive teas, luncheons, dinners, suppers and moonlight trips on the river followed by climbing over the wall into college. Willing-Denton, who spent his entire allowance in the first month, was noted for his ten-course luncheons. He and Playfair persuaded actors of the calibre of Hermione Baddeley to come down to

Oxford, and Merton Floats enjoyed a *succès d'estime* in the mid-war years when the social scene was at its height. In 1936, Neave was secretary of Floats and his friend Merritt was president. Sleeman was the grandly titled front-of-house manager. They put on two plays: *In The Zone*, a one-act play by Eugene O'Neill set on the fo'c'sle of a British tramp steamer in 1915, in which Neave played the role of Smitty; and *Savonarola*, a play of the 1890s attributed to Ladbroke Brown, in which Neave appeared as Pope Julius II. Neave also found time to make three speeches at the Oxford Union, of which no record remains. On one of these occasions he found himself debating the merits of the previous week's motion.

It was an altogether engaging life. Neave later admitted that he did little academic work at Oxford and was obliged to work feverishly at the law before his finals in order to get a degree. He graduated in 1938 with a third in jurisprudence and a BA. 'The climax of my "Oxford" education was a champagne party on top of my college tower when empty bottles came raining down to the grave peril of those below,' he wrote.[8] He remained thankful in adult life for the kindness and forbearance shown by his college during those profligate years. Life was never to be so insouciant again.

3

King and Country

In the febrile pre-war atmosphere of the 1930s, Oxford shared in the political polarisation that shook society at large. As early as February 1933, months before Neave went up from Eton, the Oxford Union carried a motion 'This House will under no circumstances fight for King and Country'. The vote was unambiguous: 275 to 153. Most undergraduates thought no more about their casual pacifism, but Winston Churchill expressed nausea at this 'abject, squalid, shameless avowal'. 'One can almost feel the contempt upon the lips of the manhood of Germany,' he added disdainfully.

Neave was not among the fainthearts. Unlike most of his university contemporaries he had seen the Nazis at first hand and did not like what he saw. However, unlike some of his contemporaries – including Denis Healey, a future Defence and Foreign Secretary – he did not embrace the fashionable left. He was emphatically a patriot and willing to fight for King and Country. Furthermore, he believed that a war with Germany was inevitable. In 1933, while still at Eton, Neave had written a prize-winning political essay analysing the probable consequences of Hitler's rise to power and predicting the likelihood of war. Leonard Cheshire recalled: 'On arriving at Oxford he bought and read the full works of Clausewitz, and when being asked why, answered that since war was coming, it was only sensible to learn as much as possible about the art of waging it.'[1] To this alarming intellectual precocity, Neave, still in his teens, added military intent. While those about him flirted with the Young Communist League, he joined the Territorial Army at the tender age of nineteen. 'It was fashionable in some quarters to declare that no one but a very stupid undergraduate would fight for his King and Country,' he remembered later. 'To be a Territorial was distinctly eccentric. Military service was a sort of archaic sport as ineffective as a game of croquet on a vicarage lawn and more tiresome.'[2] He despised the phrase 'playing at soldiers', and took some comfort in the fact that those he contemptuously referred to as 'decadents, fantastics and intellectuals' were fighting for their very lives within a few short years.

In the meantime, his reading of Clausewitz was of little help on manoeuvres with an infantry battalion in the TA summer camp on the Wiltshire Downs. Neave remembered how he lay blissfully in the grass, a wooden Lewis gun by his side, listening for the sound of blank cartridges but concentrating more on the butterflies, identifying a small copper, a fritillary and a clouded yellow as his platoon clowned around on the edge of a chalk pit. 'We were not prepared for war. We never are,' he reflected. His daydreaming was rudely interrupted by a full brigadier kitted out for the First World War who shouted 'Lie down there!' as Neave began to stand up, feeling ridiculous in plus fours and puttees covered in chalk and grass. The imaginary conflict continued under a blazing sun. In the post-mortem on this 'battle', the brigadier raged at Neave, accusing him of choosing an exposed position for his men. Why had he allowed his left flank to go unprotected? Neave answered, with more nerve than diplomacy: 'There was an imaginary platoon on his left flank, sir, I posted it there.' The brigadier was deflated and Neave was a popular subaltern in the mess that night. If he was aware that such manoeuvres were poor preparation for the gathering storm he was nonetheless proud to receive in 1935 a registered envelope from the War Office informing him that His Majesty King George V sent greeting to his trusted and well-beloved Airey Neave and appointed him to a commission as second lieutenant in his Territorial Army.

After graduating, Neave went up to London to read for the Bar. His first placement was in 1938 in the office of an old-fashioned solicitor's in the City. Here he learned the basics of law in action. It had its entertaining moments. One summer evening found him, kitted out in bowler hat and umbrella, accompanied by a junior clerk, serving an injunction on a group of thespians in a church hall in Cricklewood, north London. The play, by a local author, libelled Neave's client and the High Court injunction he served on the producer forbade its performance. The producer read the long legal document tied with green string, a familiar sight to journalists but evidently a great shock to amateur performers. 'You can't do this to us,' he expostulated. 'It's against the law!' Echoes of this farcical scene resounded in Neave's memory years later, when he was called on to serve the indictment to Nazi war criminals at Nuremberg.

Neave moved on to become a pupil in a barrister's chambers in Farrar's Building in the Temple, close to Temple Church, but beneath the superficial gaiety of the capital and the debutante season, war was rapidly approaching. In the late summer of 1939, a matter of days before war was declared, Anthony Eden, Minister for War, announced on the radio a doubling of the size of the Territorial Army. Airey and his cousin Julius were listening to the broadcast at Mill Green Park. Airey immediately proposed that they go and join up and the pair cycled off to the local Drill Hall in nearby Fryerning Lane. Julius Neave remembers that the recruiting officer said 'That's very nice of you. So, would you like to be soldiers, or officers?' They replied: 'Given the choice – officers!' Both had what was known as a 'Certificate A', meaning that they had passed a proficiency test with the Officer Training Corps at school. As a second lieutenant in the TA, Neave would quickly have been called up in any event.

He was posted to an anti-aircraft Searchlight Regiment and spent an unromantic six months in a muddy field in Essex learning his trade, before being dispatched to a searchlight training regiment in Hereford. It was hardly Clausewitz. An impatient

Neave preferred to be in the field, like Rupert Brooke and his other war heroes of history. He was soon to have all the action he wanted, and more. In February 1940 he was sent as a troop commander to Boulogne, where the uneasy peace of the 'phoney war' reigned. Lieutenant Neave was placed in charge of an advance party of 'rugged old veterans' from the First World War, mostly industrial workers with some clerks and professional men, a 'vocal and democratic lot' who did not consider themselves crack soldiers but made up for lack of infantry training with a willingness to fight. They were equipped with rifles (though many had never fired one), old Lewis guns, a few Bren guns and the new Boys anti-tank rifle which none of them knew how to use. Neave's troop, part of the Second Battery of the 1st Searchlight Regiment, was tasked mainly with operating searchlights in fields around large towns, dazzling bombers and aiding anti-aircraft gunners. The searchlight soldiers were held in little esteem, one Guards officer describing their contribution as 'quite Christmassy'. An indignant Neave kept his counsel and waited for the underdogs to show their mettle.

He did not have long to wait. Military folklore says that Hitler's decision to invade the Low Countries and France was made over lunch with von Manstein, Field Marshal of the Wermacht Gerd von Rundstedt's chief of staff, over lunch on 17 February 1940. On 2 April, the Prime Minister Neville Chamberlain confidently told the Commons: 'Hitler has missed the bus.' Early in the morning of 10 May, the Nazi Blitzkrieg on the Low Countries and France began. Under the brilliant direction of General Heinz Guderian, German panzer divisions smashed their way through the Ardennes, overrunning Belgium and striking deep into France. Within five days, Paul Reynaud, the French Prime Minister, was telephoning Churchill to say: 'We have been defeated.' It was an appalling prospect. The British Expeditionary Force numbering hundreds and thousands of men, sent to oppose any German invasion, was in danger of being surrounded and cut off in north-western France. The war for Europe was in danger of being lost before it had begun. Still, service chiefs in London judged that Hitler's lines of communication had become so extended that a frontal attack on the Channel ports was unlikely. 'It was not to be believed,' wrote war historian Michael Glover, 'that, within two or three days, they could threaten, far less capture, Boulogne and Calais. A week earlier the idea would have appeared equally fantastic to the German High Command.'[3]

On 17 May, after a depressing summit in Paris with Reynaud and the French High Command, Churchill, now Prime Minister after the resignation of Neville Chamberlain, ordered his chiefs of staff to draw up plans for withdrawal of the BEF. Guderian's panzers were racing across northern France, making for the coast and the Channel ports. Neave and his searchlight battery were in Coulogne, a few miles south-east of Calais, right in the way of the German advance. He arrived there from Arras on 20 May, having squashed himself into a tiny khaki-painted Austin Seven with his large and belligerent driver, Gunner Cooper. His troops followed behind in 3-ton army lorries. As they drove through Lens and St Omer, the tide of refugees fleeing west increased. In the ancient town of Ardres, a woman shouted that they were cowards running away from the Germans and spat at the column.

Coulogne had seen British soldiers before. In the time of Henry VIII, when the English had occupied Calais, it was an outer stronghold. In the First World War, it had been a base camp. Neave quartered himself in the Mairie, in the town square. For the first night, they were spared the bombing that had sent the French fleeing for their lives. The young lieutenant imagined that his role in the forthcoming defence of Calais would be commanding his searchlight battery. He was just twenty-four, 'unmilitary and with opinions of my own'. However, he also later vouchsafed that he and his men were 'ready to die, or at least expecting to die'.[4] The Germans did their best not to disappoint them. As he dozed under a chestnut tree in front of the Mairie in the hot afternoon of 23 May, a German light attack aircraft scored a direct hit on the building, sending tiles tumbling down over him. It was nearly fatal. More mortar bombs exploded among the refugees, killing some of them and Neave's dispatch rider, Gunner Branton. The casualties included a young girl. Neave noticed a British soldier gently drawing her tartan skirt over her knees to preserve decency even in death. The air raids were followed by panic rumours among the French that German armoured divisions were closing in, but a disbelieving Neave thought they might only be lightly armed reconnaissance groups. How could British High Command not know the whereabouts of Guderian and his tanks?

Searchlight detachments were ordered to converge on Coulogne, gathering a force of about sixty men for the defence of this 'ghastly bottleneck'. Neave's men dug trenches in the southern sector and put up rather inadequate roadblocks comprising furniture from the local school and the village hearse. Their work was hampered by the spate of fugitives from the battle zone, whose pathetic columns stretching up to half a mile long had been infiltrated by spies and fifth columnists. At one stage, Neave was forced to draw his .38 Webley revolver on a crowd of refugees threatening to break through the roadblock, prompting cries of 'Don't shoot, *mon lieutenant!*' The German tank thrust reached them in the afternoon of 23 May but was held back for five precious hours by the Searchlight Regiment's spirited defence of its HQ at nearby Orphanage Farm. Neave's Bren gunners took part in this action, but almost fired on their own side until he moved them forward. After the farm came under intense artillery fire, the order to retreat towards Calais was given at about 7.00 p.m. Neave was told to go back into Coulogne to blow up a new piece of kit known as the 'cuckoo', a sound-location device which at all costs must not be captured. With a sergeant and a sapper, he tried valiantly with gun cotton to destroy the trailer on which the secret equipment was mounted. As they tried feverishly to carry out the order, two French aviation fuel drivers set fire to their tankers alongside. The 'cuckoo' blew up and Neave's party escaped, choking on fumes from the blaze, to the Calais road.

They found only relative safety in the city. Guderian's tanks had been briefly, and inexplicably, halted the previous week on Hitler's personal instructions. His race to the sea might otherwise have been complete by this stage of the war, trapping and capturing the BEF gathering on the sand dunes of Dunkirk just up the coast from Calais. But now he was advancing at full speed and Calais was in the way of his main objective: the British army. His initial plan was to bypass the port and take Dunkirk with the Tenth Panzer Division, but a determined counter-attack by the British south of Arras on 21 May checked his drive, and the German High Command ordered Guderian to wait on the Somme, robbing him of the impetus that could have altered the direction of the entire conflict. Taking advantage of this breathing space, the British threw reserves across the Channel into Calais, elements of the Royal Tank Regiment, the Queen Victoria's Rifles and the 60th Rifle Brigade. Their orders were unclear and constantly changing. Meanwhile, service chiefs began emergency planning for Operation Dynamo, the evacuation of 330,000 soldiers of the BEF from the sands of Dunkirk by the Royal Navy and a flotilla of 'little ships'.

German artillery found their range on Calais docks as these reserves were landing and the siege of Calais began in earnest. The British High Command was in an agony of indecision: whether to fight to the death in the strategic port, dominated by fortifications dating back to the sixteenth century, or withdraw. Churchill had once described Calais as 'simply an enceinte [fortification] protected by a few well-executed outlying fieldworks . . . it could certainly not be counted on to hold out more than a few days against a determined attack'. Indeed, at 3.00 a.m. on 24 May, the War Office telegraphed Brigadier Claude Nicholson, commander of British forces in the port, that it had decided 'in principle' on evacuation. Many British soldiers, including Neave, hoped desperately that that decision would be implemented. It never was.

As Neave related in his war classic, *The Flames of Calais*, it was impossible to sleep on the night he bivouacked on the dunes to the west of the town. He was aware that Calais would be surrounded and that a battle was imminent. Yet, throughout the night, rumours of evacuation grew. Neave was frank. 'Calais had become a city of doom, and I was not in the least anxious to remain. I did not feel heroic.'[5] Later that day, Churchill counter-manded the previous decision: a War Office telegram decreed that Calais should be defended to the end, 'for the sake of Allied solidarity'. Nicholson was instructed: 'Select best position and fight on.' The garrison of Calais, recorded Glover, was deliberately sacrificed to demonstrate Britain's commitment to her allies, 'but it was the last major sacrifice that Britain was going to make in that lost cause'.[6] British troops trapped behind the nineteenth-century fortifications could not throw back Guderian's panzers. The best they could do was hold up the Nazi advance so that Operation Dynamo could be implemented.

On the ground, the men were beginning to realise the way things were going. They needed no explanation. 'It was now time to forget about evacuation and show what "non-fighting soldiers could do,' Neave reflected. With fifty volunteers from his men, he formed up with newly disembarked troops of the Rifle Brigade and marched to the eastern ramparts. As he marched, he thought of others who had moved up the line. 'This was it. Everything before was of no consequence. But would I pass the test?'

His orders were to reinforce 'B' Company of the 60th on the south-west of the town centre where a German breakthrough appeared imminent. A staff officer led them through the deserted streets to the Boulevard Léon Gambetta, which was under fire from German tanks and machine gunners advancing up the Boulogne road. Neave left his men in the shelter of a doorway and stepped nervously into the boulevard. Tracer bullets and even tank shells rained down as he made for the Pont Jourdan railway bridge. He clung for dear life to the sides of the houses as he crept towards his objective. This was his first experience of street fighting, and he was not ashamed to admit that he was acutely frightened. Reaching the bridge, he was called down to the railway tracks below by Major Poole, commander of 'B' Company. Poole ordered him to get his men into the houses on either side of the bridge and fire from the windows. 'You might fight like bloody hell,' he admonished.

Neave and his men, armed only with rifles and two Bren guns, took up position in the houses and opened fire on the German positions on the Boulogne road. Their inexperience showed, as regulars of the 60th fighting at the other side of the bridge shouted 'F—ing well look where you're shooting!' Amid the firing, the proprietor of a café at the end of the street, wearing the Croix de Guerre from the First World War, coolly dispensed cognac. In mid-afternoon, a British tank made a brief appearance, prompting a furious response from the Germans, a savage bombardment which pinned Neave down in the Rue Edgar Quintet, a normally quiet street with a girls' school, but now deserted. The only visible sign of life was the face of a frightened girl at a cellar window.

As the afternoon wore on, Neave began to feel the lack of combat training for battle: his reading of Clausewitz had not prepared him for street fighting. The heat from the sun and blazing buildings produced an unbearable thirst. He longed to get back to the café. He waited for the firing to lift and was about to cross the road when he felt a 'sharp, bruising pain' in his left side. He collapsed to the pavement, rifle clattering. A concerned soldier shouted from a window: 'Are you all right, sir?' Neave did not reply but pondered uselessly whether it was a sniper or a machine-gun bullet. He realised he could still walk, and, doubled-up, staggered across to the café. His most pressing fear was that the Germans would break through and he would be left behind and taken prisoner. It was a common fear shared by all. British combatants had a confused but horrific picture of the fate of prisoners taken by the Nazis. Death in action they understood but the stories of concentration camps made them fear capture even more. The café proprietor brought him a large measure of cognac, while a medical orderly inspected his wound. Through a half-faint, Neave heard him say: 'You're a lucky one, sir. 'Arf an inch from the 'eart.'

The orderly and a Frenchman helped him to his feet and began walking him to an aid post where they met a young officer of the 60th in a scout car, Lieutenant Michael Sinclair. Sinclair pointed out an improvised Red Cross ambulance. After an argument about where they should go, the French driver took Neave to the Hôpital Militaire, a former convent in the Rue Leveux, where he was diagnosed as having a 'penetrating flank wound' needing an operation. Neave still feared capture and was carried protesting to the operating theatre 'where grinning French surgeons in white caps, and smoking Gauloises cigarettes, awaited me'. In his recovery ward, Neave could hear the shelling intensifying. The Germans had taken the town hall, which now flew the swastika. Beside him, a mortally wounded young Hurricane pilot begged him to keep talking. He died as dawn broke on 25 May and Neave folded his arms. Shells fell closer and closer, among the mulberry trees in the hospital garden and in the street outside, smashing the hospital windows. With the other wounded, he was taken down to the cellar while the battle raged outside. Two fellow officers of the Searchlights and several gunners were killed. At 2.00 p.m. that day, 25 May, Anthony Eden telegraphed Brigadier Nicholson with the instructions to maintain his defiant stand. On this occasion, there was no mention of 'Allied solidarity', the expression which had infuriated Churchill as being entirely the wrong way of motivating British soldiers to fight. This time the appeal was to Empire and regimental loyalty: 'The eyes of the Empire are on the defence of Calais,' Eden urged. Nicholson rejected two German proposals of surrender: 'The answer is no as it is the British army's duty to fight as well as it is the German's.' Deep in his hospital bunker, Neave heard progress of the battle as more wounded were brought in. Calais was on fire. At 9 o'clock that evening, Churchill and Eden came out from dinner and 'did the deed', ordering Nicholson to fight to the end. Churchill told his doctor, Lord Moran, 'I gave that order; it was my decision, althought it sickened me to have to do it. But it was Calais that made the evacuation at Dunkirk.' For years afterwards, Churchill was unable to speak of Calais without emotion.

As dawn broke on Sunday 26 May, it was plainly only a matter of time before the Germans overran the old town and the port area where British forces were still holding out. The evacuation had been cancelled, though some wounded were still being taken off under heavy shelling by motor torpedo-boat. Stuka raids again hit the hospital. Around Neave men lay badly hurt and blinded. He recollected that the smell of wounds and fear was over-powering. Yet the British laughed and laid bets on when the bombers would reappear. In mid-morning, their position became untenable. A Stuka's bomb fell by the main doors of the hospital, blowing them in and showering debris on the wounded. Terrified that the next direct hit would bury them all alive, Neave decided to make a break for it. He could walk, with difficulty, and if he could reach the Gare Maritime he might be among the wounded being taken off. With the admonition of the French medical officer ringing in his ears, Neave and a corporal who volunteered to go with him crawled out beneath the great double doors into the burning streets. He had no idea how badly the situation in Calais had deteriorated. Whole streets were ablaze as they made their halting way northwards to the harbour station. Neave was doubled up with the pain of his wound and his companion limped badly. Thick smoke choked them both. At the junction with the Boulevard des Alliés, they turned east and continued through eerily silent Calais-Nord. Suddenly, shells burst around the pair as they passed the Courgain. Neave was not hit but the corporal 'vanished in the blinding flash and dust'. Falling to the ground, Neave crawled to the side of the street. From a cellar window, an old Frenchman offered him a bottle of cognac. He drank, and lurched on alone to the lighthouse where he encountered troops of the Queen Victoria's Rifles in front of the station, staring down their guns as he struggled to join their ranks. An officer barked at him to hurry up and listened in disbelief to his extraordinary story. Calais had been expertly infiltrated by German fifth columnists and the QVR were taking no chances. Neave's identity card was carefully scrutinised as yet more cognac was dispensed. He looked round at scenes of devastation. Amid the debris lay the bodies of dead British soldiers. He was hurried to the first aid station below the Gare Maritime, where more wounded lay. Soon after, intense shelling forced them to find deeper cover in a tunnel under the port's Bastion 1.

After the Stuka and artillery bombardment of the morning of 26 May, it was only a matter of time before the Germans took Calais. Guderian arrived in person to direct the attack, and street by street British forces were pushed back into an enclave around the port. The Citadel fell at 4.30 in the afternoon, and the commanding officer, Brigadier Nicholson, was taken prisoner. He did not surrender his forces, however. In fact, the garrison never surrendered. Split into small groups, the men were hunted down piecemeal and killed or captured when their ammunition ran out. The Gare Maritime was evacuated, soldiers taking refuge in the dunes. Some remained on top of Bastion 1, above Neave, firing on the Germans, but their position was untenable and they surrendered. Lying in one of the underground rooms, Neave could hear the hoarse shouts of German under-officers and the noise of rifles being flung to the floor of the tunnel. Through the doorway came the enemy, field-grey figures waving revolvers. A huge man in German uniform wearing a Red Cross armband put him gently on a stretcher. He was a prisoner of war. It was a sad ending to a desperately fought battle.

Outside the bastion, British troops were ordered to scatter and try to escape in small parties, an instruction interpreted as 'every man for himself'. Just before 8.00 that evening, Eden messaged his officer commanding: 'Am filled with admiration for your magnificent fight which is worthy of the highest tradition of the British army.' The message never arrived. By then Nicholson was a prisoner and the gallant stand of his men was over. Less than three hours later, troops of the BEF began disembarking at Dover from the beaches of Dunkirk.

The wisdom of the decision to hold Calais to the last man has been hotly debated for sixty years. Neave, who endured the entire bloody nightmare (and whose courage earned him a Military Cross), was naturally partisan, and devoted his most polemical book to the issue. The stand at Calais against impossible odds can be compared with other actions in the history of war, he argues. 'All through the episode there runs a thread of poor intelligence and indecision.' Reinforcements were landed too late to do little more than block the town entrances. Tanks were deployed, but not in numbers to hold back the Blitzkrieg. Neave blames those who failed to supply the War Office with up-to-date information on Guderian's dash for the coast, during which he was pursued and bombed by the RAF. 'Coordination of intelligence with the RAF had evidently a long way to go,' he remarked tersely.

Neave also complained of an air of defeatism in the War Office, whose top echelons had evidently decided that most of the BEF had already been lost and troops were needed much more urgently for the Home Front than in the defence of Calais. The fault for the loss of Nicholson's brigade, he insisted, lay with 'higher authority', the General Staff which was obsessed with getting the BEF back to Britain and had no plan for Calais. 'Indeed, it was not clear who was in charge of the operation.' In addition, few commanders 'since the days of Balaclava' had issued such suicidal orders as Lieutenant-General Sir Douglas Brownrigg, Adjutant-General of the BEF, who had ordered tanks to attack Boulogne when it had already been lost. Given Neave's ancestry perhaps the reference to Balaclava was not the most appropriate.

Churchill was in no doubt that the last stand at Calais was vital for the success of Operation Dynamo which allowed the British army to fight another day. In the British press the defenders were lionised as heroes. Writing in *The Times*, Eric Linklater argued that the death struggle waged over four days halted panzer troops who would otherwise have cut off the retreating BEF: 'The scythe-like sweep of the German divisions stopped with a jerk at Calais,' he wrote. 'The tip of the scythe had met a stone.' Guderian himself and the respected historian Sir Basil Liddell Hart disagree with this poetic verdict. In his war diaries, the German general insisted that the heroic defence of Calais, while worthy of the highest praise, had 'no influence' on the development of events at Dunkirk and did not delay his advance. Neave is withering on this point. 'One thing is indisputable, the Tenth Panzer Division was delayed at Calais for four days and not by Hitler,' he wrote.[7] Guderian, he claimed, was covering up for his failure to take the port earlier, as he had planned.

Liddell Hart argued, somewhat patronisingly, that Churchill was obliged to justify his decision to sacrifice the Calais garrison, but questioned whether it had the outcome asserted by the wartime premier. The panzer division that attacked the port was only one of seven in the area and had been deployed 'because it had nothing else to do'. The gallant stand was nothing more than 'a useless sacrifice', Liddell Hart maintained. Neave was plainly infuriated by this view. He contended: 'There was nothing useless about the stand at Calais. It hampered Guderian during crucial hours, especially on 23 and 24 May, when there was little to prevent his taking Dunkirk. It formed part of the series of events, some foolish, some glorious, which saved the BEF.'[8] Glover suggests that the truth lies somewhere in between these two extremes, though strangely he finds it 'irrelevant'. Nicholson's brigade had to be sacrificed as a gesture to shore up the crumbling Anglo-French Alliance, even though it was already doomed. 'At least it made an epic for Britain at a time when all was defeat and withdrawal,' he writes condescingly.[9]

At the time, however, the military merits of the battle for Calais were far from Neave's mind. He was about to experience at first hand what he and his men had most feared: Nazi incarceration. He nearly did not make it. On the morning of 27 May, after surviving another night in the bastion tunnel, he was taken by ambulance into the centre of Calais. En route, the vehicle was rocked by a burst of shellfire that forced the crew to take cover. Ironically, this was offshore 'friendly fire', from the cruisers *Arethusa* and *Galatea*, bombarding the investing German forces. The ambulance restarted and he was dumped on a slab in the covered market of Calais-St Pierre as if he was a piece of meat. In this makeshift field hospital, his imprisonment began.

4

Capture

Neave hated being taken prisoner, at the age of twenty-four, at the very start of the war. It was not just fear of the unknown. German front-line troops, soldiers like himself, had behaved well towards the wounded but it was the Nazis he dreaded. Furthermore, there was a psychological dimension to his capture. A prisoner of war, he discovered, suffers a double tragedy. Most obviously, he loses his freedom. Then, since he has not committed a crime, his spirit is scarred with a sense of injustice. Neave articulated this resentment as a bitterness of soul that clouded the life even of strong men. 'The prisoner is to himself an object of pity,' he argued. 'He feels he is forgotten by those who flung him, so he thinks, into an unequal contest. He broods over the causes of his capture . . .'[1]

Despite his wound, Neave determined not to fall into this psychological trap. Well-versed in the escape stories of the First World War, he quickly set himself to thinking how to avoid being sent to a prison camp deep in the heart of Occupied Europe, where escape would be much more difficult. Though hospitalised, he was still only thirty miles from England, and much of France was still free of Nazis. Flight was not impossible: Gunner Instone, of Neave's Second Searchlight Battery, was already busy escaping through France and Spain after knocking out two sentries.

His wounds were too serious, however, to attempt an escape from the hospital to which he was moved, unless he had help. Out of the blue, a French soldier, Pierre d'Harcourt, who had evaded capture from his tank regiment by posing as a medical orderly, offered a solution. Neave could abscond from the ward he shared with four other officers by posing as a corpse. Allied prisoners were still dying, and d'Harcourt, a Red Cross volunteer, could smuggle him out of the hospital in an ambulance in place of a deceased officer. It would not be easy. German guards checked the bodies before they were removed for burial in the Citadel, where Nicholson's men had fought so bravely. Nor do the plotters seem to have given much thought to disposing of the spare corpse. They hatched extravagant plans to steal a boat and flee across the Channel, but before their ideas could be translated into action d'Harcourt heard that the prisoners were to be evacuated further inland to Lille in late July. The plot had to be abandoned. Nonetheless, Neave found the experience of escape planning very good for morale. It occupied his fertile brain and gave him hope. The elusive d'Harcourt vanished to Paris, where he was active in the first escape lines for Allied prisoners through Unoccupied France before being captured. He spent four years in the notorious Fresnes prison and Buchenwald concentration camp before being liberated, half-dead, in 1945.

En route to Lille that July the German lorry carrying the wounded broke down. This mishap seemed to offer a chance to escape. While the lorry was being repaired, Neave and other walking wounded survivors of Calais wandered around the streets of Bailleul, without guards. The local people offered them food and wine, and some offered to hide them from their captors. The French spirit of resistance was already showing itself within weeks of capitulation, but Neave did not avail himself of these offers. He admitted later that he lacked not just the physical strength but also the nerve to seize the opportunity. The weeks in hospital had sapped his will. 'My vacillation cost me dear,' he wrote, 'but at this time there was no military training in such matters.'[2] In the warm summer evening, French people threw flowers and bid them goodbye from the main square of Bailleul, and Neave felt ashamed at his inaction. Subsequently, he vindicated his hesitation. Had he got away so soon, he argued, he would not have escaped from Colditz and would not have been in a position to help others emulate his example. It was perhaps a questionable piece of rationalisation after the event, to square his conscience with this unheroic episode.

Once in the Lille hospital, his thoughts again turned to flight. This time he planned to escape with Captain John Surtees of the Rifle Brigade and a Corporal Dowling of the Durham Light Infantry. A young Frenchwoman who brought food and flowers to the wounded promised to help. Once out of the hospital, they would get civilian clothes, take the train to Paris and live incognito in a Left Bank pension. It did not seem dangerous, but it was not a very well thought-out escapade for the trio had no papers and practically no money. Senior officers later upbraided them for putting the other wounded men at risk of reprisals had they got away.

In August 1940, the prisoners of Lille hospital, or at any rate those judged to be walking wounded, were taken on a long march east to their destination in a POW camp. They trudged through Belgium 'from one foul transit camp to another' before arriving at the mouth of the River Scheldt. There, they embarked on a huge, open coal barge for a three-day journey up the Waal and the Rhine to Germany. Neave felt he was on a voyage of lost souls crossing into the unknown. Life was over. As they passed under the bridge at Nijmegen in Holland, a young woman waved at the prisoners; as she did so, the wind caught her clothing, lifting her skirt and with it the spirits of the men. Neave, although overcome with despair, could not but admire the insouciance of the average Tommy, who never gave in, never lost heart.

The officers were disembarked to take up residence in Oflag IXa at Spangenburg, near Kassel. Their place of incarceration was an imposing *Schloss* with a vaulted gateway, moat, drawbridge and a clock tower. Here the men could walk round the battlements and on a clear day take in the view of farmland and distant hills.

Spangenburg reminded Neave of school – a school to which

their fathers might have been sent. In a sense he was correct, for indeed they had: the castle had been a POW camp in the first war. The new boys, like the previous generation, slept in two-tiered bunks with straw palliases and coarse blankets. It was August, one year into the war. Years of imprisonment stretched ahead of them, and initially Neave resigned himself to his fate. He filled in the time with composition and meditation, writing half a fantastic novel about the life after death of a Regency peer, a study of Shakespeare's sonnets and an essay on eccentrics for the camp magazine. He soon discovered the limits to the literary taste and sense of humour of English officers. His articles were rejected as unsuitable. The days thus passed wearily, and when he came to write his accomplished account of his adventures he preferred to draw a veil over these early efforts.

There were few attempts to escape. On one occasion, the officers who got away were captured and beaten up by drunken German civilians. Surprisingly, escape was considered bad form by the senior British officers, who had successfully imposed a pre-war army system of discipline and class values inside the camp. They argued that escape for one or two men would invite reprisals on the hundreds left behind, and even threatened unsuccessful escapers with court martial, though they were not in a position to carry out the threat. Low morale and poor rations also contributed to the 'anti-escape' attitude.

However, in the autumn of 1940, Red Cross parcels began arriving, improving health and lifting spirits. Would-be fugitives could now hoard 'iron rations' to sustain them during any planned flight. Opportunities for escape also increased in December 1940 when Neave and others were moved to a new camp in the wooded village below the castle. They were closer to a Stalag, a camp for non-commissioned officers and rank and file, who went on working parties outside the wire where the prospects for escape were more frequent. Neave, by now bored by the deadening routine of reading, talking and waiting for Red Cross parcels, sought to transfer himself to the Stalag. Life in the new camp brought new frustrations. The prisoners were closer to society and woke every morning to the sounds of the farmyard. Such proximity sometimes made them feel part of normal life but at the same time reminded them they were not. Here, Neave passed the winter 'in discomfort, but without great suffering, unless it were of the soul'. His stomach became accustomed to the meagre prison diet, and he was unable to eat a whole tinned steak and kidney pudding doled out to each prisoner on Christmas Day.

Before his plan to transfer to a Stalag could be implemented, however, Neave and his fellow POWs were suddenly transferred in February 1941 by train to Poland. Their destination was an ancient, moat-encircled Polish fortress on the River Vistula at Thorn (modern-day Torun), part of the huge encampment of Stalag XXa. (They later learned that they had been moved to this inhospitable spot as a reprisal for alleged ill-treatment of German prisoners in Canada.) At Thorn, officers were quartered in damp underground rooms, with little opportunity for exercise and none for escape. The fact that they were in Poland, a country about which they knew little, and hundreds of miles further east, made flight even more difficult. It was a soul-destroying existence, enlivened only by the daily rendition of 'Abide With Me' at sunset by a group of British orderlies on the drawbridge above the moat. Despite his imprisonment, Neave, who had been confirmed at St Ronan's, did not lose his Christian faith, as some did. He later remarked that the singing of this hymn 'was the only moment of hope and reality in all our dismal day'.

The main compound, for several hundred British NCOs and men, was three miles away. Neave quickly realised that this site was his best hope of escape. Several of the men from his own Searchlight Battery captured after the fall of Calais were in the hutted camp, and he communicated with them through working parties that came every day to the fortress. As required by camp discipline, Neave took his plan to the senior British officer, Brigadier the Hon. N.F. Somerset DSO, MC. He proposed to escape from the hut used by a captured British dentist to treat

POWs. The 'surgery' consisted of a treatment room, waiting room and a lavatory behind it with a corrugated iron roof. Neave, with his co-escaper Flying Officer Norman Forbes, planned to slip away from the dentist's hut, and then hide for a few days among the teeming throng of 'other ranks' inside the camp, before making a break from an outside working party. Neave's fellow officers in his room mocked his plan, but it was approved by Brigadier Somerset. He was 'paired' with Forbes, an RAF Hurricane pilot who had been shot down over the French coast, because he spoke fluent German. It was an excellent match. Forbes, Neave decided, was of original mind, more practical than himself and a man of great determination.

Theirs was not the first escape bid. Several other officers had tried to get out of Spangenburg, and three Canadian flying officers dressed in fake Luftwaffe uniforms had almost succeeded in stealing a German aeroplane to fly to neutral Sweden. They had swapped places with men on an outside working party to reach the aerodrome and were only detected by their ignorance of German. Tougher controls on movement in and out of the fort were introduced after that but Neave was undeterred. He bought a workman's coat and pair of trousers from a British officer who had given up thoughts of escape to read for a law degree, and a fellow officer with artistic skills made him a forged civilian pass, identifying him as a carpenter from the town of Bromberg.

Neave was not very thorough in his escape plans. For instance, he had no travel papers for the hazardous 200-mile journey across Poland to where he believed the Soviet front lines to be, nor had he much money, only a few Reichsmarks and a 'medieval faith' that his store of tinned food and chocolate would see him through. Escaping east was a doubly dangerous business. The Soviet authorities looked with deep suspicion on Allied escapers. They sometimes interned them, or worse. As Neave noted: 'Few British soldiers who reached the Russian lines during this period were heard of again.'[3] The pair planned to make contact with the Polish Resistance in Warsaw, with a view to linking up with the

Red Army on the Russian armistice line at Brest-Litovsk. Alternatively, and rather fantastically, they hoped to do better than the Canadians by stealing an aeroplane at Graudenz, north of Warsaw, and flying to Sweden. Neave had two copies of a sketch plan of the aerodrome.

As he lay on his bunk bed, day after day, Neave fantasised about freedom. His sole desire was to be free of the terrible monotony of the fort. Once outside and under the stars he imagined he would care little what happened to him. He dreamed of nights sheltering in the shade of some romantic forest, alone in the world. He would be happy if he could be free if only for a while. Such daydreaming indicated an obsessive desire to get out, one sadly unmatched by the organisational planning required to sustain a successful escape. On 16 April 1941, Neave and Forbes joined the small detachment of officers being marched to the dentist's surgery. It was a warm spring morning, with signs of new growth in the fields around. The prisoners joked with their guards: 'Back home by Christmas!' an unsuspecting German ribbed Neave. 'Certainly!' he replied, laughing.

Everything was ready at the dentist's. Under the roof of the lavatory hut, Neave's go-between, an army sergeant, had hidden bundles of wood for them to collect as part of their deception. The dentist treated Neave's gums with iodine and he divulged their escape plans. The dentist smiled and shook his hand. Back in the waiting room, Neave waited until 11.00 a.m. before asking to go to the lavatory. The attention of the guards outside was distracted by a fast-talking prisoner. Once inside the lavatory hut, Neave took off his greatcoat and hid it where the wood had been secreted and waited for Forbes. His companion swiftly joined him, and at a low whistle from the sergeant they strolled out with their bundles, wearing unmarked battledress uniforms. They walked unchallenged towards the main entrance of the camp, joshing one another as they walked, in the habit of British POWs. The German guard on the gate, who was chatting to a British corporal, showed no interest in them. He was not on the lookout for people breaking into the camp. Neave and Forbes walked casually to one of the huts, where Company Sergeant Major Thornborough of the Green Howards ushered them to their new quarters at the far end. There they discussed plans for their concealment with Neave's former Searchlight Battery Quartermaster-Sergeant Kinnear. Their disappearance would be discovered as soon as the dentist's detachment was recounted, and the pair would have to hide in the hut for several days until the German search parties were called off. They lay on their bunks savouring the moment, before Thornborough called them out to watch the entertainment. By now the guards had realised they were two dental patients short, and a hullaballoo ensued. Neave and Forbes, each equipped with a brush and pail as part of their escape props, looked on as heavily armed soldiers set off for the woods with maps and dogs, in pursuit of the men watching them from inside the wire.

Lying on their bunks, or hiding beneath them during hut searches, the escapers waited and waited, tortured by fears that a stool pigeon in the camp might give them away. It was clear from their repeated searches of the huts that the Germans believed they were still in the camp, and their helpers in the warrant officers' hut ('a homely place', Neave observed, spick and span as a British barracks) risked severe reprisals if they were unearthed. They were anxious to get someone back to England to report their plight, as rations were inadequate and some POWs had not survived the long Polish winter. 'Their selflessness touched me deeply,' Neave recorded. During their three-day stay, they mixed as equals, without reference to rank, united by a common objective to defy the enemy.

Early in the morning of 19 April, Neave and Forbes fell in with a working party of more than a hundred men and marched out of the camp into the countryside, singing 'Roll Out the Barrel' and 'The Quartermaster's Stores'. The next stage of their escape had been worked out by their camp hosts. They were to hide in a hay barn, and make a final break for freedom at night. Meanwhile, they worked under the gaze of armed guards, filling palliasses with straw. At one stage, Neave, stopping work to seek out a hiding place, feared he had been identified by a German officer who ordered him to get on with his job and kept him under close surveillance thereafter. But the day passed without incident, except that the food lorry brought two extra men to take their place on the return to camp. In the late afternoon, a corporal motioned Neave and Forbes to their hiding place in the rafters of the barn. Here they stayed until ten that night, silent and unobserved. Then they concealed their army uniforms in the hay and donned workmen's clothes, complete with Polish ski caps made from army blankets. They had now become *Volksdeutscher*, or German nationals, who had been sent to live in eastern Poland by the Nazis.

One of the barn doors was padlocked but the other was secured only by a wooden bar held in place by twisted wire which the corporal had already loosened. It was the work of moments before they were out in the open farmyard. Through the dark, they could make out the farmhouse, which was used by Germans as a mess. A dog growled and then barked, and they froze as an officer looked out to satisfy himself that there was nothing untoward, before bolting the door. Clambering over a high wooden fence, they could make out the profile of low hills where the Germans had an artillery firing range. They walked quickly across marshy ground, fearful of the noise of tracker dogs and torchlight pursuers, but they had got clean away. Neave rapturously breathed the fresh air of freedom. 'It was like walking on air,' he remembered. They stumbled through a landscape pockmarked by shell holes. Their route took them into a wood, along rides between the trees towards the town of Alexandrov, some twenty miles distant. Occasionally, they saw lights and once, near a small settlement, a dog disturbed the night silence. They hurriedly took refuge in the dark banks of trees.

It was hard work. The heavy rucksack of tinned food dug irritatingly into Neave's shoulder, while beneath his thin

workman's clothes he sweated in thick Red Cross underwear. By
4.30 in the morning they had covered ten miles, and stopped to
fortify themselves with chocolate and an apple. A cold wind sprung
up, bringing rain. Swinging his tins of sardines and condensed
milk on to aching shoulders, Neave and his companion trudged
on. There was no mistaking the amateurish nature of their
enterprise: 'These were the pioneer days of 1941, when escape
was not a science but an emotional outburst,' he admitted later. 'I
thought of an escape as a kind of hiking tour . . . as for Forbes
and myself, we were tramps or hoboes, glad to be at large.'[4]

Dawn found the pair by the railway line which ran from
Podgorz and Sluzewo, checking their compass to keep on a south-
easterly direction to Warsaw, 150 miles away. They tramped on,
bypassing Alexandrov and keeping to the fields to avoid German
patrols. The early morning rain turned heavier, soaking and
dispiriting the pair. They took refuge in a Polish farmhouse, where
two young women watched wordlessly as they stripped naked and
dried their clothes before the open fire. Resuming their march
through sodden fields, they came upon evidence of Hitler's
Blitzkrieg on Poland in the autumn of 1939: Polish army helmets
perched atop rough white crosses, burned-out farmhouses and
barns, a shattered chapel with a crucifix broken in two. At
nightfall, lost in a labyrinth of cart tracks, they sought shelter in
another Polish farmhouse. A farmworker listened to them ask the
way to Wlocawek (German Leslau), smiled and answered in
English. The farmer there was 'Tscherman [German] . . . very
bad'. He suddenly appeared, shouting at the farmworker as if he
were a dog, and the escapers fled. Deeper in the countryside, they
came on another farm, where they were welcomed by the old
man of the house and his two daughters. Neave stood awkwardly
in the living room, pointing to his soaked and torn trousers. The
old man spoke to one of his daughters and she left the room,
returning with a pair of peasant's corduroy trousers. They had no
fly buttons and Neave cut off the buttons from his painter's
trousers for the girl to sew on, which she did, blushing and giggling.

No money changed hands. Neave was conscious of the dangers the family ran in helping them. Another Pole came to warn that the German farmer was looking for them, and fear was evident in the way they talked. 'A great feeling of guilt ran through me as I witnessed their terror,' Neave recalled. 'Was it to destroy these simple lives that I had escaped?'[5] They could sleep in the barn, said the old man, but they must leave at dawn.

After a fitful night in the hay, the pair resumed their forced march to Wlocawek. Neave shaved by a stream and cooled his blistered feet. He reflected how oddly domestic it seemed, using Elastoplast to dress his sores. By mid-afternoon on their second day of freedom, they reached Wlocawek. Resting by the River Vistula, they were spotted by a German officer, who went away without speaking. Once in the town, they were overwhelmed by the ubiquity of Nazi flags and emblems, even above the doors of workmen's cottages, until they realised the date: it was 20 April, Hitler's birthday. In Wlocawek Neave witnessed an act of thoughtless Nazi brutality: a young SS thug assaulted a Jew wearing the Star of David on his back for not saluting his troop, sending the man flying into the gutter and his hat across the road. No one dared pick it up. That evening, they again sought refuge at a farm but realised they were among the enemy. The family was German, the boy of the family sporting a swastika belt bearing the legend *Gott Mit Uns*. They escaped into the cover of a pine forest and huddled together for warmth, worn out by their ordeal.

By the third morning of their escape, Neave was in a state of physical exhaustion. The regime of a poor diet and lack of proper exercise during almost a year of captivity was taking its toll. He felt that he had 'lost his feet', which had deteriorated to 'raw stumps' dragging along the ground. Their pace slowed. Hauling themselves painfully along rough tracks, they halted from time to time to sleep and regain their strength. Apart from a lonely woodman, they met no one. They crossed the Vistula by a rail bridge taking the line south from Plock, and in the evening approached the village of Gombin. It was empty and unwelcoming. They stumbled on the road to Warsaw, looking for shelter but finding none. The pair lay down in a ploughed field, endeavouring to sleep but waking regularly to keep their circulation going. Their reserves of chocolate had gone, forcing them to eat a revolting mixture of condensed milk and tinned sardines. 'I thought the night would never end,' recollected Neave.

When it did, they set off without breakfasting but with as much vigour as they could muster to reach their goal, Warsaw, by nightfall. Trudging across interminable ploughed farmland, they reached the agricultural town of Itow, thirty miles from the capital. Beyond Itow they would be in the frontier zone of the General-Government of Poland, the remnant of Polish territory left between the Russians and western Poland handed over to German nationals. They had no papers to enter this zone and only a haphazard idea of where the actual frontier lay. Three miles further on from Itow, they came to another run-down village, and asked a woman where the border was. Nervously, she replied 'It is here', and fled. Pain and weariness conspired to rob them of vigilance as they walked through the village, towards the frontier post alongside a guardhouse, which was apparently unmanned. They strode through the gate, straight into the arms of two watching German sentries sitting by the roadside, rifles by their sides. They did not have the strength to run away. The soldiers, remembered by Neave as big, stupid and fresh-faced, asked them for their papers. Forbes, the German speaker, admitted that they had none. But everyone had to have papers to cross the General-Government, the soldiers insisted. Surely these men knew that. 'We were only going to visit our mother, who is sick in Sochaczew,' said Forbes. 'This is my brother.' They were led into the guardhouse where a German official, a whip hanging on the wall behind him, bawled 'Attention, Polish swine!'

He then instructed the sentries to take Forbes outside while he interrogated the exhausted Neave, who mumbled his prepared explanation that he was a *Volksdeutsch* from Bromberg. Desperate with fatigue, his brain refused to function. He forgot his limited stock of German and spoke haltingly. The official laughed and brandished the whip in his face. Neave stuck to his story, hoping to give time for Forbes to make a run for it. 'I could not. I no longer cared that I was caught again or even if this brutal official were to flog me to death,' he admitted.[6] After a few minutes, Neave gave up the unequal struggle and brought from under his shirt the metal disc identifying him as Prisoner of War No. 1198. His enthusiastic but ill-prepared bid for freedom was over. Had his grasp of German been better, or his exhaustion not so complete, he might have bluffed his way through. It was not to be.

Pandemonium broke out. Forbes was brought back into the guardhouse, and another official woke from his sleep and joined in the general clamour. Neave's co-escaper tried manfully to cope with their accusations. 'You are not Englishmen, but Polish spies,' they cried. 'This is a matter for the Gestapo.' Neave's accuser gabbled down the telephone, his dog-tired prisoners barely understanding what was being said. They were then marched back to Itow by a soldier, who, conscious of their condition, did not hustle them. Neave noticed Forbes discreetly tearing up his map of Graudenz aerodrome, which might suggest they were indeed spies, and panicked. Where had he put the other copy? From the police station at Itow they were driven back under guard to Plock, which turned out to be a down-at-heel town swarming with SS. Their lorry dropped them outside a modern block and Neave's heart missed a beat. By the door, he saw a board carrying the legend 'GESTAPO'. Their worst fears had been realised.

The two men were taken to a small room where an SS officer and an interrogator in plain clothes asked them more questions and ordered them to empty their pockets. Pitiful remnants of their bid for freedom – bits of chocolate and bread, scraps of paper, a match box disguising a compass – spilled on to the table. The plain-clothes interrogator sorted through these items disdainfully and then seized on a small, folded piece of paper from Neave's wallet. It was the map of Graudenz aerodrome. 'So, my friends, you are from the Secret Service!' he said triumphantly. Unbeknownst to Neave, Graudenz was a bomber station, from which the Luftwaffe would attack the Soviet Union at the outset of Operation Barbarossa only two months later.

Neave was taken to an upper floor where a young, uniformed SS officer questioned him closely in English, while a typist took down his answers. Years later he confessed, 'I was in great terror, though I tried to appear calm and innocent.'[7] Neave insisted to his interrogator that he had got the idea from other prisoners, working near Graudenz, which was half true. He had been inspired by the Canadian flying officers at Thorn and had planned to escape by stealing an aeroplane, because Forbes was a pilot. 'You are lying,' said his inquisitor. 'You are a spy. You were taking this to the Russians.' Neave maintained that they were not, and told the curious officer that they were trying 'the same game' as the Canadian escape, of which his captor was unaware. The SS officer telephoned Thorn camp and received verification that there had been just such an escape bid, and that prisoners Neave and Forbes were indeed missing. Gradually, the tension eased. They were joined by another SS man, and began talking more casually about the war, referring to a map on the wall. Neave's brave sally that Britain would win the war prompted cynical laughter. They asked if Polish peasants had helped their escape, and Neave, still wearing his peasant's corduroy trousers, diverted the questioning to German mistreatment of the Poles. The SS men showed utter contempt for the Poles and their Catholicism, but they ceased interrogating him about spying. Neave's composure gradually returned. He asked his blond young interlocutor what he had been doing before the war, and, with his resentful admission that he had been at university studying for his doctorate of philosophy, the interrogation ended. Neave and Forbes were marched through the streets of Plock under armed guard to the town prison and put into solitary confinement. Their pathetic civilian disguises were exchanged for coarse grey prison clothes. Neave slept for several hours before being roused for his evening 'meal', a bowl of swill containing bad potatoes and swedes. The Polish orderly boy, in prison clothes, whispered that the other inmates knew their identity, and managed some patriotic sentiments before continuing his round.

But Neave's ordeal was not yet over. Above the door of his cell a notice identified him as 'Neave, Airey. *Spion*'. For two days, he recovered in his cell, sleeping most of the time between 'lunch' of bread and turnip soup and a half-hour exercise period. Separated with Forbes from the other inmates, he hobbled round the prison courtyard, quietly exchanging details of their interrogation. To Neave's relief, Forbes had given the same story about the aerodrome map. They had already concocted an agreed version of their escape from the camp, exonerating British other ranks. Neave's reverie was interrupted some days after the initial interrogation by his gaoler's curt insistence: 'The Gestapo wants you.'

Back in the Gestapo building, he had a new, more vicious interrogator, this one with close-cropped black hair and a scarred face. He was just finishing questioning a defiant Polish woman, to whom Neave offered a sympathetic smile. 'Go on, smile you English officer,' raged his Nazi debriefer. 'You started this war. You brought these Poles into it. Both of you are spies! Spies! Spies!' The SS man glowered at Neave, with, as he thought, 'murder in his eyes', and challenged his cover story. The Graudenz map, he shouted, must have come from a Pole. Neave reiterated that it had come from a British prisoner of war. Who? He refused to say. Then, English gentleman, added the plain-clothes SS man, he would remain a guest of the Gestapo until he thought better of his obstinacy. Suddenly the officer softened, becoming for a moment a soldier like Neave. The prisoner should not think, he said, that just because he was in civilian clothes he had not fought like the lieutenant. In fact, he had seen action on the Polish Front, and a small ribbon in his button denoted an award for bravery. 'Go, Herr Neave, and think things over,' he admonished.

Back in his prison cell, Neave contemplated his position. He trembled at the prospect of further interrogation, fearing that if physically tortured he would reveal more of the truth. He felt defenceless and alone, anxious lest he face execution like the Polish officer in the cell opposite sentenced to death for killing a Gestapo agent. He prayed, cursed and patrolled his cell agitatedly. 'I closed my eyes, and despair came over me like a great fog,' he wrote later.[8] 'I could not see a way out of the darkness.' In his dreams he was tramping through swamps of dark, stagnant water on the road to Russia, the way marked with the bones of former travellers. The next morning brought relief; he was awoken by the warder who addressed him as Herr Leutnant, and told him he was going back to Thorn 'with Oberleutnant Forbes'. Once again, he was a British officer. The attitude of his gaolers changed markedly. They were handed back their civilian clothes, including the hated rucksack with its remaining sardines and condensed milk. Neave also retrieved his pipe, tobacco and the box of matches with its concealed compass. With Teutonic thoroughness, everything had been returned, except the map that almost cost him his life. He had memorised the layout of Graudenz, however.

After ten days, the escapers were taken back by train from Plock to Thorn, along the north bank of the Vistula that had been their bearing for Warsaw. They talked amiably of the war to their guards, who knew less than they did. The POWs at Thorn had a radio receiver smuggled in in a medicine ball from Spangenburg. Their welcome at Thorn was less agreeable than their departure from the clutches of the Gestapo. A furious German officer, whose guards had allowed them to escape, drew his revolver and marched them '*Hande hoch*' to windowless dungeons in the outer wall of the fortress. When they protested at the pigsty conditions a sentry thrust his gun down the ventilation hole into Neave's cell. 'If you are swinehounds, you must expect to be kept in pigsties,' he yelled. Neave threatened to report his filthy language to the Kommandant and the gun was hastily withdrawn.

After a night in appalling conditions, they were locked in a room above the keep, without furniture but for two beds, while weighing over their failed escape bid. They came to one maddeningly simple, but vitally important, conclusion. They had tried to cross the Polish countryside too quickly and without method. 'We had, as it were, charged the barricade of the General-Government frontier without calculation,' he decided. And yet they had got so close to Warsaw. It would have been comparatively simple to skirt the ill-defined border through the woods and make their way to the capital. Moreover, in such inhospitable terrain, an escaper had to understand the strain his vulnerability would place on his spirit. 'Loneliness and physical stress undermine the most resolute,' he wrote.[9] The escaper must conserve his forces by lying up in the warmth for long periods. The lessons of this failed escape bid were not lost on him.

On being sent back to his room in the fort, Neave found that his short period of freedom had given him fresh strength. He went back to the novels of Victorian England that reminded him so much of home, and found an inner peace. One night, after he had finished Mrs Henry Wood's sentimental melodrama, *East Lynne*, he was roughly roused by a German guard and told that he was being moved immediately. 'We have had enough trouble with you,' said the guard. Gathering his few belongings in a bundle, he joined a small party of prisoners among whom he recognised Forbes. 'Where the hell are we going?' asked Neave. 'To the Bad Boys' Camp at Colditz,' came the reply.

5

Colditz

High above the Saxony town of Colditz broods an impregnable castle surrounded on three sides by sheer rock precipices, approached only by a narrow cobbled causeway over a deep moat. Infuriated by the frequent escapes of Allied officers, the Nazis decided to concentrate here, in a *Sonderlager*, or punishment camp, the most recalcitrant of the 'bad boys' from other camps in Occupied Europe. Colditz was thought to be escape-proof, and indeed it had proved to be so in the First World War when it housed Allied POWs. The logic was understandable but erroneous. By putting all the most determined officers together in Oflag IVc, the German High Command effectively established an escape academy, which scored an impressive number of 'home runs' in the five and a half years of its existence. 'We made things better for our prisoners by cramming Colditz with new escape material week after week,' confessed the camp intelligence officer in a frank post-mortem. Every new arrival brought knowledge of new methods of escape, of fresh routes, or documents, of checks on trains and the like. 'In this castle, the prisoners had the interior lines of communication, and the initiative as well.'[1]

This did not seem to be the case at all when the first British officers arrived in the autumn of 1940. Captain Patrick Reid, the chairman of the British escape committee, recollected that the prisoners could see their future prison almost upon leaving the station: 'beautiful, serene, majestic and yet forbidding enough to make our hearts sink into our boots'. *Schloss* Colditz towered over the town of the same name and the River Mulde, a tributary of the Elbe. The castle was rebuilt on much older foundations, dating back to 1014, in the early eighteenth century by Augustus the Strong, King of Poland and Elector of Saxony (known as 'the Strong' because of his tireless sexual drive: he is supposed to have fathered 365 children). The castle had seen many sieges and sackings and even its name betrayed its fortunes. Colditz is a Slav word-ending, dating from the time it was occupied by the Poles. Its original name was Koldyeze. The town, essentially an over-grown village, was situated in the centre of a triangle formed by the big cities of Leipzig, Dresden and Chemnitz. The land surrounding the castle was hilly and wooded, known locally as 'little Switzerland', and levelled out northwards into a fertile agricultural plain. It was buried deep in the Reich, 400 miles from the nearest neutral territory, Switzerland.

Since its abandonment by the Saxon royal family in 1800, Colditz had housed prisoners of one sort or another. In the 1920s it was a mental asylum, and when he came to power in 1933 Hitler used the castle to incarcerate his enemies, real or imagined, and to train the Hitler Youth. Its outer walls were 7 feet thick, resting on a rock face that rises 200 feet above the river. The inner courtyard, where the English officers were to live, rose a further 60 feet. Their cells were six storeys high with iron bars on the windows. Searchlights played on the walls all night, and in these early days at least there were more guards than prisoners. It was a truly forbidding place, designed to dishearten would-be fugitives.

The first prisoners of the Second World War were Polish officers, who arrived in the autumn of 1939 when Colditz was no more than a transit camp. With the outbreak of war in Western Europe the following year, it was designated a Special Camp, and French and Belgian officers started to arrive. The first British officers reached the castle in early November 1940. This advance guard of three Canadian RAF flying officers was boosted by a group of six army officers recaptured after escaping from a camp near Salzburg.

Colditz was designated Oflag (*Offizierslager*) IVc and came under the command of Werhmacht Group Four, based in Dresden. The Germans derived their authority to establish a special camp from Section 48 of the Geneva Convention which permitted strict surveillance, though without loss of any other prisoners' rights as provided by this agreement. 'In effect, this camp had a greater number of searches, roll-calls and so on than in the normal camps, and much less room to move around in – just a forty-yards square courtyard, and no open space except the park outside, which might only be visited for short and fixed periods daily under some restriction and much surveillance,' wrote Reinhold Eggers, latterly in charge of security at the prison.[2] Oberst Prawitz was the Kommandant during Neave's spell there. The German guards were mainly drawn from middle-aged and even elderly men called up to serve their country, though some had seen action in the First World War.

The prospect of moving to Colditz, of which he knew virtually nothing (not even where it was), contrarily lifted Neave's spirits. The atmosphere of public school and university still permeated officers' lives, and the idea of 'a camp for naughty boys, a sort of borstal' did not disturb him. He was flattered to be singled out so early in his POW career as a nuisance to the enemy. 'I was like a boy who, flogged by the headmaster, proudly displays the stripes on his backside,' he confessed later. As the British contingent passed across the drawbridge of Thorn fortress before dawn that late spring morning, he even looked forward to new adventures.

To begin with, a long train journey offered another opportunity for escape. As they travelled slowly south, the prisoners scanned the countryside and looked for weaknesses in their armed escort, but they were heavily guarded and even accompanied when they went to the lavatory. It was not a pleasant trip. When they changed trains at Posen, the POWs were spat upon. Neave cultivated the guard sitting next to him, a garrulous, middle-aged toyshop keeper from the Dresden area who had been called up for military service. Hoping to give his well-meaning guard the slip en route, Neave so shamelessly played on his feelings of homesickness that tears came to 'his stupid blue eyes'. It was not perhaps an attractive thing to do, but his manipulation of the guard showed just how obsessive the idea of escape had become.

At Dresden they changed trains again. Here, Neave took the opportunity to study the master race off guard: waiting for trains, dozing, wolfing down *Wurst* and margarine sandwiches, showing their tickets and papers to the railway police. It was a useful chance to reconnoitre the railway system. Prisoners and guards alike slept with their heads on the waiting-room tables, but an alert Neave kept up the conversation with his toy merchant. They fell into a serious discussion about what would happen after the war. The shopkeeper said there were many Communists in Dresden, and they would simply change their brown shirts for red. He asked Neave for his address in Britain, and took him to a secluded part of the waiting room where railway workers were drinking morning coffee and the conversation flowed freely. Neave was surprised at how amenable they were to his seditious propaganda. As the discourse deepened, he edged away unnoticed on his chair towards the door. He was within a yard of an impromptu escape when his guard turned round and asked: 'More coffee, Englishman?' He could not refuse and his chance had gone. Soon after they were herded out on to the platform for the train to Colditz. In later years, Neave thought often of the toyshop soldier, so genuine in his hatred for the war and his captive's tribulation. In his classic account of his wartime experiences published eleven years after that morning in Dresden, Neave wrote: 'Now I feel almost ashamed of my attempt to take advantage of his good nature.' In 1946, the shopkeeper wrote to the address Neave had given him, complaining of his fate under the Russian occupation of Eastern Germany, and asking for help. Neave replied in the most general terms to avoid exciting the attention of Communist censors. This incident provoked an unusual outburst of personal philosophy from Neave: 'Some hypocrite has called this the century of the Common Man,' he remarked, 'but in no age have common men suffered more for being human and kindly.'[3]

On the short, crowded train journey from Dresden, Neave studied his fellow passengers. In his compartment, a German officer took in the sight of British POWs in battledress uniforms and muttered nervously to his gargantuan *Hausfrau* Hilde: '*Kriegsgefangener!*' (prisoners of war). She spent the journey complaining loudly about the flight of Hitler's right-hand man, Rudolf Hess, on 10 May. Why did the Führer not stop him? Where did he get the plane? This was news indeed. Hilde was very cross. Hess had apparently parachuted into Scotland from a Luftwaffe plane, bearing a message of reconciliation to the Duke of Hamilton, and had promptly been interned. (Neave would later meet him in a cell at Nuremberg, where he served war crimes charge papers on him.) On this morning, however, the mere mention of Hess's name in front of the enemy prompted the browbeaten officer to silence his wife. The prisoners broke into smiles. Neave lit his pipe and winked at his comrades-in-arms.

The party of five 'bad boys' arrived at Colditz in the early morning of 14 May 1941. They were drawn up at the station and marched across the cobbled Bahnhofstrasse and up Badergasse, crossing the shallow but fast-flowing River Mulde by a wide, modern bridge 50 yards long. From here, they skirted the main square and trooped up the short, cobbled access road to the castle, across the moat bridge and through the great gates of the inner courtyard. 'I felt the battlements close in, enfolding us, so that I looked round in fear,' Neave recalled later. 'White faces peered at me from the windows, and men in strange clothes paced up and down in the shadows.'[4] Then he spotted John Hyde-Thomson, an officer of the Durham Light Infantry who had also escaped from Thorn, clattering along the cobbles in clogs to welcome him. He was quickly made to feel at home, not just with the contingent of twenty British prisoners but with the polyglot community of Poles, French, Belgian, Dutch and Serb

POWs. After the depression of Thorn, Colditz, for all its forbidding appearance, was like escaping from a turgid political meeting to 'a salon filled with wit and self-confidence'.

Incredibly, among the small British company were three clergymen from the Chaplains' Department. One, J. Ellison Platt, an army Methodist chaplain who had chosen to stay with the wounded at Dunkirk rather than get away, observed the new-comers. In his diary, published long after the war, Platt recorded on the day of Neave's arrival that the camp was rapidly filling up. The French contingent numbered two hundred 'and the British increase by ones and twos daily'.[5] The padres led the latest intake up a stone staircase to a large hall on the first floor, where all but the most senior British officers lived. Neave felt as if he were being ushered by masters to a school for waifs and strays. After a meal of hot stew, German bread and lard, they were escorted to smaller rooms off the mess hall where they were allocated bunks. Neave immediately fell into a deep sleep.

He was roused at 7.30 the next morning by the shouts of 'Aufstehen' (get up) by German NCOs walking through the dormitories. Thereafter he was inducted into the daily routine. Breakfast, of ersatz German coffee made from acorns, bread and margarine, was brought up to their quarters half an hour later by British orderlies. At 8.30 all the prisoners assembled in their national contingents in the courtyard for *Appell* – roll-call. After much laborious counting and saluting, the prisoners were allowed to get on with their hobbies: reading, music lessons, language lessons and exercise. The daily routine altered little, until the escapes began in earnest, when the Germans instituted more roll-calls to reduce the opportunities for getting out. 'Lunch', usually a thick barley gruel very occasionally containing pork skin, was served at 12.30, and the final roll-call took place at 9.00 p.m. Soon after, they were locked into their cells for 'lights out'. For under-graduates of Colditz academy, however, this was simply the signal to start a night shift of intense activity.

Perhaps with some overstatement, Neave later insisted that

every single officer in the castle had but a single thought – to escape. Lord Campbell of Alloway QC, then plain Alan Campbell, a young army officer who was one of the first to be sent to Oflag IVc, remembers: 'One spent most of one's time trying to escape. We were always planning escapes or doing escapes.'[6] Campbell occupied the bunk below Neave and so observed him at close quarters. 'We never quarrelled. I found him agreeable, amusing. But I never got to know him. He was a withdrawn, distant character, with a slightly isolationist, ruthless streak.' Ken Lockwood, a stockbroker in civilian life who looked after the British 'shop' and supplied would-be escapers with German money, comments that Neave in particular was keen to get out, but points out: 'We couldn't all escape. One accepted that. But the object of the exercise was to get *somebody* out of the camp and if possible get them away successfully.' He concurs with Alloway's assessment that Neave was 'very quiet, very much his own man. I don't think any of us got to know him really well.'[7]

The prisoners engaged in a restless battle with the 'goons', as the hapless German guards were known, and they were endlessly busy looking for anything that might aid themselves, or others, to get out. Neave plunged himself into this hive of industry with relish, delighted that he no longer had to fear the mild disapproval of fellow inmates content to live out the war that he had experienced in previous camps. Eggers deplored the attitude of his recalcitrant charges. 'Indiscipline, I can truly say, was the unspoken order of the day on their side: indiscipline often amounting to plain personal insolence, or at least studied offhandedness.'[8] He singled out the British as being particularly obstreperous. They even used occasional excursions to the town football ground to show off how well turned out and disciplined they could be while marching through the streets, giving chocolate to the children, until this privilege was stopped. The Germans realised they were mounting a magnificent piece of counter-propaganda, at their own expense.

Neave was not involved in the first serious attempt at a British breakout, which took place only a month after he arrived. Twelve officers, including two Poles, tunnelled their way out of the canteen, having successfully (as they believed) bribed a German guard 700 Reichsmarks to look the other way when they made their exit on to a small patch of grass beneath the parapet. The sentry accepted the down payment of 100 marks, and promptly betrayed them to the Kommandantur. The sentry was allowed to keep the money, promoted, sent on leave and given a War Service Medal.

Watching this botched escape from his window at two in the morning, Neave brooded on the shortcomings of tunnels as the best way to get out. Escapers, he concluded, must pit their wits against something frailer than the castle walls – the Germans themselves, as the last escapers had in part tried to do. The gap in their defence seemed to lie in the hope that the guards would be deceived by a bold attempt to leave by the front gate dressed in German uniform. While he pondered this plan, Neave joined 'the board' of an international tunnel, comprising British, French, Polish and Belgian officers. He had scant confidence in the project, but in a schoolboyish way he felt he had a place in the second eleven. The tunnel was started under a bed in the sick bay and went through the floor of the Red Cross parcel room below. From there, the international consortium argued about what direction to take. Nonetheless, they worked with a vigour, using broken knives, forks, door latches – anything metal they could lay their hands on – until four months later the tunnel stretched for 20 feet beneath the Red Cross room floor. Neave had no faith in its success, but he believed in the self-discipline that all escaping activity encouraged. It strengthened the spirit of POWs, occupied their mind and reduced the tedium that could otherwise drive them to distraction.

Two nights a week, Neave toiled flat on his stomach, a handkerchief over his mouth to keep out the choking dust. Disposal of the debris was the most difficult thing for most of the obvious hiding places had already been bagged by other tunnellers.

Neave and his crew stored great piles of dust and stones in the loft of the building, which eventually gave way, breaking a water pipe that showered French prisoners as they slept. While he worked away at this forlorn occupation, Neave continued to develop his own project. Through their 'goon watch', the prisoners knew all about the movement of German personnel throughout the castle. They now learned that everyone who entered the inner courtyard that housed the prisoners had to collect a numbered brass disc at the guardhouse, present it to the sentry on the inner gate, and return it to the guardhouse. Peter Allan, a second lieutenant in the Cameron Highlanders, bribed a visiting civilian painter to part with his brass pass, which went into the British cache of escaping material. However, the workman was obliged to report his 'loss', and the German officers warned their guards to be on the lookout for the missing disc.

Most importantly, Neave had to fashion for himself a 'German' military uniform that would be sufficiently convincing to get him past the guards. He had also to equip himself with civilian clothes capable of sustaining his disguise as a foreign worker all the way to Switzerland, the nearest neutral country 400 miles to the south. He thought first of bribing the very German guards he was attempting to fool to acquire a complete uniform, but he concluded that this might take years, and he was impatient to be free. So he resolved to make his own, despite admitting that he was hopeless with his hands.

Neave sacrificed a month's supply of Red Cross chocolate to buy from a Polish officer what he later described as 'an ancient tunic ... in a remote sort of way it resembled in length and design that worn by German private soldiers'. It was the wrong colour – khaki rather than field-grey – and although he contemplated dyeing the tunic, this was beyond him. Instead he employed less subtle means: he applied layers of green paint normally used for making the scenery in the camp theatre. A Polish tailor sewed fake insignia, fashioned from cardboard and painted silver, on to the left breast. Dark green cloth epaulettes with the white numerals of an infantry regiment, a forage cap fashioned from a piece of Polish uniform, white piping and an amateurish cardboard badge with eagle's wings completed this improbable disguise. He planned to wear RAF trousers for the escape, and lastly equipped himself with a pair of handsome jackboots bought from a Polish orderly with Red Cross provisions. Neave realised that his mock uniform would never pass muster in daylight. Even with the precious brass disc, he would have to pass through three sentry posts, and might also meet other soldiers who would see through his disguise.

Ellison Platt, the Methodist chaplain, noted in his prison diary for 28 August: 'For weeks Anthony Neave has had no thought for anything but tailoring and dyeing.' (After his first diary entry for 14 May, in which he uses Neave's correct first name, Platt invariably wrote 'Anthony', a clear indication that this was how Neave was known, and wished to be known, in the camp.) Platt observed that Neave's scheme was one of great audacity, adding: 'It consisted of passing out of the main gates in the uniform of a German soldier. Since the time the maggot first entered his brain, every minute has been dedicated to "getting ready".' His first idea was to steal a uniform, which might be done 'at a pinch', but could prove very unpleasant if caught in an abortive escape. 'So, on reflection, it would be better to take the long route and make it: during the period of making, nothing else has existed in the world. With an unethical fertility of invention he got hold of a mixture of several incredible substances which produce a lightish green field if applied to a khaki material.' Not quite near enough for daylight, but, under artificial light, quite indistinguishable from the real thing, he noted. 'The dyeing experiments have occupied a full three weeks.' His swastikas, woven on tunic and hat, were extraordinarily well done, as was the belt, 'a creation in tin and cardboard that deserved a better fate'.[9]

Neave was less convinced, later admitting: 'I was only too aware of the fancy-dress appearance of my uniform, fit only for amateur theatricals,' he wrote. 'Prisoners, however, develop a blind faith in the most impracticable means of escape. They underestimate the risks, believing that some kindly Providence will surely aid them. For me, escaping was still a schoolboy adventure reminiscent of the books of G.A. Henty. I had yet to learn that success can only be learned by a minute mastery of detail and a study of the mind and methods of the enemy.'[10]

For now, he had only the haziest idea how he would get back to Blighty. He imagined himself stealing a bicycle from the outer courtyard and pedalling across the moat bridge to freedom in a hail of bullets. Pat Reid was unimpressed by Neave's fake uniform but did not order him to abandon the project. It was agreed that he should go out at night, trusting to the darkness to mitigate his Gilbert and Sullivan appearance.

Then there was the problem of his 'rifle'. German guards always carried a rifle and bayonet, even the lance-corporal, or *Gefreiter*, whom he was seeking to imitate. Neave decided that making a fake weapon would be too difficult, so he determined to be a soldier on special duty reporting to Hauptmann Priem, the camp's duty officer. Even for this unlikely duty, he would need a bayonet in a scabbard. An officer in the Royal Tank Regiment, Scarlet O'Hara, carved one for him from a bed board, and decorated it with a buckle of tin foil on a cardboard belt. For civilian clothes, he dyed an RAF tunic in a vat of the lead from indelible pencils. He spent days, too, making a Tyrolean trilby, only to endure the mortification of it being seized during one of the regular German searches for escape materials. He had to make do with a sham ski cap. For the journey he believed was imminent, Neave equipped himself with a rough map of the Swiss frontier and a makeshift foreign worker's identity card. He also had a small amount of German money, around 50 Reichsmarks (the equivalent of just over £3 at the wartime exchange rate). These he was instructed to carry in a Cellophane wrapping inserted into his rectum. His attempts to practise this manoeuvre gave his fellow officers much entertainment.

He was now ready, indeed restless, to go. The project had taken over his life. Daytime was spent in a frenzied round of preparation.

By night, he dreamed of being on the run to freedom. 28 August 1941 was chosen for the break – little more than three months after he had entered Colditz in fear. The weather was very hot. Neave attended the nine o'clock roll-call wearing his British army greatcoat over his amateurish *Gefreiter* uniform. When the German officers gave the order to dismiss, the prisoners scattered to their quarters, while the guards lined up to go off duty. A fellow officer quickly removed Neave's greatcoat. Jamming the sham forage cap on to his head, he walked briskly to the massive courtyard door. There was not much light at the gate, Reinhold Eggers recalled later, for the searchlights tended to be shone on the walls above, rather than on the gate. The German guards were in a hurry to get back to the guardroom and the German NCO on duty only looked casually at the numbered passes pushed into his hand.

Here was Neave's chance. He presented his brass disc to the *Unteroffizier* at the gate and went through his carefully rehearsed lines. 'I have a message for the Kommandant from the duty officer.' He was allowed through the half-open door. As Neave turned quickly left and marched on down to the outer gate, a giddy sense of relief flooded through him. He walked quickly, his jackboots resounding with a military ring on the cobbled stones. In a virtual delirium, he imagined himself acting in a theatre without an audience, giving a performance for his own pleasure. The first archway through which he had to pass loomed up ahead.

Then, a brutal return to reality. Neave had gone left, not right, to the guardroom with the other German soldiers. And the NCO was not sure about his face. He looked again at the disc. It was the Number 26 about which he had been warned. According to Eggers, the sentry yelled 'Halt!', but 'Number 26' walked on. Other guards joined in the shouting, but 'Number 26' merely quickened his step.

Neave tried to ignore the shouts but then committed a fatal error. He turned round, and in the arc lights the painful inadequacy of his comic opera costume was plain for all to see.

The scenery paint on his tunic and the forage cap of which he was so proud glowed in the artificial light. 'I was a figure of the underworld, a demon king under the spotlights in a Christmas pantomime,' as he later confessed.[11] Neave turned back and ran towards the archway and the bicycle that was to take him to freedom. But from the archway came a second, firmer voice: 'Halt, or I fire.'

Realising that further resistance was pointless, Neave turned back again towards the guardroom and put his hands in the air. The archway guard stuck a rifle in his back and all the soldiers in the guardroom gathered round in great excitement, shouting, gesticulating, waving rifles and revolvers as if caught up in a major military incident. One *Unteroffizier*, enraged at Neave's audacious impersonation, screamed: 'This is an insult to the German army! You will be shot!' The mayhem died down with the arrival of the Kommandant, Oberst Prawitz. The impeccably dressed Prawitz looked Neave up and down disdainfully, took in the details of his amateurish uniform, remarked on the impertinence of the escape bid and ordered that he be taken away to the cells.

Chaplain Platt argued that Neave's failure lay not in his comic opera uniform but in the way he behaved in trying to escape. Once outside the gates, the German guards stood about waiting to fall in and march back to their quarters. 'Neave couldn't possibly do that,' Platt wrote in his diary. 'His only hope for success lay in an unobtrusive disappearance from the immediate scene, and then to walk rapidly down the causeway to the outskirts of the village.' Alas, his quickstep departure aroused suspicion. Neave had not made sufficient distance to warrant making a hit-or-miss dash for the open country, Platt commented. 'There wasn't a chance in a million that he would get twenty yards without being shot. So failed a very worthy effort.'[12]

In the cells Neave was thoroughly searched – 'more thoroughly than usual' according to Eggers. They discovered the Cellophane container stuffed with money, which was a disconcerting find. It showed that the prisoners had access to German currency, an invaluable aid to escaping. Neave was led roughly away to solitary confinement, where he took off his makeshift cardboard belt and wooden bayonet and hurled them to the floor in a fit of temper. It was hours before he could sleep. Years later, he would reflect on his dejection at being caught, on his fall from self-made hero to a sad joke in a burlesque German uniform. Perhaps he was too hard on himself. It was not his uniform that had given him away, nor necessarily his behaviour, but the brass disc that the British contingent had coaxed out of the civilian painter. Had they copied the disc, and engraved a different number, the ruse might have worked. Even so, and as Chaplain Platt observed, Neave had not thought through his tactics after getting over the first big hurdle, the castle gate. His passion for flight was the rage of youth. He was still only twenty-five, perhaps older than his years but still lacking in a strategic grasp of the science of escape. Neave had proved he could get out of Colditz, but not clear away from Nazi Germany. Being a loner was his nature, and it was not enough. It never would be. He needed others, allies with a greater instinct for the long range.

In the morning after his failed bid, the guard brought him the usual ersatz coffee. Gravely, he warned Neave that he was about to be court-martialled and shot. Neave snorted with derision. He was no longer afraid. He felt only foolish and unaccountably 'liverish'. Later in the morning, he was frogmarched to the Kommandant's headquarters, where in a formal, wood-panelled gallery, he was inspected by Colditz officers one by one. The reactions to his uniform varied from derision to wrath. Kommandant Prawitz ordered him to stand to attention and salute, German fashion. Neave was beside himself with rage and made a poor show of a German salute. Prawitz ordered him to do it again, this time properly. The other officers sniggered and Neave saluted again. It was a humiliating experience. He was made to stay in the gallery, under guard, for the rest of the morning. From time to time, police officers from the village and soldiers came in to gape at him as if he were an exhibit in a zoo. Then, an elderly photographer from the town was brought in to take his picture. Neave posed for the camera, perspiring profusely beneath his lurid uniform. 'I had reduced all escaping to a ridiculous farce, a music-hall turn,' he raged. 'I grew crimson with mortification as the old man doddered about the gallery exchanging feeble jokes with the soldiers. It seemed hours before the comedy was over.'[13] The photograph he took survives to this day and it does Neave more credit than he realised at the time. He stands, half at ease, left arm behind his back so that the scabbard for his 'bayonet' is clearly visible. He stares coolly at the camera and it is impossible to imagine him thinking anything but: 'You may have got me this time, but there will be another.'

After the embarrassing charade of being photographed, his fake uniform was removed, thereafter to take pride of place in the Kommandant's personal museum. The threat of court martial for impersonating a German officer was quietly dropped. Instead he would serve the customary indignity of imprisonment in the town gaol when a cell became available, there being constant pressure on accommodation due to frequent escape bids.

Neave's humiliation was not complete. At the evening roll-call, Hauptmann Priem, the officer to whom Neave was supposed to be taking a message during his escape, announced to the crowded courtyard: 'Gefreiter Neave is to be sent to the Russian Front.' Everyone joined in the laughter. 'It was friendly towards me,' recalled Neave, 'but it was not music to my ears.' Eggers remembers the incident slightly differently, recording that Priem announced: 'Gefreiter Neave is posted to the Russian Front.' Eggers also recalled: 'There was an almighty roar of laughter. Lieut. Neave looked very rueful. Six months later, though, he had the last laugh.'[14] Following Neave's daring bid, the camp authorities tightened security. All escapers and new arrivals were subject to mouth and body – i.e. rectal – examination. All military personnel had to carry a printed pass, signed and stamped by the camp adjutant, which was to be shown to all sentries. However,

not even the German guards observed such Teutonic thoroughness. They were often too deferential to higher ranks and the rule
was never completely observed. Roll-calls, too, were extended,
and a new system of counting introduced to make deception
harder.

Before the year was out, Neave was caught once again, this
time in the Polish orderlies' quarters on top of the old sick bay
when he should have been in bed. German guards who picked
Neave and a fellow prisoner up on the night of 23 November
assumed, wrongly, that the miscreants were helping an escape bid
by two Canadians found on the roof. Chaplain Platt noted
enigmatically in his diary: 'Actually, they were pursuing interests
of their own.' They were thrown into the *Schloss* prison, but, gaol
space being at such a premium, Neave was locked in an unheated
double cell with two fellow officers. Their cigarettes were
confiscated and 'they thought themselves to be holy innocents
exposed to the harsh winds of a cold, hard and unjust world'.
They determined on a protest notice, which read *'Achtung! Dieser
Tat ist eine Schandtat'* (Attention! This is a scandal). Reasoning that
it was of little use to write out so high-minded a notice unless it
could be suitably displayed, the trio picked the lock of their cell
door, pinned the notice at eye level on the outside, then locked
themselves in again and went to sleep. Episodes like these, amusing
though they were, drove the German guards to despair.

6

Escape

Neave was sentenced to the usual twenty-eight days' solitary confinement for his escape attempt. Several weeks elapsed before he could serve his term in Colditz town gaol, and he spent the time staring disconsolately from the British quarters as the weather turned colder. In early October he was taken under guard along the route by which he had tried to reach freedom. The sentries joked that the new white barrier at the final gate was a tribute to his audacious bid. His books and tobacco wrapped in a blanket, Neave was in no mood for entertainment.

Then, by his own account, he spotted another way out of the castle. Looking over the parapet of the moat bridge, he noticed a rough pathway leading across the tumbled stones of the dry moat towards the German married quarters. A small wicket gate stood half open in the moat bridge wall. If he could gain access to this gate, he was free of the barbed wire, with only a fence round the married quarters and a 12-foot high wall around the park beyond to negotiate. Excited, Neave crowed with delight, puzzling his guard with his air of elation. Neave's version of events is contested by Pat Reid, who said he himself had spotted the small garden gate on his arrival at Colditz a year earlier. The energetic Dutch, always on the lookout for escape possibilities, also claimed to know of its existence.

Banged up in his municipal cell, Neave still thought of escape. The tiny barred window was beyond reach. He climbed on to the massive East European-style stove and contemplated cutting through the ceiling, breaking out of the roof and letting himself down to the gravel courtyard with a blanket rope. Thus occupied with thoughts of flight, he was surprised by the gaoler who roared with laughter: 'So soon, Herr Leutnant! You must stay with us a few days longer.' Next day, they moved him to a cell on the ground floor. He endured his spell of confinement remote from the worsening fortunes of the war, smoking on his bunk in the company of Jane Eyre and the Duchess of Wrexe. On his way back to the castle twenty-eight days later, he noticed again the little wicket gate, which by now appeared in his dreams as 'the gateway to the land beyond the Blue Mountains'.

Some weeks earlier, Pat Reid had also had an inspiration. A trained engineer, he understood architectural drawings and had the happy knack of mentally being able to take buildings to pieces and put them back together again. It occurred to Reid that the wooden stage of the camp theatre, on the second floor of a building occupied by the most senior Allied officers, offered escape potential. It was constructed over a room leading to the top of the German guardhouse outside the prisoners' courtyard. This corridor was sealed off from POW quarters by heavy locked doors and bricked-up windows, but it might be accessible from above. Together with 'Hank' Wardle MC, a Canadian in the RAF, he reconnoitred the theatre and found that by removing wooden steps from a dressing room he could move freely about under the heavy stage. There were no floorboards, only rubble on top of a lath-and-plaster ceiling over the corridor.

Reid and Wardle sawed a 2-foot square through the ceiling and found the room below disused and empty. To disguise their activity, they constructed an ingenious device known as 'the shovewood'. This was a plaster-covered hatch fixed from above with turn-buckles resting on the ceiling joists. It was virtually invisible from below, and in any event no guards ever went there. This was Neave's 'magic entrance'. As Reinhold Eggers later lamented: 'We had left the prisoners a very simple barrier, no more than a floor-ceiling between their quarters plus a door into a passage on our side to get through.'¹ Reid clambered down on a rope made from a mattress cover, padded down the corridor in carpet slippers and picked the lock of the door. Beyond, a passage ran over the courtyard gate – the most difficult barrier to negotiate – and ended at another locked door. This yielded easily to his skills and Reid found himself at the top of steps leading into an attic above the guardhouse. The sounds of laughter and noisy drinking drifted up from the German Officers' Mess below. If an escaper could disguise himself as a German officer, the guards at the gate would scarcely give him a second glance, because this time he would be approaching from the right direction.

What is more, the prisoners were planning to put on a Christmas pantomime within weeks, offering the perfect opportunity to mount an escape. Reid began a search for the right officers. He quickly whittled his list down to six, including Neave. He told them 'casually' that he could get them out of Colditz if they could acquire convincing German officers' uniforms. Neave and Lieutenant John Hyde-Thomson, who had already tried to get out in a consignment of palliasses, were finally chosen to make the break, in company with two Dutch officers.

There were compelling reasons for cooperation with the Dutch. First, their command of German was much better than that of the British, second, their long blue-green army greatcoats bore a striking resemblance to the Wermacht uniform, and third, they were inveterate escapers. They had already made four 'home runs' via Switzerland. This Anglo-Dutch entente had been operating for some months through Reid and his opposite number, Captain van den Heuvel, invariably known as 'Vandy'. He finally settled on a brave young officer of the Netherlands East Indies Army, Second Lieutenant Toni Luteyn, to accompany Neave. In 1940, the Dutch army had capitulated to the invading Germans. Its officers were required to sign an oath of non-combatance, or face internment for the rest of the war. Virtually all signed, with the exception of a contingent of sixty-seven colonial army cadets who had just passed out of Breda Military Academy. Luteyn, aged twenty-three, was one of them. He was interned in a camp at Zossi on the Dutch–German border, but when one of them escaped they were moved deeper inland to Oflag VIIIc in Poland. After more escapes, the whole lot was dispatched to Colditz in July 1941, arriving soon after Neave. Until now Neave and Luteyn had scarcely met. They were thrown together by calculation rather than friendship. Despite being the younger of the two – he was only twenty-four – Luteyn was the senior partner because of his command of German. 'We had some exercises, because Neave did not speak German, except *jawohl*,' Luteyn said years later, 'but going through the guardroom there was quite a chance somebody would talk to us, and they would talk to the highest ranking officer. So I was "promoted" to Hauptmann and he was a first lieutenant. We practised that exercise for a week in the courtyard. He had to march on my left-hand side. If he didn't wheel to my left, I shouted at him.'[2]

Meanwhile, both would-be escapers were rehearsing for the camp pantomime, *Ballet Nonsense*. Neave later dismissed the 'pathetic futility' of the entertainment, insisting that although such performances keep prisoners from brooding on their fate, the actual performances were ghastly. But at the time he threw himself energetically into the show, writing and producing a three-act sketch with the improbable title 'The Mystery of Wombat College', which was clearly based on his experiences at Eton. Neave played the principal character, the unpleasant headmaster Dr Calomel. The other parts were equally nasty, as befitted the obscene dialogue and cynical performance. The chaplains complained about the 'unsuitability' of the sketch and Neave thought it a 'wretched little piece' but it brought the house down in Oflag IVc.

A photograph of the full cast shows him striking a pose in gown and mortar board of black paper and steel-rimmed spectacles, made up to look like a beetle-browed, leering Groucho Marx. While Neave busied himself on stage, Reid and Wardle were hard at work beneath his feet creating the 'shovewood' escape route through which they planned to send several Anglo-Dutch teams. Neave and

Luteyn would go first, followed twenty-four hours later by Hyde-Thomson and Luteyn's fellow officer Lieutenant Donkers. At one point in rehearsals, when Neave was pacing the boards in a scene where Dr Calomel expels the son of a duke, Reid and Wardle emerged from beneath his feet, covered in dust.

Neave acquired a Netherlands Home Army uniform overcoat, which he hid, wrapped in sacking, beneath the floorboards. The prisoners had hundreds of these hides, some of which are still giving up their secrets today, sixty years later. With the help of camp experts, he then set about converting it into a German officer's uniform. Epaulettes, fashioned from linoleum cut from the bathroom floor, were painted silver to match the officers' silver braid. He gave himself a gold regimental number. Neave promoted himself to Oberleutnant Schwarz and Scarlet O'Hara carved gold wooden stars to denote his rank. O'Hara was one of the unsung heroes of Colditz who sat in their primitive quarters day after day helping others to escape. The selflessness of men like him helped twenty officers to escape from the 'impregnable' fortress, eleven of them British – the best escape record of any camp in Nazi Germany.

Then came the problem of the buttons. O'Hara and Neave went to Pat Reid in some distress. Neave told him the project was running short of lead. O'Hara's reserves of lead piping – 'thin German stuff' – had been used up. As they spoke O'Hara eyed longingly the alcohol still that the British officers were using to make their Christmas booze. Reid took fright: 'What are you looking at? I hope you're not hinting.' O'Hara demurred but pointed out that the only other source of lead piping was in the lavatory block. With only three lavatories to serve forty officers breaking one up might trigger a revolt, so the still's lead coil was removed, melted down and poured into white clay moulds carved by a Dutch officer. 'Oberleutnant Schwarz's' belt and leggings were made from cardboard, as was his revolver holster, stuffed with nothing more dangerous than newspaper. The finishing touch, a cap of an *Offizier* of the Third Reich, was converted from

Neave's own dress uniform cap by Squadron Leader Brian Paddon. It was an impressive sight: the shiny black peak bent Nazi-style, with a design of leaves, a red and white roundel, eagle's wings and a swastika on the front, all made from linoleum, the whole thing finished off with white piping sewed to the edge of the brim. Neave was delighted. 'With such a uniform I could face the arc lights once more with confidence,' he remembered.[3] Even Reid was impressed. At a passing-out test, he complimented Neave and his helpers. The uniforms would pass in any conditions other than broad daylight at close quarters.

Neave was by now impatient to go. He harried Reid about the readiness of the escape route and was told to keep his hair on. Meanwhile, rehearsals for the pantomime went ahead. Providentially, Luteyn was in the camp orchestra. Neave remembered him as a drummer, but Luteyn insists he played the double bass, which he bought from an English officer. A unique photograph of the show's line-up confirms that in this performance he played the double bass. The escape was planned to take place a few days before Christmas. The weather was deteriorating rapidly and Neave was anxious to avoid freezing to death on a German hillside. A combination of circumstances, however, forced a delay. According to Neave, their uniforms and false papers were not quite ready but Luteyn recollects that the postponement was due to a seasonal increase in train controls because so many German soldiers were going home for Christmas. Either way, the escape bid was postponed until the new year. *Ballet Nonsense* was a huge success; it included a new scene at Wombat College in which Dr Calomel gave a burlesque Nazi salute three times, to the discomfiture of German officers in the audience. Chaplain Platt noted in his diary: 'After the interval, Anthony's [Neave's] public school farce delighted the British and fogged the foreigners . . . The public school farce was redolent of masters' perceived interest in small boys, though one could plainly see that the intention was a take-off of a well-known schoolmaster.'[4]

After the pantomime, sloshed on bootleg alcohol, the men danced, fell dead drunk to the floor or vomited. In the midst of this revelry, a German officer came in to wish them a Happy Christmas: 'The laughter ceased abruptly and there was a silence so deliberate and terrible, that it struck the German like a blow in the face,' related Neave. 'He looked blankly about him, saluted and disconsolately withdrew.'[5]

Escape day was set for 5 January 1942; the phoney uniforms and civilian clothes had already been concealed beneath the stage. Reid decided to send out two pairs of escapers on successive nights, immediately after the change of sentry in front of the guardhouse, so the guard would be ignorant about officers' movements during the previous two hours. The break would take place after the nine o'clock *Appell*. Snow was falling during the roll-call, but Neave was roasting under his usual combination of battledress and sweater over civilian clothes, plus RAF trousers – and the black-painted cardboard leggings. Looking over to the Dutch contingent where Luteyn was similarly attired, Neave had an overpowering sense that this was his last evening in the castle.

On the order of dismissal, Neave and Luteyn mingled with senior officers as they moved into their quarters and went straight up to the theatre above. Fumbling their way in the dark, they ducked below the stage. Reid carefully opened the 'shovewood' trapdoor, and the three let themselves down noiselessly on a mattress-cover rope into the room below. There the escapers discarded their British uniforms and dusted down their German disguise. Reid led the way in stockinged feet through the first door until they were across the bridge and outside the final barrier: the locked entrance to the loft above the German guardhouse. Here, the escapers put on their boots and waited, fear and exasperation mounting, while Reid fought with the obstinate lock, at one point even admitting: 'I'm afraid I can't get it open.' But after he fiddled for ten minutes with his patent wire pick-lock, the heavy door creaked open.

Reid told Neave they must not move for exactly eleven minutes, the time it would take him to retrace his steps to the theatre. Neave accepted the order but warned he would not 'hang around' after that. The pair would take the first opportunity of a quiet spell in the guardhouse below. Reid reminded them of their 'escape theatre': on reaching the guardhouse door, they were to stop in full view of the sentry, calmly pull on their gloves, swap casual remarks and walk smartly down the cobbled ramp to the outer gates. 'We waited ten or fifteen minutes, and went down the stone stairs,' recollected Luteyn. 'On the first floor, where the officer of the guard was quartered, someone had just put on the radio. The door was ajar, but he didn't hear us, and couldn't see us because we nipped through very quickly. If he had seen us, it would have been finished. When we came out of the guardroom, the soldiers jumped up and stood by the door. A sergeant opened the door for us. Our hearts were pounding!'[6] Their cameo German performance was unnecessary.

They strode out to the snow-covered outer wall, Neave doing his best to adopt a Prussian military manner. Unfortunately, despite all the practice, he still marched with his hands behind his back, every inch a British officer. Luteyn hissed: 'March with your hands at your sides, you bloody fool.' By the gate into the outer courtyard, the first sentry saluted and said 'Nothing to report.' They thanked him and walked on to the second sentry by the outer gate. Luteyn ordered him to open the door which he did. They were now outside the main castle, on the moat bridge, from which the wicket gate led down into the moat and up the other side towards the German married quarters. By now it was snowing heavily and as they stumbled down a German soldier came towards them. He halted, staring at the 'officers'. Neave hesitated and was ready to make a run for it, a reminder of his earlier sense of panic once beyond the castle gate. Luteyn, with great presence of mind, demanded forcefully: 'Why do you not salute?' Open-mouthed, the soldier did as he was told and the escapers hurried on up the other side of the moat and round the married quarters to a high oak fence. Surmounting this, they were at last in tree cover. Neave's cardboard belt was ripped apart in the climb and his 'holster' disappeared into the snow.

The final obstacle was a high, moss-covered stone wall, overlaid with snow and ice. 'Here, we made our first mistake,' remembered Luteyn. 'I helped Neave up with my hands so he could sit on it and pull me up. We should have done it the other way round, because I was much bigger and more powerful.'[7] Every time Neave tried to pull his companion, he fell backwards in a confusion of snow and stone. Eventually, he caught Luteyn under the arms and they struggled to the top, panting heavily. They sat on the coping for a minute, then jumped 12 feet to the broken ground below. Neave was bruised, shaken and frightened. They leaned against the trees, breathing in the sharp, cold January air before Neave urged them on. They tore off their lovingly prepared fake uniforms and threw them into the river that wound its way below the woods.

In his diary entry for 5 January, Chaplain Platt recorded: 'Anthony Neave and a Dutch officer, Second Lieutenant Luteyn, escaped ten minutes ago. It was a scheme requiring the boldest initiative and at least eight weeks' preparation. It was carried out with the utmost secrecy, and already they are outside the castle.' During 1941, only two British officers succeeded in getting clear of the castle, and they had both been recaptured. 'The British are due for a success, and the seven people who so far know of Anthony's break are fairly confident that this is it.'[8]

Clear of the castle, Neave and Luteyn set off to walk to the town of Leisnig, six miles away. They would be less noticeable in this manufacturing centre than in the town of Colditz, where they risked recognition. The plan was to take an early morning workmen's train to Leipzig, thirty-five miles to the west. Thence, they would proceed south by train via Ulm and Nuremberg to Singen on the Swiss border, where they would walk to freedom. The imaginative Dutch had bribed a Colditz guard to secure a railway timetable, so the escapers knew that the first train left at 5.00 a.m. They thus had seven hours to kill in the freezing dark.

Mercifully, although the thermometer read minus 17 degrees Celsius, the snow was abating and the moon aided their progress across frozen fields until they reached the country road to Leisnig. With rising confidence, they struck out for the station. Neave was dressed in a blue jacket. Fashioned from an officer's uniform of the Chasseurs Alpins, this was the gift of Capitaine Boris, a Jewish reserve officer in the French regiment, in recognition of Neave's support of the small Jewish contingent in Colditz. His RAF trousers were turned down over his Polish boots and the civilian guise was completed by a ski cap made from a blanket.

The escapers had forged papers showing them to be Dutch electrical workers, with permission to change their place of work from Leipzig to Ulm. It was a plausible cover. By 1942, foreign workers had been drafted all over Germany to aid the war effort. They had no papers for the journey to Leipzig but hoped that early morning stupor would lower the guard of the railway authorities. They walked steadily for two hours before coming to the outskirts of Leisnig, where the presence of a sentry outside what appeared to be barracks forced them to take to the country once more. 'We couldn't stand still, because it was too cold. We walked through farms,' said Luteyn. 'The only thing we heard was the barking of dogs. We got the money out of our bodies [stored in their rectums as before] and cleaned it with snow.'[9]

Neave remembered that it was too cold to talk. They waited until the train was almost due and then walked down the main street to the station, exchanging greetings with another early traveller. The still little town, with its spires and snowy rooftops, reminded Neave of an illustration in Beatrix Potter's *The Tailor of Gloucester* and its description of the snowy, sleeping city in the early morning. There was nobody on duty at the station, where they sheltered from the cold behind a wooden hut. Neave and Luteyn stood apart from each other until the arrival of the train when everyone surged forward to the ticket office. Being much the better German speaker, Luteyn bought two workmen's tickets to Leipzig on the 05.45 service.

In the warm fug of the partially blacked-out train, Neave soon nodded off. Luteyn, however, stayed awake. He was horrified at one point to hear Neave murmuring in English in his sleep and kicked him smartly on the shins. The relationship between the two men was a curious one. Thrown together by the fortunes of war only weeks previously, they were now utterly dependent on each other. Yet it was not a close relationship, not even friendship. Luteyn said: 'I didn't know him, and he didn't know me.' Neave has left behind a generous portrait of his fellow escaper in *They Have Their Exits*, praising him as a strong and buoyant character, with Dutch thoroughness and staying power. His superior knowledge of German enabled him to take each fence with aplomb, while his 'gay, attractive manner of speaking' got them both out of the many dangerous situations that were to follow. 'For my part, rebellious by temperament though I was, I found him easier to work with and we seldom argued with each other.'[10] Indeed, they spoke little, for fear of drawing attention to themselves.

The workmen's train got them to Leipzig by six o'clock where they shared in the station lavatories using Neave's safety razor. Their next destination was the medieval city of Ulm, birthplace of Albert Einstein, more than 200 miles away. In Neave's recollection, there was no train until 20.52. According to Luteyn, there was a morning service, but they decided to wait for the night train so that they would have somewhere to sleep. They bought coffee at the station refreshment room and took it to the waiting room. Neave took in the poor, run-down travellers sitting 'silent and obedient' amid their families and luggage, and he felt a surge of pity for the victims of Hitler's war. 'The hopelessness in their faces brought a stark realisation of suffering,' he recorded later. The gaucheness of camp life almost gave them away at this stage. Unaware of what he was doing, Neave took out a slab of Red Cross chocolate and began eating it. Although POWs were quite liberally supplied with chocolate, German civilians had not seen such a delicacy for months. One young woman gaped at him and spoke quickly to an old woman beside her. The crowd stared in a hostile manner, muttering '*tchokolade, tchokolade*', and Luteyn shot him an angry look. Embarrassed, the pair shuffled out of the waiting room and into the streets of Leipzig.

The city looked as if it was under military occupation, which in a sense it was, but by the country's own army. Military vehicles crammed with personnel ploughed past in complete indifference to civilians, while the field-grey of the Wehrmacht and the mauve-blue of the Luftwaffe dominated the pavements. Civilians, Neave noted, looked 'hungry and unhappy'. They made their way through the crowded streets to a park, where a further recontre with a German civilian almost unmasked them. As they sat on a park bench in the winter sun, Luteyn reading a newspaper, a German girl came and sat close to Neave. He remembered her as young, blonde and obviously working class. Gazing through prominent blue eyes, she addressed him: 'Good morning.' It was the first time for almost two years that he had been so close to a woman. 'She wanted to approach him,' says Luteyn. Neave, tense with the knowledge that he could not and dared not get into a conversation, tried to remain calm. When he did not respond the girl became irritated, accusing him of being unsociable. Luteyn stood up and motioned to him '*hier gehen*' (come here) and they walked quickly away. 'She was goddamn angry,' said Luteyn.

The pair then took refuge in a cinema, reasoning that in the dark they would be undetectable among the crowd. It would also be warm. But in the cinema, Neave made another of those curious errors of judgement when he lit up a cigarette, it was English, POW issue. 'You could see people smelling it in the air, wondering "what the hell is that?".' All these things were little mistakes,' recalled Luteyn.[11] It was a dangerous moment, especially as they were sitting among German soldiers and sailors and their girlfriends in the cheapest seats; Neave promptly switched to Polish cigarettes. They sat through a newsreel of Rommel's campaign in Libya, which showed panzers in action and the downing of a British plane. The captured pilot was filmed waving encouragement to those of his fellow airmen still in action. Neave, overexcited by this display of British verve, gripped the seat in front so firmly that he earned a sharp rebuke from its occupant. There followed film of the German advance into Soviet Russia, but the appalling conditions being endured by the Wehrmacht, Neave thought, came as a shock to the audience.

After the newsreel, the lights went up and to loud martial music the audience began singing Nazi songs, among them 'We Are Marching Against England!', though by this stage the Battle of Britain had been lost and Hitler's invasion plans had been shelved. The song was familiar to both men, who were used to singing it, albeit derisively, in the camp, so they joined in lustily with, Neave insisted, 'a faint grin on our faces'.

All too soon they were back out in the cold of the Leipzig streets. Snow was falling, and the pair had to double through back alleys to shake off an inquisitive policeman. They took shelter in another cinema, watching the same war newsreel for a second time among German troops on leave. Then came more propaganda, this time Hermann Goering calling for a boost in the war effort. The film ended with scenes of goose-stepping Nazis, prompting some of the audience to start the Horst Wessel song. Neave thought the singing cheerless and half-hearted.

Back out in the streets, they tramped about in the blackout before making for the railway station. Luteyn bought tickets for the journey south towards Switzerland. He remembers booking only to Nuremberg although Neave believed he booked right through to Ulm, not far from the Swiss frontier. They waited 'tired, cold and anxious' in the station waiting room, Neave again observing his fellow passengers closely. Some, mostly civilians, were poor and infirm; others were soldiers, army clerks in uniform and SS men, marching around 'like locusts' requisitioning food and newspapers. 'Such is total war,' he reflected.

Military police were checking servicemen but allowed civilians straight through on to the platform. The two men stood by their train until it was time to board; finding all the seats taken they stood in the draughty corridor. As the train progressed south, passengers got off, making space in the compartments. Neave and Luteyn were, however, reluctant to take up the empty seats for fear of being discovered during a chance conversation. At one point an SS officer with a compartment to himself invited them to join him. Not for the first time Neave's and Luteyn's recollections differ. Neave recorded that the officer first asked them if they were Jews but Luteyn denies this.[12] It does seem an odd question. At this stage of the war, barely 150,000 Jews survived in Germany, all of whom were required to wear the yellow star. 'He asked us in, and it would have been dangerous not to do so,' said Luteyn. 'We went inside and I put Neave in the corner where he could sleep.' The SS officer spoke to Luteyn, who told him they were Dutch electrical workers travelling to Ulm. 'This is how it should be – working for Germany,' said the officer. He volunteered that his destination was Munich, and then Vienna for a conference. They nodded politely, and took it in turns to sleep. More passengers came in, eyeing their down-at-heel appearance contemptuously, but when the military police asked for their papers, the SS man waved them away with the explanation that they were Dutch *Fremdarbeiter* (foreign workers). As Luteyn slept, Neave counted off the stations: Zwickau, Plauen, Hof and Regensburg, where they changed trains. They sat in the waiting room, heads resting on a table like the other travellers, until the connecting service took them on to Ulm.

Here, they were in a sensitive border area, with officials on the alert for suspicious looking individuals. Luteyn tried to buy two tickets for Singen, a German town less than twelve miles from the Swiss frontier. The female booking office clerk understood from Luteyn's language that he was not German, and asked for their papers. She studied them sceptically before telling them to wait while she called the station police. They stood nervously in a queue in front of the booking office window, the Germans eyeing them 'as if we were scoundrels', said Luteyn. He edged Neave towards the door, but when they were almost outside a fat red-faced railway policeman halted them. Luteyn tried to explain that they were electrical workers based in Ulm and were on an excursion to visit an aunt in a village near Singen. The policeman refused to listen, and marched them across the station yard to a police office, where a more senior officer examined their papers. Their Colditz-manufactured documents, 'stamped' by the Leipzig police confirmed that they were Dutch voluntary workers being transferred to Ulm. The police lieutenant could make neither head nor tail of the papers but he was impressed by Luteyn's genuine Dutch passport, issued when he left Batavia (now Jakarta), capital of the Dutch East Indies, in 1936 to enrol in Breda Military Academy. 'Is this yours?' he asked, and began to talk in a relaxed manner about the East Indies. Neave kept quiet. The officer sent them under armed police guard to the nearby State Labour Office, a two-storey building 'guarded' by men in brown uniforms with spades. On the way, Neave was frantically eating his *Ausweis*, thinking it would not stand up to further scrutiny. 'He thought if they saw it that it would be extra time in prison, so he tore pieces off in his pocket and ate the whole thing,' remembered Luteyn.

In the reception room of the Labour Office there was a list of offices. Room 26, where the policeman was to take them to verify their identity, was on the second floor. There were no lifts. Their police escort had clearly had enough. 'You go up there and fix your business, and I'll find you quarters,' he said, trustingly. Neave and Luteyn had had enough, too.

They went up one flight of stairs and found themselves in a long corridor with a metal staircase on one side leading down into a coal shed. They clambered down, climbed through a window, jumped a fence and made good their escape through an open window into the side-streets of Ulm. They crossed the River Donau, unchecked by military guards on the bridge. Luteyn bought a motoring map of the surrounding area and they began walking to Singen. It was still bitterly cold.

Entering the town of Laupheim further on, they encountered a tramway going in their direction. Night was falling, and in the market square they bought tickets to Stockach, the village nearest the frontier to which they dared book passage. They sat undisturbed, though the object of rustic curiosity, on a bench waiting for the train. Once installed in the wooden compartment, fell asleep, worn out by their exertions. Clattering through the village of Pfullendorf, they reached Stockach at about nine in the evening of 7 January 1942. Watched by an inquisitive railway official, they walked among the white-painted cottages towards Singen. The road became steeper and dense woods hemmed them in on both sides. Great banks of snow lined the route. They walked all night to reach Singen. At one point, they met a Frenchman on the road driving a horse and wagon. Neave challenged him in French: 'Can you turn round and take us to Switzerland?' The alarmed Frenchman demurred. From their bearing, he guessed that they were Allied officers. 'No. It is too dangerous for me. You as officers can have a good time, but if they get me I will be put somewhere rotten. I have a good life on the farm. You can hide. I will not say anything.'[13] They continued to hike through the intense cold all night, and before dawn encountered four German woodcutters walking with lanterns to their work in the forest. The men challenged them, asking if they were Poles from a labour camp in the vicinity. Luteyn said they were. The woodcutters did not believe them and sent one of their number off by bicycle to fetch the police from Singen. As on the previous occasion of his escape in Poland, fatigue almost did for Neave. He was all but ready to give himself up. His feet felt like blocks of ice and he hardly cared that they had come so far only to be recaptured. He could only think of warm fires and beds.

As the fourth man pedalled off, the three remaining men looked uncomfortably at their charges. Then Neave and Luteyn realised that the woodcutters were as scared as they were, if not more. Sensing their opportunity, without saying a word the pair sprinted into the woods at the roadside and continued until they could run no further, sinking at last exhausted into the snow. Regaining their breath, they stumbled on through the forest. According to

Luteyn, Neave was by now hallucinating, imagining he was back at university. Neave admits to suffering 'a kind of delirium, between sleeping and waking', and thinking he was on the parade ground talking to his colonel. Luteyn snapped him out of it, but it was vital that they find somewhere to rest up for the day before making their final bid for freedom. It was snowing heavily again. Then, crossing a clearing in the trees, they came to a woodman's hut. They approached it walking backwards, to give the impression that someone had left it rather than entered. They climbed in through an open window and found a couch. Utterly drained, they crawled under a blanket together and slept until mid-afternoon. They were woken at one point by dogs barking, but otherwise they were not disturbed.

However, one further calamity occurred – this time involving Luteyn. He had taken off his soaking wet shoes before falling into deep sleep. In the bitter cold, they had frozen to the floor. Without shoes, he could go nowhere. They both got down on to the floor and blew on Luteyn's shoes until the ice melted. All the while they could hear the distant noise of traffic on the road to Singen. From their little map, they gathered they were only two or three miles from the border town. Neave recorded a further meeting with two Hitler Youth, and recalls his readiness to kill them to ensure his freedom. Once again, however, Luteyn does not remember this incident.

During the night the two men passed through Singen, skirting a great coal heap in the blackout. Neave recorded in his official report on the escape, now in the Public Record Office, how they walked west from Singen as far as a signpost showing 'Gottmadingen 4 km'. From there they travelled north and skirted a large wood fringing the Gottmadingen–Singen road, eventually travelling south over the railway line that ran north of the road to a point where the road and frontier met for about 50 yards. An open space lay before them with woods all around. Less than 100 yards away, they saw a German sentry at a barrier stopping cars. At 00.30 on the morning of 9 January, Neave and Luteyn, walking and crawling through deep snow, crossed the road and the open space and thus passed over the frontier. 'We saw no Swiss guards and no lights,' Neave reported. After accidentally crossing back into Germany, 'which we discovered by observing a sentry on our left – i.e. to the east, we followed a compass line to Ramsen and were there interned at 01.00 hours'.[14]

Both Neave and Luteyn also left less formal accounts. 'We knew exactly where to cross,' said Luteyn. 'We shook hands and said "OK, let's go".'[15] He recollected that it was about four in the morning. They navigated a big ditch and floundered across country for a mile or so before entering a forest they knew to be Swiss. 'Nobody shouted at us.' It was absolutely quiet, apart from their laboured breathing. Neave's boots were weighed down with ice, and the effort of wading through deep snow was sometimes too much. They lay down, panting and cursing. Luteyn was blabbering in Dutch and at one point had to be pulled from a deep drift that buried him up to his ski cap. 'Then,' recollected Neave, 'it was my turn to flounder, helpless and distraught, murmuring with a last attempt at humour that Patriotism was not enough.'[16] Coming out on to higher ground, they heard a clock chime five and they stumbled on to a road. The dark shapes of buildings materialised on either side, and soon they found themselves in a rural street ending in a church tower. Neave spotted an advertisement for a circus. By the flame of his cigarette lighter he read that it was being held in Schaffhausen, which was in Switzerland. They were in the Swiss village of Ramsen. They had made it.

7

Operation Ratline

Safe in the knowledge that he had reached freedom, Neave's first instinct was to pray. 'I thought of kneeling in the snow and thanking God for our deliverance,' he said later. Luteyn and he shook hands again. At this point, their accounts diverge once again. Neave recollected that they heard the sound of army boots ringing down the street and backed into the shadows in case it was a German patrol. On being challenged, however, they realised it was a Swiss frontier guard and announced their true identity, before performing an impromptu dance together in the main street. Luteyn remembers that they sat down in the snow shouting: 'Hey Swiss, come on out! Come and get us!' until a sentry came to investigate.[1] On this occasion, unusually, Luteyn's recollection is the more romantic. Both concur that the Swiss guards took them into their frontier post and warmed them with mugs of hot chocolate.

Neave was ecstatic. 'Never in my life, perhaps, will I ever know such a moment of triumph,' he reflected. Almost imperceptibly, the partnership between the two escapers began to dissolve. A Swiss official requested their personal details, and asked if anyone in Switzerland could speak for them. Neave offered the name of Madame Paravicini, wife of the former Swiss Minister in London, who had been sending parcels and letters of encouragement to Neave and other British POWs for many months. Luteyn could not emulate his social connections. The escapers were taken under guard to Ramsen police station, and allowed to sleep until dawn.

A Swiss policeman offered Neave a razor and 'the great escaper' was shocked to see his reflection in the mirror: a grey face with cracked black lips and ears raw with chilblains. His eyes were defiant, but he still noted fear.

The fugitives had one last contact with Nazi territory. The little Swiss train from Ramsen to Schaffhausen ran through a neck of Germany. Its carriages had balconies down each side, guarded by Swiss guards in plain clothes on one side and a German sentry on the other. Safely in the police station at Schaffhausen, the pair were questioned individually. Neave's interrogation was conducted in French and generally reflected curiosity about life under the Nazis. Having been a closely guarded prisoner of war he could tell them little, though he expatiated on the shortage under the Third Reich of that Swiss delicacy, chocolate. He concluded his interview with a long denunciation of the Germans, whom he described contemptuously as *Boches*. A highly diverted police official asked him to remember he was now in a neutral country.

As the first escapers to reach Switzerland in 1942, Neave and Luteyn were welcomed by the burgomaster of Schaffhausen and promptly placed under 'hotel arrest' in the Hotel Schwarn, as regulations required. They were not to let it be known that they were escaped prisoners, as the Dutch and British embassies had first to be informed. This quickly proved to be an impossible injunction to observe. In the hotel dining room the escapers sat down to their first proper lunch for two years. Steak and wine were served, and the proprietor joined in the merrymaking. Neave became so drunk he started to speak in a meaningless polyglot language, mixing English, French, German and a few words of Polish. The hotelier soon realised the two men could not handle alcohol and bundled them to an upstairs room where they slept off their meal. The days of 'hotel arrest' that followed were amiable in the highest degree. Curious Swiss would come in and buy them drinks, sharing their stories of derring-do in Germany. Neave found the memory of prison slipping rapidly away, except as a topic of conversation with his hosts. He did not forget his arrangement to report his escape, however. He sent two postcards back to Colditz, one in code under an assumed name to a fellow prisoner, the other in English to Oberst Prawitz, the Kommandant. 'Dear Oberst,' wrote Neave, 'I am glad to be able to inform you that my friend and I have arrived safely for our holiday in Switzerland. We had a pleasant journey, suffering the minimum of inconvenience. I hope that you will not get sent to the Russian Front on my account. My regards to Hauptmann Priem. Yours sincerely, A.M.S. Neave, Lieutenant, Royal Artillery.'

The cards were not posted for several weeks, to give time for the two other escapers, Lieutenant Hyde-Thomson and Lieutenant Donkers, to get out of the castle by the same route taken by Neave and Luteyn. Not until 7 January did the camp authorities find that *four* officers had actually flown the coop. Nor could they find the escape path. However, on 12 January, three days after Neave and Luteyn crossed into Switzerland, Hyde-Thomson and Donkers were recaptured in Ulm, posing as Dutch electrical workers and trying to buy tickets to Tuttlingen in the frontier zone on the same train. After the first party's daring getaway from the State Labour Office security at the station had been increased and RAF bombing of the city put the authorities on alert for downed air crew. Railway police soon saw through the disguise of the second pair and arrested them. Thereafter, Colditz escape managers adopted a new policy, that no more than two fugitives would travel the same route. After a diligent search, 'shovewood' was found by the Germans on 13 January and closed. 'The horses, however, had bolted,' mourned Reinhold Eggers. 'Two never came back.' He nonetheless got a week's leave and a bottle of champagne from the Kommandant for discovering the unusual theatre exit.

Comfortable as it was, hotel arrest began to pall. Just as they were becoming increasingly impatient, the police came and told them they should pack. From Schaffhausen they were escorted by train south, where they were separated, Neave going to the British embassy in Berne and Luteyn on to Geneva. Despite the intensity of their eighty-four-hour escape ordeal, they were to meet again only three times, once in Switzerland and then in Holland and London many years after the war. Their ordeal did not make them lifelong friends, a testimony, perhaps, to Neave's self-containment.

In Berne, Neave was taken through the legation to a side door in the garden leading to a small house next door used by the British military and air attachés, where he was welcomed by Colonel Henry Antrobus Cartwright, the military attaché and a war hero in his own right. He had made repeated attempts to escape from captivity during the Great War, succeeding the fifth time, and chronicled his exploits in *Within Four Walls*, published in 1930 and exactly the kind of reading enjoyed by the young Airey. 'I greatly respected him,' he wrote subsequently. 'His book was a classic and had inspired a new generation of escapers. As a small boy, I had read it with romantic pleasure, and it played a great part in forming my philosophy of escape.' Cartwright, who served as British consul in Bratislava for two years from 1920, was recalled to government service in the Sudetenland in 1938 before being posted to Berne on the outbreak of war in September 1939. His work as military attaché was useful cover for his role with MI9. MI9's role was to organise the repatriation of escaped and evading British officers and other ranks from Occupied Europe. It was an offshoot of MI6, the British Secret Intelligence Service (SIS). Apart from its quasi-humanitarian mission, MI9 was heavily engaged in gathering military intelligence for the war effort. Neave was immediately given a short interrogation, at which point he delivered his assessment of Graudenz aerodrome, the destination of his unsuccessful escape bid the previous year. His volunteering of such useful intelligence material may simply have been an act of soldierly zealousness. It seems unlikely, however, that an officer of Neave's background would not appreciate the impact of his communication. He had been accused by the Nazis of being a spy and here he was acting like one. Innocently or otherwise (probably otherwise), he was offering himself as a prime candidate for intelligence work. In his first contact with the secret world of the security services, he acquitted himself well and his performance was duly noted.

Cartwright found Neave some better civilian clothing – 'an awful green tweed suit of Swiss design' – and took him home for the night. He then stayed with Cartwright's assistant, Major Fryer, (who would also have been in the know) and his wife for a couple of nights, attending the legation in the mornings 'for various papers to be put in order'. In the jargon of a later generation, he was being talent-spotted by MI9. In the afternoons, he wandered around Berne, smoking *Stumpen,* small Swiss cheroots, for which he had conceived 'an eccentric passion'. After nearly two years of incarceration, it was some time before he got used to traffic and the ways of a busy city. Cartwright sent him for a medical examination by Dr von Erlach, a Swiss doctor who by extra-ordinary coincidence had first met Neave in Spangenburg camp in 1941. Baron von Erlach, a senior official in the Red Cross and also a colonel in the Swiss army, had led a deputation to the camp. There he had conveyed a message from Madame Paravicini to the young British officer: 'Your family are well and send you their love,' he told Neave. Now, von Erlach found him reasonably fit but prescribed three weeks' rest at his own home, Rosengarten, an agreeable chalet situated near Gertenzee. Here, Neave celebrated his twenty-sixth birthday and pondered his future. He had not thought beyond the enormous challenge of escape. Nothing, he imagined, could match the elation of freeing himself from the clutches of the Nazis. Transferred to a hotel in Fribourg, under close watch by the Swiss police, he lived a life of 'mild dissipation', waiting for a summons. He drank absinthe, mixed with Polish officers interned in the area and made up for lost time in the company of young women, some of them, by his own admission, 'alleged female spies'. He also attended one lecture on architecture at Fribourg University.

In March 1942, the summons came. He was recalled to Berne, where Colonel Cartwright gave him a dressing down for mixing too freely with 'unreliable' girlfriends who could indeed be spies. As a veteran of Gestapo interrogation, Neave prided himself on being able to deceive any female agents of the Third Reich. The interview must have gone well because he was brought back on 15 April. Expecting another lecture on security, the young lieutenant was 'astonished' when the military attaché growled: 'We're sending you back first, Neave. MI9 have asked for you.' In retrospect, it seems more remarkable that Neave was so unsuspecting. He was an obvious candidate for recruitment to an escape and intelligence service for he had made the first successful British breakout from Germany's most impregnable fortress. Unbidden, he had offered a military assessment of Graudenz aerodrome. He had survived the attentions of the Gestapo, and of course he had the right social background. The intelligence services relied heavily on personal recommendation. New entrants were usually 'one of us'. As a generation of upper-crust British spies for the Soviet Union was discovering, it was unquestionably a matter of who you knew, not what you knew.

Over an 'uneasy' meal, culminating in port, nuts and fine cigars, Cartwright told Neave that he would be leaving for neutral Spain the very next day. Neave was shocked. He had expected regimental orders to go to the Unoccupied Zone of France, but Cartwright was adamant: 'We are sending you out before the others, even though they escaped from Germany before you.' Eight other British officers were still enjoying Swiss hospitality. He was being given priority, though the journey through France, over the Pyrenees and across Spain to Gibraltar, was fraught with danger. British officers on similar sorties had been captured by collaborationist Vichy police and handed back to the Germans. As Neave contemplated the 'sheer excitement' of his new odyssey, Cartwright said calmly: 'MI9 have sent orders for you and Hugh Woollatt to cross the Swiss frontier as soon as possible. We have sent one or two people through before. But you are still guinea pigs.' Woollatt, a regular officer in the Lancashire Fuseliers, had escaped from Oflag Vc at Biberach in southern Germany at the

end of 1941. He would be killed in action in the battle of
Normandy in 1944. Neave had suspected that he and Woollatt,
who was equally enthusiastic about his social life, might be sent
back first. 'Perhaps MI9's like Cartwright's real fear was that we
might become entangled with beautiful Gestapo spies,' he
admitted later.[2] There were indeed grounds for anxiety. Several
attempts had already been made to discover how Neave had
reached Switzerland. The delights of Fribourg might be fun but it
was dangerous there too. He knew it was time to leave. Neave was
instructed to leave Berne by the early morning train to Geneva.
In true cloak and dagger fashion, he was to approach a man in a
dark felt hat at the station bookstall who would be reading the
Journal de Genève and make himself known. It was nearly midnight
when he parted from Cartwright armed with the password '*Je
viens de la part d'Aristide!*'

Rising early the next day, Neave was impressed when Cartwright turned up in his dressing gown to see him off. 'I could see
that he secretly envied me,' he observed. Neave watched to see if
he was being followed but the train journey was uneventful,
despite sharing his compartment with two German businessmen
and their fat wives. He met his contact, 'Robert', at the bookstall,
noticing that he was reading the newspaper upside down. They
shook hands, had a reviving glass of Pernod in a nearby bar and
motored out to a nondescript hotel in the old sector of the city,
which turned out to be little more than a brothel. Here, Neave
met Woollatt, a tall dark-haired man, 'very alert and courageous'
but also blessed with a good sense of humour. Neave signed the
register as Oscar Wilde. Not to be outdone, Woollatt wrote Herr
Albert Hall. They were shown to a small, bare room and spent
several hours smoking, drinking champagne and joking about life
in a brothel, before 'Victor', a slim Englishman, appeared during
the afternoon with a suitcase of new clothes. At last Neave could
discard the ridiculous Swiss tweeds, if only for a blue suit that had
seen better days. 'Victor', who was Cartwright's man in the British
embassy in Geneva, also brought a change of identity for the pair.

Henceforth, they journeyed as Czech refugees bound for a reception centre in Marseilles. They had new papers which permitted them to travel in Occupied France. Neave's photograph, taken after his arrival in Berne, was 'far from flattering', but it was his appearance in the fresh set of clothes that concerned him more. With his dark skin, Woollatt looked the part but Neave's fair hair and boyish looks shouted 'English'. The embassy envoy solved the problem by jamming an old green workman's cap on his head, which gave him a flavour of *mittel Europa*. Their efforts to pronounce incomprehensible Czech cover names reduced the party to fits of laughter. Looking back, Neave found it extraordinary that they should have treated the occasion with such levity.

That evening they went out for a stroll by Lake Geneva and ate curry with lager beer before holing up in the hotel bedroom for zero hour, set at three thirty the following morning. A Swiss policeman in plain clothes would knock on their door and they were to follow his instructions. He would give the rather transparent password 'Mr Churchill expects you'. Neither man could sleep and the hours passed with interminable slowness until at the appointed time there came a knock at the door and an archetypal plain-clothes detective said with feeling, '*Vive* Winston Churchill. He wants you back.' He hurried them to a waiting car. The party travelled south-west, to a graveyard surrounded by a flint wall on the outskirts of the city. Here, they hid among the tombstones, Neave's curry still troubling him. Over the wall lay a broad band of barbed wire, separating Switzerland and France.

At five o'clock, as dawn broke, the Swiss policeman gave them his final instructions. They were to cross the barbed-wire barrier with care and climb up the grassy bank to a small white house where a road sign pointed the way to the frontier town of Annemasse. There they would be met by an old man in classic French attire – sabots and beret – sporting a clay pipe in his mouth, upside down. They shook hands with their Swiss helper and vaulted the cemetery wall. As they picked their way through the wire, Neave tore a gaping hole in his 'Czech' suit and had to borrow Woollatt's raincoat to conceal the telltale evidence. Once again, it was as well that he was not travelling alone. They swiftly made their rendezvous, only to find the traffic was almost entirely made up of men dressed exactly as their contact, most of them smoking clay pipes. Eventually, a middle-aged man with silver-grey hair stopped, leaned his bicycle against the signpost and, after a careful, deferential look, announced himself. 'Good morning, gentlemen. I am Louis Simon, formerly of the Ritz Hotel, London.' He walked them along the road to Annemasse, reminiscing about his years as a waiter in the West End. He thought their disguises poor. He could see that they were gentlemen. Neave was equally unimpressed by Louis' country smock, picturing him instead in his black tailcoat moving self-assuredly among diners at the Ritz.

Their walk along the road to the *douanier* more resembled a gentle morning stroll in the Haute-Savoie than that initial frightening passage from enemy territory to Switzerland. When they reached the border post, it was raining hard and the escapers mingled with early morning workmen while Louis chatted to the frontier guard. The sun came out as they strode into France and a mile later they came upon Louis' red-brick villa set back from the road. His wife had prepared an enormous repast of ham, eggs, toast and coffee, which she set before them as 'a special London breakfast'. They saw from her face that she was worried, and she admitted that she had not slept the night before. She was relieved that they had got this far. Monsieur and Madame Simon, and many other brave people like them in Occupied Europe, were taking the most terrible risk in sheltering Allied servicemen. If Neave and Woollatt were recaptured they could expect to be sent back to Colditz for another month in the town goal. The French couple would either be shot or sent to a concentration camp, which often amounted to the same thing. Both were death sentences.

At this point in the war, April 1942, the escape routes organised

by MI9, known as ratlines, were still in their infancy. Several
hundred Allied airmen, soldiers and sailors were being held by
the Vichy authorities at two prison fortresses, St Hippolyt-du-
Fort, near Nîmes, where the French began interning British
personnel from the spring of 1941, and Fort de la Revère at La
Turbie, outside Monte Carlo. Here were imprisoned Expeditionary Force survivors from Dunkirk who had got over the
demarcation line only to be interned by the French, together with
RAF aircrew shot down over France and other Allied servicemen.
The first escape line had been set up as early as the summer of
1940 by a Belgian army medical officer, Albert-Marie Guérisse,
who had escaped to Gibraltar after the fall of Paris. This
exceptionally courageous man had, with a French naval officer,
commandeered a cargo vessel, *Le Rhin*, and sailed her to the Rock.
She was taken over by the Royal Navy, renamed HMS *Fidelity* and
pressed into service ferrying escapers from southern France to
Gibraltar and infiltrating SOE and MI6 agents. On a mission in
April 1941, Guérisse, codenamed Pat O'Leary, was captured by a
Vichy French patrol near the Spanish border and incarcerated in
St Hippolyt. He escaped, but instead of fleeing to England stayed
behind to set up a ratline, named the Pat line after his pseudonym.
It was down this line that Neave and Woollatt were to be
repatriated.

The escapers were taken by a second guide, Mademoiselle
Jeanne, a 'quiet, mystic young girl', no older than eighteen, from
Simon's villa to the backstreets of Annemasse. Jeanne did not
speak until she had taken them to the safety of a run-down house
where they were once again fed with coffee and fried eggs. Neave
tried to engage the girl in conversation about the escape route
and its organisers, but she confined her reply to: 'All I ask of you
is that you should send a message on the BBC if you get back to
England to safety. Here, everyone listens to the BBC.' Bowed by
her transparent faith in her duty, the British pair sat in silence as
she left. The experience made a powerful impression on Neave.
He detected 'a strange light' in her eyes, recording that 'Nothing

could have expressed more powerfully the spirit of resistance to Hitler ... I never forgot this first revelation of the courage of ordinary French men and women in helping us to escape.'[3] His admiration of the girls who carried out this dangerous task grew and unquestionably reshaped his attitude to women. Neave grew up in a male-dominated household but his wartime encounters inspired respect – reverence even – of women. He was well ahead of his time in what would now be called gender politics.

The escapers waited an hour after Jeanne left, sitting over coffee made in the dingy kitchen watched by an alarmed housewife and her two small children. Their reverie was broken by the arrival of Alex, a portly Frenchman who cheerfully announced himself as a well-known black marketeer. His daytime profession was perfect cover for aiding escapers. Alex drove an antiquated Citroën powered by a charcoal burner. In this, they banged and rattled off through Ugine towards Annecy. En route, there was a scare when *les flics* roared towards them, horn blaring. Neave and Woollatt took to their heels among bushes by Lake Annecy. As Alex predicted, the police stopped briefly but ignored him, and the trio bounced noisily into Annecy, coming to rest under an archway by a large square. Here, announced the black marketeer, was the home of Pierre and Cécile. Their flat was above the archway and the woman of the house had prepared another substantial meal. Cécile, Neave noticed, had none of the quiet courage of Jeanne. Her hands were shaking as she served the food. Fear stalked her every move and she behaved like a frightened animal. 'A sense of family duty alone kept her from panic,' Neave observed later. 'She was courageous in her weakness, seeking to struggle on for the sake of her husband.'[4] The meal continued over liqueurs into the afternoon while Alex questioned them about their phoney Czech papers and they expressed fears about their fate if questioned by the police. The atmosphere grew tense and Neave sought to ease the strain by talking about life under the Pétain regime. They heard sobbing in the kitchen and raised voices: Pierre was quarrelling with his wife over the risks they were taking. The escapers sat in a taut, guilty silence until Alex and Pierre led them from the dingy flat to the *gazogène* Citroën for the next stage of their underground journey to Chambéry. As they left, Neave discerned 'forlorn and defenceless' Cécile, her face smudged with tears.

The party spent a few hours at a safe house near the station before boarding a crowded overnight train to Marseilles. Clutching their battered briefcases, the escapers and their minders fought their way into a carriage. Neave wore his Geneva suit and a French tweed cap; Woollatt had acquired a grey Homburg, a size or two too small. They attracted no attention until Neave, unable to sleep, left the compartment to get some fresh air in the corridor. He was immediately aware of a young, blond-haired officer of the Milice, the Vichy police, standing next to him. Lacking confidence in his Czech cover story, Neave implored Alex with his eyes to take his place. He did so, drawing the policeman into conversation, but Neave found the officer's cold blue eyes still on him when the crowded train steamed into Marseilles at seven in the morning of 17 April. They hurried out into the bright sunlit boulevards, making for the Canebière district where the guides expected to find shelter before the final stage of the escapers' journey from Vichy France to neutral Spain. Their first effort drew a blank. After a nightmare quest through the filthy back lanes of the port, they were thrown out of the 'safe' address by an enormous prostitute enraged that the men were not seeking her favours. They moved on to a second address given by 'Robert' in Geneva, and after noon found themselves, drained and famished, in the Café Petit Poucet, a working-class restaurant on the Boulevard Dugommier. A waiter motioned them to a table, but when Neave asked for 'Gaston' he looked around in fear and shot through glass double doors. The patron, a short, balding man, was not pleased to see them. He ordered them into a back room and demanded the password. Then, to the consternation of the escape party, he brought a young gendarme in through a side door. Neave, fearing a trap, demanded to know who he was. The patron told him to mind his own business. The gendarme, Jacques, was clearly a trusted man who would bring someone to talk to them. They waited, Alex and Pierre silently fuming. It was clear that, by barging in so ostentatiously, they had upset their host. 'Gaston' relaxed, ordered them coffee and drinks, and a short time later a slightly built, sharply dressed man of middle age sporting a neat grey moustache entered the room.

He introduced himself as 'Maurice' and demanded the password. Satisfied with the response, he addressed the escapers in perfect English, asking about Geneva and their journey through Vichy France while their guides looked blankly on. This was the mysterious Louis Nouveau, a rich Marseilles businessman, who both funded and organised the Pat evasion line. 'Maurice' joked about taking messages to his solicitor in England, and of taking a bottle of champagne home to give to his broker in the City. The two men gazed in astonishment at this extravagant figure, for whom even their exotic travels had not prepared them. 'Maurice' made an elegant joke about Pierre Laval ('there must be something wrong about a man who always wears a long white tie') and debated the merits of Pimms No. 1 before warning them of the dangers still ahead. Not until 1969 did Neave reveal that Nouveau was a well-known merchant banker who served as one of the most faithful and devoted workers of the Resistance. He even gave the Pat line £5,000, a small fortune in 1942, from his own funds.

Their elegant new guide took over from Alex and Pierre, instructing Neave and Woollatt to follow him at thirty paces and stop when he stopped. Nouveau led them through the marketplace to a modern block of flats by the harbourside. After a false alarm over a watching gendarme, he lifted his hat and wiped his brow as a signal for them to enter the apartment block. Nouveau's flat was on the fifth floor, commanding a fine view over the Old Port and the Mediterranean. They stayed here for a week while arrangements were made to smuggle them over the Pyrenees and across Spain to Gibraltar. Staring through the picture windows of the flat, Neave considered his position. He was more than halfway home but embattled Britain was still 800 miles away. They idled their time away, shuffling round in heavy felt slippers to deaden the sound of their presence from occupants in the flat below, who were suspected Vichy sympathisers. In his ridiculous furry slippers, Neave felt vulnerable to sudden police raids. He also chafed at being a 'parcel' on the mysterious Pat escape route. He did not yet know the true identity of Pat O'Leary; he felt claustrophobic, with no control over his destiny, and even considered making a bolt for it alone. But wiser counsels prevailed, and one afternoon his organisers turned up in great secrecy. They were a truly international crew. A photograph of this meeting round a window seat in Nouveau's flat shows them relaxed but serious. 'René', alias Francis Blanchain, an Englishman of Neave's age, had been born in France and spoke the language fluently. Then came 'Solon', a middle-aged Greek businessman who exuded confidence. His real name was Mario Prassinos and he was clearly in charge of the operation in the absence of 'O'Leary', who was in Gibraltar negotiating with MI9 for money, a wireless operator and arms. Finally, they were joined by Timon, also Greek, tall, dark and accompanied by his silent wife, a German Communist.

A few days later, René took them back to Marseilles railway station for the journey to Toulouse, a staging post to the border city of Perpignan. They were joined by other fugitives including Poles, two Canadian priests and two more Britons, the elderly Mr Roberts, and his eighteen-year-old son. Roberts *père*, aged sixty-five and born in Liverpool, had been employed in Paris by a ticket-printing company. He was initially interned as a civilian and then released into the Unoccupied Zone. Usefully, father and son also had Irish passports and spoke French fluently. The party found seats in a cramped third class compartment also occupied by a gendarme and his boisterous family, giving Neave fresh fears for his safety. However, the policeman soon fell asleep in the spring heat. They arrived at Toulouse in the middle of a military inspection of a French air force guard of honour, which helpfully delayed their exit because their forged Czech papers were not examined in the mêlée of passengers forced to wait until the comic opera proceedings ended. The party was quartered in the Hôtel de Paris, a run-down establishment where Neave and Woollatt were compelled to stay a further week, leaving only for scanty meals. The city authorities believed the hotel was hardly functioning and never looked at the upstairs bedrooms where a veritable foreign legion of Britons, French, Poles and even Australians was gathered for the final assault on freedom.

Francis Blanchain supplied his party with a new set of papers. They had forged instructions to report to a centre for refugees at Banyuls-sur-Mer, close to the Spanish border. Then, after more frustrating delays, twelve escapers took the train in two groups to Narbonne, where they had to change. Neave and Woollatt were shadowed by a gendarme as they walked round the town with their unnecessarily new suitcases. They went into a café and his companion cautioned Neave: 'Don't get drunk.' Why not? he asked. 'You look so appallingly suspicious when you do,' insisted Woollatt. 'So do you,' shot back Neave. So they sat in grumpy silence drinking an occasional brandy until the time came for the last stage to Port Vendres. In truth, Neave often felt an obvious fraud, attracting suspicious looks from officials and policemen. At Port Vendres station, he was stopped by a gendarme who looked at his papers and accused him of being British. It was an anxious moment but the policeman initially let him go. Minutes later, as the group were loitering on the seafront, reassured by Neave's explanation that he had shaken off his inquisitor, the gendarme came hurtling after him on a bicycle with what looked suspiciously like two fellow officers. The little congregation dithered on the shingle until their guide René shouted 'Meet at José's house!', the emergency safe address he had given them when they were in Toulouse. The party scattered across the beach, jumping over rocks and jetsam in their flight to low woods in the hills. A ragged cheer went up from French promenaders, but the gendarmes did not pursue them and Neave was quickly reunited with Woollatt.

When night fell, they found the safe house where all but one of the escapers were already assembled, eating sandwiches and drinking rum, fortifying themselves for the ordeal ahead. Their mountain guide, José, presented himself and asked for payment in advance. Large bundles of cash were handed over, René paying for his Pat line charges. José, a wiry little man with cunning eyes, was a professional smuggler. His trade had prospered mightily since the war began, since there were so many people desperate to escape the war zone. José made them leave any superfluous luggage behind. Neave took only dry socks and chocolate. He and Woollatt bid farewell to René at midnight as the party began the long haul. Up and up they went, following José's white boots. After four hours of climbing, they rested beneath a rock face. Neave, although relatively fit, was exhausted. They reached the summit at daybreak and breakfasted off cheese, hard-boiled eggs and brandy. A storm burst as they prepared to leave and fine rain and strong wind whipped the escapers pitilessly for hours as they stumbled along mountain paths. When Roberts *père* collapsed, Neave took turns with Woollatt and the man's son to carry him on their backs. It was midday before the rain gave way to fog as they reeled down the Spanish side, following shepherd tracks to the lower ground. Through open farmland they tramped exhaustedly all day, avoiding the green-uniformed guards of the Franco government, who would have interned the entire party at a camp in Miranda. José's white boots finally led them to a village at one o'clock the next morning. They were handed over to a well-built, sharply dressed man on a wooden railway platform who showed them to rough bunks in a wooden shed. 'Welcome to Spain, gentlemen. Rest yourselves. The train for Barcelona arrives at six.'

8

Secret Service Beckons

In the spring of 1942 Barcelona was a city still recovering from the horrors of civil war. Although Spain was technically neutral, Franco had received massive help from the Germans in his successful three-year military insurrection that ousted the left-wing government elected in 1936. The British consulate in Barcelona, headed by Harold Farquhar, had inadequate funds to finance the operations of MI9. The Consul also had to contend with the downright hostility of the ambassador in Madrid, Sir Samuel Hoare, who feared this hazardous work would imperil his diplomatic standing. Initially, Hoare pretended that the ratlines were nothing to do with Britain's presence in Spain. His Nelsonian attitude made the already insecure work of his officials in Barcelona even more difficult. Historians of MI9 speculate that Sir Harold, as he later became, spent much of his own money on the safe conduct of escapers until the policy changed in favour of bringing servicemen home whatever the cost.

Neave was still on dangerous ground. He was only vaguely aware of the professionalism of the Pat line, and only hazily conscious that he had been singled out for service in this most secret arm of His Majesty's Secret Service. A young Englishman from the British consulate met Neave, Woollatt and the two Roberts at Barcelona station and took them for breakfast. Everywhere they looked, they saw secret policemen lazing in doorways or leaning against trees, noting their movements. The Englishman, who, Neave noted with satisfaction, was wearing the tie of his own regiment, the Royal Artillery, treated their presence with a disconcerting nonchalance. Such things were only to be expected in a police state, he shrugged. Neave, who had had uncomfortably close acquaintance with the less amiable side of secret policemen, was shocked.

Consular staff took the details of the two British officers, kitted them out with loud green-blue tweed suits and dispatched them to a sympathetic anti-Franco worker's house in the suburbs of Barcelona, where they were confined indoors. Their food was brought to them daily by a young woman from the consulate. Now, almost four months into their escape, they chafed at being kept virtual prisoners, demanding daily to be taken to Gibraltar. Then, without notice, at dawn on 1 May 1942, two men in a Bentley bearing diplomatic number plates came to pick them up. Neave recognised their Foreign Office manner and style of dress, and admired their soft brown hats and their well-manicured hands. They ignored their charges sitting in the back, but, as they bowled through the hinterland to Madrid, Neave began to relax. 'I felt for the first time in those long, dangerous months that I was home.'[1] The party stopped halfway to the capital for lunch of red wine and sandwiches, Neave and Woollatt taking cover behind a pile of rocks whenever another vehicle sped by in a cloud of dust. They arrived at the British embassy just before dusk, in time to join a party of two dozen other Allied escapers of every nation in the embassy garden. Neave protested that he had valuable military information to hand over, but the First Secretary insisted: 'What you need is a drink.' At this rather masculine tea party, Neave was startled to hear his name called and turned to recognise Major Philip Newman MC of the Royal Army Medical Corps, who lived in the same Essex village. Extraordinarily, they had both been in Oflag IXA/H at Spangenburg, near Kassel. Now they were retracing their steps to Ingatestone together.

The embassy at Madrid was a key staging post on the road to freedom. While the ambassador was deeply uncomfortable about the illicit trade in Allied servicemen, one of his attachés, Michael

Cresswell, was, in the words of MI9's historians, a tower of strength who undertook a great deal of the delicate and difficult work of ferrying British evaders and escapers round Spain. His codename was 'Monday'. That night, Neave was blissfully happy. The next morning, he was equally moved by a service of communion conducted by the Bishop of Gibraltar before the boisterous band boarded a gaudy orange bus for the last lap to Gibraltar. Their new cover maintained that they were students, under the care of Mr Roberts *père* who had fully recovered from his mountain ordeal.

The party stayed overnight at a hotel in Cordoba, still under the intense scrutiny of Spanish police checking their fake registration. The men talked of what they would do when they got back to Blighty. One specified three pints of mixed – mild and bitter – while another promised himself a motor drive to the Downs. Generally, their longings were not of a spiritual nature – mostly fit young men in their twenties, they felt that for their efforts the world owed them all the women and the beer they had missed during their years of imprisonment. Down through the mountains to Malaga, and then along the twisting coast road to the frontier post at La Línea, they caroused their way to freedom. Frontier guards disputed their papers but quickly succumbed to the afternoon heat and waved them through.

If they expected a hero's welcome on British territory, they were much mistaken. The Gibraltar base authorities had not heard of them and left them to kick their heels outside the orderly room, guarded by two military policemen. The drama of escape was somewhat lost in the administrative tedium of arriving back at camp. Watching RAF planes take off and land at the new aerodrome, Neave found time to laugh at his predicament. The smile faded when he met the intelligence officer, who pointed out sharply that they had arrived inconveniently, on a Saturday afternoon. In the British army, Neave remarked to Woollatt, only Sunday was more sacred to officers. He did not know then that the intelligence officer in question was Donald Darling, whose cover name was 'Sunday'. Darling had been moved from Lisbon to Gibraltar on the day of Neave's escape from Colditz, and stayed there until late 1943, officially as a civilian liaison officer, though the civil population had been evacuated earlier in the war. Darling ran a one-man interrogation office which was of inestimable value for MI9. He took each fugitive through every move of his escape, building up a complete picture of the ratlines.

Neave and his companions made full use of the entertainment that the Rock had to offer in wartime. Still clad in his improbable Spanish tweeds, he drank pink gins and slowly absorbed the sights and sounds of freedom, albeit in a heavily fortified war zone. In the officers' mess at base, he found himself something of a hero. Young officers stood him rounds of beer to hear his escape exploits, but at his back he felt the gimlet eyes of the intelligence officer, and when he came to security-sensitive information Neave clammed up. At lunch, Darling sat next to him, offering his congratulations on Neave's conversational skills while hoping that he would not say too much. Security-conscious Neave beamed with pleasure. 'It was like receiving a school report that was better than one hoped,' he recalled later.

Two days after their arrival in Gibraltar, the escapers, impatient in new battledress without rank or number, were embarked on a troopship bound for Britain. Apart from a U-boat scare, the journey to the Clyde was uneventful, and in bleak, misty weather on 13 May 1942 they were landed by motor boat at Gourock. Neave found nothing welcoming in the barren streets of Clydeside. He, Newman and Woollatt went to a dreary pub for their first ritual pint on home ground, where one of the escapers prompted horse laughter in the bar by asking for a ham sandwich, something virtually unknown by this stage of the war. They had only a sketchy idea of the privations of the Home Front and the Nazi bombing of cities. Neave was also surprised to see a huge liner carrying American troops steaming up the Clyde: when Japan attacked Pearl Harbor in December 1941, he had been in Colditz town gaol reading Charlotte Brontë. The USA was now engaged in the war, which was reaching a critical phase. While he was on the run across Occupied Europe, Singapore had fallen to the Japanese. British forces were being pushed back in the Western Desert, though Malta had withstood Axis efforts to bomb the island into submission. In Russia, the Red Army was still retreating from the hammer blows of the panzers. While in prison, Neave, like his fellow officers, was able to follow the main events of the war through a contraband wireless. He had not, however, grasped the sheer scale of change at home. He and his companions left the Gourock pub disconsolate and embarrassed, 'unable to recapture the old world or understand the new'.

Sitting later in a Glasgow hotel restaurant that evening, waiting for the overnight train to London, Neave, still trying to come to terms with his new surroundings, was astounded to see his younger sister Rosamund. She had been on holiday in Scotland and was returning south on the same train. Brother and sister greeted each other with incredulity, while Neave reflected on the series of chance reunions that had accompanied his flight: meeting the Swiss doctor, von Erlach, who had visited him in Spangenburg; the reunion with Philip Newman in Madrid, and now this unexpected rencontre with Rosamund. It seemed to him that Fate had placed these friends at stages to help him along his way. Neave also used his influence to help others. When his party went to board the night train, a tough little corporal among their number who had staged a one-man escape found he had been omitted from the travel warrant. The military police barred him from the platform and a furious row ensued. Neave and his fellow officers intervened. Other-rank escapers joined in the argument, as did his sister Rosamund. Attracted by the mêlée, a full colonel supported his MPs, and an enraged Neave stormed: 'If this man is left here I shall see to it that the War Office is informed of this scandal. Surely you can accept the word of officers who have escaped from Germany!' The colonel suggested that Neave and his colleagues could themselves be German agents, prompting hoots of laughter. Neave produced his documents signed by

Donald Darling in Gibraltar. When the guard blew his whistle the escapers rushed the barrier, hauling their prize corporal with them on to the night express.

On arrival at Euston on the morning of 14 May, three and a half months after walking out of Colditz, Neave sat in his carriage alone long after the train had emptied, savouring the atmosphere of being home again. Little details gave him particular delight: the leather buttons on the carriage upholstery; the handle of the heat regulator; sunlight filtering through the smoke-stained roof of the station; women in tweeds hailing porters – the rich mosaic of a traditional British station, redolent of things familiar even in wartime.

Neave's immediate instructions were to report to the Great Central Hotel, Marylebone, which had been requisitioned by the War Office. Before the war, he had enjoyed drinks in the same hotel at four in the morning, before the milk train took him back to Oxford. Now, it was protected by sandbags and guarded by MPs with fixed bayonets. In place of the pretty blonde of former days, a sergeant manned the reception desk. He informed Neave that he was in the London Transit Camp and asked where he had come from. 'Germany,' said Neave. 'Then you'll be wanting MI9,' the imperturbable sergeant replied.

Despite its secretive name, MI9 turned out to be a large double room on the second floor, with trestle tables where the imposing brass beds of his youth had once stood. Two officers interrogated him about his escapes, in an apparently languid sort of way that irritated Neave, who was later to learn, when he was asking the questions, that escaped POWs often found it hard to talk about their experiences. Reluctantly, he gave his interrogators details of the Pat line and then escaped to the hotel lounge which now masqueraded as an officers' mess. It was still only eleven in the morning, and in keeping with the British traditions that he had been so happy to reacquaint himself with a few hours earlier, the bar was shut. Neave chafed at the delay in getting home to his family in Ingatestone, though telephoning his father that morning had revealed the unchanging diffidence between them. Sheffield Neave was busy shaving and could find little to say to his son.

MI9, however had not finished with him. As Neave twiddled his thumbs in a dowdy armchair, a slightly built, moustachioed officer wearing the uniform of the Coldstream Guards approached, instantly recognisable as Lieutenant-Colonel Jimmy Langley. Neave had last seen Langley in a makeshift hospital for British prisoners of war in Lille in the summer of 1940. In the interim, Langley had lost his left arm, amputated because of his wounds. He had escaped from the hospital with the aid of a mysterious escape line known as the 'Institut Mozart', first to Paris and then into Unoccupied France where the Vichy Armistice Commission declared him unfit for military service and repatriated him home via Spain. Langley congratulated him on his escape and invited him to lunch with 'someone important'. They went off to Rules in Maiden Lane, then, as now, a quintessentially English eating place, where Neave was introduced to Brigadier Norman Crockatt, head of MI9. Neave was immediately taken with this smart, handsome man with an undisguisable military bearing, wearing the tartan uniform of the Royal Scots and ribbons of the MC and DSO. Crockatt gently probed him for information, then suddenly became serious. 'You've seen the people who work for us behind the lines,' he said. 'They need money and communications. Do you want to help them?' His thoughts full of Maurice and other Pat line operatives, Neave needed no second bidding. It was, he later recalled 'the one job I should like to do'. Crockatt was relieved and said that, subject to security clearance, he could begin working for Langley's organisation IS9(d) in Room 900 in the War Office. He would have the rank of captain. His work would involve secret communications with Occupied Europe and the training of agents. He did not elaborate, except to observe that it would not be a bed of roses and he should keep his mouth shut and get results. Lunch was abruptly terminated and Neave was left behind in Maiden Lane trying to come to terms with his sudden recruitment into the

Secret Service. Before him lay the prospect of 'another great adventure'.

Before taking the train out to Essex from Liverpool Street, Neave made his way down the Strand and into Fleet Street, making for Farrar's Building in the Temple where he had been a pupil in chambers before the war. He discovered the Temple Church in ruins, and his old offices badly damaged, but found the old clerk Charles Hiscocks still installed in his brief-cluttered room. Hiscocks turned pale when Neave appeared at the door: 'You can't come in here, sir! You're supposed to be dead!'

Neave travelled back to Ingatestone in company with Newman through the familiar Essex suburbs. They exchanged few words, the scenery passing as in a dream. The station features appeared as 'faint images' to Neave, who left a poignant recollection of his homecoming. 'My father was alone on the platform. I walked up to him and we said nothing for a moment. It was not a time for words. No sentence which I could have selected would have seemed appropriate. I shook hands with the stationmaster, and then I was in the car travelling through the hedgerows until we came to the white gates of Mill Green Park.'[2]

It was also a time for some mild self-indulgence. His army back pay had been accumulating in the bank throughout his incarceration and he now had money to spend. Neave went window-shopping in St James's Street, as a man about town would, with £20 burning a hole in his pocket. He bought tobacco and cigars and ordered himself two expensive shirts. Then, on 26 May 1942, ten days after his return to London and the second anniversary of his capture at Calais, he presented himself in his new captain's uniform at Broadway Buildings, a discreet stone building crammed between the Old Star and Crown pub and offices in Broadway, opposite St James's Park underground station. This was the headquarters of MI6, alias the Secret Intelligence Service, headed by the formidable Colonel Claude Dansey. Neave reported to his boss, Colonel Jimmy Langley, in Room 900, which turned out to be a tiny office that had formerly been used to make the tea in.

Initially, the two of them formed the entire complement of IS9 (Intelligence School 9) and it never numbered more than four officers. It was primarily concerned with facilitating escape and evasion by Allied servicemen and worked directly with Crockatt who operated from MI9 headquarters in Beaconsfield, the Buckinghamshire town where Neave had spent much of his childhood. Langley explained that Room 900 was subject to 'dual control' by MI9 and the Secret Service. Neave gave little away during his lifetime about this close connection with MI6, but he did write a first-person piece in the *Observer* in 1974 in which he said: 'The latter [SIS] supplied communications and training facilities for agents that were paid for by MI9, our nominal employers.'[3] His use of the word 'nominal' clearly indicates that his real employers were MI6, and from this time forward he was a member of the intelligence community, from which there is no retirement.

On his first day, Neave described being summoned into the presence of Dansey, a bald, iron-jawed man who shot him a freezing glance and growled: 'These escape lines are very dangerous.' His new captain was well aware of that, having been passed through their hands across Occupied Europe, but Dansey meant the danger that the ratlines might pose to his military intelligence units. The SIS chief illustrated his point by arguing that the First World War heroine Nurse Edith Cavell should not have compromised her information-gathering work in Brussels by hiding escaped British soldiers in her clinic. Neave, who had firsthand experience of the courage of young women on the escape routes, bridled. Dansey, he felt, did Nurse Cavell an injustice. She had been shot for harbouring prisoners and she had not been a spy. A generation later, her legend was still inspiring nurses that she had trained to work for the escape lines in Belgium. In Neave's view the motives that made men and women help evaders on the run were quite different from, and often superior to, those of professional spies. Dansey singled out one agent, a young Belgian woman named Dédée, about whom he entertained doubts, though by that stage she had already brought out thirty British servicemen into neutral Spain. He lectured Neave on the need to recruit couriers and train them in codes and wireless communication. Finally, he declared sarcastically that all the escape lines in Occupied Europe were 'blown' and known to the Germans. With a final grimace, the downbeat briefing was brought to a close and Neave was back in the corridor. 'I was dismayed by his attitude,' he confessed later. 'In war and peace one cannot be too careful about security. But his harsh judgements were difficult to accept. I thought of those who had risked their lives to get me back to England.'[4]

Deflated by his encounter with Dansey, Neave returned to Room 900 to begin his secret work. His first task was to choose a codename, and for the next three years he became 'Saturday', though the War Office assigned him other names, including Anthony Newton. Langley showed him the files, which confirmed Neave's impression that, though small, MI9 was a professional operation. As early as July 1940, only a fortnight after the fall of France, it had set up the escape line through the Iberian peninsula, to the benefit of the many British soldiers who had not got away at Dunkirk and had then poured down into Vichy France.

MI9 was nothing if not original in the way it operated. Lacking local contacts in the South of France, the organisation sent out Nubar Gulbenkian, son of the hugely rich and well-connected oil billionaire Calouste Gulbenkian, together with his valet, first to Lisbon then Barcelona and on to southern France to set up the evasion and escape lines. Being an Iranian diplomat, he could travel unhindered, and the Gulbenkian mission was highly successful. In Marseilles, Captain Ian Garrow of the Seaforth Highlanders played the role of 'stay behind' organiser brilliantly, recruiting among others Louis Nouveau, who had set up Neave's escape. Throughout 1941, MI9, manned only by a handful of officers, perfected its operations, bringing dozens of men back through Spain to Gibraltar. There, like Neave, they were briefly interrogated before being sent back home to continue the war. Some were also interviewed by MI9 in a first-floor flat in London's

arrested and he was returned to Paris in the custody of the Americans. Cole escaped yet again and hid with a woman friend, but neighbours informed on him as a suspected deserter and he opened fire on two gendarmes sent to arrest him. He wounded one, but was shot dead by the other. Neave regarded Cole as one of the most selfish and callous traitors ever to serve the enemy in time of war.

Room 900 struggled against official indifference to its work. Until the summer of 1942, organised evasion was a low-ranking priority with the RAF, without whose cooperation they could not parachute wireless agents into enemy territory. They were also short of funds, until Room 900 discovered a Mr Gosling, a local manager of the British textile firm, J. & P. Coates, who was hiding in southern France with six million French francs belonging to his company. MI9 arranged to credit the firm in London, while the 'Gosling millions' financed its operations for more than a year. One of its highest profile escapers was Whitney Straight, the American racing driver, who was rescued with thirty aircrew from a beach near Perpignan in late July 1942. Similar operations in September and October netted more than a hundred other escapers. MI9 was in business.

Neave's work had another, less flamboyant, dimension. He was tasked with interrogating Allied nationals fleeing their Nazi-dominated homeland. The grillings took place at the Royal Victoria Patriotic Asylum for the Orphan Daughters of Soldiers and Sailors killed in the Crimean War (the RVPS), a grim building in Clapham, south London, built in 1857. In 1939 it was commandeered as the MI5 Interrogation Centre for non-British arrivals. Here, enemy agents were sometimes exposed, 'broken down, so I supposed by endless cups of War Office tea', Neave observed later. After questioning, Room 900 could pluck their recognised agents from this forbidding place and whisk them off to safe houses for hot baths and the best food that rationing would allow. Here, Neave went to identify Louis Rémy, a Belgian air force officer who had swum the Bay of Algeciras to seek sanctuary in Gibraltar. Fortunately, Neave could identify him as an ex-inmate of Colditz.

There were other surprises too, among them Leoni Savinos and his German Communist wife, whom Neave had met in Marseilles in his transit through the Pat line, and who came through the processing machine of the RVPS. (Leoni had at that time been introduced to Neave as Timon.) A bewildered Neave took the couple to dinner in London in August 1942, reflecting that the underground movement defied all ideological barriers. 'There were no politics in this humane form of warfare,' he deliberated. He was to show much less sympathy for the left in post-war years. Savinos and his wife had to be extracted from under the noses of the Gestapo, who arrested him in Paris on a mercy mission for the escape lines. The Nazis threatened to take Madame Savinos hostage unless he agreed to work for the Germans. Savinos agreed to spy on the escape lines, but unbeknown to the Gestapo he acted as a double agent for the Allies. He and his wife were brought out in a Room 900 sea operation and Savinos returned to Europe for the SOE in 1943.

Throughout the winter of 1942, the Pat line continued to bring out escaping servicemen on the route followed by Neave, despite the German occupation of Vichy France on 30 November. In its heyday, the line had hundreds of people working for it, bringing Allied aircrew and soldiers back from collection points in northern France. Room 900 had regular radio contact through a courageous young Australian operator, Tom Groome. Yet over the operations hung the spectre of the double agent Harold Cole. When conditions became too hot, Louis Nouveau, who had sheltered Neave, closed down his safe house in Marseilles early in 1943 and took over the Paris end under an assumed name. Activities were moved to Toulouse. Conscious that the net was tightening, Neave and Langley hatched plans to extricate key operatives. Ian Garrow, the founder of the Marseilles group, was snatched from Fort Meauzac prison camp. Like Neave, he walked out in enemy uniform, on this occasion as a French gendarme. Garrow escaped through Spain, but safely back in Neave's Elizabeth Street flat he warned that Cole's treachery had put the entire organisation at risk. His alarm was fully justified. First, Groome was captured while sending a radio message from a remote farmhouse; then Nouveau was arrested bringing five airmen through the Gare d'Austerlitz in Paris. Finally, O'Leary himself was picked up by the Gestapo on 20 March 1943 and Neave's most efficient evade and escape system was in ruins. His best agents disappeared into Nazi concentration camps and the Germans tried, without success, to use Groome and the captured radio set to deceive Neave and Langley into sending further air drops and agents into southern France. The Pat line ceased to exist, though it had helped more than 600 Allied servicemen to their freedom. The price paid was heavy. Over a hundred brave helpers were gaoled, some paying the ultimate price. O'Leary himself survived three concentration camps, and Nouveau lived through the horrors of Buchenwald.

Back in London in Room 900, Neave was distraught. Rival services, never slow to criticise MI9, heaped scorn on their efforts. 'For many weeks, Langley and I lived under a cloud until we almost believed that we were solely responsible,' he later confessed.[6] Neave blamed higher authorities for refusing to sanction more agents and radio transmitters. The need for MI9 was greater than ever, he reasoned. The big RAF raids on Germany were under way, and the number of crews shot down and evading capture had increased proportionately. It was very expensive to train fresh crews, and therefore cost-effective to bring back as many of the downed airmen as possible. Moreover, the impact on morale of a flying officer shot down over the Continent later walking back into his aerodrome mess was enormous, as Neave could personally testify. These comebacks also persuaded aircrew to take evasion and escape more seriously, with a consequent rise in success rates.

Nonetheless, Neave conceded that they had made mistakes. Their organisation was unlike any orthodox security service. It dealt with men on the run, using civilian helpers and impromptu systems of escape. There was much enthusiasm but not enough professionalism. The early escape lines had grown too quickly, weakening security and making the organisation more vulnerable to infiltration by the Germans. The rolling-up of the Pat line forced a major rethink of strategy. As the war went into its third year, MI9 was sending in agents to create smaller groups of helpers tasked with specific evacuations, by land, sea and even light plane. Sitting in Room 900, Neave never ceased to be amazed at the courage of local civilian volunteers. He was now responsible for the Comet line, started in 1941 by a petite young Belgian, Andrée de Jongh, a schoolmaster's daughter from Brussels. Known invariably by the diminutive 'Dédée', she began by bringing two Belgians and a British soldier over the Pyrenees on foot, presenting them to an astonished consul at Bilbao. He put her in touch with 'Monday', the Madrid embassy attaché Michael Creswell, and so began one of the most daring and successful collaborations of the war. Dédée insisted on running her own operation, funded by MI9. 'It was an informal, even high-spirited escape line and she wanted it that way,' he conceded. 'She did not like to be regarded as a spy.'[7] Her youthful but nonetheless effective methods were difficult for the old War Office intelligence establishment to stomach (as suggested by Dansey's doubts about her) but the airmen she rescued were often moved to tears by her courage. She was being sought by the Gestapo, along with her father Frédéric, who had also joined the cause. The numbers of Allied airmen passing along the Comet line rose exponentially as the saturation bombing of Germany and the occupied territories intensified. In all, 337 crews of all Allied nations were rescued in this way. Neave could not repress his admiration for the 'little cyclones', as he called his women volunteers. One, Madame Elvire de Greef (codename Tante Go, after her pet dog), enlisted her entire family. Her husband Fernand, an interpreter at the local Kommandantur, stole identity cards and passes, and her son and daughter acted as couriers. She and his other little cyclones were 'wonderful examples of the triumph of willpower and feminine subtlety', he wrote later.[8]

The war brought many women into positions where their courage was tested and often found to be at least as good as that of men, but Neave felt he had experienced something special. He visited his former agents after the war and devoted his second book, *Little Cyclone*, published in 1954, to them. On the title page, he quoted from the last stanza of Wordsworth's 'She Was a Phantom of Delight':

> *The reason firm, the temperate will,*
> *Endurance, foresight, strength and skill;*
> *A perfect Woman; nobly planned,*
> *To warn, to comfort, and command.*

He made little of it in his books but Neave had quickly found such a woman – Diana Giffard – at a party soon after his fateful meeting with Crockatt at Rules. Diana was a member of one of England's oldest families. An ancestor, Sire de Longueville, came with William the Conqueror in 1066 and later took the name of Giffard. It was love, if not at first, then at third sight, for after meeting her only three times Neave proposed and was accepted. They married on 29 December 1942 at the parish church of Brewood, Staffordshire, near her family home, Chillington Hall. He was twenty-six, she was twenty-three. He gave his occupation as captain in His Majesty's Army, while Diana was described as a divisional secretary of the British Red Cross, which gave nothing away. Airey's father was registered as a Doctor of Science and Diana's father, Thomas Giffard, as 'landed proprietor'.

Diana Giffard, a linguist, was also in the Secret Service. War work took her initially into nursing at an RAF hospital, but, like Neave, she was talent-spotted by a Foreign Office scout and was moved into intelligence. She worked for the Political Warfare Executive, which conducted secret broadcasting and black propaganda to Occupied Europe in close liaison with the BBC.

The PWE was based at the riding school at Woburn Abbey and at Bush House. She also worked secretly for the Polish Ministry of Education. Many years later, Diana admitted that while he (Neave) 'commanded agents in the field' she worked on 'equally secret operations'. A subsequent account suggests that, so intense was the secrecy of their respective war work, it was only when they lost one of their mutual agents that they discovered they were both involved in intelligence. This is hard to credit, since they moved very much in Secret Service circles, professionally and socially, and MI6 looked benignly on relationships within the service because they reinforced the ring of discretion. Neave himself used to tell a story that he met his new bride in a restricted area 'and we had one of those ludicrous "what are you doing here?" confrontations'. His anecdote is the more credible.

Neave described Diana as 'a beautiful auburn-haired girl' and could not believe his luck. In the depths of his despair in Room 900 'she restored my will to fight on and complete my part in this story'. Patrick Cosgrave has said she had an elfin beauty, great charm and a ready wit. Like other wartime marriages, particularly where both individuals worked for the Secret Services, happiness had to be seized whenever it offered itself. In a foreword to one of his books, Diana wrote: 'We both understood the dangers, fully aware that the Gestapo would have no mercy if Airey were caught in enemy territory. It was a bittersweet time, when the gnawing anxiety would be relieved by the joy of a sudden reunion and our unflagging optimism that the war could not last forever.'

The Neaves had a short honeymoon in January 1943 and returned to London to live in a flat at Ebury House, further down Elizabeth Street, belonging to an aunt of Diana's. Here, he continued to bring agents for debriefing, Diana playing her part by providing 'the best wartime hospitality'. Among the field operatives who sipped sherry while recounting their harrowing experiences was a twenty-year-old Belgian girl, Peggy van Lier, who had just escaped the clutches of the Gestapo. Jimmy Langley fell in love with her as she stepped off the plane and they too married.

Despite personal happiness for Neave at home, MI9 operators were struck by successive blows in 1943, not least when Dédée was finally captured. In London, Neave felt the agony and frustration of the remote, chairborne commander, unable to do anything except wait for news from clandestine wireless contacts. At this stage he decided that he would return to France if he could. Dédée had been taken by the Gestapo at a hideout on the French–Spanish border, betrayed by a farmworker for money. Despite Room 900's policy of not reinforcing escape lines once they had been broken, Neave personally resolved to get Comet back into operation. He parachuted two young Belgians, one a wireless operator, back into Brussels. They were excited at the prospect of adventure. Neave had a heavier heart, feeling responsible for their young lives. 'War is dangerous, especially behind enemy lines,' he wrote later. 'What is inexcusable is not to feel for the safety of others.'[9] Neave saluted his brave Belgians as they boarded an RAF bomber in Bedfordshire. They were dropped in 'blind', without a reception committee. A few days later, however, both were arrested in a roll-up of the Brussels organisation that captured Jean Greindl, codename Nemo, MI9's head of operations in the Belgian capital. Greindl's son Albert escaped and Neave took him to the Goring Hotel near Victoria for a late-night debriefing, after a special request to relieve him of the unpleasant quarantine of the RVPS. The service discussed the possibility of a neutral country interceding on behalf of Jean Greindl and Neave later observed that, had there been many German agents to exchange, then something like the late twentieth-century spy swaps between the West and the Soviet Union might have taken place. But in 1943, such an initiative would have been pointless: the Nazis had captured too many Allied agents and any move of this nature by MI9 would merely have confirmed their guilt. Jean Greindl died in captivity, ironically the victim of an Allied air raid on the artillery barracks at Etterbeek. It was a grim time for the escape and evasion business.

9

Enemy Territory

Neave took over Room 900 in September 1943, following Langley's promotion to joint commander of IS9 (Western European Area) as preparations began for the Allied landings in Europe. At this stage of the war, the mass bombing raids on Occupied Europe meant more and more airmen were being shot down, and their successful repatriation was vital for the war effort. The escape and evasion business moved into higher gear. Amid escalating preparations for the forthcoming Allied invasion, Neave looked for more agents and fresh escape routes.

He flew out to Gibraltar with a senior MI9 officer, Colonel Cecil Rait, to discuss the new arrangements with 'Monday', Donald Darling and Baron Jean-François Nothomb. Known by the codename Franco, Nothomb was a handsome and courageous young Belgian, the son of a senator and novelist, who had picked up the dangerous reins of the Comet ratline in Paris. According to Darling, Neave thought Franco was too young for the mammoth task.

The flight, via Lisbon (Portugal remained neutral) on a KLM plane on charter to BOAC, was a farce. Under War Office instructions, Neave travelled in civilian dress, carrying his uniform in a suitcase. His passport described him as a barrister, which was accurate enough for he had been called to the Bar although he had not yet practised. As he waited for the flight at Bideford aerodrome in Devon, an agitated Special Branch detective called him to the telephone to speak to Room 900 'about the lesbians' false teeth'. Amazingly, this was not a coded message. Brigadier Crockatt was furious that two elderly Parisian ladies who had escaped to England after hiding evaders in their flat had ordered new teeth on Neave's account. The bill came to the not inconsiderable sum of £70 and Neave insisted that MI9 paid it, in view of the ladies' bravery. In Lisbon, a disbelieving customs officer saw straight through his civilian 'disguise'. 'Good luck, Major Neave, and a pleasant journey,' he said.

On the day after his arrival on the Rock, Neave took Nothomb for an audience with the Governor of Gibraltar, Lieutenant General Sir Noël Mason-MacFarlane, in recognition of his outstanding gallantry in rescuing so many servicemen via the Comet line. Mason-MacFarlane received the bemused Belgian aristocrat in bush shirt and khaki shorts, congratulating him on his work and promising that 'the day of Liberation will soon come'. Neave feared that if Nothomb returned to Paris, he would suffer the same fate as Greindl and Dédée. Nothomb rejected Neave's proposal of rest and recuperation in England and was smuggled back across the frontier into Spain in the boot of Darling's car. Darling later wrote: 'We both felt inwardly that Franco could not much longer avoid the attentions of the Paris Gestapo, though we did not then know that one of Comet's guides was a traitor, which made the Belgian's arrest inevitable.' Neave felt certain that he would never see Nothomb again. Franco made three more escape journeys, bringing his personal tally of rescued servicemen to 215, before being arrested by the Gestapo six months before D-Day. He was sent to a concentration camp but survived the war to become a priest.

Working with MI9 continually brought Neave into contact with some remarkable men and women. He was particularly impressed by Ghita Mary Lindell, the Comtesse de Milleville, a woman with a passion for adventure equalled only by her ardour for plain speaking. Mary arrived in London in the summer of 1942, after bringing a wounded captain in the Welsh Guards from Paris to Vichy France where he obtained Irish papers and escaped back to

England via Portugal. She presented herself to Neave in the St James's Street flat, 'very definitely English and used to getting her own way', asking to be returned to France where she had lived since 1919 with her husband and three children after serving with great distinction as a Red Cross nurse in the Great War. Mary, then forty-five, had already served a nine-month prison sentence in the notorious Fresnes jail for helping Allied servicemen on the run. Released in late 1941, she found herself on the run but still working for the escape lines. Her keenness to return to the fray overcame Neave's anxieties for her safety, and she became his first female agent to be dropped back into Occupied Europe in October 1942 armed only with a French Red Cross identity card forged by MI9 in the name of Ghita de Melville. Neave drove her to RAF Tangmere in the autumn dusk, confident of her ability to succeed, but with a heavy heart. He feared the risk of degrading torture, which distressed intelligence officers of his generation. 'It was an attitude which many women agents scorned as Victorian,' he later recalled, 'and perhaps it was.'

But the bold comtesse went on to rescue a number of servicemen, including two of the famous 'Cockleshell Heroes' after the daring commando raid on Bordeaux harbour. MI9 had collaborated in the planning of Operation Frankton, a raid on enemy shipping in the harbour of Bordeaux in December 1942. Five two-man canoes were launched from a submarine off the mouth of the River Gironde, and two got as far as Bordeaux where they fixed mines on seven ships, causing great damage and infuriating Hitler. Neave was involved in the operation because the men knew they could not return to the submarine and would have to escape as best they could or accept capture. They were told to make for the town of Ruffec after their mission, where they would find an organisation able to smuggle them home. Neave was very anxious about giving the raiding party details of the escape line contacts, fearing that the commandos might reveal the secret under torture. Death was the usual fate of French civilian helpers at the hands of the Nazis. It seemed to him the worst of both worlds. There was no guarantee that the commandos would make contact with the comtesse or her agents, and she had not been forewarned of the raid. In the event, only two of the ten men got away after the mission, Major H.G. 'Blondie' Hasler, an Atlantic yachtsman and leader of the party, and Marine Sparks. With the aid of special maps and compasses supplied by Neave, they walked nearly a hundred miles across enemy territory to Ruffec and made contact with the escape line by giving a note to the sympathetic *patronne* of a small hotel. The comtesse took them under her wing, on one condition: 'NO GIRLS. From past experience we know that once they meet a pretty girl everything goes to hell.' After considerable adventures, Mary got her charges across the Pyrenees into Spain. She continued her escape work on unconventional lines that had the men of Room 900 tearing out their hair, until she was arrested by the Germans at the border railway station at Pau in late 1943. Brutally treated by SD (*Sicherheitsdienst*) officers, her life was saved by a German surgeon, only for her to be transferred to Ravensbrück concentration camp in September 1944. But Mary Lindell not only survived: she worked in the camp hospital and saved several women from the gas chamber, including an SOE agent. Neave found her intractable and often unlucky, but her pertinacity and daring were 'almost without precedent'.

Room 900 dispatched only one other woman to Occupied Europe. In 1943, Neave parachuted Beatrice 'Trix' Terwindt, codename Felix, into Holland. Tragically, and unknown at this time to the War Office, Britain's SOE operations in Holland had been successfully infiltrated by German counter-intelligence, the Abwehr. Many years later, when he came to chronicle the work of MI9, Neave still found it difficult to write about her. In February 1943, he took her out to Tempsford aerodrome and they shook hands before she climbed into the Halifax bomber. From a captured radio transmitter, the Nazis knew an agent was coming, but not that it would be a woman. The Dutch reception committee were collaborators, who tricked her into giving the name of her contact in The Hague. When she realised that she was in enemy hands, Trix tried to take her suicide pill but her captors thwarted her. She was interrogated virtually non-stop for three days, then gaoled. Trix did not talk: she endured imprisonment in Ravensbrück and Mauthausen before being released through the Red Cross a week before the end of the war. Neave considered this 'tragic failure' to be one of the saddest episodes in Room 900's history of human success and sacrifice. 'I never sent a woman on a similar mission from England during the rest of the war,' he recalled.

Wartime security was so strict that Neave himself was not allowed to go back into Occupied Europe. As an organising officer he knew too much and the War Office could not risk him being captured. Yet the Germans were aware of the existence of Room 900. They had a file on Jimmy Langley, and even knew that he was a member of Brooks's Club. They had a photograph of him and were acquainted with MI9's operational arrangements.

After Neave took charge of Room 900 from Langley, his first big exercise was Operation Shelburne, a new escape organisation bringing back escapers by high-speed motor gunboats from a beach codenamed Bonaparte, near Plouha on the north Britanny coast. Despite the official ban on intelligence officers going into the field, Neave wanted to be with his evacuation teams. 'I do not pretend that I had any desire to risk recapture by the Germans,' he admitted. 'It was not only my escape from Colditz, but the possibility that my name was known to them through the arrest of others that finally led Crockatt to forbid me to go to Britanny.'[1] Operations began in January 1944, and in a brilliant debut the gunboats running out of Dartmouth brought back nineteen men: four RAF crew, thirteen American airmen and two Frenchmen seeking to enlist. A month later, Neave and his Room 900 French agents brought out twenty more, including sixteen USAF flyers. In March, a further thirty got away, more than half of them American survivors of the massive daylight raids. Shelburne continued until after D-Day, bringing out a total of 135 men and women. Almost a hundred more were spirited across the border into Spain.

Neave, however, was never satisfied that he was doing enough. With the Allied landings imminent, he considered how MI9 could shelter and supply from the air large groups of men who would be on the run in Occupied Europe, unable to make neutral territory because of the destruction of the rail system in northern France. Neave's answer was Operation Marathon, a scheme to concentrate downed aircrew in hidden camps well away from the battle zone. Hiding places were identified in France, Belgium and Holland, usually in heavily wooded areas, where the men could hold out until the Allied advance reached them. He reckoned on concealing 500 men at a time, in sites where they could be supplied by air drops. It was an ambitious plan and attracted criticism that it was 'too risky', especially the sending out of advance forces to set up the camps. But the Air Ministry, which had scoffed at MI9's operations earlier in the war, now recognised the value of getting aircrew back and gave valuable support. Neave recruited a magnificent team of French and Belgian agents to create the camps in Rennes and Châteaudun, north of the Loire valley in France, and in the Ardennes, Belgium. The first agents were sent out into the field in late 1943, after a particularly exacting party thrown by Neave at the Embassy Club in London, during which a French veteran escape organiser was seen to swing on the chandelier. The war did not diminish Neave's enjoyment of life. Amid the high jinks, he had been nicknamed 'Napoleon' and this was used by the advance parties in France to identify themselves.

The date of the Normandy invasion was a closely guarded secret but Neave worked on the assumption that it would be in the late spring of 1944. In the intervening months, he set up a shadow organisation. The first site chosen to concentrate men on the run was in the Forêt de Fréteval, north of Tours. It was designed to hold men who could not be got out via Operation Shelburne. Neave sent out his agents in April to prepare the ground, and set in motion Operation Sherwood. He appreciated that his radical plan involved great risks, but the area was a stronghold of the Resistance and local farmers and shopkeepers were sympathetic to the Allies. Increasing movement of German troops made travel around Occupied Europe more dangerous and difficult, but in late May the first downed aircrew were brought along the Comet line to this secluded spot. Neave arranged air drops of tents, medicines, clothes and food to supplement provisions bought locally. The diet was surprisingly generous for a clandestine camp surviving virtually under the noses of the Nazis. Neave's agents calculated that the men should get 500 grammes of bread per day, plus two eggs, a litre of milk, 100 grammes of meat, 400 grammes of potatoes and fresh fruit whenever possible. By the end of July, six weeks after D-Day, the camp held over a hundred men. A month later, the figure had risen to 152, and a second camp had to be established six miles away. The men maintained some military discipline, rising at six and camouflaging their tents with branches. Boredom was a serious problem, though they fashioned a rudimentary golf course among the trees. Their chief distraction was listening to the progress of the war on the wireless. As the battering of the Wehrmacht intensified, smaller camps were established in northern France.

Neave decided that he should personally liberate the camps. He persuaded his superior officers that IS9, the Anglo-American (Western European Area) outfit, should be responsible for this operation. IS9 was attached to the intelligence staff of Mont-gomery's 21 Army Group, Langley was posted as General Staff Officer (Intelligence), or GSO1 (I), and Neave became GSO2 (Planning) of IS9, and therefore GSO2 (I) of 21 Army Group. These glorified titles disguised his real underground activities, he later confessed. He never went anywhere near 21 Army Group, leaving the links to Langley, but concerned himself entirely with rescue operations until the British army reached and finally liberated Holland in May 1945. Donald Darling was brought back from Gibraltar to run Room 900, and Neave sailed to Normandy on a motor torpedo-boat, disembarking at Courseulles in July 1944 just weeks after the Allied landings. IS9 was based in Bayeux, near Caen. They were a motley crew, with a headquarters staff, two interrogation sections and four field sections, one English, two American and one Canadian, equipped with jeeps. However, they were lightly armed and if there was any serious risk of fighting, they would have to call on special troops, including the SAS and commando units. For nearly a month, while the invading Allies struggled to break out of the Normandy beachhead, Neave and his fellow officers had little to do. He put up an idea for sending French and Belgian guides – 'retrievers' – through the enemy lines to contact downed airmen and, if possible bring them back, but the proposal was rejected as too dangerous. As they kicked their heels in Bayeux, Neave's outfit attracted criticism from staff officers that IS9 was a 'private army' and not their affair. This was a misunderstanding, traceable to the division between orthodox military intelligence in a combat area and Room 900's clandestine operations. However, it was a distinction that appealed to Neave's sense of the adventurous and unconventional. It was not genuinely 'private warfare', of course. Neave was an officer in an invading army and had to obey orders but there was a freelance feel to his military activities.

When the American army broke through to Brittany at the beginning of August 1944, Neave was determined to be right behind them. He loaded his jeep and took the American sections of IS9 to Rennes, expecting to find a group of airmen. The drive through villages offered a dreadful prospect of war: dead German soldiers, smashed vehicles and the bodies of horses littered the road, while ambush by retreating Wehrmacht units was a constant danger. They were often cut off from the American forces but Neave's blood was up. 'The exhilaration was unforgettable,' he recorded. 'The restraints of London and the beachhead were past and the smell of pursuit was in the air.'[2] To his chagrin, the evaders at Rennes had already gone. Leaving one section to look after any stragglers, he wheeled about to follow Patton's Third

Army to Paris. On 10 August, Neave reached Le Mans, less than fifty miles from the camp at the Forêt de Fréteval. He and his men received a rapturous welcome from local people, and Neave based himself in the Hôtel Moderne, which had only just been evacuated by the Germans and was now full of Free French troops and war correspondents toasting the liberation of the city in white plonk. Neave was unable to join in the jollity, fearing that the American thrust towards the Falaise Gap that would destroy the German army west of the Seine would also deprive him of back-up transport and troops to free his camp of evaders. He drove north of Le Mans to the XV Corps headquarters, and implored the American staff officer to spare him lorries and light tanks to carry out his mission, pointing out that many of the evaders were Americans. He argued that they were at great risk from the retreating Germans, who were simply ignoring the rules of war in their headlong, murderous flight. But the Americans were adamant that they could spare nothing in the build-up to the push for the Seine, and Neave returned empty-handed to his hotel. There, to his infinite relief, he found a squadron of the SAS drawn up in the courtyard, a force of thirty officers and men under the leadership of Captain Anthony Greville-Bell. He immediately agreed to undertake the operation and got permission from his seniors at SAS headquarters, incidentally restoring Neave's radio contact with Darling in Room 900, who for several days had been frantically scouring France for 'Saturday'. On 11 August, the Resistance supplied Neave's little force with requisitioned charcoal-burning buses, but they still could not find drivers. Reports from inside the Fréteval camp suggested that the men were very restive and might try to break out on their own, putting themselves and any French who might help them at great risk from SS reprisals. Neave sent orders that they were to stay put and wait.

At this point, a captain in IS9 (WEA), Peter Baker, volunteered to go to the camp ahead of the main group. This young man, later, like Neave, to become a Conservative MP (for South

Norfolk), was to figure substantially, and fatally, in the operations of IS9 in the coming months. Baker claimed in his autobiography, an exculpatory exercise written after the crash of his business empire, to be 'an old and esteemed friend' of Neave.[3] The feeling was not entirely reciprocated. Neave knew that Baker had visions of changing out of uniform into civilian clothes and making his way to Paris to write an article on his derring-do for the American press. He was doubtful about Baker, but also loath to curb 'such dash and enthusiasm', and after some hours' delay finally allowed Baker and five SAS men under one of their own officers to go on a reconnaissance mission to the Forêt de Fréteval camp. By Baker's account, there were only four of them: himself, Gunner Mackenzie and two armed Frenchmen. Most of the Germans had fled, and in one village after another they were welcomed as liberators. However, as they neared their objective, Baker's party came under machine-gun fire, and had to take refuge with the Resistance. Technically, at least, they were still in Occupied France.

Back in Le Mans, Neave chafed at the lack of transport, until he received a mysterious summons to one of the city's main squares, where, drawn up under civilian armed guard, was a motley assortment of sixteen buses and lorries, decked out with flowers and French flags. The operation by now seemed comic but he decided to brook no further delay. They set out after breakfast on 14 August 1944, a gaudy convoy headed by an SAS patrol. Not much more than an hour later, they reached the rendezvous point where Neave's agents had been told to collect the men. They were jubilant at being rescued. Operation Sherwood had come to an end. Luck was still on his side. That night, German patrols reappeared in the forest, alerted by Neave's charabanc army. By that time, however, the evaders – Americans, Canadians, New Zealanders, Polish and British – were enjoying a hot meal in Le Mans. This was the military exploit of which Neave was most proud, not comparable to the activities of the Long Range Desert Group in North Africa or the SAS in Europe 'but none the less impressive', not least because of the way his 'private army' had been treated. His initiative had brought together well over a hundred evading servicemen, many of them valuable aircrews, in a hidden camp supplied from the air under the noses of the retreating Germans. The exploit is commemorated by a plain stone memorial at the edge of the forest, unveiled amid full military honours by a French government minister for war veterans in 1967.

Bolstered by success, but still anxious about the fate of up to ten evaders unaccounted for, Neave sent Baker back to the Forêt de Fréteval later in the day to search for the missing servicemen, only to discover that they had joined a tank unit of the advancing American army. The French capital was now everyone's goal. Neave wanted to take his 'private army' twenty miles beyond Châteaudun to Chartres. His ostensible purpose was to recover more airmen known to be in hiding in the region, but he was also anxious about rumours of revolution and massacre reaching him from Paris. He feared for the safety of French people recruited to work for the Room 900 ratlines. The Americans disapproved of his intention to race ahead of the main force, deprecating him as a 'bandit', a term his appearance did nothing to disprove for Neave had lost his helmet and now wore corduroy trousers. He obediently followed the conquering US Third Army to Chartres, where minor fighting was still taking place. Though he does not mention it anywhere in his own writings, Neave was involved in a remarkable incident in the thirteenth-century Gothic cathedral at Chartres, a building generally recognised as one of the crowning achievements of Western civilisation. According to a record kept at the parish church of St Mary's, Longworth, Oxfordshire, where he is buried, Neave and de Blommaert, his Room 900 agent, arrived in the *place* in front of Notre-Dame Cathedral, which was crowded with American jeeps and troops. When they returned in the evening, it was deserted but for three US tanks. Gunfire echoed round the side streets. De Blommaert recalled: 'A frantic young Texan sergeant came up to Airey and explained that German troops were said to be hiding in the spire, and his captain had returned with orders to blow up Chartres cathedral. Airey calmly went up to the captain and asked if he could really justify opening fire on such a monument. He said: "My orders are to demolish rather than risk a single American life." '

Neave replied: 'I am in charge of Special Services in this sector. This is a special case. Wait five minutes before opening fire, no more. I will go in and look myself, and wave my handkerchief if all is clear.' Neave entered the cathedral unarmed, and de Blommaert followed with his rifle at the ready. Neave told him: 'Keep your distance, so we don't offer a double target up this damned spiral staircase, and if you must shoot, try not to hit me!' There were no Germans in the spire. He waved his handkerchief to the troops below as arranged and the cathedral was saved. This story has almost certainly gained something in the telling, but essentially it rings true, and it is unlikely that de Blommaert would have lent his corroboration to a fantasy. Admirers of French Gothic architecture owe more than a passing debt to Neave.

Neave's irregulars (he admitted they could best be portrayed as 'paramilitary', and evinced every sign of satisfaction at the description) continued on the road to Paris, picking up stray evading airmen en route, before landing in Rambouillet, where Peter Baker had set up a forward post. There were few soldiers in the town but many war correspondents, among them the towering figure of Ernest Hemingway, waiting to cover the liberation of Paris. The American halted their advance to allow the French under General Leclerc to free their capital. At this point, Baker's memoirs insist that 'Airey had been ordered back to England',[4] but Neave logs no such order. He records spending time with French officers working out how best to extricate his helpers in the Comet and Shelburne organisation, whose arrest and deportation he still feared, though there was also an element of wanting to be in the front ranks of the liberators. 'The desire to be first in the city was mingled with the more responsible objective of getting them out of danger,' he admitted.[5] He and Langley, who had joined him at Rambouillet, drew up a list of names and addresses for the rescue operation. Langley recorded that his fellow officer was in command of 'what was indubitably a private army'.

As they waited in the hot sunshine for permission to leave the grounds of the great chateau at Rambouillet, Langley heard dark rumours that Paris was burning, that Leclerc was being pushed back and the Nazis were murdering civilians. However, on Liberation Day, 25 August, Neave was on his way, driving with one of his men through Versailles and entering the city by the Porte d'Orléans before tearing down the Champs-Elysées, round the Arc de Triomphe under fire from French snipers who mistook them for Germans, to the Hôtel Windsor where he set up a temporary headquarters for IS9. Baker suggests that he preceded Leclerc by two days, though Neave, again, makes no such claim. To have admitted such an action would have been to acknowledge a breach of orders, of course. His first act was to rescue two Germans from an angry crowd. Over succeeding hours, he found that most of his helpers were safe and well. The following day saw, as he put it, 'the wildest scenes of shooting, jubilation and drinking'. Langley reported that Neave and his private army were fully engaged in collecting snipers, contacting helpers, routing out suspected enemy snipers and German collaborators. Baker also observed that Neave was in his element: 'The people of Paris had greatly exaggerated his importance, and crowds of them assembled at our hotel each morning to bring information or complaints to "The Chief of the British Secret Service".'[6] To Baker's reply that they had come to the wrong HQ, they would exclaim: 'Oh, but we heard General Neave was here.' The hotel began to resemble a bizarre scene from a Graham Greene novel, with men offering to assassinate Hitler or Pétain. Obscure French politicians and self-styled Russian agents demanded appointments with the mysterious Mr Neave. They refused to believe the ostensible reason for Neave's presence, dismissing it as a cover story. All this Neave found entertaining, but it was difficult to compose his thoughts in such bedlam. Apart from volunteers offering to serve in IS9, some came demanding British decorations for their part in the war. Others simply asked for food. 'Airey and I wondered if we would ever get all our problems sorted out and cursed the letters "IS" in the unit's name since the French instantly assumed they stood for Intelligence Service.'[7] Officially, it was Intelligence School, but the difference was basically semantic, and it reported to MI6.

From London Crockatt sent Donald Darling over to Paris to open an Awards Bureau for the hundreds of French nationals and others who had helped escapers, but Neave was keen to follow the Allied advance into Belgium, where, he assumed, there would be substantial numbers of Allied airmen in the Marathon camp he had ordered to be set up in the Ardennes. After only a few days he took off, without his SAS back-up who had been ordered to return to their unit. His 'paramilitaries', consisting of a small group from IS9 (WEA), were now officially known as Rescue Teams, though, as he later pointed out, they were ill-equipped to conduct rescue operations. In the event, due to internal rivalries in the escape and evasion lines, there was to be no repeat of the Châteaudun initiative. Room 900's Belgian agents working the Comet line viewed the Marathon programme with suspicion, and the supposed camp at Bastogne did not exist. It had never been set up. Neave followed hard on the advance towards Brussels, searching for his 'missing airmen' but found nothing. They were hidden in safe houses around the Belgian capital.

Neave accompanied the liberating tanks of the Guards Armoured Division into Brussels on 3 September, amid further scenes of wild elation. With difficulty he reached the Hôtel Métropole where MI9's agents had been asked to gather. They sat in the lounge, drinking champagne 'on Uncle Sam' at the behest of an 'American colonel' who looked suspiciously like a war correspondent with a sense of humour. A large bill of nearly £200 was settled by SHAEF (Supreme Headquarters Allied Expeditionary Force) only under protest, but on the following day more than a hundred flyers and as many Belgian helpers reported to Neave. 'I found it moving to see them celebrate and later take leave of those who had risked so much for them.'[8]

Neave did not bask in the reflected glory for long. Similarly urgent duty called in Holland, where British undercover operations had so fatally been undermined by Abwehr infiltration. Despite the Germans' best endeavours, Room 900 had managed to parachute in Dignus 'Dick' Kragt (codename Frans Hals) who established contact with the Comet line and sent back more than a hundred airmen before Operation Market Garden, the airborne attack on Arnhem, in September 1944. Pushing north to link up with his Dutch agents, Neave reached Nijmegen, on the River Waal, in the first week of October. The bridge over the Waal, visible from his headquarters in the outskirts of the city, was under constant German shelling. He took his life in his hands every time he crossed the bridge, while recollecting the hot summer's day in July 1940 when he had passed under it in a coal barge on his way to prison camp. Close by the bridge, Neave made a vital discovery in the city's electricity generating station. It was still in contact with sister stations in enemy territory, through a direct telephone link across the Waal and the Rhine further north. The Dutch Resistance was already using the line to talk to its people and Neave saw a golden opportunity to get in touch with evading airmen and the remnants of the force that had taken part in Operation Market Garden. Initially, Neave's superiors blanched at the idea of telephoning across enemy lines, but the Dutch power engineers assured them that the circuit was safe from prying Nazi ears, and IS9 got approval from 21 Army Group to take full advantage of this opportunity. In Nijmegen, Neave was joined by Major Hugh Fraser of the SAS who became second in command of IS9. They became firm friends, nightly making a hazardous journey to the power station to draw up a plan with the Dutch Resistance to bring out the Arnhem survivors. The operation, codenamed Pegasus, relied on the Allied evaders being brought by underground guides to the Rhine near Wageningen before winter rain made crossing the river by small boat too dangerous. Neave's operations did not usually prompt critical comment from the army High Command, but on this occasion clearance was accompanied by a message to Langley which read: 'The Field Marshal hopes this will not be an Imperial Balls Up as if it is it will be the last IS9 will make under its present Commanding Officer.'[9]

On 6 October, Neave wrote to Langley at IS9's Brussels headquarters asking permission to send an officer through enemy lines on a reconnaissance mission to the Dutch underground. In *Saturday at MI9* he declined to identify this agent, codenamed Harrier. He was in fact the turbulent Captain Baker, evidence of whose devil-may-care bravery had already been seen in the Forêt de Fréteval. Langley consented to the plan, as long as Baker promised to remain in British army uniform and never to wear civilian clothes or leave the safe house in which they would be hidden. It was as well for Neave that he retained this correspondence with Langley because Harrier disobeyed orders, with fatal results. Baker was excitable and romantic, and 'fancied himself as a secret agent, for which he had no training', Neave wrote later. With a small patrol from the Highland Light Infantry, Neave and Fraser escorted Baker and his companion, a young American soldier, across no-man's-land to the River Waal on the night of 11 October, after a long march across farmland and dykes. The canoe that took Baker and the US private into enemy territory also brought out a Dutch representative, Herman van Roijen (later Netherlands ambassador in London) with vital intelligence for his government in exile. Neave escorted the VIP to Nijmegen, pointing out in his record of events that he and Fraser were now in charge of secret intelligence.

He waited anxiously for Baker's return. Operation Pegasus was now ready to go. Canadian army engineers, protected by troops from the 101st American Airborne Division, would row Market Garden survivors back in assault craft. Neave expected at least a hundred men to make their escape, but on 18 October he received distressing news. Baker and the American private accompanying him had been spotted in civilian clothes. First, and incorrect, reports said the Germans had arrested and shot them. Why were they in civilian clothes, despite orders to the contrary? In his account, Baker insisted that his Dutch hosts in the town of Tiel made him wear 'civvies'. 'There was no argument I could offer,' he wrote. 'I could only place myself in their hands.'[10] The Dutch Resistance took the pair to a farm where they were well treated and even taken for walks under the noses of the Germans. Here, Baker stayed for twenty-four hours, guests of the Ebbens family, before a treacherous tip-off brought the Wehrmacht to the farm. They were not harmed but both were taken prisoner; their unfortunate hosts were shot by the Gestapo for harbouring the Allied servicemen. Baker was later found in a POW camp. Of the American soldier nothing was ever seen again. Neave was deeply troubled by this blow, which harmed relations with the Dutch Resistance and prompted a post-war enquiry. 'The ultimate responsibility must always remain with those in command, but I had reason to feel that the tragedy was unnecessary,' he recorded. Langley and he were cleared of responsibility.

This setback did not affect preparations for Operation Pegasus, which went ahead on schedule on 22 October. From their clandestine telephone links, IS9 now knew the number of men of the 1st Airborne Division in hiding was much greater than first envisaged. Assault boats were carried to the banks of the Rhine under night cover. Meanwhile, alerted by the Baker episode, the Germans increased military activity on the other side of the river and began expelling Dutch civilians. For Neave, Pegasus had become an operation combining 'military planning and secret intelligence'. He plainly revelled in the latter. His communications lines through Room 900 and IS9 worked at fever pitch to ensure the success of the enterprise. Neave and Fraser went to the forward command post at a farmhouse near Randwijk on the Allied side, to act as 'beachmasters' to the incoming human cargo. A Bofors gun firing ten rounds at intervals signalled the start of the operation, and soon after midnight Neave watched the Canadian engineers embark. A Morse code signal from the other side was 400 yards from where he expected it, but within twenty minutes of the launch the men began to return, bringing 138 evaders, including several Dutchmen. Neave recognised two of the latter: they were fellow escapers from Colditz.

They entire party got through enemy territory with remarkable ease, bringing information that a further 150 evaders were still at large, some of them badly wounded. Neave came under pressure to mount a second operation – Pegasus II – to bring them out. This would not be so easy. Enemy reinforcements had moved into the area north of the Rhine, and unfortunate publicity given to Pegasus I by jubilant survivors on their return had also alerted the Germans. However, he began planning a second mercy mission, provisionally fixed for 16 November. The crossing point this time would be the village of Heteren, four miles east of Randwijk and closer to the Arnhem battle zone. Autumn rains now ruled out the use of rowing boats, and Neave wangled a dozen flat-bottomed 'storm boats' fitted with silenced outboard motors from the Canadians now occupying Nijmegen. Even so, he began to harbour doubts about repeating the success of Pegasus I. With so many Dutch evaders making their way into Allied territory under their own steam, there was an obvious risk to security. But it was decided to go ahead six days later than originally planned. The Rhine was running high on the night of 22 November. It was very dark and windy. All night Neave's party, under fitful shelling from German batteries, watched for the Morse signal from the other side that would indicate they were on their way. It did not come, but at 3.00 a.m. on 24 November they heard an Irish voice carry across the river. A storm boat hurried across and came back with three men: an RAF sergeant and two Dutchmen, all in civilian clothes. It transpired that they were all that survived from a group of 120 men who had set off to walk in stockinged feet to the crossing place two days earlier, only to be ambushed by a German patrol that opened fire, killing several and taking the rest prisoner. Only seven got away. Later that night, another voice called across the river and an American lieutenant insisted on paddling a canoe across the treacherous current. Neither he nor the mystery caller came back. Neave confessed to being deeply depressed by the failure of his mission. It had been a grim disappointment and marked the end of large-scale rescue attempts until the following spring. On reflection, he decided, 'only a miracle could have prevented disaster'. The unwise publicity given to Pegasus I had put the Germans on a high state of alert.

Neave returned to London in December 1944, leaving Hugh Fraser in charge of IS9 at Nijmegen. His task now was to organise a small-scale crossing of men still at large and the dropping of supplies to MI9's agents in Holland. To Neave's obvious pleasure, his old unit reverted to clandestine operations supplying the British and Canadian forces with military intelligence. 'This was not the accepted function of IS9 (WEA) and the War Office would have protested had they known about it,' Neave mentioned with some satisfaction.[11] His own operations from Room 900 brought out more than thirty more officers and men of the 1st Airborne through the maze of Dutch waterways. Among them was Brigadier (later General Sir) John Hackett, badly wounded while commanding the 4th Parachute Brigade at Arnhem, who strongly supported Neave's bid for extra equipment, particularly wireless sets for his agents.

However, the war in Europe was drawing to a close and with it the need for Room 900's evasion operations. Crockatt and Neave debated a number of alternative ideas, including an incredible plan to send paratroopers into prisoner of war camps, including Colditz, to forestall wholesale killings by the retreating Nazis. Neave fondly imagined himself landing in the courtyard of the castle whence he had escaped three years earlier. The plan was dropped on the grounds that it would put POWs' lives at risk. Neave returned to Holland in the first week of April 1945 and crossed the Rhine into Arnhem in the wake of the German retreat. Two days before the official VE Day, he contrived to get permission to cross the German lines after a truce was signed at

Wageningen, and drove at breakneck speed to Amsterdam and The Hague in search of his MI9 helpers. Their hour of thanks and reward had come. Neave was ordered to set up an Awards Bureau in The Hague for Dutch nationals who had risked their lives to help Allied servicemen. This 'congenial task' kept him occupied for almost five months.

It also brought to an end his wartime involvement with IS9, which, according to Jimmy Langley, was concentrated at Bad Salzufflen in the British Occupation Zone in July 1945 prior to being disbanded. He also recorded that MI9 was disbanded. However, the work of both organisations continued in a discreet manner long after the war, and under a different name it continues today. Neave continued to have a key role in these peacetime activities. He took keen satisfaction in the work his organisation had done, not merely in freeing Allied servicemen from their captors but combating totalitarianism in all its forms, particularly Soviet Communism. In his memoirs of MI9 service, he paid tribute to the – mostly young – people who, inspired by a sense of outrage, resisted tyranny and oppression. In an illuminating sentence, he argued: 'Their counterparts can be found today all over the world, especially among the opponents of Soviet imperialism.' Neave paid tribute to the young Czechs who chalked swastikas on tanks in defiance of the Red Army. 'The difference is that, in war, these emotions have to be organised.'[12] IS9 (TA) did precisely that, in preparation for a possible war with the Soviet Union. Neave lectured widely, including to the SAS, in the techniques of combat survival.

The work of IS9/MI9 remains little known, except among military historians. It was, said its leader Jimmy Langley, 'a brilliant conception, not so big as to give rise to the criticism that it was an unnecessary appendage to the invading forces, not too little so as to be ineffective. It met and solved the problems of escape and evasion to a triumphant conclusion.'[13] Overall, more than 3,000 Allied aircrews shot down over France, Belgium and Holland before D-Day were successfully returned. The number of Room

900's helpers who died – shot, tortured or starved in concentration camps – will never be known. Langley argues that it is far in excess of the 500 recorded names. Every returnee probably cost the life of a helper.

10

Nuremberg

The Britain that Neave found on his return from a Europe restored to peace was a very different landscape from the pre-war society that he had fought to preserve. While hostilities still raged across Europe, social reforms were afoot to make Britain 'a land fit for heroes'. As part of the wartime coalition government, the Conservatives played a key role in this radical change. R.A. Butler introduced the 1944 Education Act, which brought free, compulsory secondary education and raised the school leaving age to fifteen, a measure widely regarded as the most important social reform of the first half of the twentieth century. It was supplemented by a White Paper presaging the establishment of a National Health Service, another strong contender for the accolade. A wind of change was blowing through the nation. After so much sacrifice, there was a widespread feeling that things could not – and should not – ever be the same again.

On 5 July 1945, the British people turned their backs on Winston Churchill and elected a Labour government by a landslide. The new Prime Minister, Clement Attlee, was, like Neave, a major, but there the similarities ended. Neave was a natural Tory. His upbringing, education and preference for the Territorial Army and the Junior Carlton Club rather than fashionable causes of the left in the thirties marked him out as a man who would tread an orthodox political path, if he took to politics at all (his forebears had not). If his pre-war days among the Myrmidons at Oxford had exposed a dilettante side, his clubland. The flat, No. 5 St James's Street, opposite Prunier's, the fish restaurant, was Jimmy Langley's home. It was here that Neave and Langley met returned POWs and interviewed likely recruits to be sent into the field as agents of Room 900.

Neave's life now fell into a more regular pattern. In June 1942, he rented a flat in Elizabeth Street, Belgravia. It was, he mused, accommodation 'fit for Bertie Wooster with twentyish furniture'. He lived the life of a man about town here for six months, passing the evenings drinking whisky and talking tactics with Langley, ever alert for a telegram or phone call that would recall them urgently to Room 900 to hear of another batch of escapers. 'It did not seem a soldier's life,' he reflected later. 'Sometimes I felt, thinking of those I had left behind in Colditz, that I had no right to this luxury.'[5]

However, the intense period of MI9's activity was only just beginning. While Neave had been hiding in Marseilles, Langley, Darling and O'Leary had met in Gibraltar to plan a big upgrading of the escape effort. Before they could implement these plans, however, they had to try to eliminate a traitor on the ratlines, Harold Cole, an army sergeant in his late thirties, who was masquerading as a captain. The British police knew him as a small-time crook, with a string of convictions for housebreaking and fraud. He had absconded from the British Expeditionary Force with the sergeants' mess funds just before the battle for Dunkirk and mysteriously reappeared as a courier in the Allied escape routes from Lille and Paris over the demarcation line. Cole was a womaniser and was suspected of using escape funds to promote his disreputable lifestyle. But much worse, he was also a traitor, a double agent who betrayed to the Gestapo an estimated 150 French men and women working for the Allies, to save his own skin. Cole was eventually cornered in a Marseilles flat but escaped through a bathroom window to continue his ruinous treachery. He was later jailed by the Vichy regime for spying. At the end of the war he was still on the run, posing as a British intelligence officer in the American zone. The British had him wartime ordeal as a prisoner of the Nazis and subsequent experience in the secret services fired the serious side of his nature. He abhorred the totalitarian state and by sustaining his links with IS9 he signalled a readiness to fight that challenge from wherever it came.

On the international front, a new world order was already taking shape. In October 1944, the four great powers – America, Britain, China and the USSR – announced the setting up of the United Nations, a global security body to supersede the discredited League of Nations. New international financial institutions, the World Bank and the International Monetary Fund, were established to avert a post-war economic collapse that might plunge the world into fresh political instability or even war.

Much thought was also given to the question of punishing Nazi war criminals. An Allied body, the United Nations Commission for the Investigation of War Crime, went to work identifying those who should be brought to book. The Allied powers could not agree on how to dispose of the guilty men. Initially, Churchill favoured summary execution of Hitler and his clique, and some senior advisers to Franklin D. Roosevelt shared this view. Indeed, the American President, reacting to the mass slaughter of French civilians as early as 1941, had warned: 'One day, a frightful retribution will be exacted.' The Soviets preferred a show trial, at which they were expert, followed by the firing squad. Stalin had his own little list comprising 50,000 members of the German General Staff. More sober counsels prevailed when Roosevelt, Churchill and Stalin met in Tehran in November 1944. The big three agreed to take Hitler's fiends through a judicial process, though no court of international law to try them yet existed.

The Americans swiftly set about drawing one up. At its heart was the novel crime of conspiracy to wage war. While it had long been a feature of British law, conspiracy was a concept alien to US and European jurisprudence. But in the context of Hitler's subjection and maltreatment of millions, it had obvious advantages. The Nazis had engaged in a criminal enterprise to wage aggressive war and proof of participation in this conspiracy would ensure a guilty verdict. Initially, the British were reluctant to go down this road. On 12 April 1945, the day Roosevelt died, the War Cabinet confirmed its view that 'executive action' was the right way to dispose of the top Nazis. The new US President, Harry Truman, however, pressed the case for an international tribunal and by early June the American view prevailed. Furthermore, Washington insisted that 'if we are going to have a trial, then it must be an actual trial' not a judicial confirmation of a political decision to convict. There would have to be genuine, compelling evidence of war crimes. Fortunately, the advancing Allies were accumulating masses of captured documents tracing the proof of responsibility for atrocities which the Germans had recorded in minute detail. Robert Jackson, a US Supreme Court judge charged with setting up the International Military Tribunal, reported to a London conference of ministers: 'I did not think men would ever be so foolish as to put in writing some of the things the Germans did put in writing. The stupidity of it and the brutality of it would simply appal you.' In late July, Nuremberg was chosen as the venue for the greatest trial of the century. Despite saturation bombing by the Allies, which killed two thirds of its 450,000 population, the city where Hitler staged his greatest pre-war rallies still had a courthouse, a luxury hotel, a prison and agreeable houses for the 600 Tribunal lawyers and staff. Here, the twenty-three top Nazi war criminals would be put in the dock, in the city where their hideous decree depriving Jews of their rights and forbidding them to marry Aryans had been promulgated in 1938.

The Allies' first priority was to bring together the damning evidence. And despite the official disbandment of MI9 and his return to London, for Neave the war against Nazism was not quite over. In August 1945, he was appointed to the British War Crimes Executive. It was an appropriate decision. His Oxford degree in jurisprudence had given him a grasp of international law, though he could not have been familiar with the new dispensation created to punish Nazi war crimes. He spoke some German and he had personal experience of the Gestapo. His work with MI9 had also drawn him into the wider European theatre. But Neave did not take the job in any spirit of personal revenge. He felt he had had his triumph when he escaped the Nazis' clutches in January 1942. The requital he sought was post-humous justice for the agents he had lost, some in the most appalling circumstances in concentration camps.

Neave's initial task was to gather evidence to incriminate Gustav Krupp von Bohlen und Halbach, head of the firm that was the engine of Hitler's war machine. In line with the novel doctrine of war conspiracy, he had to substantiate the charge that Krupp participated in military and economic preparations for war, and committed war crimes and crimes against humanity involving the use and abuse of slave labour. Neave reached the bombed-out city of Essen in late August 1945. The giant Krupp Works was largely a ruin, demolished by RAF raids culminating in a devastating 1,000-bomber onslaught five months earlier. Walking around the shattered factory, he found the silence oppressive. That evening, his unit ensconced itself in the Villa Tegelmann, a modern house in a middle-class suburb that had survived the attentions of 'Bomber' Harris. Promptly the next morning, he began his investigation at the Villa Huegel, the Krupp family mansion set in its own grounds overlooking the city. This overblown monstrosity, with 200 rooms and a 100-foot reception hall ornamented by larger-than-life family portraits, was built by Alfried Krupp, the firm's founder, in 1870. Neave's assignment was to make it give up its secrets.

It was not an easy task. The firm's remaining staff stayed stubbornly loyal to their boss, who was not even a Krupp himself but the scion of a minor Prussian diplomatic family who had married the formidable Bertha, granddaughter of Alfried Krupp. Their marriage in 1906 was attended by Kaiser Wilhelm himself, who urged Gustav to help make Germany a great military nation.

He needed no bidding and boasted of being 'the nation's armourer'. After the First World War, he had been indicted as a war criminal in the ineffectual campaign to demilitarise Germany. Sentenced by a French court in 1923 to fifteen years' imprisonment, he served only five months before returning to become Hitler's munitions manufacturer. His production lines turned out the Panzer tanks that spearheaded the Nazi Blitzkrieg. Neave painstakingly assembled evidence that Gustav had secretly rearmed Germany for offensive war in defiance of the Treaty of Versailles. He was helped by Krupp's own swagger, for he had several times boasted in speeches and articles of his support for the Führer. A family album contained photographs of Hitler in the grounds of the Villa Huegel, and of his deputy, Rudolf Hess, awarding Gustav with the Nazi 'Gold Banner of Industry' for his contribution to the war effort in 1940.

Within a matter of days, nearly a ton of Krupp documents was in Neave's hands, and on 9 September he was instructed by the War Crimes Executive to arrest the firm's directors and executives. Accompanied by members of the British Field Security Police ('scholarly sergeants in spectacles, very different from the Gestapo') and an armed guard from the Manchester Regiment, Neave's diminutive force of four armoured cars and jeeps rolled into the Essen plant. They locked in the entire staff, who stood by their desks in a quasi-military show of disobedience. Neave was amused by their Prussian contempt for the victors but angry at their pretence that slave labourers had not been maltreated and starved to death. Nine directors were arrested in their homes the next day, an exercise that Neave found 'rather pathetic'. Neave housed them in the cellars of Essen's bombed-out gaol, but he could not make them talk. Through their lawyer, the Krupp bosses protested about the 'inhuman and illegal' conditions of their imprisonment. An enraged Neave received the lawyer after reading a report by a Krupp director about the extremely bad conditions in which foreign workers had been kept: forced to walk barefoot in winter, eating only bad meat and suffering a quadrupled rate of

tuberculosis. Neave turned on him with fury. Very young children
had been employed by his clients in much worse conditions, he
assured the disbelieving lawyer, whose protests went unheeded.
In the immediate aftermath of war, and the exposure of so much
Nazi brutality, it was as difficult for him as many other British
officers to accept the German habit of denial: that they had not
known or they were only carrying out orders. In fact, Krupp had
employed 70,000 of the 4.8 million foreign workers driven into
slavery by Hitler. Some of them came from Auschwitz to
manufacture weapons, among them Jews forced to labour in a
plant named Berthawerk after Gustav's wife.

Neave's British unit was joined in the second week of
September by an American team, many of German-Jewish origin,
who had a consuming interest in their work. Together, they filleted
Gustav's diaries and correspondence, searching for testimony that
would convict. Much evidence had already been destroyed,
burned before the Allies invested Essen in April. A painstaking
search of the Villa Huegel for secret hiding places revealed nothing
until Gustav's private secretary finally disclosed the existence of
two secret safes, one in the bedroom, the other in Gustav's dressing
room, embedded in concrete in the wall of the house. They could
not be opened. Neave wrote to his superiors, pointing out that it
was impossible to find a professional safe-cracker, and requesting
permission – duly given – to use REME engineers to break in. It
promised to be the best free theatre in Essen and a crowd of
senior officers gathered for lunch in late September to watch.
Alas, an afternoon of exhausting efforts to cut through steel,
copper, more steel and then concrete bored Neave's distinguished
audience and still the doors remained firmly shut. A week passed
before the patient REME experts eventually cut their way in.
Neave rushed in, to find nothing but old bills and envelopes.
Bertha's safe contained empty jewellery cases. The Krupps had
foiled them. Neave and his fellow officers saw the funny side of
the episode and went back to the tedious work of gathering
incriminating files. He took responsibility for evidence relating to

the conspiracy to prepare for war, and shipped a further ton of material back to the War Crimes Executive at Bad Oeynhausen. Neave's verdict was straightforward. Gustav was guilty. He had offered his support to Hitler in 1933 when he became Chancellor, and was deeply enmeshed in the preparations for war thereafter. In 1936, Neave discovered, Gustav had even admitted that his firm's 'gratifying rise in profits' was 'inseparably bound up' with the fate of the Fatherland, and expressed satisfaction that his firm shared in the rearming of Germany. Neave wrote repeatedly of his anger in his record of those months. It was a bitterness born of the knowledge that Hitler could not have prosecuted his war of subjugation and cruelty without men like Gustav Krupp.

Unfortunately, his tireless zeal was largely in vain: Gustav Krupp von Bohlen was judged too ill to stand trial. The evidence against him was overwhelming, but Colonel Harry Phillimore (later Lord Justice Phillimore), head of the War Crimes Executive, accepted medical testimony that Gustav was senile and 'virtually dead'. He was tracked down to his hunting lodge, where he was found to be unable to feed himself and suffering from senile dementia, muttering '*Donnerwetter!*'. Nonetheless, he survived until 1950. The Americans, cheated of their prey, argued that Gustav's son Alfried, who actually ran the great armaments plants, should be indicted in his place as a representative of the German industrial class that had collaborated with Hitler. But the Nuremberg bench rejected this argument, with the British prosecutor Sir Hartley Shawcross arguing that the trial was 'not a football match in which we could field a substitute'. Seeking to indict Gustav was a mistake. Three years later, Neave had the satisfaction of seeing Alfried Krupp convicted of war crimes, substantially on the evidence he had gathered that hot, dusty August in Essen. However, Alfried served only five years and returned to rebuild the family empire, still a source of some resentment to Neave decades later.

Neave was obliged to abandon his investigation into the Krupp outrage shortly after finding Bertha's empty jewellery boxes. The momentous trial of the Nazi hierarchy was about to start, and he was head-hunted for a position of judicial aide to the International Military Tribunal. It was a posting he 'least expected' and he was not slow to appreciate the irony of his position. Here he was, summoned to Nuremberg to act as a liaison officer between the Tribunal and the defendants, men once looked upon as military demigods and now reduced to the status of common criminals, much as Neave had been during his years of incarceration at their hands. Nor did he relish the prospect of meeting these men, he later confessed. 'I was afraid to meet them, as they awaited trial. To all ordinary people they were objects of nightmare,' he wrote. 'I imagined them crouching in their cells like wounded beasts. I feared to approach them as a man backs from a corpse.'[1]

He travelled from Bad Oeynhausen in low spirits. In Nuremberg, he was oppressed by the overpowering smell of disinfectant spread everywhere to disguise the stench of putrefying corpses, estimated at between six and thirty thousand, buried in the ruins of the city whose cultural history stretched back through Albrecht Dürer to the Meistersingers and the real Tannhäuser of the thirteenth century. At dusk, the army bus deposited him in front of the Grand Hotel Fürstenhof, an oasis of electric light in a desert of darkness. Next door, Hitler's personal 'Guest House' was being linked to the hotel to accommodate the hundreds of tribunal officials.

Neave had been brought into this unique legal circus by Sir Geoffrey Lawrence, the British judge at Nuremberg and president of the Tribunal. Lawrence, a compromise choice, was waspishly described by Sir Hartley Shawcross, his Chief British Prosecutor, as 'better known as a country squire with a good stable than as a great lawyer'. On the advice of Phillimore, Lawrence proposed Neave to the members of the Tribunal at its first (and only) meeting in Berlin, held there at the insistence of the Russians who had wanted the trial to take place in their zone of occupation. Neave's appointment as assistant to the General Secretary of the Tribunal, Harold B. Willey, was confirmed. It was not what he had been looking for. He was not even sure what the job entailed.

Neave had been on the point of taking up another legal post with the Control Commission when he was told to go to Nuremberg and await the arrival of two American judges. The meeting took place in the foyer of the Grand Hotel on 18 October. Francis Biddle, the senior of the two, a former US Attorney-General and a Supreme Court judge, appeared a frightening man: smart, spare and sardonic. He looked Neave up and down and asked: 'Is this Major Neave?' Receiving the affirmative, the judge added: 'You look remarkably young.' He was twenty-nine, trying to look older but defeated by what the historian Sir John Wheeler-Bennett, described as his 'cherubic countenance which made him look even younger than he was'. Perhaps to counterbalance this, he recollected, Neave 'affected a somewhat fierce and austere manner'.[2]

Biddle came straight to the point. 'Are you ready to serve the indictment?' he asked. Neave most certainly was not and his face showed it. This was the first he had heard of the awesome responsibility that was to rest on his young shoulders. He was to bring the instrument of justice to the top war criminals, personally, to their cells. Moreover, he was to do it the next day. He had not even seen the historic document of arraignment. Biddle continued, as if speaking in court, instructing Neave that under Article 16 of the Charter governing the activities of the Tribunal, the defendants had a right to a fair trial and to counsel of their own choice. 'We have appointed you to advise them of their rights and select them German lawyers,' Biddle concluded. The interview was over. 'Mr Willey will explain everything to you. Is that okay, Major?' he asked. 'Yes, Judge,' replied the dumbfounded Neave. 'Bully,' said Biddle, striding into the dining room.

Neave, feeling the measure of his inexperience, tried to stay calm, but somewhat theatrically imagined this was 'the most dangerous situation since Colditz'. It was not, of course, but it was to be the most affecting episode in his life after Colditz. Time and again he would return to it in his electioneering remarks to voters as he strove to secure a seat in Parliament, and in his own account he tried to rationalise these 'several minutes of unreasoning panic'. He felt as if he had been suddenly invited to sing at Covent Garden, or lecture in higher mathematics. Far from being elated at such a great honour he was anxious about the lack of clear instructions. 'I knew that this was a moment of history, that I should be the envy of other delegations,' he admitted. But like many other young men who had gone through five dangerous years he had become cautious. His insouciant days as a Myrmidon seemed far off.

He found Willey in the hotel's Marble Room that evening listening to a German singer doing her folk routine to a largely indifferent audience of officers and secretaries, including the staid pinstriped British contingent sitting in a corner. Willey was more confident than he was. The indictment had been drawn up, and was being translated into German by the American prosecutor's office. It would be ready in the morning, and in the afternoon Neave could simply 'shove the bundles into the cells'. This did not sound like the service of the most important legal document in the history of mankind: it sounded more like a newspaper round. Nor was Neave happy with the Article that made him responsible for supplying the accused with a list of German defence lawyers. He expected serious difficulties in persuading the Nazi High Command that they would have a fair trial. Had not justice been a hollow mockery in their own country for more than a decade?

Nonetheless, he was seized of the necessity of doing things right. He may have lost friends to Hitler's brutal regime who never had a chance of a trial, but in this new war, a war of civilised values, Neave was determined that, whatever Churchill's views, 'the tradition of the Temple' must triumph at Nuremberg. He spent a fretful night in the suburban house in Zirndorf where he and other War Crimes Executive officers were billeted. At dawn on 19 October, he was smoking and drinking coffee in the front room, pondering his confrontation with 'these monsters'. He presented himself in best service dress to the Tribunal

Secretary in the Palace of Justice, and was relieved to hear that, on judge's orders, Willey would accompany him. The weighty stack of documents on his desk made fascinating reading. Each indictment carried the names of the four big powers – the USA, France, Britain and the USSR. The charges named the twenty-three defendants as being members of specific groups – the Reich Cabinet, the Leadership Corps of the Nazi Party, the SS, the SD, the Gestapo, the SA and the General Staff and High Command of the German Armed Forces. The indictment then went on to accuse them individually of war crimes.

Once again, Neave felt a sense of awe. Furthermore, though he had some German, from his time spent in Germany in 1933 and as a POW, he was not confident of being able to translate to Willey everything the defendants said. A German-speaking American officer was therefore brought in. Then there was the matter of procedure, to which no thought had been given. It was agreed that Neave would introduce himself by name as the officer appointed by the Tribunal to serve the indictments, hand over the documents and offer to answer questions a day later. Over lunch, it was the talk of the mess that the indictments were being served that afternoon, and Neave told a fellow diner, 'I hope I shan't make a balls of it.'

The daunting figure of Colonel Burton C. Andrus of the US Cavalry was there to make sure he did not. Andrus, formerly head of the American army's toughest stockade at Fort Oglethorpe, Georgia, was a fearsome disciplinarian who carried a riding crop tucked under his arm. His black eyes bored through steel-rimmed glasses, and a pencil moustache completed the grim visage. Neave, Willey, Andrus, the interpreter and two soldiers detailed to carry the heavy sheaf of documents led the way down a silent row of cells in the prison. Another American security officer, a psychiatrist, a chaplain and several military policemen in white helmets brought up the rear. It was quite a posse.

The Palace of Justice in which this drama unfolded was one of the few buildings still standing in Nuremberg after seven Allied air raids in the closing months of the war. A solid, municipal structure, it had been the scene of a last stand by remnants of the SS, and machine-gun cartridges were still scattered about the courtyard. Inside, the courtroom was being enlarged to accommodate the teams of lawyers, guards translators, visitors and journalists. Here, only a year before, Hitler had conducted the show trial of some of the minor plotters in the abortive July conspiracy against his life. Now, some of his captured SS fanatics were put to work reconstructing the court to bring their former leaders to book. Outside, American tanks faced the Fürtherstrasse along which cowed civilians trudged, and heavily armed soldiers stood guard behind sandbags inside the corridors. The new occupiers were taking no chances. Rumours of a fresh Nazi uprising circulated in Nuremberg, the 'last refuge of evil'.

Behind the courthouse was a prison where the war criminals were incarcerated in a three-storey block linked to the courthouse by a covered way. Here, where Hitler's opponents had been gaoled, Neave began the process of retribution. At the far end of the first row, Andrus announced simply: 'Goering.' Neave looked through the grille as the door was unlocked. He scarcely recognised the short, fat man who got up from his bed as though from sleep. Was this the First World War air ace, rival of Baron von Richthofen? The founder of the Gestapo and Hitler's deputy? Years of drug abuse had taken their toll, but his gaolers had weaned him off pills and the prison diet had slashed his weight from 20 to 15 stone. His grey Air Force uniform, shorn of rank and other insignia, hung loosely on him. The indictment party crowded in the narrow 13 by 9-foot cell making Neave feel claustrophobic. When their eyes met, Neave found he was no longer afraid, despite the 'air of evil' that Goering exuded. Stripped of his voluptuous surroundings, his flunkeys and the panoply of office he was just another prisoner who ate out of a GI mess tin. But he was still a consummate performer. 'Hermann Wilhelm Goering?' asked Neave. '*Jawohl*,' he growled. Neave handed over the indictment and read out the offer of defence counsel. Reality suddenly dawned on the former Reichsmarschall. 'So it has come,' he breathed. 'So it has come.' Neave handed him the list of lawyers, which Goering studied indifferently. He did not believe they could do much for him. Would it not be better to defend himself? Neave heard the voice of the Temple saying: 'I think you would be well advised to be represented by someone.' Goering thought his situation pretty hopeless, but insisted on reading the document thoroughly, adding with sudden defiance: 'I do not see how it can have any basis in law.' Neave found his voice soft but threatening. 'Despite his apparent despondency, he never lacked courage. He was ready to fight,' he recalled. As the trial proceeded, Neave felt that, alone of the accused, Goering was the only man who might have been capable of governing Germany.

Colonel Andrus tried to hurry things along but Goering again remonstrated: 'Lawyers! They will be no use in this trial.' He demanded a private interpreter. Neave told him to take it up with his counsel, and indicated that the interview was over. Goering leaned forward in acknowledgement. The posse walked out and Neave felt a great sense of relief that the hardest part of the day's ordeal was over. Yet it had been a strange anticlimax. Half expecting to meet a legendary monster of cruelty and vice, he found he had crossed Europe to meet 'a decayed and gloomy voluptuary'.

There were nineteen more indictments to serve that day (two of the defendants had managed to commit suicide, despite being under close guard, and Gustav Krupp was only a technical defendant). Next came Rudolf Hess, co-author of *Mein Kampf* and Deputy Führer until his mad solo flight to Scotland in May 1941, allegedly to sue for peace through the Duke of Hamilton. Again, Neave studied his subject through the window grille as the door was unlocked. He was shocked by the white-faced, shabby creature, whose sunken eyes beneath heavy brows gave the appearance of a skull. 'I immediately felt sorry for him,' Neave recorded. He handed over the papers and explained the accused's rights. Hess asked if he could defend himself, was told that he could, but that Neave advised against it. It would be in his own interest to have a lawyer. In truth, he knew the judges would be appalled at the prospect. Hess's sanity was uncertain. And, mad or not, Neave immediately formed the view that he looked it. For now, all he wanted to know was whether he would be tried with 'other party comrades'. Informed that this was so, Hess said: 'I do not like to be tried with Goering.'

Von Ribbentrop, former German ambassador to the Court of St James, Hitler's Foreign Minister, and co-signatory of the treacherous pact with the Soviet Union, came next. He was another deflated figure. Neave felt nothing but contempt for this sloppily dressed, self-pitying 'Second Bismarck' in his untidy cell. He scanned his face, while von Ribbentrop refused to look him in the eye, hunting round the tiny room as if seeking an escape. Scribbled notes drifted from his table while Neave was once more filled with disgust at the sight of a political legend reduced to a balding wreck shuffling about in carpet slippers. He answered to the phoney aristocratic name he had given himself – Joachim von Ribbentrop – and with tears in his eyes implored his captors to tell him where he could find a lawyer. He knew only Dr Scanzoni, a criminal barrister he had met at a cocktail party in Berlin many years earlier. He proffered Neave a list of names, among them members of the British aristocracy who, he insisted, could testify to his desire for peace. An impatient Neave told him they would be sent to the Tribunal office, and strode out.

Julius Streicher, the most notorious Jew-baiter of the Third Reich, hissed as Neave and his Jewish-American interpreter entered the cell he occupied. His enthusiasm for the 'Final Solution' was common knowledge in the Palace of Justice, where a substantial proportion of the Tribunal officers and staff were German or American Jews. But Streicher, the foulest anti-Semite in Hitler's entourage – so unspeakably vile that even the Nazis disowned him – still goaded his captors, even when threatened with a sentry's blackjack. Strongly built and half-demented, he screeched at Neave: 'I need a lawyer who is anti-Semitic. A Jew could not defend me.' He dismissed the list of lawyers as too Jewish sounding and the judges as Jews. With an obscene wink to Neave, he implored 'The Herr Major is not a Jew,' until silenced by Andrus. Neave stifled his disgust and asked if he knew any lawyers in Nuremberg. Streicher mentioned a Dr Marx and Neave promised to make enquiries before quitting his revolting presence.

Not all the interviews were so stomach-turning. Baldur von Schirach, Hitler's Youth Leader and Governor of Vienna, was a smartly dressed man in his late thirties with a teasing bisexual manner. He tried to turn the indictment process into a social occasion. Neave imagined him at ease beneath the palms in Cannes in co-respondent shoes, but he saw through the soft persona to the well-groomed enthusiast for Hitler's racial solutions who referred to the monstrous Nazi tyranny as a 'misfortune'. Alfried Rosenberg, the Nazi 'philosopher' who celebrated his master's thinking in the party's ideological bible, *The Myth of the Twentieth Century*, was a seamy contrast to the effeminate von Schirach. His stinking cell was littered with torn papers, and his pompous rejection of the indictment for conspiracy gave way to a whining request for help, and a meeting with Hans Frank, the Butcher of Poland, next on Neave's list. Frank, a lawyer who insinuated his way to the top by defending Brownshirt thugs in the late twenties, made an unctuous bid to enlist his sympathy. 'I regard this trial as a God-given world court, destined to examine and put an end to the terrible suffering under Adolf Hitler,' he began, before Colonel Andrus cut him short. Neave found his legal protestations as unconvincing as his conversion back to Roman Catholicism. 'I had no faith in his remorse,' he remarked. Frank sweated, mumbled and seemed on the point of nervous collapse. In Neave's view, this man, who once wrote a marginal note on a memorandum saying '1.2 million Jews will perish', was 'far the most execrable' he met that afternoon. 'He was the one man whom every soldier shunned like a leper, despite the claims of priests that he was saved,' he recorded.

Two other 'Fs' remained: Walter Funk, the former President of the Reichsbank, and Wilhelm Frick, Hitler's sinister Minister of the Interior. Funk wept uncontrollably as Neave read out his script. 'Be a man, Funk!' barked Andrus. 'Listen to the Major!' But the former financial journalist who rose to become Plenipotentiary of the War Economy was also personally responsible for ordering the confiscation of valuables from Jews as they were herded into the concentration camps, and for stealing the gold from their teeth when they succumbed 'for Germany's war effort'. Funk pulled himself together and asked to see his counsel at once. 'I have a great interest in the outcome of this trial,' he told an astounded Neave. So, he was tempted to say, had the relatives of those whose gold teeth were deposited in the Reichsbank. Frick, who had studied law and became a police official before realising that the Nazi Party offered the best route for his talents, was the man who stripped Germans of their civil rights and set in train the extermination of the weak-minded and insane. He dismissed the indictment of conspiracy as 'fictitious'.

It was getting dark as Neave moved on to his next 'client', Ernst Kaltenbrunner, the most wanted member of the SS after the suicide of Heinrich Himmler. At 6 foot 5 inches, Kaltenbrunner was the very worst kind of Nazi, an alcoholic sadist, built like a bull, violent and devious. He had directed extermination units against the Jews and taken personal charge of executing the leaders of the plot to kill the Führer in 1944. He had also signed the death warrants for British and American POWs in Mauthausen concentration camp. He put down the revolt in Warsaw with exemplary savagery and razed the city. But when confronted with Neave and the redoubtable Andrus, he was reduced to silent tears and begging for electric light. For the other defendants, Neave had managed to keep a diplomatic face, but with 'the Lord High Executioner' the mask slipped. First, he read out his prepared text, and then extracts of his war crimes from the indictment itself. Asked why he had done so, Neave replied grimly: 'Because of Mauthausen. And because of Warsaw.' Rage aside, he felt that he had come to speak for the dead that fearsome afternoon. The Tribunal would 'speak for the civilised world', but he had already seen compelling evidence of Kaltenbrunner's crimes. 'I was furious with this man for crying like a child,' he recollected. 'The Poles had died gloriously, but this savage Austrian lawyer, born in the next village to Hitler, was a coward.'[3] There was a clear distinction in Neave's mind between soldiers who fought for their country and the militarist Nazi politicians who did not fight but caused the deaths of millions. So, he had some admiration for Admiral Canaris, chief of the Abwehr, who was strangled with piano wire on Kaltenbrunner's orders for his complicity in the plot to murder Hitler. Canaris was a 'chivalrous adversary on the other side', while Kaltenbrunner was scum. Yet he tried to argue that he was a soldier. Perhaps he believed it, Neave reflected contemptuously.

The burden of bringing these evil men face to face with their crimes began to tell on the young major. He doubted if he could take much more but he led his posse into the cell of Dr Robert Ley, head of the German Labour Front, the Nazi usurper of free trade unionism. This 'slobbering creature' had connived in the slave labour programme, yet confronted with the indictment he claimed: 'The whole thing is preposterous.' The following evening, he hanged himself with a towel from the toilet lever in his cell, the sounds of his choking deadened by his underpants stuffed into his mouth. Fritz Sauckel, Ley's fellow slave-trader, or 'General Plenipotentiary for the Employment of Labour', and also a general in both the SS and the SA, turned out to be a little bald man with a feeble Chaplin moustache and stupid brown eyes. He, too, shed tears, prompting Neave to ask himself: were they all going to cry, except the genuine soldiers?

It only occurred to him later that his tour of the cells at Nuremberg terrified the defendants. They assumed, because that was what they were accustomed to, that the trial would be short and sharp and they would soon be dead. It was a belief shared by some on the Allied side. Even the chief American prosecutor, Robert Jackson, thought they would all be home by Christmas

1945. 'I did not realise that day how many of these defendants regarded the service of the indictment as the moment of doom,' he wrote later. 'It was as if I had come to read the death sentence.'

Neave next moved on to Albert Speer, Hitler's architect who became Minister of Armaments. He found Speer a gifted and compelling man. Speer thought Neave's style was 'unceremonious'. Neave could not trust Speer but he was initially impressed, believing him to be a man of integrity. Speer spoke English very well and offered that 'the trial is necessary' as he took the indictment. But despite his advice to the Führer in March 1945 that the war was lost, he had been at Hitler's side for more than a decade, and Neave had no doubt that without his formidable organisational skills, the Third Reich could never have become so powerful or lasted so long. Neave was ambivalent about this brilliant man. He seemed the one civilised man among the Nazi leadership. He was the only member of Hitler's inner cabinet who did not lose his will or reason, yet he deployed his great talents to make the Nazi dream a reality. Speer smiled pleasantly at Neave's offer to find him a lawyer, and Colonel Andrus frowned, evidently uncomfortable about the bond that appeared to be springing up between prosecutor and defendant. Neave understood. They must not fall under the spell of Speer, a man perhaps even more dangerous and beguiling than Hitler. Speer himself did not share this analysis. Long after the war, in his memoirs, *Inside the Third Reich*, he disclosed his dismay at being included in a general arraignment. 'In my naïvete, I had imagined that each of us would receive an individual indictment,' he wrote. 'Now it turned out that we were one and all accused of the monstrous crimes that this document listed. After reading it I was overwhelmed by a sense of despair.'[4]

Baron Constantin von Neurath, Hitler's pre-war Foreign Minister and Reichsprotektor for Bohemia and Moravia after the Munich crisis, presented no such difficulties. He was a diplomat of the old school, who betrayed the traditions of the German Empire to insinuate himself into the Nazi hierarchy. Von Neurath, by now aged seventy-three, had won an Iron Cross (First Class) in the First World War, and rising in the diplomatic service he had been ambassador to London for two years in the early thirties. He spoke to Neave as though he was a Foreign Office courier, rather than the angel of death as others feared. 'I am much obliged to you, Major,' he responded to the service of the indictment. He was also gracious about the offer of defence counsel. 'I was always against punishment without the possibility of a defence,' he murmured. Neave was furious at being patronised by the former 'Protektor'. 'You will have every opportunity to put forward your defence,' he retorted angrily.

Franz von Papen, his next quarry, Chancellor of Germany before Hitler, and subsequently the Führer's Vice Chancellor, was equally disdainful, if not more so. He spoke to Neave in smooth Old Etonian English, affecting to misunderstand his situation. 'I cannot imagine why I find myself in this situation, Herr Major,' he submitted. Neave advised him to read the indictment, accusing him of conspiracy to wage aggressive war, and he would see exactly why. He found von Papen untrustworthy, long before evidence emerged that, for all his diplomatic standing, he was a born liar.

Steeling himself for the next confrontation, with Dr Artur Seyss-Inquart, Reichskommissar of Holland for the entire war, Neave moved down the prison hall in fading light. His experience of the Netherlands war theatre and the atrocities meted out to the anti-Fascist Dutch primed him to meet a 'thin-lipped monster, a murderer with a limp'. The limp was there, but he was otherwise shaken by the wan figure wearing thick glasses who waited in his cell: the 'gentle Judas' of Austria who had betrayed his country to Hitler for personal advantage did not live up to his cruel image. Yet there was a cold fury in his eyes. Seyss-Inquart, who presided over the liquidation of four-fifth's of Holland's 150,000 Jews – including the fifteen-year-old Anne Frank – and the slaughter of Dutch hostages, bowed to Neave and smiled: 'Last act of the tragedy of the Second World War, I hope.'

Despite the demeaning confines of his narrow cell, Dr Hjalmar Schacht, Hitler's banker, retained an impressive bearing. He talked down to Neave, with a withering promise to read the indictment 'but, *of course*, I expect to be acquitted. I am, after all, a banker.' The white-haired former president of the Reichsbank could not browbeat the young British major. Neave took an instant dislike to the man who had funded the Nazi terror. He believed Schacht was lying about his relationship with Hitler, even though he had belatedly defied Hitler. Neave's next client, General Alfred Jodl, Chief of the Operations Staff of the German Armed Forces, shared some of Schacht's doubts, but continued to carry out orders. Neave, with his customary sharp eye for detail, described him as 'a trim little man, like a Leach cartoon of a Victorian coachman' with 'fierce blue eyes, a strawberry nose and huge ears'. Nonetheless, he was every inch a high-ranking officer, addressing Neave as if he were his junior and questioning him closely about the qualifications of the German lawyers chosen to defend him. Were they experts in criminal or international law? Neave equivocated. He did not know and Jodl was perfectly aware of that. Hitler's reluctant ex-chief of staff demanded stationery to prepare his defence and showed none of the self-pity of some of his fellow defendants. He considered himself above all a soldier, doing his duty to his country. 'He did not believe himself guilty of any crime,' recorded Neave. Not even the shooting of POWs, which he had sanctioned. Jodl, the tidiest of the prisoners, protested at being stripped of his marks of rank, but Neave rejected the complaint. In his soldierly way, he did not think Jodl was evil, though he was part of a criminal government and took a leading role in its military organisation. Jodl's fault, Neave concluded, was an obsessive loyalty to Hitler, who they thought would recover Germany's lost pride. 'They pretended not to understand politics and in fact they did not do so,' wrote Neave.[5] Here, Neave's lifelong ambiguity with regard to values is laid bare. As a man of arms himself, he admired soldiers and soldierly virtues, and was contemptuous of Hitler on the simple grounds that 'he never cared a fig about his soldiers'. Yet he insisted that soldiers should also understand politics, and Nuremberg was the greatest example of civil society seeking to make soldiers understand the nature of their actions and their responsibility to recognise political right and wrong. In his own life, the soldier–politician Neave was not always so scrupulous. He vigorously propounded the virtues of liberty and democracy but flirted dangerously with quasi-military groups in Britain determined to halt what they saw as a drift towards Communism. For the most part, the politician was in charge, but sometimes the soldier took over, as in his attitude to Northern Ireland much later.

Field Marshal Wilhelm Keitel, Chief of the High Command of the German Forces, was a man Neave had come a long way to meet. Keitel, the 'square-headed murderer', had signed the order for the execution of the captured 'Cockleshell Heroes' in May 1942 and British commandos captured at Stavanger later that year. The conqueror of Europe had been a figure of hate in Colditz and Neave told him the story of his abortive escape from the camp dressed as a German corporal. 'Yes. I remember the camp,' replied Keitel. 'Your comrades in Colditz were a trouble to us.' Yet, Neave reflected, he might owe his life to this toady of the Führer. His soldiers had guarded Colditz and they had respected the Geneva Convention. The SS would have thrown him into a concentration camp for impersonating an officer of the Wehrmacht.

Neave analysed Keitel's claims to be a 'real soldier' in some detail, confirming his acute interest in differentiating between the real thing and the fake. He concluded that this man with stupid eyes had fawned on Hitler and betrayed his fellow officers for personal gain. Had he not also instructed his commanders on the Russian Front to execute fifty 'Communists' – civilians, in fact – for every German soldier killed? If he had not sold his soul to the devil, he would never have gone beyond the rank of colonel before retiring to a small estate. American combat GIs crowding outside the cell shared Neave's revulsion at this sweating, purple-faced creature who sought to excuse his crimes by claiming he was 'only a soldier'.

Two German admirals – Karl Doenitz and Erich Raeder – were more difficult clients. They attracted substantial sympathy from US and British naval officers, who argued that they had fought an honourable war and should not be tried for war crimes. Neave did not share their reservations. He was astounded that the apologists for Doenitz did not know he was the Führer's chosen successor: a man who spoke of Hitler as the new Napoleon, and demanded that the war be fought to the bitter end when it was quite clear that it was lost. Over and above the general crime of conspiracy to wage aggressive war, he was charged with violating the rules of war at sea. Neave had personal experience of Doenitz's ideas of total war: an officer friend, his wife and baby had drowned when the British passenger liner *Laconia* was torpedoed in the South Atlantic in 1942. Days later, Doenitz issued War Order 154, forbidding the rescue of survivors because such action could put the submarine at risk. That was his idea of chivalry. Yet still he puzzled Neave, who kept repeating to himself Doenitz's words, 'Compared with him [Hitler] we others are worms', as he emerged from the long ordeal of indictment service. Taking a deep breath of fresh air, Neave hurried off to make his report to the Tribunal.

However, he reckoned without the momentous journalistic nature of the story that was now unfolding. The American GIs' paper *Stars and Stripes* picked up a fairly accurate account of Neave's activities, particularly the reactions of the Nazis. It came not from him, because he was wary of the press, but from his accompanying US guards, and perhaps even officers, who were not so reticent. From the *Stars and Stripes*, the story moved rapidly to daily newspapers, and after breakfast on 20 October, barely hours after his ordeal, Neave was ordered into the presence of a very angry Judge Biddle. If the defendants were to have a fair trial, any statements made by them were confidential. There must be no more leaks. Furthermore, demanded the judge, had Neave given

notice of the trial date? He had not, for the simple reason that he
didn't know it. 'Jesus!' expostulated the judge. They must be told,
forthwith, that the trial was to start on 20 November. Neave must
meet these monsters all over again. He and Burton Andrus served
notice of the date, leaving aside the question of defence counsel
until the next day.

By then, the condition of some of the defendants had
deteriorated even further, though they could still not shake off
their Nazi past. Goering retained his composure, but Keitel was
'woebegone' and Kaltenbrunner attended in a 'most emotional
state and wept during part of the interview', Neave recorded in a
memorandum to Willey. Sauckel also cried and pleaded for a
Nazi lawyer. Hess was indifferent to the choice of a lawyer, so
long as the court did not appoint a Jew. Doenitz called for naval
experts, 'anti-Semites and persons who were not Marxists or
pacifists'. The banker Schacht was in good form, demanding
'immediate action' to find a Dr Dix of Berlin (he was promptly
found). Over the succeeding weeks, Neave put together a formidable team of defence counsel, though he still found personal
dealings with them distasteful.

He also had to face the eight judges several times, in private
session in an ante-room in the Palace of Justice. Neave found
these hearings wearying, particularly the Soviet judges' perplexity
over Western legal values. For them, Nazi war guilt had already
been decreed by order of Stalin. They objected strongly to lawyers
who had been Nazi Party members but their objections were
overruled. This was Neave's first appearance in a court of law
since he had defended a young soldier on a charge of accidentally
shooting a woman civilian cycling through Armentières during
the phoney war of 1940. Now, despite 'looking twenty, being
thirty, acting forty' (in the words of a colleague), he was appearing
on behalf of the men who had incarcerated him and enslaved
Europe. 'This reversal of fortunes was not lost upon the judges as
they considered my pleas,' he later reflected.[6] Neave was charged
with securing pleas from the defendants before the opening date

of the trial. German lawyers worked frantically to meet the deadline, badgering the office where he operated with a bevy of beautiful German-speaking Wrens. However, the trial opened on schedule under the presidency of Sir Geoffrey Lawrence, a jurist for whom Neave had boundless respect. In his wing collar and bowler hat, he embodied the British virtues of correct appearance, conduct and values. A barrister since 1906, and a judge in the King's Bench Division of the High Court since 1932, he lived contentedly in rural Wiltshire. 'Lawrence could be sharp, biting and stern,' observed Neave, 'but I always found him impeccably just.' His arrival at the Palace of Justice every day in black coat and striped trousers was one of the sights of ruined Nuremberg. He was more than equal to prosecution and defence, and even won over the defendants who came to look on him in high regard. 'Without his quiet wisdom and personal charm,' Neave decided, 'the trial would have collapsed in mockery and Allied recrimination, at a time when the Cold War had already begun.'[7] Norman Birkett, Lawrence's 'warm-hearted and fair' alternate, also impressed Neave.

The American judges were more difficult to fathom. Initially, Neave found Francis Biddle, the senior of the two, sardonic and frightening, but came to respect his formidable inquisitorial style. Biddle nursed his own private secret during the trial: an affair with Rebecca West, the British writer and long-time lover of H.G. Wells. He had known West for twenty years and became what she described at the time as 'certainly my last lover'. She was then fifty-three and was briefly but 'gloriously happy' with Biddle at Nuremberg while reporting the trial for the *Daily Telegraph*.[8] She also enjoyed Neave's company. Her biographer, Victoria Glendinning, says: 'The best friend she made among the British delegation was the future MP, Airey Neave',[9] though given the twenty-four-year age difference it is unlikely that they were anything more than good friends.

Biddle's alternate, Judge John J. Parker, offered something of a parallel to the British pair: alongside his brilliant, distinguished

and sophisticated senior, he cut a large and warm figure, remind-
ing Neave of the homely judges of Hollywood's imagination. 'He
symbolised those Christian values which the Nazis had so
ruthlessly destroyed,' recorded the young major. The French
judges disappointed him with their inscrutable inactivity throughout the trial, whereas the Soviet judges and prosecutors fascinated
him. Neave had more than a jurist's interest in them. As he freely
confessed in his record of Nuremberg, he was there not only as a
legal officer of the court, but as a spy reporting back to London.
Neave described the senior Russian judge, Major-General of
Jurisprudence I.T. Nikitchenko, Vice-President of the Supreme
Court of the USSR, as a man of sharp intelligence who was
principally there to carry out Moscow's instructions. Nonetheless,
he was friendly and civilised towards Neave 'when the secret
police were out of the way'. Nikitchenko won the admiration of
other Allied lawyers for his liberal views, not to mention his
phenomenal capacity for vodka. He had a genuine legal background, having graduated from Moscow University and lectured
on criminal law at the Military Jurisprudence Academy. The same
could not be said of Colonel Alexander Federovich Volchkov, the
Soviet alternate judge. Volchkov 'was said' to be People's
Commissar for Justice and Professor of International Law, yet he
refused to take his turn in the chair at a private session in the
absence of his superior, pleading lack of qualifications. 'The
intelligence services of the Western world, *whose representatives at the
trial included myself*, made reports on him,' wrote Neave (author's
italics). 'That he was close to the secret police is certain. Perhaps
he had been appointed to watch Nikitchenko.'[10] Volchkov was
uncommunicative and rumour had it that he was an officer of the
NKVD. Not only that, it was also suggested that he was com-
mandant of a Soviet concentration camp in eastern Germany –
based in Colditz castle. Neave offered no further evidence for this
extraordinary suggestion. His own reports on the Russians, and
perhaps on the other Allied powers' representatives, presumably
went back to his old employers, MI6. They were interested in

anything he could glean about intelligence and security organisations, and particularly concerned to know about what information was going back to the USSR from Nazi records on the Eastern Front. Much post-war intelligence of the east derived from Luftwaffe aerial photography. The records might also yield information of possible German/Soviet collaboration in the use of agents against the Allies at the beginning of the war, before Operation Barbarossa. MI6 had an omnivorous appetite.

The trial opened promptly at ten o'clock on the morning of 20 November. Earlier optimism among the American legal team that they would be home for Christmas had by then evaporated. The proceedings would go on for 284 days before Hitler's henchmen were finally brought to book. On the first day, Neave sat below the judges' bench to hear Lawrence in his opening statement describe the trial as unique in the history of jurisprudence and of supreme importance to millions of people all over the globe. It would carry a 'challenge of hope to posterity'. But the main part of Neave's work was now over and he was, frankly, bored. The defendants had cheered up considerably since he had served the indictment on them, realising that it was a genuine trial, and that some might get off, or at least avoid the gallows.

It took junior members of the Allied prosecution two days to read out the full indictment, more than 20,000 words long. Under the lash of its chilling detail, some of the monsters on trial hung their heads, while others breathed defiance. For Neave, who was free to come and go as he pleased, the indictment seemed to have no end. 'I could not sleep that night for thinking of a myriad corpses,' he recorded. Next day, all twenty defendants in the dock (Kaltenbrunner was in hospital) entered a plea of 'not guilty'. Neave had instructed them how to plead. He was unimpressed by the way some of these vain men gilded their plea with appeals to God. Their defence lawyers had a near insuperable task, faced with the damning testimony that followed. Any sympathy they might have had dissolved after the showing of film of terrible scenes of suffering uncovered by the advancing Allied forces.

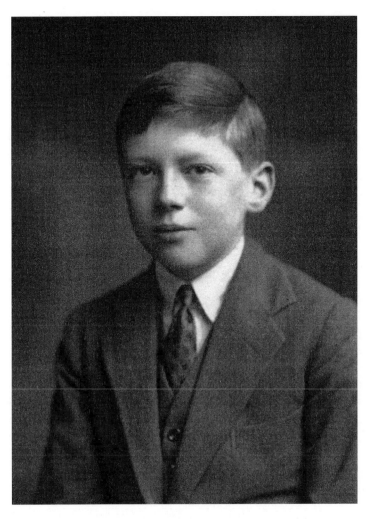

Young Airey (he hated the name) as a pupil
at St. Ronan's prep school, Worthing.

Neave as a public school master in the Colditz Christmas pantomime of 1942. His fellow escaper, Dutch officer Tony Luteyn, is in the band. The pair escaped from below this theatre stage.

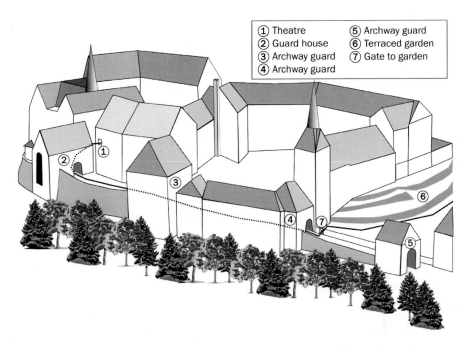

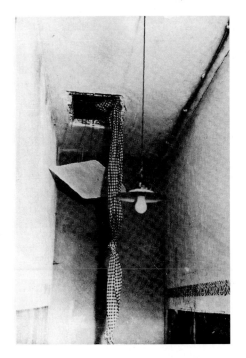

① Theatre	⑤ Archway guard
② Guard house	⑥ Terraced garden
③ Archway guard	⑦ Gate to garden
④ Archway guard	

Colditz Castle from the East: Neave and Luteyn's escape route from the theatre out of the gate.

The ingenious 'shovewood' escape hatch down which the pair got away.

Neave in the uniform of a German soldier worn on his first, unsuccessful escape bid.

Neave (second right) in Marseilles just after his escape with fellow
British officer Hugh Woollatt and the 'ratline' organisers.

Reunited: An RAF Escaping Society reception in 1967
where Neave meets the brave women who helped Allied
servicemen through Occupied Europe.

The cells in Nuremberg prison where Neave served war
crimes indictments on Nazi criminals.

Monsters in the dock: the court at Nuremberg where Hitler's henchmen
stood trial.

Airey Neave, Abingdon MP.

2 November 1975: Margaret Thatcher, the new Conservative Party
leader, is guided from the House of Commons by Airey Neave,
who organised her campaign.

Margaret Thatcher chatting with Irish premier, Jack Lynch. Michael O'Kennedy (Irish Foreign Minister) and Airey Neave look on, after talks in February 1977.

Margaret Thatcher was visiting her North London consituency when she heard of the car bomb explosion. She was yet to know that the man who died was Airey Neave.

How the shocking story was told: Fleet Street was
united in its condemnation of Neave's brutal murder.

Neave was tortured by that experience. On the day he looked in vain for signs of remorse for these heinous crimes. 'They wept for themselves, not for the dead,' he noted. More than thirty years later, he still suffered bad dreams.

Rudolf Hess, for whom Neave had felt sorry when serving the indictment, sought through his counsel, Dr Gunther von Rohr-scheidt, to demonstrate that he was unfit to plead, on grounds of total amnesia rather than insanity. Neave listened intently to the prosecutors' arguments that Hess was fit to stand trial, and detected a growing restlessness on the part of Hess, who was alone in the dock during this hearing. Hitler's co-author suddenly stood up and admitted that his loss of memory had been a tactical sham. He would henceforth accept responsibility for all his actions. Neave noticed that he was 'extremely pleased' at the sensation his little pantomime had caused, while accepting that some of Hess's amnesia was not in doubt. 'With me, he was always lucid, courteous, even witty, but definitely abnormal,' Neave added. And when von Rohrscheidt fell on the ice and broke his leg, Hess sacked him and turned to Neave for advice. He insisted on defending himself, and 'fenced amiably' for hours with Neave, who finally persuaded him to accept another German lawyer. This experience drew the old soldier–politician and the young major close together. 'He seemed to understand and confide in me,' Neave wrote. 'I think he did not want to be bothered with reading trial documents but preferred his novels.' The lawyer Neave found, Dr Alfred Seidl of Munich, still represented Hess decades later, when he was the lonely prisoner of Spandau.

Britain's turn to confront the Nazis came on 4 December 1945, when Sir Hartley Shawcross, the new Labour government's Attorney-General, made his speech for the prosecution. The cultured British lawyer cut a commanding presence and Neave listened to his 'persuasive and deadly' arguments the whole day. Shawcross met and demolished the key argument of the defence: that they had only been acting under orders. It was no excuse for a thief to say he had been told to steal and the principle held good even where the crime was mass murder. Political loyalty and military obedience might be fine things but they did not justify wicked acts. Neave concluded that the British prosecutor's 'lethal moderation' unnerved the defence.

After the four opening speeches of the Allied powers, Neave had little business inside the court. He had to look after the many practical difficulties thrown up by the efforts of the German defence counsel, including the discovery of witnesses among the confusion of the Occupied Zones. He took some well-deserved Christmas leave at home with Diana and in the New Year of 1946 returned to work promoted to Lieutenant-Colonel in a new post with a commission supportive of the Nuremberg legal process. This body was charged with gathering evidence to defend those charged with membership of Nazi organisations 'deemed to be criminal'. It was an enormous task, as Article 9 of the Charter under which the accused were charged gave the Tribunal power to declare criminal any group or organisation. On the face of it, this catch-all provision could have several million members of the Nazi Party and its allied organisations in the dock. His burden was greatly eased by the Tribunal's decision that membership alone should not be grounds for prosecution. It was still a daunting task for a thirty-year-old middle-ranking officer.

Neave was appointed Chief Commissioner of the new legal entity and in mid-May began the mammoth task of hearing evidence. He sat in a room reminiscent of a London magistrate's court and a steady stream of witnesses culled from internment camps and the bombed-out cities of Germany appeared, under armed guard, to give testimony. In June, it was clear that sitting alone he would never complete the task of interviewing several hundred witnesses and four assistant commissioners from each of the Allied powers were appointed. A second commission began work. Neave considered that his mission went to the heart of the Nazis' 'only obeying orders' defence. He was not a soft touch. He rejected all defence grounds for being a member of outfits such as the SS except physical intimidation. Neave had no legal precedents to guide him, only the wording of the Charter under which the Tribunal operated. He had to sit through many hours of vexatious pleading from German lawyers, seeking to prove that the Nazi Party, or the Gestapo, or the SD, were not actually engaged in a criminal conspiracy as defined in the Charter. Neave thought most of the defence submissions were bogus or worse, and the Tribunal shared his view, expressed in what came to be known as the Neave Report, delivered to the court in August 1946. He was particularly sickened by the lies and excuses offered by defence lawyers acting for former SS officers, among them that prisoners in Auschwitz, Buchenwald and Dachau were well fed and guards were forbidden to strike them. 'There was a ghastly humour about the proceedings in my little courtroom as if I were acting in a little horror film,' he remembered.[11]

However, when it came to the German High Command, things were very different. Was the General Staff a criminal conspiracy? Neave took evidence from the top military figures, including six field marshals. He observed these formidable figures curiously, noting how they retained an authority despite being stripped of their uniforms and decorations. Yet some of it was mere show. Under questioning, Field Marshal von Brauchitsch banged the table and told Neave, 'You do not know what a military genius Hitler was!' With yet more banging, he insisted that only someone who had known the Führer could understand his hold over others. An angry Neave told him to shut up and he apologised for his lack of composure. In his report to the Tribunal, Neave summarised the case for the defence: officers belonging to the High Command and General Staff did not form a defined group in the sense alleged by the prosecution. They had not conspired with Hitler to plan an aggressive war, had not influenced the Nazi leadership and had mostly kept clear of politics. They had not conspired with the Gestapo or the SS to commit war crimes or crimes against humanity, and particularly after 1941 could not have resigned their commands without fear of serious consequences for themselves and their families. The Nuremberg judges decreed

that the German General Staff and High Command were not a
'group' or an 'organisation', a verdict with which Neave agreed.
But four categories of officers could be indicted, chiefly the heads
of the three services. They, along with the other criminals of the
Nazi state, heard Sir Hartley Shawcross tear their defence to
pieces in the prosecution summing up in late August 1946. Neave
thought it was 'a great speech'.

During a month-long recess to consider their verdicts and
sentences, the judges decided that only the most heinous of the
Nazi organisations – the Gestapo, the SD, the SS and the Corps
of Political Leaders – were 'criminal'. To the fury of Stalin, the
Reich Cabinet, the General Staff and High Command and the
SA were excluded from this category. The otherwise intelligent
and honourable Nikitchenko, under pressure from the Kremlin,
set forth a dissenting judgement. The stress showed plainly. He
appeared drunk at dances. The Western Allies looked the other
way but Neave recollected 'a clear vision of Nikitchenko with his
maroon and gold epaulettes, staggering round the room'. London
was no doubt informed. He was not heard of again after returning
to the Soviet Union.

In the afternoon of 1 October 1946, the judges filed back into
the courtroom to hand down their verdicts. To their disbelief,
three – Fritzsche, Schacht and von Papen – were acquitted.
Sentence of death by hanging was delivered on Goering, von
Ribbentrop, Keitel, Kaltenbrunner, Rosenberg, Frank, Frick,
Streicher, Sauckel, Jodl, Seyss-Inquart and Bormann (*in absentia*).
Hess, Funk and Raeder got life, Speer and von Schirach twenty
years, von Neurath fifteen years, and Doenitz ten years.

The dramatic sentencing process over, Neave flew back to
England in Francis Biddle's private Dakota. He was keen to pick
up the traces of civilian life, after seven years in uniform, and
resume his truncated career as a barrister. He was not present at
the executions on 17 October, after appeals for clemency had
been rejected by Western leaders, but he was amused to read in
the *Evening Standard* that Goering had cheated the hangman by

committing suicide with poison in his cell. In the controversial
aftermath of the Nuremberg Tribunal, Neave never weakened in
his conviction that it was right, for political and psychological
reasons, to hold the trial. Unsurprisingly, given his own close
involvement, he believed that the trial was fairly conducted. He
also drew a general moral lesson from the experience. 'The sight
of these once-powerful Nazis,' he wrote 'will always be an
illustration to me of the true dangers of authoritarian rule.'

II

Lawyer Candidate

Returning to civilian life was an unsettling experience. Post-war Britain, with its shortages and a Labour government dedicated to state ownership, was for Neave a poor reward for the sacrifices he and those like him had made. He determined to enter politics but first he had to find a job to support a growing family. His daughter, Marigold Elizabeth Cassandra, was born in May 1944, at Chillington Hall, the home of his wife's family. Neave appears on the birth registration as a major in the Royal Artillery and barrister-at-law, though he was not practising. Two sons followed: Patrick Richard was born in the same place in 1947 and William arrived in 1953. There was nothing of the Neave tradition in the boys' first names: no Sheffield, no Airey, for the first time in three generations. The family still had the flat in Pimlico but also lived at Mill Green Park.

Neave had been called to the Bar in 1943, though unable to practise because of the war. He found himself a pupillage with Gerald Thesiger, who later became a judge. Because of the extensive war damage, accommodation for young barristers in the Inner Temple was very scarce and Thesiger could not keep him after his pupillage. Looking around for an alternative berth he alighted on Frederick (later Lord) Lawton, who was also a casualty of the bombing. Lawton had been invalided out of the army in 1941 after an accident. The son of a prison officer, he was no stranger to politics, having flirted with Communism as a Cambridge undergraduate. He moved to the ultra-right on coming down, joining the British Union of Fascists and becoming prospective Mosleyite candidate for Hammersmith in the late thirties. Returning to the Bar, he found his chambers in Essex Court destroyed by the Blitz and its members dispersed. Lawton therefore became a wartime refugee in Norman Birkett's chambers at 3 Temple Gardens on the understanding that when the other members of the chambers returned from the services he would move on. Lawton duly did so in 1946, setting up his own chambers with two young lawyers recently called to the Bar. They shared accommodation on two floors of 5 King's Bench Walk, a listed seventeenth-century building situated in a quiet square between Fleet Street and the Embankment. Bomb damage had been roughly repaired, and the offices were 'exceedingly primitive', but it was an agreeable spot.

Here was an opening for Neave. Lawton recollected: 'One of the consequences was that for some time after the war I had more accommodation in my chambers than I could usefully fill. That got round, and when Airey finished his pupillage he asked me if I would take him in and I did.'[1] He was to remain there until he became a junior minister almost a decade later. Lawton's chambers were characterised by bright young men, including Robin Day, later to find fame as a broadcaster. Margaret Roberts, later to become rather better known as Margaret Thatcher, was one of the bright young women.

The law in the late 1940s was not particularly lucrative for a young barrister making his way in the profession. Neave's expenses in chambers were quite low, only £100 a year. Tradition required that tenants pay only a small contribution to the running of chambers, while the head made up the balance. But the income was also low. Neave might earn only four guineas for an appearance at the magistrates' court, and seven guineas at the Quarter Sessions where more serious cases were tried. If he took on a case under the Poor Prisoners' Defence Certificate scheme, he would receive only £3 5s 6d for a day in court, and if the case went on longer, no matter how long, another £2. 'He was certainly not earning big money,' said Lawton. 'I doubt if he was earning a thousand pounds a year. He was not a great success as a barrister, and there were so many of them chasing a comparatively small amount of work.' Neave did mainly criminal work, flogging around the courts prosecuting or defending petty crooks on the Eastern Circuit. Shoplifting cases were unduly prominent.

It was clear that his real interests lay elsewhere. Lawton recollects that Neave never had any interest in the law. His abiding passion was politics. When the partners drifted off to the local Kardomah café for a convivial chat at the end of the day, he would not be among them. Nor did he join them in El Vino's, whose back door was conveniently close by, or the Feathers, a pub in Tudor Street where lawyers mixed with Fleet Street journalists. 'Almost every night he was off somewhere down to Essex,' remembered Lawton. 'He was determined to get into Parliament, and a lot of people pulled his leg.' But his fellow barristers were impressed by Neave's single-mindedness. He gave them to understand that whatever he decided to do, he was determined to do.

His first big break came in his native Essex, where the Conservatives selected him as prospective parliamentary candidate for Thurrock in the General Election that would have to be held some time in the first half of 1950. Thurrock was, and remains, a slice of working-class south-east England. Then, as now, it was dominated by its docklands, though Bata Shoes had a large factory there. Before the war, the electorate was split between the divisions of South-East Essex and Romford. Rapid population growth compelled a revision of boundaries and the Thurrock constituency was carved out of these two seats during a wartime redrawing of the political map.

In 1945, Leslie Solley, a barrister who had clawed his way up to the Bar by scholarships from an elementary school to London University, won Thurrock with a majority of 13,262 over his Tory rival, Major Tom Adams. But Solley proved to be a left-wing thorn in Attlee's side and was expelled from the Labour Party in

1949 for defying the government's foreign policy. In the coming General Election, he would be standing as an Independent Labour candidate. He had a substantial level of support from the unions, including the mineworkers, though the nearest pit was many miles away in Kent.

The official Labour man was Hugh Delargy, a political refugee from Manchester where he had been MP for the now defunct Miles Platting division for five years. Delargy, aged forty-one, had been educated in France and Italy and by turns had been a teacher in a private school, a journalist and a labourer. He had had a good war, rising in the Royal Artillery from the ranks to staff captain at General Eisenhower's headquarters. The Liberals also fielded a candidate, W.H.N. Siddons, an actor and descendant of Sarah Siddons. He had been a flight lieutenant in Bomber Command and won the DFC.

Thurrock was nowhere near a marginal seat, though Conservative membership was steadily on the increase and the party association could boast seventeen branches. Neave's only hope was that the two Labour candidates would split the anti-Conservative vote, allowing him to sneak in through the middle. The growing unpopularity of Clement Attlee's socialist government, which had been in power for four and a half years but had not yet managed to end wartime rationing, suggested that the Tories under Churchill might be in with a chance of forming a government. By now Churchill was seventy-five but as *The Times* guide to the election pointed out 'his weight of years diminished not at all his zest for the fight or his robust leadership of the anti-government forces'.

At first sight, there was much common ground between the parties. Plans for a great improvement in social services had been drawn up by the wartime coalition and implemented by Labour. Family allowances, pension and health benefits were extended right across the nation. The 'welfare state' was born. However, there were deep divisions over the Attlee government's determination to take over the commanding heights of the economy.

With their majority of almost 150, Labour pushed through nationalisation of the coal industry, civil aviation, the Bank of England, the railways, gas, electricity, large parts of the road haulage industry and cable and wireless communications. Nationalisation of the steel industry was approved in principle, despite a wrecking campaign by the Conservative-dominated House of Lords which prompted a further curtailment of their legislative powers. Neave shared the general Tory hostility to state ownership of industry, and had serious reservations about Labour's conduct of foreign policy, though the Opposition had by and large supported the government in the post-war period, particularly the establishment of NATO.

Worsening economic conditions, including a massive devaluation of the pound in 1949, forced Attlee into heavy cuts in public spending and investment, adding to the air of expectation that the government would have to go to the country before the end of its statutory five-year term. Attlee resisted pressure to hold an election in the autumn but was finally obliged to ask the King for a dissolution on 11 January 1950. Polling day was fixed for 23 February.

On 21 January, shortly after his thirty-fourth birthday, Neave offered his personal manifesto to the voters in the *Essex and Thurrock Gazette*. He dived directly into a controversial statement of political philosophy. 'What you people who call yourselves Labour must remember is that Labour is a socialist party. Socialism means nationalisation of all the means of production, distribution and exchange,' he wrote. 'They call it "public ownership", but it's the state that makes you pay its losses. If you let them take over cement and insurance, where will it stop? I believe it will end in the state making a monopoly out of clothes, shoes, and even your beer. They will be able to charge what they like. What is more, the so-called socialist state will then be a Communist state.'

Neave conceded that coal, gas, electricity and the railways would have to remain in public hands (not least because of huge losses), but demanded denationalisation of air transport, road haulage and the steel industry. He also favoured breaking the link between trade unions and the Labour Party by abolishing the law that required union members to 'contract out' of paying the weekly political levy which largely financed the party and gave the unions a powerful influence in determining its policy.

Pledging himself to work for peace, and to provide adequate defence against oppression, Neave proposed building up the regular armed forces, reducing numbers conscripted by National Service and doing more for the Territorials. Taking a further swipe at the Labour Party, he suggested that it had been prepared to seek a compromise with Communism in 1945 and compared Labour's HQ, Transport House, with Goebbels, the Nazi propaganda chief. England would only be great again when she had dropped socialism – 'No one has much faith in it – and it doesn't work.'

A few days later, Neave used the annual meeting of the Thurrock Division Conservative Association to take the fight to the enemy, revelling in Labour's internal wrangling between 'the Solleyites' and the supporters of Delargy. The election would decide 'perhaps for ever' whether the prestige of Old England would be restored. He attacked the post-war record of the Attlee Cabinet, recalling Sir Stafford Cripps's encouragement of the workers not to make munitions – and thus starve the armed forces of weapons – and took a dig at the 'class war' of socialism, concluding that socialism spoilt the country both economically and spiritually. In post-war Thurrock, this was a brave but foolhardy furrow to plough. Thurrock was the stronghold of the Transport and General Workers and other unions, and such declarations did not play well in the letters columns of the *Essex and Thurrock Gazette*, where correspondents concentrated more on the Conservatives' past record, and unflatteringly so. One voter referred Neave to the 'good old days' of oppression, pawnshops, starvation, the dole and means tests.

Neave was confirmed as parliamentary candidate in the Conservative Club Hall in Clarence Road, Grays, on 3 February, in the middle of an energetic round of nightly public meetings around the constituency. Invariably, he was billed as A.M.S. Neave DSO, MBE, MC. His military rank of lieutenant-colonel, with which he had left the army, was not mentioned. His meetings were well attended but not on the scale of Hugh Delargy's, who asserted 'without conceit' that he would win because he was the Labour candidate and the people wanted Labour. With little more than a fortnight to polling day, local coverage of Neave had been reduced to a two-paragraph item on his views about the other candidates. He fared rather better as the papers went to press for the last time before polling day, but not in the best light. At South Ockendon, a packed hall in the local school greeted him with organised heckling, forcing him to shout above the din, 'I've met far tougher audiences than you!' In a girls' school in Grays he warned an audience of 170 people: 'If you value your freedom, look out! Your trade unions will have no right to strike!' He did not believe for one moment that 'the working man' would vote socialist just to save red-faced masters. Then, contrarily, he admonished: 'It won't be much use waking up in five years' time and finding yourself in a completely Communist state. You must decide now!'

Neave's fellow lawyers would have been surprised at the venom of which their reserved colleague was capable on the hustings. He had no compunction about raising the spectre of Communism as the natural culmination of an old-fashioned Labour government. In this he was only following his leader. Winston Churchill claimed that an Attlee government would 'have to fall back on some kind of Gestapo' because his party found the concept of a free Parliament 'odious'. Neave's hatred of totalitarianism had been sharpened by his war. 'The whole experience had a deep influence on my future life,' he admitted. It would have been odd had it been otherwise. But also, and crucially, he had noted the behaviour of the Russian lawyers at Nuremberg. At the diktat of the Kremlin, they had subjugated the rule of law to political ends. No doubt he made this point in reports from Nuremberg to MI6, when post-war policy was already focusing on the threat from Communism as the Soviet Union swallowed up the states of Eastern Europe one after another. Churchill first referred to an 'iron curtain' descending over Europe in a cable to President Truman ten days before polling day in 1945. The ensuing Cold War dominated not only the thinking of the security services and the military, but the political classes and the nation as a whole. Neave's political attitudes and development have to be seen in that context. He may have been born in the countryside but he was no traditional knight of the shires. His politics derived more from contemporary influences, not least his continuing connection with IS9 and the clubby secret service world in London where anti-Communism was the norm.

Neave required little goading to exhibit a gut hatred of Labour, to whom he invariably referred in the Conservative style of the day as 'the socialists'. There were occasions, too, when he talked down to the electorate, equating a vote for Labour as a blind, unthinking step down the road to Stalinism. The politics of contempt did not go down well in working-class Thurrock, as he discovered on polling day. The turnout was high: 85 per cent in mild, generally fine winter weather, and just above the national average. Delargy easily retained the seat for Labour with 22,893 votes, a majority of 9,587 over Neave, the runner-up, with 13,306 votes. On Neave's part, it was a fair performance. He polled around 3,400 votes more than the Tories had achieved in 1945, but Delargy dropped only a few hundred and the combined Labour/Independent Labour vote (Leslie Solley, the Labour radical, had polled 4,250 votes) actually increased by more than 4,000. Neave put on a brave face, vowing that the battle would continue. It did, but without him. He moved on to greener pastures. Thurrock would not fall into Conservative hands until 1987, and then only for one parliamentary term. Across the river, his fellow lawyer Margaret Roberts, the twenty-four-year-old political prodigy, fared no better, losing at Dartford, Kent.

Neave's performance looked even more modest when set

against the national outcome. In a Commons reduced by boundary changes from 640 MPs to 625, the Tories and their associates won almost a hundred constituencies. Labour shed sixty-nine and the Liberals also fared badly. Attlee was left holed below the waterline, with an overall parliamentary majority of only six. When the Commons returned, the Prime Minister admitted that the House was more evenly divided than at any time in the previous hundred years.

Attlee was determined to soldier on but a new general election was clearly on the horizon. Neave busied himself looking for a more promising seat and became prominent in the Conservative Candidates' Association. This organisation, a useful proving ground and a good source for political gossip, met a couple of times a year. In 1950, Neave was elected secretary of the CCA, a largely honorific post, but a useful boost to his profile.

Edward du Cann, another Tory hopeful who had had a good war – in his case, in motor torpedo-boats – met him at the association's annual general meeting in Abbey House, off London's Victoria Street. They numbered around 150. Du Cann remembers Neave then as 'a solid but not dull man with an impression of competence about him'. He shared Neave's belief that the Labour Party had failed the country in the post-war period, that Britain had somehow missed the spoils of victory. They were fired with an enthusiasm to change things.[2]

Neave's search for a winnable seat was concluded with remarkable swiftness. In the first week of May 1950 he was adopted as prospective parliamentary candidate for Ealing North, a comfortable suburban stretch of west London. Ealing North contained some manufacturing industry, including strongly unionised firms like Hoover and vehicle builders AEC, and a number of large council estates, but it was a classic Labour marginal, ripe for shaking. The incumbent Labour MP, Jimmy Hudson, had had a majority of only 2,404 over the Tory candidate, Mrs Elsie Olsen, in the General Election of that year. Hudson, a former schoolmaster and Labour pioneer who represented a Huddersfield seat in the 1920s, could not have offered a greater contrast to Neave. An elderly man of pacifist views, he was almost better known as secretary of the National Temperance Federation than as an MP. He had never got beyond parliamentary private secretary – an unpaid post at Westminster – and his ministerial career had ended twenty years previously.

Accordingly, Neave was in his element when he spoke to the Northolt Conservative Association two weeks after his selection. 'I shall fight like a tiger,' he promised. 'I will put up a fight you will never forget. I am going to fight right the way through.' His martial style was greeted with prolonged applause. His rally to arms, which made the front page of the *Middlesex County Times*,[3] posed the question of what younger people would have to look forward to in the second half of the twentieth century. The great danger of the present day, he claimed, was that Britain was breeding a race of professional politicians instead of men and women who got to know others by meeting them on their doorsteps, in their clubs or 'even in the pubs', a sly dig at his teetotal rival. His vigorous defence of Tory policy brought new heart to his audience. The outgoing chairman, Councillor F.E. Thomas, said, 'I think in him we have a candidate who at last is going to crack the hard shell of socialism in this district.'

At Westminster, the Opposition harried Attlee's hard-pressed administration, putting down three motions of censure in the first month. But Labour survived, regrouped and pressed on, despite the loss through ill health of the Chancellor, Sir Stafford Cripps, and the death of the Foreign Secretary, Ernest Bevin, a bulwark of the Cabinet. Twice the government survived only by the casting vote of the Speaker, and it was outvoted five times, though never on an issue of confidence. Churchill called again and again for a general election to give the country a firm, stable – that is, Conservative – government.

In Ealing, Neave pursued his political prize relentlessly. In June 1950 he addressed the Rotary Club of Greenford, drawing on his experiences at Nuremberg. 'Someone has called this the century of the common man,' he told the assembled Rotarians. 'Never have such brutalities been perpetrated upon him. The men who did these things under Adolf Hitler were, with few exceptions, very ordinary men.'

A fortnight later he was on his feet again, speaking to his association chiefs, but more for public consumption. This was the height of the Cold War and Neave was keen to discredit his rival's pacifist ideals. 'Korea may be Stalin's rehearsal for West Germany,' he warned. 'Old-fashioned pacifism will not stop Communist tanks . . . However sincere a pacifist may be, it is no use being a pacifist in 1950 until you can turn Stalin and Molotov into pacifists.' He also supported the Schuman Plan (for integrating Europe's iron and steel industries, put forward in May 1950 by the French Foreign Minister, Robert Schuman, and the nucleus of the European Community), arguing that it would lead to a pooling of output without change of ownership. Britain should at least discuss the issue of European iron and steel 'instead of standing sheepishly aside. Then we could put our case and demand our conditions. As it is, we are going to be left looking very silly.'[4] On this issue, Neave was ahead of public opinion and attitudes within his own party. The war had made him a convinced European, in strategic terms.

Over the ensuing months, Neave delivered more set speeches on foreign and domestic policy. They were a mixture of serious Merton College-type lectures with occasional dashes of *Ballet Nonsense*, along Colditz lines. Overall he was grave, warning that 1951 presented the nation with the very last chance of preventing another war. Six months earlier, Communist North Korea had invaded the US-backed South. American forces, supported by the United Nations, opposed the invasion and the first British troops began arriving in late August 1950. The Communists were thrown back into the north, but China joined the war in November and after bitter fighting the UN forces were driven back. Britain also faced a threat to her interests in Egypt, where King Farouk demanded withdrawal of British troops there to guard the strategic Suez Canal. It was not a time for faint hearts.

'I am a positive man and I will speak my mind,' Neave declared. 'This is the year that will bring the decision.' He accused the beleaguered Attlee government of 'a hideous state of muddle', pursuing a miserable Micawber-like policy of hoping that something would turn up. Labour had known perfectly well that the Soviet Union had not demobilised after 1945, yet the government had allowed the country's defences to deteriorate into muddle. He accused them of not heeding the gathering storm. Neave moved his attack to 'socialist controls' of business, which threatened to turn private enterprise over to 'spivs and barrow boys', before returning to his favourite theme: 'That is not the way to stop Communism.'[5]

Neave's sense of impending doom did not quite match the national mood. The Festival of Britain, opened on London's South Bank by the King and Queen in early May, was a huge success and lifted the spirits of a people still feeling the brutalisation of the war and years of austerity. The House of Commons, devastated by German bombing, had reopened. Unemployment was little over a quarter of a million, the best peacetime figure of the century. But underneath, the political ice was breaking up. Labour was weakened by the resignation of Nye Bevan, the Minister of Labour, and Harold Wilson, President of the Board of Trade, over the introduction of charges for NHS glasses and false teeth. Pressure on British forces in Korea diminished, but intensified in Egypt and a new dispute broke out with Iran, where British oil interests were threatened with nationalisation. A scandal seriously embarrassed the government when two British diplomats working in Washington, Guy Burgess and Donald Maclean, defected to Moscow. They had been spying for the Soviet Union since their pre-war days at Cambridge.

Returning from holiday in August 1951, Neave reverted to his ruling passion: the war against Communism. Speaking to the Ealing South Conservative Political Centre, he made a powerful plea for rearmament. Pointing to 215 Soviet divisions allegedly poised for war, he accused Attlee of paying lip service to defence while, in the Middle East, Russia was probing to see how far she could extend her influence short of provoking war. Since 1945, the British government had shown itself unwilling to stand firm in the maintenance of British interests. 'All this in the name of peace and brotherhood, but resulting in one international crisis after another.' Everyone but the Communists accepted the principle of rearmament, he insisted. 'Then let us make a proper job of it.'[6] The next eighteen months would be the testing time, he concluded. He would not have to wait anything like so long. In fact, the figure of 215 Soviet divisions was substantially a myth, being an improvement on the 175 divisions earlier asserted by Churchill. By this stage of the Cold War, British intelligence did not believe there was going to be a land invasion because the Red Army was taking so long to recover from its terrifying losses in the war.

On 19 September 1951, with King George VI sinking fast, Attlee used a personal broadcast after the nine o'clock news to announce a General Election on 25 October. Wearied of governing with a tiny majority, he would ask the people for a vote of confidence to deal with important issues at home and abroad, including the Korean War. As he had promised, Neave came out fighting. At a packed meeting in Ealing Town Hall, he warned that the election would be 'a battle for the life and soul of the country'. Privately, Attlee and most of his MPs had already conceded the outcome, but the enemy was vigorously engaged. Neave's battleground was a 'very good, winnable seat for the Tories,' Michael Elliott, later a Labour MEP but then a nineteen-year-old party activist, admitted, 'but Jimmy Hudson was well dug in, and well liked. Loyalties were more rigid than they are now, and swings tended to be a lot less. Neave was regarded as a bit of a toff – not the sort of person who would appeal to the Labour vote of 1950. On the streets he was referred to as "Hairy Knees", and people used to scrawl that on his posters.'[7]

In the short, fierce campaign that followed, Labour attempted to portray the Tories as warmongers, but the voters were more interested in housing and the cost of living than in war and peace. The Conservative promise to build 300,000 houses a year struck a chord with the electorate. Winston Churchill defended himself against the 'false and ungrateful' charge that the election of his party would hasten the prospect of a third world war. He had only stayed in public life to avert such a tragedy, he said in his last election speech. 'It is the last prize I seek to win.' The voters granted his wish, returning a Conservative government with an overall majority of seventeen. But not in Ealing North. On a remarkable turnout of 88.99 per cent, it was a photo finish between Neave and Hudson. On the first count, Labour had a majority of 125, and after a recount, of 120. Hudson polled 25,698 votes to Neave's tally of 25,578. From the balcony, the relieved Labour victor was greeted with derisive remarks and some booing, while Neave received prolonged and enthusiastic cheering. He urged local Tories to continue the fight, though their applause did little to abate his indignation at losing.

But a man who has walked out of Colditz does not give up easily and Neave's position as secretary of the CCA kept him in close touch with political opportunity. If anything, and certainly in retrospect, it was a blessing in disguise not to scrape into Westminster as MP for a highly marginal constituency that would swing back and forth between Labour and the Conservatives with the consistency of a metronome for the rest of the century. He was looking for something more solid: a seat on which he could rely and preferably in a more agreeable spot.

He did not have long to wait. The largely rural constituency of North Berkshire became available within months of the General Election, through the decision of its sitting member, Sir Ralph Glyn, not to stand again. With a fine disregard for the niceties of public life, Sir Ralph had announced his decision to leave politics during the general election. It was widely expected that he would be translated to the Lords by the new Conservative government, having sat continuously since 1924. In retrospect, his action (unthinkable today) was plainly influenced by the proximity of a Tory administration, which alone could be counted on to reward him with a peerage.

North Berkshire's main town was Abingdon. Created a borough in 1556, with the right to send a Member to Parliament, it had the occasional high-profile MP and frequently stormy elections (in 1753 a 'very considerable' brewer had tried to buy the seat for his son by throwing open the public houses to the electorate), and John Wesley, the Methodist preacher, he found the citizenry 'so stupid, senseless a people, both in the spiritual and natural sense, I scarce ever saw'.

For all that, for Neave Abingdon was a political godsend, a classic slice of conservative England. It enjoyed low unemployment, high owner-occupation and was predominantly middle class. Apart from the towns of Abingdon, Wantage and Didcot, the constituency was made up of villages with Olde English names like Hinton Waldrist, East Hendred and Kingston Bagpuize. At the 1950 election Sir Ralph had a majority of almost 4,000 over his Labour rival. Surprisingly, a Communist Party candidate took 396 votes, trailing a long way in fourth place behind the Liberals. In 1951, Sir Ralph bequeathed an increased majority of 4,883 in a straight fight with Labour.

The selection procedure to choose a prospective parliamentary candidate was set in motion within months of the poll. A long parade of hopefuls was narrowed to a shortlist of six. They were called to a selection conference at Didcot Conservative Club on 18 March 1952. Neave was nominated by the Kingston Bagpuize branch of the Conservative Association. On the night he was an easy winner, taking an overwhelming majority of the votes. The *North Berkshire Herald and Advertiser* carried a page lead reporting his selection, and introducing the thirty-six-year-old London barrister with a distinguished war record. Unusually, it also disclosed that Neave had been with 'the Special Intelligence Unit' between 1945 and 1946, after the war was over. He preferred to be addressed as plain 'Mister' rather than by his rank.

Neave caught Labour on the hop. They were still looking round for a candidate and appeared still to be committed to J.E.G Curthoys, who contested the seat unsuccessfully in 1951. While Neave was building up his support in the constituency Conservative Association, Curthoys was reduced to defending Attlee over the leadership ambitions of Nye Bevan and 'a slight difference of opinion' in the party hierarchy about the exploitation of British migrants to the colonies. Neave lost no time in establishing his credentials. In May, he spoke to Abingdon and District Rotarians about his role in the Nuremberg war trials. The following month he was busy praising the new Conservative government at a rain-hit Whit Monday party fête in Faringdon, in the west of 'his' constituency. He insisted that the cost of living was already coming down, citing lower prices for shoes, and he promised to take advantage of this by launching Operation Shoeleather, in which he would take his political message to the voters. He was dismissive of the post-war Attlee administration, telling the people that if they voted for Labour they would get a welfare state that the nation could not afford, no defence against Russia and 'that fatal thing – unbridled, deliberate class warfare'.[8] Quite why he felt the Faringdon Conservatives needed to be reminded of this frightful prospect was unclear. He was on firmer ground when he urged them to 'Give us four years to do the job. We will finish it and this country will be great and prosperous again'.

Neave scaled down his political activity during the long, hot summer of 1952, but the prospect of a by-election in the constituency revived interest sharply in the autumn. Labour had chosen as its candidate Ted Castle, originally a local man, the son of a gardener and a prominent journalist on the *Daily Mirror*. He was also married to the left-wing firebrand Barbara Castle, MP for Blackburn East. Tall, dapper, balding and with a neat moustache, he looked more (even to his wife) like the actor David Niven than an orthodox politician. Here was an opportunity to go on the offensive and Neave lost no time in taking it. Labour's influential left wing in parliament was at this period led by Aneurin Bevan, flamboyant post-war architect of the National Health Service, and his adherents were invariably referred to in the Tory press as Bevanites. They had emerged as a powerful faction at Westminster in March 1952, when fifty-seven Labour MPs defied party leaders and voted against the Conservative government's defence policy. Playing on his rival's name and fears of the Labour left, Neave said at the conclusion of a brains trust in the village hall at Sutton Courtenay that: 'The Bevanites are building a castle in Berkshire. But it may be you will find it not particularly strong when the election comes, because Bevanism is to a great extent out of date.'

Castle, campaigning in Wallingford the following month, sought to turn the tables by asking voters 'Are you a Glynite or a Neavite?' He was talking about an embarrassing move by Sir Ralph Glyn on the bill to denationalise transport then going through its Commons stages. The outgoing Abingdon MP called for the Transport Bill to be subject to a commercial enquiry, prompting Ted Castle to claim that he supported Labour's view that the legislation was an unnecessary waste of time. Neave hit back swiftly, arguing that Conservative MPs had greater freedom of conscience than Labour members. Party leaders did not spit in the face of back-bench dissidents, he claimed, in unusually demotic style. 'Socialist agitators against the Bill would do well to note Sir Ralph's statement that transport should be removed from the cockpit of party politics, and cease their trumpetings about renationalisation,' he added. Castle's half-hearted point that the Conservatives had two representatives in the constituency – a lame-duck MP and his impatient successor – did not have the same muckraking appeal as Neave's adroit linkage with the Bevanites. Sir Ralph was a respected figure, whereas Nye Bevan was a bogeyman.

Sir Ralph Glyn was duly given his peerage, choosing to become Lord Glyn of Farnborough, and the by-election was set for 30

June 1953, three weeks after the coronation of Queen Elizabeth II. International tension was easing, with the death of Stalin and his replacement by Nikita Krushchev, and the ending of the Korean War with an armistice, but Churchill was under increasing strain. Anthony Eden was recovering from surgery in an American hospital, and the Prime Minister, now nearly eighty and in failing health himself, took over the Foreign Office. The workload was too much. Four days before polling day in Abingdon, he suffered a stroke that paralysed his left side, but the news was kept secret and he retreated to his country home, Chartwell.

Neave's by-election was a three-cornered fight against Labour and the Liberals, who were represented by George Allen, a thirty-year-old agricultural economist from Oxford. Much as he tried, Ted Castle found it hard to shake off the 'Bevanite' charge and equally difficult to dent Neave's robust defence of the Tory record on housebuilding, the economy and defence. Turnout on polling day was within a whisker of the General Election. Seventy-eight per cent of the 56,543 voters went to the polls, against 79.9 per cent, an unusually high turnout for a by-election. In scenes reminiscent of earlier, more excitable days, a crowd of around 600 thronged the Market Place in Abingdon for two hours, waiting for the returning officer to announce the result at lunchtime on 1 July. It was predictable enough. Neave was in with an increased majority. He took 22,986 votes (53 per cent of the total), a majority of 5,860 over Ted Castle, who polled 17,126 votes (39 per cent) for Labour. The Liberals took 3,060 votes (7 per cent) and lost their deposit.

An exuberant Neave addressed the crowds from the balcony of the Queen's Hotel. At the same time he also sought to mend his fences with the Opposition. 'One word to the Labour Party,' he said. 'Now that I am your member, whether you voted against me or not, I want to make it clear that I will work for every one of you, whatever your politics may be. I made that promise and I will keep it now.'

This is the customary note of inclusiveness that most successful parliamentary candidates offer their opponents. In Neave's case, it may also have been tinged with guilt about the tactics his party had used in the by-election. Ted Castle complained of unscrupulous exploitation of whispers against both him and Barbara, including an eve-of-the-poll suggestion that he was a conscientious objector. As a tabloid newspaper journalist, Ted Castle was more attuned to open disclosure than to Airey Neave's secretive world of wartime and post-war disinformation. The charge of being 'a conchie' could still damage, even eight years afterwards. During the war, when Neave was engaged in all manner of heroics, Castle was night editor of the *Daily Mirror*, though he was no stranger to danger. As he walked to his newspaper one day in 1944, a V1 rocket landed on a crowded bus in front of him. He picked his way coolly through a macabre scene of severed limbs and was violently sick on reaching the office.

Some new MPs do their utmost to deliver their maiden speech in the Commons as soon as possible. Others, particularly after a General Election when many seats have changed hands, wait months. Neave erred on the side of celerity. At 5.44 p.m. on 29 July, just four weeks after his by-election victory, he rose during a defence debate to make his first address. It established his position for the rest of his quarter century in the House. Neave pointed out that his constituency contained a number of defence establishments, including the Military College of Science at Shrivenham, and the top-secret Atomic Energy Research Establishment at Harwell. He offered the hope that his view would not be very contentious. 'I served for a long time in the Territorial Army, recently leaving it when I retired two years ago, and I specialised in the last war in military intelligence. As a consequence, I want to lay emphasis on training in that sphere.'

It was clear to all MPs that a certain amount of radical rethinking was required upon defence policy, Neave argued. He was particularly concerned about retaining National Servicemen in the TA, arguing the case for 'large and skilled reserves' available to the regular army. 'My first point is that the training of Territorial intelligence officers should be encouraged. That is a type of military service which would be highly suitable for certain types of men who might volunteer to remain on in the Territorial Army.' A certain amount of machinery for that purpose already existed, he agreed, in the field security units, 'but it should be carried much further'. In the war, no branch of the armed forces had a higher proportion of civilian soldiers than military intelligence. Many men came from offices and factories to undertake this thoroughly interesting work.

Neave sat down at 5.54 p.m. to fulsome praise from Colonel George Wigg, Labour MP for Dudley and a confirmed intelligence freak. He had impressed the House with the breadth of his knowledge, and MPs would look forward to many further contributions from the Member for Abingdon, 'much more lengthy and more contentious'. As his latter remark signals, Wigg was being too kind. Though it lasted only ten minutes, Neave's speech was windy, repetitious and circumspect. The points he made concerning the TA could have been made more vigorously in a third of the time. And for an old soldier used to the terse language of war, it was a curiously tentative offering. There was 'a certain amount' of this and 'a certain amount' of that. He had shown himself much sharper on the by-election hustings. However, he had established himself as a Tory soldier–politician, one who would bring specialised knowledge of, and concern for, the role of military intelligence to the Commons.

12

The Greasy Pole

The summer of 1953 was an opportune moment for a young Conservative to enter Parliament. The Queen had just ascended the throne and a New Elizabethan age was promised. Her coronation in Westminster Abbey, watched on new-fangled television by millions of her subjects, was crowned by the news that a Commonwealth expedition had conquered Everest. It was a good time to be a patriot. The economy was doing well and Britain was struggling to find a new, independent path for her colonies, particularly in Africa.

In one of his first speeches to the Commons as peacetime Prime Minister, Churchill called for a lull in party strife and several years of quiet, steady administration 'if only to allow socialist legislation to reach its full fruition', a statement hardly likely to endear his strategy to Neave. However, the Labour Party was exhausted, drained by years of rule during post-war austerity and infighting thereafter. It opposed Conservative cuts in food subsidies, but in the face of compensating increases in pensions, benefits and family allowances made little political headway. The second Budget from the Chancellor, R.A. Butler, in 1953, cut income tax by 6d in the pound, increasing the Conservatives' popularity to the point where they were able to take Sunderland South from Labour, the first time a government had won a seat from the Opposition at a by-election for almost thirty years.

After his maiden speech, Neave did not seek to make much of a splash on the back benches. Instead, he continued to mark out his chosen territory: defence and related issues. He was on his feet in a debate on the Navy, Army and Air Force Bill later that year, speaking up for his favourite unit, the Territorials. On 17 November, he raised a number of arcane points about the Bill's distinction between Territorials and reservists, and to urge the army to keep track of the jobs now being done by men who faced the call-up. He had an argument with the prickly Labour MP for Brixton, Lieutenant-Colonel Marcus Lipton, about the exact date of the 'embodiment' of the TA in 1939, and sat down. It was not a brilliant exercise, though it did mark out his political interests and he followed up the intervention with a written question in February 1954 about training for the 'Terriers'. The following month, he began a long parliamentary involvement with the atomic energy industry and its professionals. In the second reading of the Atomic Energy Bill, Neave observed: 'We have reached a stage in the history of atomic power at which we can take stock of the achievements of our scientists.' He praised the 'mental stimulus' of his own constituents employed at the Atomic Energy Research Establishment at Harwell: here (though Neave did not say it) they not only sought peaceful ways to harness the power of the atom but also built Britain's atomic bomb. Neave commended the 'not very sensational or revolutionary Bill', but urged that more homes be built for the staff at Harwell, and conveyed their anxiety about recognition for their trade unions and staff associations. Telling the House 'I speak as a lawyer', he also urged the right of appeal for atomic staff who might be suspected of some kind of security offence.[1] It was a creditable speech, worth more than the sarcastic rejoinder of John Freeman, Labour's brilliant rebel, that Neave was simply 'rolling a log' for his constituents.

Like any new member, Neave found the social side of Westminster attractive. Inside the safe confines of the Palace he could relax in the company of his own. He drank with fellow Tories in the MPs' bars, and he also mixed in the circle of parliamentary journalists, where his tastes were surprisingly catholic, extending to the liberal *Manchester Guardian*. Neave operated on the principle that it was better to know what 'the enemy' was up to. His writing also progressed well. *They Have Their Exits*, the record of his wartime adventures, was greeted with critical plaudits, sold remarkably well and was still available in paperback twenty years later. Neave followed up this triumph in 1954 with *Little Cyclone*, a collection of true stories of the women and men who risked their lives in MI9's escape organisations. The *Sunday Times* thought his second book ranked 'with the very best of its kind', though it did not meet with the same popular success as his first. For Neave, it was more than a book. It was an admiring tribute, and war hero Douglas Bader praised him for establishing a monument in words to their memory.

His showing in the Commons had still not attracted any attention outside the Westminster village. Andrew Roth, the veteran parliamentary observer, noted: 'Airey Neave did not set Parliament afire.' Despite his interest in military matters, he had nothing to say in the House about the war in Indo-China that culminated in the defeat of the French at Dien Bien Phu. Nor did he mark the end of the Korean War. As a new boy, he might be expected to keep his counsel about Anthony Eden's lacklustre foreign policy. Yet surprisingly, in view of his pedestrian parliamentary performance, he had clearly impressed his political superiors. In February 1954, only eight months after being elected, he was appointed parliamentary private secretary to Alan Lennox-Boyd, the new Secretary of State for the Colonies. This was the lowest rung of the ministerial ladder. A PPS is merely the eyes and ears of his master in the Commons, and unpaid to boot. But at least he had his hands on the greasy pole of promotion.

The argument over nuclear weaponry gained fresh impetus in late 1954 when it was disclosed that the United States was experimenting with the hydrogen bomb, a device infinitely more awesome than the atomic bombs that ended the Second World War. A bomb tested in the remote Pacific atoll of Bikini was six hundred times more powerful than the atomic devices that devastated Hiroshima and Nagasaki. The government's revelation, in the Defence White Paper of 1955, that Britain would participate in this massive extension of nuclear capability, was music to Neave's ears and those of his Tory colleagues. It split Labour from top to bottom. Nye Bevan, dissatisfied with Attlee's explanation as to whether Labour would use the H-bomb, led sixty-one MPs in a mass abstention from the official Opposition amendment. The parliamentary whip was withdrawn from Bevan, prompting widespread protests in local Labour parties.

The Conservatives, sensing the public mood moving their way, decided to go on the offensive. On 5 April, Churchill tendered his resignation to the new Queen, who asked Sir Anthony Eden, the Foreign Secretary, to form a government the next day. In a broadcast from Chequers on 15 April, Eden announced that parliament would be dissolved on 6 May, and a General Election would take place on 26 May. Eden's place at the FO was taken by Harold Macmillan, who as Housing Minister had more than honoured the Tories' promise to build 300,000 houses. Butler's final Budget on 19 April announced tax concessions and the Conservative manifesto, *United for Peace and Progress*, dwelt heavily on social issues but also promised (to Neave's satisfaction) a programme of nuclear power stations.

His third General Election as a candidate, but first as incumbent MP, found Neave with two new rivals. Labour, runners-up in the 1953 by-election, chose Mrs Margaret Reid, a school teacher and veteran of two parliamentary polls. The Liberals fielded George Allen, an economics lecturer at St Edmund Hall, Oxford, who had served with the Northants Yeomanry during the war. Neave addressed seventy-five meetings across the 300 square miles of his constituency, and his diligence was rewarded with an increased majority of 8,634 over Labour, benefiting in part from an increased turnout. Diana Neave was also very active, speaking for her husband 'on a large number of occasions', the local newspaper noted. Neave returned to a slightly enlarged House of Commons firmly under Conservative control. Eden had a majority of sixty

over all other parties. His first move was to impose a State of
Emergency on 31 May to counteract a national strike by
railwaymen.

Neave had been a PPS for little more than a year and could not
expect rapid preferment in Eden's new government. Nor did he
get it. Instead, he soldiered on as a back-bencher, steadily building
a reputation in the fields of defence and atomic energy. Just before
Christmas 1955, he championed the salary claims of scientists
and engineers working for the Atomic Energy Authority. The
Minister of Works, his friend and fellow former MI6 officer Nigel
Birch, who was on the point of moving on to the Air Ministry,
was non-committal.

The Commons considered defence spending in the spring of
1956, almost a year after the Soviet bloc had solidified its military
effort into the Warsaw Pact. Public opinion was shifting towards
Neave's view of a strong NATO. Even the Labour Party had been
converted to German rearmament. Across Europe, vast concen-
trations of firepower confronted each other, while Britain still
had to contend with insurrection in Cyprus, Kenya and Malaya.
In the debate on 20 April, Neave called for a radical rethinking of
the whole defence programme, urging the need for scientific
development. Given his continuing connections with his old
comrades in the security services, it must be assumed that he was
better briefed than he let on. He did not dispute the government's
plan for smaller and better equipped forces, but he pointed to
scientific advances in the Soviet Union and insisted that 'technical
expenditure and training will be of much greater importance'.
Nonetheless, he was in favour of keeping unconventional weapons
until new ones were ready. It was a broad-brush speech lasting
fourteen minutes and was not particularly distinguished. Perhaps
the timing – he was on his feet just after 1.00 p.m. – suggests that
lunch was waiting.

Abolition of the death penalty was a very live issue in that
parliamentary session. Sydney Silverman, the Labour MP for
Nelson and Colne, had put forward a widely supported private

member's bill to end judicial execution, the alternative being an automatic life sentence. Neave was much exercised. During the committee stage of the bill on 25 April, he argued for more judicial discretion in sentencing those involved in so-called 'mercy killings'. But a month later, he demanded retention of the death penalty for murders carried out during the commission of rape, just as he had unsuccessfully proposed the noose for murder committed during burglary, housebreaking or any violent crime. A vigorous debate with the abolitionists ensued, which Neave and his cohorts lost.

In the big parliamentary debates later that year, on the Russian invasion of Hungary and the Suez débâcle, Neave was again silent. As a junior member of the government, his duty was to speak when instructed. He could not simply get up and intervene in debates. British troops began leaving the Suez Canal base in June 1956 and Egypt's President Nasser promptly nationalised the canal. Anthony Eden characterised the move as a threat to the very life of Britain, which relied on the free passage of oil from the Gulf. National pride was also at stake. The canal had been 'British' since Disraeli had pleased Queen Victoria with the purchase of a majority shareholding in 1875. Popular opinion, stoked by tabloid vilification of Nasser as 'another Hitler', set the stage for a joint Anglo-French invasion of Egypt on 31 October. Operation Musketeer, as it was christened, was a disaster, inviting international opprobrium and allowing the Russians to put down a revolution in Hungary a few days later with exemplary ruthlessness. Throughout this tumult, which shook the country and the Tory Party, Neave kept his counsel, though his support for the government was unwavering. There was never any question of a high-profile resignation over the issue. Being a member of the government, however lowly, limited his opportunities to speak in the House, even on such an issue. Not until he returned to the back benches six years later did he offer that Eden's action had averted a third world war.

The Suez crisis forced Eden to resign and brought the

Chancellor of the Exchequer, Harold Macmillan, into Downing Street as his successor in January 1957. This was Neave's opportunity. When the new government was constituted, he was appointed joint parliamentary secretary to Harold Watkinson, Minister of Transport and Civil Aviation. Loyalty and unostentatious good work had been rewarded. He was part of the new order. He may only have been one of four (including John Profumo, later Minister of War and the most high-profile victim of the Christine Keeler scandal) but he was firmly on the ministerial ladder. Satisfaction at his promotion may well have outweighed the sense of being at the centre of power. Neave's first task as a minister was a mundane one: replying to a motion for the adjournment about faulty lifts at Hampstead Underground Station which had resulted in a fellow Tory MP and twenty other passengers being trapped for half an hour.

If this was Neave's introduction to ministerial responsibility, there was to be more of the same, much of it just as uninspiring. Questions answered included those concerning newspaper deliveries to the Middle East and the problems of the Aberdeen Flying Club. In July, Neave, a serious cigarette smoker, also refused to ban smoking on British European Airways routes, despite medical evidence of a link between cigarettes and lung cancer. Throughout, his style was polite, firm and unflappable. Some might have found it a touch sardonic, though he showed little of the combativeness he was capable of displaying as a back-bencher.

Neave's years of office continued in much the same vein. He was a loyal member of the government. While the government weathered a brief but fierce economic storm, he steered the Milford Haven Conservancy Bill through the Commons, a measure allowing large-scale petrochemical and shipping development in the biggest natural harbour in South Wales. He also had to deal with the occasional brush fire. On 7 November 1957, an MP complained in the Commons about noise created by a Soviet TU 104 jet airliner taking off from Heathrow at four o'clock in the morning. Neave sympathised with the complaint, but rejected, in the nicest and most long-winded manner, claims for damage to property. There would be no free lunches while he was in charge.

Politically, 1958 opened with a bang. On 7 January, Macmillan lost his entire team of Treasury ministers – Chancellor Peter Thorneycroft, Enoch Powell and Nigel Birch – all of whom resigned in protest at rises in public spending they considered imprudent. Macmillan, not yet the 'Supermac' of the cartoonists, was publicly unperturbed. He embarked on a six-week tour of the warmer Commonwealth countries, explaining: 'I thought the best thing to do was settle up these little local difficulties, and then turn to the wider vision of the Commonwealth.' Neave, however, while attracting attention as a safe pair of hands, did not profit from the ministerial reshuffle that followed.

He built on his reputation during the year, using a fat file of statistics and civil service arguments where he could, and polite rebuttal where he could not. February's work included support for a Merchant Shipping Bill, promoted by two MPs from Northern Ireland, to extend the liability of shipowners, and a debate on the future of air transport development. In the latter, he promised 'a fair crack of the whip' for independent operators seeking to compete with the state airlines. However, these remained Britain's flag carriers. There was no hint that one day they, too, might be in private hands. A political consensus, discredited by the term 'Butskellism', still operated between the main parties on the wisdom of retaining air traffic in state hands.

Throughout 1958, Neave continued to polish his reputation and his dry humour. In May, Dame Irene Ward, the formidable Tory MP for Tynemouth, taxed him on the issue of dry docks. 'Dry docks are very important,' he replied, 'but they are not my responsibility.' 'A bad reply,' shot back the old dragon. There were some compensations for office. In May he travelled on the inaugural flight of BEA's new service to Warsaw, and used the trip to revisit the Gestapo headquarters where he had been interrogated after his unsuccessful escape from Stalag XXa in 1941. Otherwise, he performed competently, without showing genius or originality either in his departmental or parliamentary work, but in Andrew Roth's (perhaps ambiguous) view he was 'a decoration to any Conservative platform'. In June, he ruled out the installation of telephones on trains and aeroplanes, describing them as 'gimmicks'. In July, he led a debate on the accounts of the British Transport Commission, as the state railway system was then known. He was evasive about the closure of unremunerative services. In November, he defended the government's decision to close Croydon Airport, taken in 1953, and to expand Prestwick Airport in Scotland.

1959 was to prove a momentous year. On 16 January, Neave was promoted to Under-Secretary of State at the Ministry for Air. It was a useful move up the greasy pole but it still did not make for more exciting politics. His main role remained that of answering MPs' questions from the front bench. On 5 March, he replied to a debate on the Air Estimates, thanking MPs who congratulated him on his new post. There was, he said 'general goodwill' towards the RAF, before running into an argument about the value of the British atomic bomb. He pushed the government line that 'the possession by this country of an element of nuclear power might, in certain circumstances, be a decisive factor in preventing war by miscalculation', fending off an intervention about the circum-stances in which Britain might use the deterrent independently of the USA. The whole issue of Britain and The Bomb had assumed a much higher profile since the USAF had stationed nuclear weapons on British soil the previous year, prompting the establishment of the Campaign for Nuclear Disarmament (CND) and the first Easter march on the government's Atomic Weapons Research Establishment at Aldermaston, in Berkshire. With his heavy constituency involvement in atomic science, and his keen interest in defence policy, Neave was utterly hostile to CND. He talked instead about the need for more pilot recruits, more women and more dentists, but he did confirm that the government was going ahead with Blue Streak, a liquid-fuel, land-based rocket capable of escaping the earth's gravitational pull. This was designed to become Britain's independent nuclear deterrent. There were tetchy exchanges with Geoffrey de Freitas, Labour MP for Lincoln, in which Neave was forced to apologise. Neave also went on to laud the merits of the proposed TSR2, a tactical strike and reconnaissance aircraft, capable of supersonic speeds. (The TSR2 would be aborted, in 1965, by a Labour government.)

The new minister commented briefly on press reports about missile warning stations and anti-missile developments generally. He had nothing to add to what other ministers had told MPs, 'namely that we are collaborating closely with the Americans on this difficult problem'. It was not a very satisfactory response to an issue of public and media concern, nor was it a particularly satisfactory speech, for all its length and broad range. On 10 March, he was once more on the defensive about the RAF's budget, but the various appropriations went through without a vote, as they customarily do. It was not exactly a baptism of fire, but the parliamentary process tested Neave's ministerial skills as they had not been at Transport. He managed oral answers a week later with confidence, though skirting a series of awkward questions about the ill-fated Thor missile bought from America. Roy Mason, Labour MP for Barnsley and a future Defence Secretary, asked if the nuclear warhead would be a permanent feature of the missile, now in operation only for training purposes. Neave was compelled to admit that he could not give an answer; he was to be quizzed again in the subsequent months but could be no more enlightening.

Neave's last recorded contribution as a minister came on 8 July 1959, when he answered a written question on conditions at RAF station El Adem. He admitted that this was 'not a comfortable place to serve' but promised a new airmen's club and the extension of messes. As the long summer recess beckoned, the future looked mildly promising. He had not committed any major gaffes. At the age of forty-three, he was a middle-ranking minister with prospects: the kind of traditional Tory politician who might just make Cabinet rank. His home life was also secure. The family was living in the Old Vicarage in Ashbury, below the Marlborough Downs on the western edges of his constituency. Neave's daughter Marigold remembers the period as probably their most settled: 'It was home for us all to go to, a very nice five-bedroom Georgian house next door to the church.' Neave often read the texts there during Sunday service. The village was close to the site of the battle of Ethendune, and a ring of sarsen stones in the old rectory garden rekindled a sense of England's prehistoric past. Neave 'liked the place very much'. It was his kind of Betjemanesque Britain.

Then, in the late summer of 1959, he had a heart attack: not massive, but sufficient for his doctors to order him to rest. 'He wasn't able to work,' recollects Marigold. The family speculated that it might have been brought on by his wartime experiences, but it was more likely that quite heavy smoking and his fondness for drink, exacerbated by the stress of ministerial office and a largely sedentary lifestyle, caused his cardiac event. He had been absent from parliamentary business in January 1959, pleading 'indisposition', and in the same month he admitted to a 'slight leg injury' that had prevented him from carrying out his duties. In April, he was again absent, on this occasion laid low with flu. Whatever the cause of his heart attack, it changed his life, and, arguably, the politics of the late twentieth century. For the children it was a difficult time. 'It was spoken of in hushed tones,' remembered Patrick. 'We were packed off to stay with our grandparents, and mother got in a nurse. None of his condition was discussed with us, and I never asked.' Neave was ordered to give up smoking and alcohol, and take more exercise. For this purpose, he incongruously kept a rowing machine under the bed in the 'dressing room' of the Crescent Mansions flat in Fulham that was now their London home.

By far the greater impact was political. While still convalescing, Neave was compelled to go out and fight for his constituency for the third time in only six years. Nationally, the Conservatives were in a good position. On the international front, Macmillan's visit to the USSR had raised his profile as a statesman. Cyprus had been granted her independence, with the UK maintaining sovereignty over two military base areas. At home, economic recovery proceeded apace. Income tax was down, as were beer prices. Macmillan judged it profitable to announce the dissolution of parliament on 9 September, with polling day set for 8 October. In Abingdon, Neave faced the familiar hazard of a three-cornered contest, with two new opponents. Labour fielded Philip Picard, a barrister, like Neave, and the Liberals chose Mrs Verdun Perl.

The Conservatives romped home with an overall majority of 100 seats – a remarkable achievement by 'Supermac' who had taken over the leadership of his party in 1957 when its fortunes were at their lowest after the Suez débâcle. Neave increased his majority substantially, to 10,972.

On his return to Westminster in late October 1959, Neave did not pick up the reins of ministerial responsibility, returning instead to the back benches. His explanation to the voters of Abingdon concealed more than it revealed. 'I have resigned from the government and returned to industry,' he wrote in the weekly column he contributed to the *Abingdon Herald*. Newspapers were a great deal more reticent about revealing the private lives of public figures in those days and readers had never been told that he had suffered a heart attack.

Most subsequent accounts argue that Neave quit office because Edward Heath, the Chief Whip, told him his political career was over. There was not much love lost between the two men. Heath was an occasional visitor to Neave's constituency. Marigold remembers with some asperity being told that her parents could not come to her school sports day in Wantage because the Chief Whip was speaking locally. 'My father and Heath didn't like each other. Heath was not an easy character.' The received version of what happened next is put simply by Heath's biographer, John Campbell, who argues: 'He made a lifelong enemy of Airey Neave . . . who returned to Westminster after suffering a coronary, expecting to be welcomed back with congratulations on his recovery, only to be told bluntly by Heath that he was "finished".'[2] Another biographer, this time of Sir Keith Joseph, related a similar story. Neave had to resign because of a minor heart problem, wrote Morrison Halcrow. When he reported his medical problem to Heath, 'the Chief Whip had tersely commented, in effect, "That's the end of your political career, then", and Heath had acquired yet another enemy.'[3]

In his autobiography, Heath went out of his way to demolish the 'myth' of Neave's desire for revenge for the alleged spiteful comment about his health. 'There are absolutely no grounds for claiming that I was unsympathetic towards him,' insists the former Prime Minister. As a junior minister, Neave had informed Heath 'that his health had broken down and that his doctor had told him he should resign'. Heath further asserts that he expressed his sympathy, told him he must recover his health and urged him to come back as soon as his doctor confirmed that he could accept another appointment. As his health improved, Heath adds, Neave took up various business interests, but never indicated that he wanted to come back into government. 'There is absolutely no justification for these false stories about my telling Neave that he was "finished". I would never behave in that way towards a colleague.'[4]

In an interview with the author, Heath elaborated: 'He had this illness, and he told me he couldn't carry on. So I told him this was very sad, but I quite understood and if he regained his health then we could give him another job – not necessarily the same one, but a similar one, and he could go on climbing the ladder.' The story of their fall-out in 1959, Heath believes, was 'an invention after the Thatcher [leadership] election to justify what he had done. He never came and said he was fit enough for office again, or he could have had a job.' Heath's opinion of Neave as a minister and a parliamentary performer was not high. 'He did the job perfectly well. He was competent. He didn't blunder.'[5] In private, to friends, he was more forthcoming, telling Michael Jones, assistant editor (politics) of the *Sunday Times*, that Neave was 'a shitbag'.

A third explanation was offered by Andrew Roth, in his reference book *Parliamentary Profiles*. 'Some of his colleagues thought his request was coupled with an incident in which he was arrested as intoxicated in charge of a vehicle. This incident received virtually no publicity.' Even in those more censorious times, it is unlikely that a minister would be compelled to surrender ministerial office for such an offence. It would have added to the sum of his tribulations but could scarcely have been decisive. For whatever motive, Neave left no explanation, other than his curt announcement of resignation in the *Abingdon Herald*. In the absence of his own clarification, the evidence of the other players in the drama has to be preferred. Neave drank and smoked too much, took little exercise and was a classic candidate for cardiac failure. His later attempts to justify deep personal and political hostility to Heath on the grounds of the Chief Whip's alleged brutal ending of his career sound like exculpatory reasoning long after the event. Airey Neave was more likely the architect of his own ministerial downfall and could not bring himself to terms with that fact. That his long-nursed resentment would have such a tumultuous outcome does not begin to justify it but does explain it.

13

Locust Years

The 1960s were for many people a decade of wider freedom and boundless expectations. National Service was abolished and higher education became more widely available to a new generation. Unemployment began to feel like a scourge of the past and trade unions were more 'bolshie' in their wage demands. Harold Macmillan proclaimed 'a wind of change' blowing through the British Empire, which would sweep away the nation's colonial heritage. Yet Airey Neave, the product of an earlier and largely hostile generation, was on the margins of this revolution. Still a relatively young man in his early forties, he was languishing on the back benches at Westminster, the victim, as he saw it, of unfeeling treatment at the hands of his own party.

Accordingly, like many a Conservative MP before and after, he turned to business. Soon after giving up ministerial office in 1959, he joined the West Midlands manufacturing firm of John Thompson. The company was based in Wolverhampton not far from the stately home of Chillington Hall owned by Diana's father. Some colleagues at Westminster alleged that his wife's family got him the post in this key company, though his keen public interest in science had been evident for years. He also became a governor of the Imperial College of Science and Technology in London. The John Thompson Group manufactured power station boilers and pressure vessels, chiefly for the state-owned Central Electricity Generating Board. Neave went to Thompson as legal and parliamentary adviser, with a seat on the main board. It was common practice of the day for MPs to have such outside interests, and there was no compulsion to log these lucrative 'extras' in the Commons Register of Interests as exists today. His knowledge of the nuclear power industry, derived from contacts in the atomic science industry, would also have been very useful, as indeed would his security service background. The nuclear industry was regarded as a prime target for espionage and subversion, and with his background Neave needed no vetting. John Thompson was one of the two top firms in Britain specialising in this field (the other being Babcock & Wilcox), and it had offices in Tavistock House, in the Bloomsbury area of London, where Neave ensconced himself in some comfort with two secretaries, Joy Robilliard and Hannah Hulme. The company built Berkeley nuclear power station in the Severn Valley. Brian Mares, the firm's office manager at the time, remembered him well: 'He took a great interest in that [the nuclear side] because a lot of the know-how came from Harwell, which was in his constituency.'[1] Mares also recollected that Neave did a great deal of his constituency work in his company office, 'because he didn't have an office in the Commons'. At that time, it was quite common for back-bench MPs not to have a room at Westminster.

Neave did not speak in the Commons again until 3 March 1960 and when he did there was a note of nostalgia not unmixed with envy in his voice. He did not intervene again until late April, in a debate on the increasingly ill-fated Blue Streak missile. On this occasion, he was obliged by parliamentary protocol to declare a personal interest. As a director of Thompson, Neave had inside knowledge about Blue Streak. There was 'nothing wrong' with the project, he stated. Blue Streak was well made, had good range and considerable accuracy. He argued that the rocket could still be used for space exploration as part of a wider European programme. Neave was also keen to stress that an abandonment of Blue Streak (as was threatened) did not end British involvement in the nuclear deterrent against the Soviet bloc. He read the House a long, strongly worded lecture on ballistic missiles, interrupted from time to time by two of Labour's most inveterate peacemongers, Sydney Silverman and Emmanuel Shinwell. He concluded that 'a large number of V-bombers fitted with Skybolt [an American air-delivered missile] would present an effective deterrent'.

Loss of office had clearly diminished Neave's enthusiasm for Westminster. It was almost seven months before he made a further contribution of substance in the Commons, this time in the debate on the Queen's Speech in November 1960, when he made a passionate appeal for better scientific education. The nation's future was bound up with the rate at which it could produce trained technologists, he insisted, also finding Cold War reasons to back up his assertion. Nikita Krushchev had recently told the United States 'we graduate three times as many engineers as you, and whoever has the knowledge has the future at his feet'. In pure science, Neave claimed, the West was ahead of the USSR, lagging only in technology and applied science. He put his new-found interest in science to good advantage, becoming vice chairman of the Conservative Backbenchers' Science and Technology Committee.

Some of Neave's political ardour returned just before the winter recess, when he led a debate on the British communications satellite programme, or, more precisely, the lack of one. He criticised the Post Office (then in charge of all telecommunications) for dragging its feet on the commercial use of satellite communications. Speaking from his lofty position as chairman of the All-Party Committee on Space Research, he called for a Cabinet-level body to push through an 'historic decision' on the issue. His committee had held talks with the leading aviation and electronics firms, and the British Interplanetary Society, and Neave now called for a British initiative to forestall US domination of the world telephone market. He was years ahead of his time anticipating that satellites would come to dominate international communication, but his policy was becoming familiar to MPs. It rested on reactivation of the Blue Streak missile, taking a payload of 300 lb. or more into orbit 5,000 miles from earth. Once again, he declared 'I am a director of a firm which has a financial interest in Blue Streak', but enthused over a £243 million programme spread over twenty years, which he described as 'an economic proposition' offering cheaper international telephone calls. Although he inspired Woodrow Wyatt, the maverick Labour MP and socialite, who found it a 'most excellent and comprehensive speech', British involvement in space communication had to wait many years.

The pace of change quickened in 1961. Abroad, John F. Kennedy was ushering in a new era in the USA. At home, Macmillan brought together unions, employers and government ministers into a National Economic Development Council ('Neddy') in a bid to roll back wage inflation. Neave pursued his customary concerns of science and industry, a happy marriage of constituency, personal and business interests. In February that year, he advocated an accelerated nuclear power station building programme, even though nuclear power stations cost three times as much as conventional coal-fired stations. In a Commons debate, he was once more obliged to declare an interest, of being 'directly connected with this industry'.

In March 1962, he also introduced a private member's measure, the Carriage By Air (Supplementary Provisions) Bill, extending rights and protections of air passengers. In the debate, he told MPs: 'I am not an international lawyer. Indeed I have ceased to practise law . . .'[2] This was the first public indication that he had turned his back on his chosen profession, though it was true he had not practised since entering Parliament nine years previously. The government supported Neave's Bill, and it passed into law that summer. He had a talkative summer, debating science and industry and proposals for Britain to join the Euratom project. At least he had a better summer than many Cabinet ministers: seven were sacked by a physically ailing Macmillan in the July 'Night of the Long Knives'.

As the year drew to a close Neave welcomed Dr Beeching's

'new and constructive' plans to rationalise the state railways, despite the pending closure of the only rail link to Abingdon in the heart of his constituency. In January 1963, shortly after the death of Hugh Gaitskell, leader of the Labour Party, Neave was compelled to lead a late-night adjournment debate on the rail closure, describing it as 'a clear injustice'. The two events were unconnected but had a common background. The years of 'Supermac' were drawing to a close, along with his efforts to draw both sides of industry together into a common cause against inflation, especially on pay. A General Election was not much more than a year away. The Tories were losing by-elections all round the country, including in Orpington, Kent, where the Liberals had overturned a massive Conservative majority in their suburban heartlands. Neave had lost one of his constituency's largest employers with the shutdown of the Didcot Ordnance Centre. Now the railway was going and the political future was uncertain. Gaitskell was replaced by the sharp-witted Yorkshireman Harold Wilson, whose slogan 'Thirteen Wasted Tory Years' was beginning to resonate with voters. Neave did not like what he saw of Wilson. The new leader originated in the Bevanite left of the Labour Party, and conspiratorial elements in the security services considered him a crypto-Communist. Moreover, George Brown, the right-wing contender for the leadership who now became deputy leader to Wilson, had been in contact with the security services during party infighting over nuclear disarmament in the early 1960s. In the view of Stephen Dorril, 'He [Wilson] also knew that as late as July 1963 his deputy, George Brown, was still in contact with MI6 and its head "C".'[3] So was Airey Neave. He had never severed his connections with the intelligence community, and his later link up with the shadowy campaign to destabilise the Wilson government had its seeds in this change of leadership.

For the moment, however, he publicly sustained the image of a hard-working back-bencher, speaking quite regularly in debates about parliamentary reform, space satellites, the railways, science and education. On one issue he was seriously preoccupied: prisoners of war and compensation for those who had suffered. At 4.22 a.m. on 15 July 1963, he raised the case of Miss G.M. Lindell (the Comtesse de Milleville), a lady of British birth domiciled in France who had endured the horrors of Ravensbrück. She was one of Neave's 1S9 agents, but she had missed out on the compensation paid to victims of Nazi persecution by the German Federal government in 1953. Neave had first raised her case in 1954 but nothing had been done to help her. Peter Smithers, Foreign Office Under-Secretary, promised him the Lindell case would be pursued with 'vigour and expedition'.

In the autumn of 1963, it became clear that Macmillan could not go on. From his hospital bed on 10 October, after an operation for prostate cancer, he sent a message to the Conservative Party faithful gathered in Blackpool for their annual conference. He was stepping down, and, in the manner of the Tories in those days, 'soundings' were taken. The Foreign Secretary R.A. Butler was the Cabinet's choice, while the constituency parties wanted Lord Hailsham. MPs favoured the much younger Reginald Maudling. None of them came near; instead, Lord Home emerged as Macmillan's successor. Labour leaders could scarcely believe their luck. The government had been on the rack for months over various spy scandals: the Profumo affair, involving Neave's former ministerial colleague at the Air Ministry; the defection of Kim Philby to Moscow to join Burgess and Maclean; the unmasking of John Vassall, a homosexual spy in the Admiralty; and the gaoling in Russia of the businessman-spy Greville Wynne. An enquiry into the Profumo affair by Lord Denning sharply criticised the government, which was now to be led by a Scottish earl who looked like a throwback to the Victorian era. Lord Home had to renounce his peerage and fight a by-election as a commoner. Only then could he begin to mobilise a badly shaken Conservative Party for a General Election. He was duly returned for Kinross and West Perthshire and the countdown began.

In the months following Macmillan's démarche, Neave was

more active at Westminster. He asked questions about the so-called 'brain drain' of scientists from the UK to the USA and Canada, discovering that the numbers were low and that many subsequently returned home. He took up the theme in a debate on 24 February, accusing some of the migrant scientists of being in cahoots with the Labour Party to attack government funding of the universities and the Medical Research Council. Neave had robust exchanges with several leading Labour figures, including Richard Crossman and Mrs Judith Hart. The Opposition was making much of the running on science, particularly since Wilson's 'white heat of technological revolution' speech in Scarborough the previous autumn. It was an issue they felt was a natural for Labour, facing a Tory Party led by an earl who famously used matchsticks to work out awkward sums. Neave was equally determined that they should not get away with this tactic, particularly as state supervision of scientific research lay behind it. 'I am not a scientist,' he admitted, 'but I have met a great many scientists, and I believe that fundamental advances in science are not the result of a plan. They are the result of the creative ability of individuals with freedom to do that research. Any interference with their creative ability would be extremely bad and would be unlikely to produce new or better products. It is particularly true of research in industry where, in my opinion, there could not possibly be remote control from Whitehall.'[4] A more cogent Conservative view of the role of the scientists would be hard to find. When his emotions were engaged, as they all too rarely were, he could speak convincingly without the need for a civil service brief. And the politics showed through, as in his peroration that day: 'I do not believe that a socialist policy can be right for industry or for government research.'

When Blue Streak was finally launched at Woomera rocket range in the Australian outback on 5 June, the Aviation Minister Julian Amery was quick to claim a 'technical success' in the House, and Neave was equally swift to congratulate the government on this 'very significant technical achievement'. Excitedly (by his standards), he asked whether ministers had plans for advanced means of space propulsion 'through atomic or electrical power'. They had not. Nor did the test launch of Blue Streak take Britain into the space age: it flew for only 147 seconds before thrust was terminated. Later that year, Blue Streak was ignominiously cancelled under pressure from the United States. Harold Macmillan was seriously embarrassed by America's subsequent cancellation of Skybolt, which it had been pushing in its stead.

Neave also continued to harry the government on its failure, as he saw it, to win proper compensation for the victims of Nazi persecution. In particular, he sought satisfaction for the relatives of the fifty RAF officers executed on Hitler's orders after recapture following the 'Great Escape' from Stalag Luft III in 1944, and other British nationals who had died in the concentration camps. Ministers, including R.A. Butler, stonewalled for months, refusing even to publish a full list of those deemed to qualify. Finally, on 9 June, shortly before the summer recess and the start of the election campaign, Butler came to the House to confirm that the Federal German government was to pay £1 million to compensate British victims who had suffered loss of liberty or damage to their health at the hands of the Nazis, and to their dependants. Neave was called first, after the Shadow Foreign Secretary, Patrick Gordon Walker, in recognition of his long campaign. He welcomed the statement with 'very general relief'.

Polling day for the 1964 election was set for 15 October. Neave faced another three-cornered fight, with Mrs Perl making a reappearance for the Liberals and Labour fielding a new candidate, Frederick Riddell, a schoolmaster. When the votes were counted, Neave had performed a little less well than in 1959, but a great deal better than his party did nationally. The 'Thirteen Wasted Tory Years' were over. Labour's overall share rose by only 0.6 per cent, but the Conservative share slipped by 6 per cent and Harold Wilson was in Downing Street with a majority of five over all other parties. In Abingdon, Neave's majority fell to 6,373. On his return to Westminster, Neave persevered with his special interests: science, technology and the defence and communications implications of space exploration. Wilson had promised '100 days of dynamic action', but on 5 November, the newly returned member for Abingdon accused Labour of not living up to their promises. During the election, he said, many scientists were persuaded that a Labour government would go ahead with a technological revolution and harness science to socialism. 'Within a fortnight of taking office they have done exactly the opposite,' he complained, alleging that Concorde, the supersonic aircraft, would be scrapped. It was not, but his other fears about Blue Streak and the Black Knight missiles were realised. Neave was particularly unimpressed by Labour's choice as Cabinet Minister for Technology, the elderly Frank Cousins, 'on loan' from the Transport and General Workers' Union where he was general secretary. Cousins, a former lorry driver, had not even been elected an MP, being obliged to enter the Commons via a by-election. 'There is no special merit,' he argued, 'in setting up a new ministry. The problems will not be solved merely by doing that.' In a debate on the Science and Technology Bill, Neave repeatedly demanded what plans he had for nuclear science and the power station industry, not omitting to mention his personal interest as a director of Thompson. He was relieved that Anthony Crosland, Secretary for Education and Science, accepted an amendment guaranteeing the pensions of government scientists. The Tories might no longer be in power but detailed measures such as this sustained his political credibility back in the constituency.

In the ballot for private member's bills, Neave won twenty-second place, a difficult site from which to launch new legislation, but he used it to pursue justice for the very elderly who had been excluded from a key provision of the welfare state. He tabled a National Insurance (Further Provisions) Bill aimed at giving pensions to older people not covered by the 1946 National Insurance Act. After a parliamentary spat over precedence, Neave finally rose to introduce his Bill on 25 March 1965. His measure sought to give state pensions to 250,000 elderly men and women (mostly from the professional classes) who had been excluded from the scheme at its inception in 1948. Most were over eighty. The average age was eighty-four. It was a popular measure, though it would cost £30 million a year if implemented in full. Since announcing his intentions nearly five months previously, he had received nearly 2,000 letters.

Neave conceded that his own party had continued Labour's post-war policy of refusing to give state pensions to this dwindling group, but argued that the time had come to remedy an injustice to the very old. He appealed to Miss Peggy Herbison, the Minister of Pensions and National Insurance, for 'action and humanity'. The minister was sympathetic but specific in her compassion. Some of the intended recipients were genuinely badly off: ex-teachers with small pensions, former ministers of the church and the like. But others were businessmen and landowners who had deliberately opted out of National Insurance, while almost half of them were already covered by National Assistance and would not benefit financially. The total cost would be nearer £100 million, which would mean higher National Insurance contributions from employers and workers. Neave's Bill was deliberately filibustered by the government on 26 March, by ministers who continued a debate on the Consolidated Fund all night until eleven on Friday morning, thus killing off private members' business. Richard Crossman, Minister for Pensions, recorded in his diary that the press found this tactic a 'parliamentary outrage'. In truth, however, even the Shadow Cabinet had doubts about the measure. Sir Keith Joseph, the pensions spokesman, agreed to meet Neave to try to get him to play down his campaign, 'but felt he was unlikely to be successful'.[5]

Neave was deeply distressed by these wrecking tactics and his public profile for the rest of that parliament was much lower. Besides, the Conservative Party had a new leader, Edward Heath. Lord Home had resigned in July 1965, triggering a contest for the leadership under new rules introduced only six months previously.

Instead of the mysterious process of the leader 'appearing' from high-level horse-trading, MPs now chose their own man. Under the new rules, to be elected at the first ballot a candidate had to win an absolute majority of the votes cast plus a margin of 15 per cent over his nearest rival. If the election went to a second ballot, a simple majority sufficed.

Heath, the Shadow Chancellor with some notably good performances in the Commons under his belt, was determined to be the front-runner from the beginning. His supporters were off the mark before the starting gun was fired. In late June, they leaked stories to the Sunday newspapers about a group of 100 MPs demanding change at the top, and Home was put to the embarrassment of repeated denials that he was about to quit. When the pressure became too strong to withstand, the Tory leader announced to a shocked 1922 Committee on 22 July that he was standing down. The pressure came chiefly from 'the Heathmen', who saw the Shadow Chancellor as the right man to take on Labour on the economy. Harold Wilson had inherited a nightmarish balance of payments deficit, forcing tax rises, public spending cuts and eventually 'voluntary' curbs on wages. The man who bequeathed him this mess, former Chancellor Reginald Maudling, was Heath's main rival for the leadership. He was the clear preference of the voters, especially Tories, but Heath had the backing of the City, party activists and the media. His campaign manager, Peter Walker, proved a formidable operator. Indeed, his *modus operandi* differed little in organisation from Neave's own campaign to unseat Heath ten years later. In the first ballot, Heath won 150 votes, Maudling 133 and the maverick Enoch Powell, 15. Maudling immediately conceded. There was no second ballot and Heath took over on 27 July 1965.

There was no room in Heath's Shadow administration for Airey Neave. He was now marooned on the back benches, ploughing his favourite furrows as Labour looked for signs that an early election might yield a bigger majority. A famous by-election in Hull North on 28 January 1966 showed a swing from the Tories to

the government of 4 per cent. It was enough. Harold Wilson
unveiled a raft of popular measures, including cheap mortgages
for those on low incomes, relief for council ratepayers and better
pension arrangements. All this was marketed under the confident
slogan 'You Know That Labour Government Works'. It certainly
worked for Wilson. On polling day, 31 March 1966, Labour was
returned with a majority of ninety-seven. Neave's majority in
Abingdon was slashed to 3,302 in yet another three-cornered
fight. On this occasion, his Labour opponent was one of the
nuclear scientists whose cause he had so consistently championed.
Alan Matterson, a thirty-six-year-old scientist at the Atomic
Energy Research Establishment, Harwell, and a member of
Abingdon Borough Council, polled 24,447 votes to Neave's 27,749,
while the Liberal, schoolmaster Denis Case, took 7,703. At the
rate of decline since the late fifties, Abingdon was in danger of
becoming a marginal seat. At a by-election it would not have
been reckoned safe for the Tories. The swing against Neave was 3
per cent.

Politically, these were Neave's darkest days. Not even the
work he had put in for the over eighties was properly appreciated. Soon after the election, in late April 1966, Michael Foot,
Leader of the House, accused Neave of not being in the chamber
when the parliamentary progress of his National Insurance Bill
was being discussed: 'I do not know where he is. Apparently he
is so eager to support the proposition that he is not here at
all. He is not here tonight as he was not here for thirteen years.'
He had only turned up to please the elderly 'when he thought
it would embarrass the government'.[6] Conservative MPs were
furious. Neave had been there all the time and Foot was
compelled to apologise. Little more than two months later,
this measure came back to haunt the government, this time
piloted by Dame Irene Ward, the daunting Tory MP for
Tynemouth, with Neave powerfully in support. It failed again.
Neave did not give up. He was on the attack again in July 1967,
moving an amendment to the National Insurance Bill in the

teeth of ministerial hostility. That, too, met a sticky end.

Neave also proved to be a constitutional thorn in Labour's side. He argued persuasively for the Prices and Incomes Bill, which froze pay and dividends for six months and prices for a year, to be debated on the floor of the House, that is, by all MPs and not a committee drawn from each party in accordance with their parliamentary strength. The government proposed to give itself 'very serious and arbitrary peacetime powers', he argued during the committee stage of the Prices and Incomes Bill. Quoting *The Times* in support, Neave declared, 'We may be bidding goodbye for some time to economic freedom.'[7] In the face of such a large Commons majority, he was kicking against the pricks. The government had its way, but Neave could fairly claim to have established a reputation as 'a Commons man', an important distinction at Westminster.

Neave kept up the pressure on the victims of Nazi persecution, raising the case of fourteen British prisoners held in Sachsenhausen concentration camp. They included fellow POW escapers, among them Sydney Dowse, organiser of the 'Great Escape' from Stalag Luft III. Their claim for compensation had been rejected by the Foreign Office on the grounds that, while the cells in which they were incarcerated were in 'geographical proximity' to the camp, they were not inside the perimeter wire. Neave, who had met the Foreign Office minister George Thomson privately a number of times to press his case, now publicly attacked this 'most pedantic and unreasonable decision'. Thomson claimed that Neave had failed to persuade Tory ministers to back his claim, and refused to go back on the FO ruling. Neave promised to fight the case. It would prove to be a long battle, but he would ultimately win it. He raised the matter again on 7 November, in oral questions to the Foreign Secretary George Brown, who fobbed him off with the 'floodgate argument' that any concessions to the Sachsenhausen prisoners would lead to many other and bigger claims which would stretch beyond reason the cash available for compensation. Neave responded by putting down an early day motion on the issue, which was signed by 275 MPs from across the political spectrum. On 4 May 1967, Richard Crossman, the new Leader of the House, refused to give time for a debate, but the government was beginning to shift. Ministers urged Neave and his all-party group of supporters to refer the issue to Sir Edmund Compton, the newly appointed Parliamentary Commissioner for Administration – the 'Ombudsman'. If he found in their favour, there would have to be a debate. The Ombudsman duly found in their favour and was sharply critical of the Foreign Office in a report published just before Christmas 1967.

At this point, it would be useful to make a chronological leap to February 1968, when George Brown was obliged to ask the Commons to 'take note' – that is, approve – the Third Report of the Parliamentary Commissioner which found the FO guilty of maladministration. In the three-hour debate, Brown paid tribute to Neave's pioneering work, while sheltering behind the cloak of ministerial responsibility to operate the 1964 Anglo-German Agreement which laid down strict provisions for eligibility. He rejected outright the Commissioner's allegation that Foreign Office officials had failed to supply ministers with the correct information. If things had gone wrong, it was the fault of ministers, not civil servants. 'I am the one who got caught with the ball when the lights went up,' he confessed. The Sachsenhausen fourteen were gallant men but 'borderline cases'. No one had blundered or bungled. However, the Ombudsman ruled that his judgement was wrong. Brown accepted that, with bad grace, and reversed his decision.

Scathing in his response to Brown, Neave was praised by Labour veteran Emmanuel Shinwell, a War Office minister in 1929 who had dealt with similar cases from the First World War, for his courage and tenacity in starting and seeing through the two and a half year campaign. His actions had helped re-establish the authority and dignity of Parliament, and he had cleared gallant officers of any doubt that might have hung about their names. Neave could scarcely ask for more. Certainly, he did not get it from Crossman, who closed the debate without mentioning him by name in the group of 'a few back-benchers' to which he casually referred.[8] The motion was agreed and the war heroes got their money.

Perhaps unexpectedly, Neave showed himself on the side of the modernisers in the great debate of that parliament: whether proceedings of the Commons should be televised. In late November, he spoke in favour of televising, insisting that the presence of cameras would have little or no effect on proceedings, but would make them available to a wider audience. He showed common sense where others became agitated over prima donna MPs, convinced that the mass medium of television was the best way of informing people about what went on in Parliament. Neave also linked televising the House to the growing habit of the Wilson administration of operating through the media, rather than the Commons. The term 'spin doctor' had not yet been invented, but Neave correctly discerned the trend towards government by news management. 'I do not want to see Parliament bypassed by other methods of publicity,' he argued. The very existence of Parliament as a forum of the nation depended on giving the fullest information to the people. The motion was carried and the televising of debates rapidly became as much a feature of the parliamentary scene as *Hansard*, the official record – and one as little watched as the other is little read. The only exception was the twice-weekly stand-up theatre of Prime Minister's Questions, which pitted the party leaders in Commons combat. Cameras or no, it had been a busy year for Neave. He was active in debates on the 'brain drain', care of the elderly, nuclear energy, toll bridges and the foot and mouth epidemic among English cattle.

The year 1968 found Neave on familiar ground, arguing the case for pensions for the very elderly, reform of Parliament, enquiries into railway accidents, town planning (the great Abingdon gasholder dispute, which he won), the Abingdon by-pass and the future of cutbacks in nuclear power research at

Culham Laboratory. On the latter, he initiated a debate at six o'clock in the morning that went on for three quarters of an hour. His constituents could not say he was short-changing them. In May of that year, he was back on his feet challenging the Technology Minister, Tony Benn, arguing the case for nuclear energy (and declaring his own personal interest in the industry). Whatever he thought about Benn's undoubted enthusiasm for science and technology, Neave was forming a deeply suspicious opinion about the nature of his politics, and indeed those of the Labour government as a whole, wrongly believing that they formed a threat to democracy.

Maurice Macmillan, the Tory MP and son of the former Prime Minister, picked up the gauntlet on pensions for the very old in 1969, introducing Neave's original private member's bill for the fifth time. It had, said Neave, become an 'embarrassing and painful episode' to come to the House year after year only for the government to vote down pensions for people whose average age was now eighty-five, despite countrywide backing for the measure. Their numbers were now down to 125,000 he told MPs. Four died every week, yet they did not have the benefit of the death grant. Speaking with feeling, he added: 'They are too old for pensions. They are too old to die, in the eyes of the state.' Neave reminded MPs that after the filibuster in 1965, Labour had promised a minimum income guarantee instead of pensions. 'I had a very sharp and acrimonious correspondence with the Prime Minister on the subject, and reproached him very strongly about it,' he went on. But nothing materialised. The debate on 7 February was equally acrimonious, with Neave interjecting 'Rubbish' at times. His passion was to no avail. The Bill was denied a second reading.

After his success with Sachsenhausen, Neave took up the case of Rudolf Hess, the last of the leading Nazi war criminals still in gaol, and a man who had so fascinated him during the Nuremberg trials. Hess was normally incarcerated in Spandau prison, guarded by twenty-five men and one officer, at the intransigent insistence of the Russians. Britain, together with France and the USA, would have allowed his release. In February 1970, Hitler's former deputy was ill, lying in the British Military Hospital, Berlin, with an ulcer. Neave asked if Professor Rudolf Zenker of Zurich could examine Hess, but the Foreign Office minister George Thomson said Hess was responding to treatment and independent medical examination was unnecessary. Neave insisted that this was 'a question entirely of humanity' and asked if the Prime Minister could take up the matter on his next visit to the Soviet Union. Thomson agreed to consider that point, continuing: 'I think the time has come for humanitarian considerations to prevail.'[9] They did not.

Some Labour MPs contrasted unfavourably Neave's concern for Hess with the plight of other 'political' prisoners around the world, not least the African nationalist leaders rotting in Rhodesian detention camps. But Neave would not be the first politician to be selective in his sympathy and it would be pointless to argue that he should have behaved like his critics. They had an entirely different, indeed opposite, agenda. Neave was a Conservative of the old school, with a caring streak that made him unusual for the Tory Party, but in most aspects he was a classic product of his time and background. The shifts and changes in British society of the decade largely passed him by. He did not see the 'swinging sixties' as a welcome debunking of authority and a release of people power. He was at home with the Conservative condemnation of strikes, particularly the miners' strike of surface workers in late 1969, which presaged the convulsions that were to come.

Superficially, 1970 opened as a good year for Wilson's second government. In January, the Chancellor Roy Jenkins reported to the Cabinet that economic growth would be up by half to 3 per cent, and the economy would have a healthy balance of payments amounting to £500 million. The Conservatives, under Ted Heath, saw their lead in the opinion polls begin to slip away. But pressure for relaxation of pay controls was building up, strikes became more common, and Jenkins's cautious Budget of mid-April dismayed MPs looking for election bribes. However, a strong

Labour recovery in the local elections in May, coupled with a poll showing the government ahead by seven points, convinced Wilson that a snap poll would give him a third term in office, albeit with a reduced majority. There was also a fond hope that England's footballers would repeat the 1966 World Cup win in Mexico. Some of the winning sheen had rubbed off on Labour in the previous poll. On 18 May, Wilson took a gamble and called the General Election for 18 June.

Heath was caught on the hop and initially his nerve faltered. Labour exploited an improving economy to the hilt and forged ahead in the polls. Heath's call to the nation to 'wake up – or lose the future' did not chime with that summer's sense of confidence. In Abingdon, Neave faced not only his usual three-cornered fight but a much bigger electorate. His constituency now numbered almost 86,000 voters, a growth of 20,000 in only fifteen years. His rivals on this occasion were Norman Price, a thirty-four-year-old scientist standing for Labour, and for the Liberals, Caradoc Evans, who described himself modestly as a broadcaster, company director and teacher.

Labour's composure was rudely shattered only three days before polling day when trade figures showed Britain sliding back into the red. Ministers tried to talk their way out of this bad news by claiming it was a one-off deficit caused by the state airline's purchase of four jumbo jets, but the balance of payments figures, coupled with a demoralising defeat by Germany in the quarter-finals of the World Cup, changed the nation's mood virtually overnight. The last opinion poll, on polling day, put the Conservatives one point ahead. When the votes were counted, it was clear that Heath had pulled off a sensational victory. Labour's 100-seat majority had been overturned to a Conservative majority of thirty over all other parties. Heath's biographer John Campbell rightly described the outcome as 'the greatest upset in British politics since Attlee's victory in 1945'.

In Abingdon, Neave romped home with a hugely increased majority of 13,073 over his Labour rival. His share of the poll also went back up to its high-watermark level of 54 per cent, and the swing towards the Conservatives in his constituency was – at 6.7 per cent – much higher than the national average of 4.8 per cent. It was a very satisfactory result and the Neave family celebrated. But the return of a Conservative government led by his old enemy was a mixed blessing: there would be no place in a Heath government for Airey Neave. At fifty-four, he was firmly on the political shelf, while his old sparring partner in the CCA, Margaret Thatcher, immediately entered the Cabinet as Education Secretary. Some saw Thatcher as 'the token woman', but Neave later insisted that prejudice against women in the House of Commons was a thing of the distant past. 'This is not a place where women aren't treated as colleagues. They are, and have been for many years since Lady Astor.'[10]

Neave used the debate on the Queen's Speech to revive political interest in pensions for the very old. Death had brought down the number excluded from the state pension scheme to 110,000, so he welcomed the government's decision, heralded in the Conservative manifesto, to do justice at last. A National Insurance Bill implementing the reform was brought to the Commons within three weeks, and its first clause gave pensions of £3 a week to single people and £4 17s to married couples left out of the 1948 pension scheme. It was not equivalent to the full state pension, but it was a victory of principle. Labour MPs accused the Tories of 'lifting' a proposal that they had made just before going to the polls, incensing Neave. But recognition came from an unexpected quarter – the Opposition benches – where Jack Ashley MP, the Labour campaigner for the disabled (who is himself deaf), paid tribute to Neave. 'Irrespective of what one thinks of the arguments,' Ashley told the Commons, 'the hon. Member for Abingdon can take great satisfaction from the influence he has had in pressing his government on an issue on which he feels so strongly.'

Later that year, Neave again took up the case of Rudolf Hess. In Foreign Office questions on 16 November, he asked for a statement, and the FCO minister Geoffrey Rippon disclosed that the British ambassador in Moscow had made an approach to the Soviet government on behalf of the Three Powers almost nine months previously, on 23 February. It was unsuccessful. Since then, however, the Russians had agreed to improvements in Hess's conditions of imprisonment. The government would continue to watch for 'an appropriate moment' to raise the issue again. Neave was not satisfied. Would the Foreign Office initiate new, high-level talks with the French and American governments with a view to a fresh approach? Rippon was somewhat more forthcoming, but not much. He did, however, praise Neave's assiduity. 'There is certainly no man in the House or outside who has a better claim to press this matter,' he oozed.[11] Five months later, Neave raised the stakes, calling on the government to take unilateral action to free Hess from his 'cruel and pointless detention' as the sole prisoner in a 600-cell gaol. The Foreign Office fobbed him off on that occasion, and several more times during the parliament. Hess died alone, a broken man, in Spandau prison in 1987.

For the rest of that parliament, Neave stuck to his favourite topics: benefits for the very old, atomic energy, defence pro-curement and research, and science and technology. He became chairman of the All-Party Select Committee on Science and Technology, and as such a respected back-bencher. His committee produced four reports, which informed ministerial policy-making in this field. James Prior, Leader of the House, praised the 'enormous importance for the well-being of our country' of Neave's work. One instance suffices. Neave showed himself remarkably progressive on the issue of birth control, arguing the case for a completely free family planning service on the NHS, including advice and the supply of contraceptives. He argued that social and environmental problems would multiply without a population control policy involving 'all income and age groups'. His select committee urged this course of action, which was eventually implemented.

But the bees in his bonnet did not stop buzzing. He took up

issues dear to his wife's heart, such as the level of government relief for distressed Polish ex-servicemen and controversy over the murder of 4,000 Polish prisoners of war in the Katyn Forest in the closing months of the war. The Russians insisted that this outrage was the work of the Germans. Neave was convinced it was the work of Stalin, and he asked the FCO to place the issue on the agenda of the United Nations. He was rebuffed with a polite 'No'.

On the really big issue of the day – Europe – Neave found himself at one with his Prime Minister. He supported British entry to the European Economic Community, as it then was. On 21 October 1971, the Foreign Secretary Sir Alec Douglas-Home moved a Commons motion approving in principle the government's decision to join the EEC. Two hours into the debate, Neave rose to support the motion. 'I wish the whole venture well, but I do not think that it will succeed unless there is successful exploitation of British scientific and technological effort in conjunction with the Common Market,' he contended. In retrospect, this argument had an inadequate feel to it, compared with the great economic and political opportunities the British people were being asked to embrace. But Neave was on his hobby horse and there was no stopping him. After declaring his interest in the nuclear power industry, he waxed lyrical: 'Science is, and was long before the Common Market was dreamed of, essentially international.' Within the new psychological structure of the EEC, scientists could work for the common good and compete with the superpowers. He then got down to business, urging collaboration with France and Germany on the building of nuclear reactors. He envisaged that by 1985 most new electrical capacity would be nuclear, due to rising oil prices, and the industry would be dominated by perhaps two or three large European companies. He urged the government to give more attention to this development. A week later, he was among 356 MPs (a fifth of them Labour rebels) who supported entry into the EEC, in the teeth of opinion polls showing evidence that the British people opposed the move.

Apart from this momentous vote, events outside parliament dominated the news. After the dock strike came a nine-week stoppage by postal workers, which crippled communications by land. That was followed by a one-day walkout by 1.5 million workers to protest against Heath's ill-fated Industrial Relations Bill, which sought to put the trade unions in a legal straitjacket. The legislation, based on a blueprint prepared by the Inns of Court Conservative Association to which Neave belonged, set up an Industrial Court with authority to order 'cooling off' periods before a dispute could begin. It also had powers to fine unions and imprison recalcitrant strikers who defied the court. More strikes followed, in the state-owned steel industry, on the railways and in the civil service, culminating in the threat of an official one-day General Strike called by the TUC when five London dockers were gaoled for contempt of an Industrial Court. Neave shared the anxiety of many Conservatives that a breakdown of civil society could be imminent. In less than four years of office, Heath was compelled to declare a State of Emergency a record five times. Unrest culminated in the first national miners' strike since 1926, which began in January 1972 and lasted for seven weeks. The dispute, and secondary picketing of power stations, brought electricity blackouts and serious disruption to industry. Moreover, the police admitted that they could not cope with the impact of mass picketing. At the notorious 'battle at Saltley Gates' in Birmingham on 10 February 1972, police chiefs closed down a vital coke depot rather than risk a riot on the streets. Heath was forced to cave in, appointing a Commission of Enquiry under Judge Lord Wilberforce to award inflation-busting rises exceeding 20 per cent to the men. They only accepted after hours of face-to-face talks in Downing Street with the Prime Minister, at which miners' leaders drank most of his whisky. Weeks later, the same treatment was given to workers in the power supply industry who went on a crippling go-slow.

Yet Neave showed a public imperturbability at the rising tension in the coal industry. When the OPEC countries quadrupled the price of oil, and the miners announced a nationwide overtime ban, he was busy arguing the case for nuclear energy without reference to the impending crisis. In a Commons debate on the economy and the energy situation on 18 December 1973, he spoke five times, urging (after yet again declaring his business interest) the merits of ordering British-built reactors. He never mentioned the looming pit strike, even though Heath had just declared a three-day week for industry starting on 1 January 1974 to conserve dwindling coal stocks. On 7 February, the day the Prime Minister called a General Election to ask the voters 'who rules – the government or the miners?', Neave was busy leading a Commons debate on the pay of civil service scientists. These 'creative and brilliant people' were 'having a very bad time', he told the House. He had very strong views about the miners and their insurrectionary campaign, but he did not give them public expression. Privately, he shared the views of some former army officers and ex-members of the security services that the state was losing control of events.

Polling day was set for 28 February. The bookmakers made Heath an odds-on favourite to win. The opinion polls gave the Conservatives a lead varying from two to five points. But beneath the surface, voter confidence in Heath's premiership was ebbing away. It was not possible to hold the election to the simple constitutional challenge of 'who rules?'. The miners, secure behind an 81 per cent secret ballot for strike action, cannily played down their industrial action. Picketing was strictly limited and there was no repetition of the battle at Saltley Gates. Labour successfully broadened the campaign to encompass the Heath government's economic record, which was weak. Growth was stagnant, and double-digit inflation made nonsense of the Tories' claims for price stability. Heath's statutory pay policy was unpopular, and his Industrial Relations Act was so discredited that even the director-general of the CBI, Sir Campbell Adamson, suggested it be repealed and replaced with legislation more acceptable to trade unionists. Despite the peril into which the nation was plunged, the Act was not used against the National Union of Mineworkers.

In Abingdon, Neave's high-profile championship of the 1,300 civil service scientists in his constituency plainly did him no harm. Despite a one-half per cent swing against the Conservatives, his majority went up by 670 votes to 13,743, largely as a result of an increased turnout and a collapse in the Liberal vote. The Liberal candidate, Michael Fogarty, Professor of Industrial Relations at Henley Staff College, saw his vote tumble by more than half to little over 10 per cent of the total, while Labour's man, television director Denis Moriarty, increased his party's share. Way out in front, however, was Neave, with a comfortable 54 per cent.

Nationally, however, the picture was very different. Heath's biographer described the result as 'the strangest of modern times'. The Tories' comfortable majority disappeared. The verdict of the voters was that, whoever ran the country, it certainly was not the Prime Minister. They gave Labour 301 seats, and the Tories 297. The Liberals won fourteen seats, nine Nationalists were returned in Scotland and Wales. With the twelve MPs from Northern Ireland and two others, no party could command a majority in the Commons. Heath tried desperately to cling on to power, offering a pact on electoral reform to Jeremy Thorpe if the Liberals would support a Tory–Liberal coalition. His advances were spurned and on 6 March Harold Wilson returned to Downing Street at the head of a minority Labour administration.

In a fit of socialist emulation, Neave's scientists caught the mood of militancy, staging half-day strikes and demonstrations over their pay claim. At Westminster, Neave supported their campaign for 'catch-up' pay rises of up to 25 per cent, while subtly sustaining his demand for the state-run Central Electricity Generating Board to order English nuclear reactors not American 'light water' reactors. His intervention in a debate on 13 March earned the approval of John Stonehouse MP, who declared his speech 'attractive'. (Months later, however, Stonehouse faked his own death on a Florida beach, and after being extradited from

Australia was sentenced to seven years for fraud, theft, forgery and conspiracy.)

The new Labour government duly abolished the Industrial Relations Act, and big pay rises were granted to public servants, particularly nurses and teachers. However, Wilson could not continue governing for long without a clear majority. Heath was in the political doldrums, unlike his much-loved racing yacht *Morning Cloud* which actually sank in a storm off Shoreham, a portent for the poll that was confidently predicted for the autumn. Two weeks after this personal disaster for Heath, Wilson called a General Election on 10 October.

In Abingdon, Neave faced the same two rivals over whom he had triumphed a little over six months earlier. Voters never like being called out to elections held so soon after they have given their verdict, and this was no exception. The turnout in Neave's constituency fell from 83 per cent in the February poll to 75 per cent. His own vote fell by more than 4,000 to 31,956, but he increased his share of the vote. He returned to Westminster with a comfortable majority of 10,637. Again, nationally the picture was calamitous. Heath had performed well on the Tory manifesto, *Putting Britain First*, but his party lagged in the opinion polls throughout the short campaign and at best he limited the damage done to the Conservatives. Harold Wilson returned with an overall Commons majority of only three. He would be highly vulnerable to a reorganised and revitalised Opposition, but of the two party leaders Heath was the more immediately threatened. He had now fought four general elections and lost three of them. 'With the best will in the world it was hard to see how the party could contemplate a fifth under his leadership,' wrote his biographer John Campbell.[12] In Neave's view, the time for contemplation had come and gone.

14

A Very Spooky Coup

Heath's double defeat within seven months was Neave's opportunity to begin the process of change at the top. He had already begun to lay the ground for a coup against his old adversary after the débâcle of the 'who rules?' election. In March 1974, as Tory MPs returned to Westminster, this time in Opposition, Neave was elected to the powerful executive of the Conservative 1922 Committee, composed of all Tory back-benchers. When not in government the '22 excludes only the leader and the Chief Whip. This was the body – 'the men in suits' – that could make or break a Tory Party leader. It was an unforgiving instrument of power, interested only in success. From 1972, its chairman was Edward du Cann, Neave's old comrade from the campaigning days of the 1950s. As far as these hard men were concerned, Heath was on trial for his political life. If he won the election, his tenure of office was secure. If not, his ousting was simply a matter of time and procedure.

Du Cann set the note for the 1922's approach with a deliberately ambivalent speech to Tory candidates in the opening stage of the second election campaign. He was complimentary about his leader – 'you not only lead but command our party' – and thanked him for a cogent explanation of the theme 'on which you will fight the election'. John Campbell detected a subtly backhanded ambiguity to the address. It loaded the entire responsibility for success or failure on to the leader, thereby preparing the way for a swift defenestration. Du Cann was not a Heath fan. He had resigned

amid acrimony from the chairmanship of the Tory Party, to which
he had been appointed by Sir Alec Douglas-Home, shortly after
Heath became leader. His task as chairman of the 1922 was not
made easier by the Prime Minister's refusal to make any concessions to political fellowship. 'Ted was very unpopular with the
rank and file in the House,' he recollected. 'And we had a very
difficult time with him.'¹ Du Cann's attempts to forge closer links
between the 1922 Committee and the Prime Minister proved
fruitless. At a dinner in Downing Street, Heath was in a grumpy
mood with his MPs. He wasted this opportunity to spread goodwill
through the parliamentary party, an omen of his downfall. 'He
couldn't even be bloody polite to us,' remembered du Cann. 'We
did our best to keep the party behind him, but after the second
election it was absolutely hopeless. We all knew he had to go. The
only question was when.'²

Four days after polling day in the October election, before the
new Parliament had even convened, the 1922 executive met in du
Cann's house in Lord North Street, ostensibly to discuss the
routine business of election of officers. As the chairman expected,
MPs were not interested in such mundane stuff. They wanted an
inquest into the election disaster, and they were 'clear and
unanimous' about one demand: Heath should stand down as
leader as soon as possible. The executive instructed du Cann to
convey this message in person to Heath immediately. Heath was
aware of the clear and present danger. The press was full of
speculation. His candid friend James Prior warned him his only
chance of carrying on as leader lay in submitting himself to an
early election through the 1922. Heath snubbed Prior's advice,
insisting that he would not submit himself to a leadership election
'because he was determined to fight the right wing'. This was
scarcely a time for ideological warfare, but his reaction showed
just how out of touch Heath was with the gathering pace of
events. Du Cann found him similarly unbending. Prior was with
Heath in the leader's room when the chairman of the 1922
reported the mood of senior back-benchers. 'Don't they realise

what they are doing to our party?' rasped Heath peevishly.

Du Cann, not an artless man, had an idea up his sleeve. As presently constituted, the party rules did not admit of a challenge to an existing leader. Heath could not be forced to stand down and resubmit himself for election. The notion of an insensitive leader refusing to quit had never occurred to the party hierarchy when the rules were changed in Alec Douglas-Home's time. Du Cann accordingly suggested that Heath should reconstitute the rules committee, and introduce a new provision for a leadership election to be held 'if required as a matter of routine' at the beginning of each new Parliament. This move would at least buy Heath some time to regroup his forces. Du Cann was too disingenuous by half. He knew that such a reform would be the end of the Heath era, and Heath realised as much. The proposal came from an enemy, but he promised to think it over.

Events accelerated his deliberations. On the morning of the next day, 15 October, the 1922 executive met again, this time at du Cann's City office, the headquarters of Keyser Ullman in Milk Street. They entered singly and unnoticed for secret talks around the boardroom table and endorsed du Cann's crafty initiative, adding the rider in a letter to Heath that he should step down. As a member of the executive, Neave was privy to all these machinations. He had, as yet, no settled view as to who should succeed Heath, only a fixed determination that he should go. There was no obvious heir apparent and the list of possibles looked like the entry for the Grand National in an optimistic year. No-hopers like Christopher Soames rubbed flanks with favourites such as Willie Whitelaw and Keith Joseph. Margaret Thatcher was not highly fancied, indeed she had ruled herself out of the race the day after the election, telling the London *Evening News*, 'You can cross my name off the list. I just don't think I am right for it.' *The Economist* noted drily that she was 'a lady Joseph, but without the intellectual drive and with a more restricted suburban appeal'.

Neave's political instincts were divided. He saw some merit in

Edward du Cann, who had wide ministerial experience at the Treasury and the Board of Trade, leading the party, but he was also attracted to Keith Joseph, the Tories' new-found ideological guru. In the view of Joseph's biographer Morrison Halcrow, the two were 'not really on the same wavelength. Joseph was a man who was at home in an atmosphere of privacy, not secrecy.'[3] Halcrow sourced the mystery and secrecy behind Neave's 'engaging' personality to his wartime exploits, which called for ingenuity, boldness and circumspection, qualities of inestimable value in the coming campaign.

After the shambles of Heath's first (and only) administration, Joseph, a cerebral Jewish millionaire Fellow of All Souls, Oxford, and a successful businessman in the family construction firm, Bovis, set out to take the Tories on a different path, towards the free market and monetarism. He had, by his own account, become 'converted to Conservatism' in April 1974. According to John Ranelagh, a member of the Conservative Research Department in the late 1970s, Neave was present at a post-mortem on the February election held in Heath's rooms at the Commons during the summer of 1974.[4] He shared Joseph's views on the free market, and therefore went along with his condemnation of the Heathite philosophy of pragmatism and hostility to 'right-wing', anti-welfare, anti-union nostrums. Joseph went on to found the Centre for Policy Studies, a right-wing think tank and the intellectual engine of what was to become known as Thatcherism. The CPS found no difficulty in attracting funds, some from the hard-liner James Goldsmith, the chairman of Cavenham Foods. Joseph was already testing the water for a bid to unseat Heath in the days before the election was called. In a speech in Preston on 5 September entitled 'Inflation is caused by Governments', he excoriated the post-war political consensus and argued the case for monetarism. It was a coded attack on Heath and all he stood for.

Neave's initial choice as leader was Edward du Cann, an option that the chairman of the 1922 found both flattering and awkward.

'I was extremely embarrassed to find my name being mentioned,' he claimed later.[5] Neave was part of a group under Nigel Fisher, the moderate Tory, four of whom signed a letter to du Cann urging him to stand. They maintained they could get a hundred signatures. Du Cann, whose City profile with Lonrho and Keyser Ullman was, to say the least, controversial, said: 'It was obvious to me this was not a sensible thing to do in my personal circumstances. If I had stood against Ted Heath and beaten him easily, I would have been open to the charge that I had been fixing the rules to suit myself.'[6]

If not the king, then the kingmaker. As they left du Cann's office, the 1922 executive plotting their party leader's downfall ran a gauntlet of photographers and reporters. Someone in the Heath camp (believed to be Sarah Morrison, wife of Charles Morrison MP) had learned of the meeting, and talked about it. A Conservative Central Office press aide, identified by du Cann as Maurice Trowbridge, tipped off the press. The plot was now out in the open and the schemers were promptly dubbed the 'Milk Street Mafia'. Heath's contacts in the media rubbished the conspiracy, a move that proved counter-productive. When Parliament assembled later that month, feeling against Heath was running high in the parliamentary party. A crowded meeting of the 1922 Committee on 30 October gave vent to those passions, and increased the pressure on Heath to accept the du Cann plan for a fresh look at the leadership rules. Two weeks later, on 14 November, Heath gave way and announced the formation of a committee chaired by Sir Alec Douglas-Home to review the election procedure. He had been compelled to go ahead with the stratagem designed to bring him down.

Neave swiftly accepted the general, and du Cann's own, view that the chairman of the 1922 was not an appropriate candidate. According to Ranelagh, 'within days of the General Election' Neave asked Joseph to stand against Heath, and Joseph considered doing so, writing to Ian Gow MP on 18 October that, 'If Ted does decide to resign, I shall certainly allow my name to go forward.'

Unfortunately, Joseph felt that Shadow Cabinet loyalty required him to inform Heath of Neave's approach. This move made Neave uneasy. 'He said to his friends that when Heath learned of the extent of the operation to find a replacement leader, "He'll kill us! He'll kill us!" '⁷ Nothing better illustrates Neave's instinct for working in the shadows.

But the day after his letter, 19 October, Joseph committed a spectacular *auto de fe* on his political ambitions in a speech in Edgbaston, Birmingham. In it, he suggested that people in socio-economic classes four and five should not have children, on the grounds that they were least fitted to bring children into the world, were of low intelligence and low educational attainment. 'The balance of our population, our human stock, is threatened,' he warned. 'These mothers, under twenties in many cases, single parents from classes four and five, are now producing a third of all live births.' His remedy was greater birth control. The speech brought predictable headlines of the 'Sir Keith In "Stop Babies" Sensation' variety, and cast him in the role of a heartless propounder of eugenics. It was, by his own admission, 'jolly clumsy' for a prospective leader of a great political party. The reception given to his speech reinforced Joseph's natural self-doubts. On 21 November, he withdrew from the contest. Later, he admitted: 'I was flattered by the idea and was willing to be swept along. But I was a joke, a useful joke.'

Deprived of their standard bearer before the flag could even be raised, Neave and his colleagues had to cast around for another candidate. It was only at this stage that the name of Margaret Thatcher began to emerge seriously. Joseph called on Thatcher in her office at Westminster on the day of his decision to quit the race. 'Well, if you won't stand, I will,' she declared and immediately went to Heath's office to tell him. Heath listened to her two-minute statement in his usual undiplomatic manner. He is said to have told her brusquely 'You'll lose', and carried on with his paperwork. She may not have appeared a formid-able rival. Her only experience of Cabinet office was in the

Education Department, where she was principally remembered for abolishing free school milk: 'Margaret Thatcher, Milk Snatcher!' was the slogan of the left. In his Shadow Cabinet reshuffle the week before, Heath had appointed her deputy to Robert Carr, the Shadow Chancellor, giving her an opportunity to shine on the Treasury benches which she was to exploit to the full. But she had no organisation behind her in the parliamentary party, and she also faced the additional hurdle that no woman had ever scaled the topmost heights of the Conservative Party. That might work to her advantage, however. Du Cann recalled that she was 'strikingly attractive, obviously intelligent, a goer'. He invited Thatcher and her husband Denis round to his house in Westminster. 'They sat on a sofa together, rather like a butler and housekeeper seeking employment,' he recollected, while concluding that she would be the best candidate.

Heath, however, was still regarded as the front-runner, both in the party and the media. A poll of constituency party chairmen found a majority in his favour, and another showed 54 per cent of Tory voters wanted him to stay. However, Heath's backers had underestimated Airey Neave. With the benefit of hindsight, politicians and historians alike have identified his entry into the fray as the turning point in the fortunes of the Conservative Party. 'Airey wanted to be rid of Heath,' said Ian Gow, 'and Airey would use whatever was the best weapon that he thought was available.'[8] Gow, newly elected in 1974 as MP for Eastbourne, was later to become a close political ally of Neave.

Neave's next step was to approach Thatcher and offer to be her campaign manager. It was an act of courage rather than calculation. The omens were not promising. Heath had enlisted John Peyton, the canny strategist, and Peter Walker came back on board as his campaign manager. 'But,' recollected James Prior ruefully, 'we reckoned without the persistence and almost obsessive scheming of Airey Neave.' Someone who had been determined enough to escape from Colditz was unlikely to be put off his objective by losing a couple of candidates. Prior, who was to offer himself as a candidate, thought that Thatcher, while ambitious, really did not believe that her time had yet come. He saw the campaign at close quarters, as his office in the Commons was directly opposite Thatcher's, which became Neave's headquarters. 'There was a constant flow of MPs to see them, and I began to realise that these were drawn from a wide cross-section of the party,' he recorded. 'Airey Neave's exercise was carried out by a combination of promises and flattery, and was brilliantly master-minded.'[9] There was more to it than that. Neave brought to the campaign a secret agent's understanding of psychological operations: disinformation, manipulation and misrepresentation. He was far from being the only ex-MI6 member in the Tory ranks. His former comrade-in-arms Hugh Fraser had joined him in the House, and other Tory members with an intelligence background included Sir Stephen Hastings, Julian Amery, Maurice Macmillan, Harry Kirby and Cranley Onslow. But Neave was a uniquely 'natural spy'. In the words of one former MP: 'He had a lot of intelligence even the whips didn't discover. He never imparted a piece of bum information. His power lay there.'[10] Neave's information network was unsurpassed. 'Airey, with his efficient intelligence service, knew better than anyone precisely what the score was,' observed Halcrow. He was better informed than the whips, who were constrained by loyalty to the leader.

Neave next approached Sir William Shelton, MP for Streatham and longstanding admirer of Thatcher, with an offer to 'bring over his troops' if they could come to an agreement on who was running the show. 'I'm older than you are, so I'm number one, and you're number two,' Neave insisted. The pair had lunch and Shelton recalled: 'Ted didn't ever believe a woman could challenge him for the leadership. He felt very safe.'[11] As the leadership campaign got under way, the IRA's bombing campaign in England dominated the front pages. The Birmingham pub bombs, which killed nineteen and injured 182, exploded on the day Thatcher disclosed her intention to challenge Heath. Six days later, the Home Secretary Roy Jenkins outlawed the IRA and rushed through the Prevention of Terrorism Bill. It was a sombre backdrop to proceedings, but few could have imagined that republican violence would eventually get much closer to home.

The Tories gave their full support to getting this legislation through, before turning to their own political crisis. The Home Committee finally reported in the week before Christmas 1974. It proposed radical reforms, beginning with a requirement that when in Opposition the party leader should be subject to re-election at the start of every parliamentary year. Potential challengers would need only two nominations. This was the answer to Heath's critics who said the leadership was 'a leasehold, not a freehold'. New methods of consulting the party in the country were also proposed, though the franchise would still be restricted to MPs. More significantly, Home proposed a three-ballot process. To win in the first ballot, a candidate would have to secure an absolute majority plus a 15 per cent margin of all those eligible to vote. This was a critical raising of the fence from the rules promulgated in 1965, which required only an absolute majority plus 15 per cent of those voting. Heath would not only have to secure 139 votes from the electorate of 278, he would have to garner forty-two votes more than his nearest rival. Senior Tories not involved in the reform committee immediately realised that the Home reform could cripple Heath in the first ballot. It signalled that a candidate could be denied victory by large-scale abstentions, and increased the odds on a second or third ballot. And if no one won in the first round, other candidates could enter the race in a ballot held a week later, a provision promptly dubbed the 'Cowards' Charter', because it enabled a vacillating would-be leader to wait until Heath was mortally wounded before entering the fray. If the contest went to a third ballot, it would be decided by a single transferable vote. The new rules made it much harder for Heath to sustain his position and the Thatcher camp determined to exploit them to the hilt.

In December Neave held a party for Thatcher in his flat in Westminster Gardens, inviting new MPs to meet her. He was not a natural schmoozer, but he could stage a discreet cocktail party as well as the next politician, if not better. Thatcher was still far from being the preferred candidate, but her readiness to take on Heath where others had wavered (including Willie Whitelaw, also approached by Neave at one stage) gradually began to impress back-benchers, particularly the 'anybody but Ted' brigade. It was a tense period in public life. On Sunday 22 December, the Provisionals returned to the attack, this time aimed at Heath's home in Wilton Street. A bomb, thrown from a passing car, exploded on the first-floor balcony of a room where he often worked. It caused serious damage but Heath was not in the house. At the time of the outrage, he was driving home over Vauxhall Bridge after conducting a carol concert in Broadstairs. He did not allow the terrorist attack to prevent a planned visit to Ulster the next day, when he reaffirmed his belief that a majority of people in Northern Ireland wanted power-sharing.

Margaret and Denis Thatcher spent that Christmas with William Deedes, ex-Tory minister and influential editor of the *Daily Telegraph*, sometimes known as the house journal of the Conservative Party, at his country home in Lamberhurst, Kent. Over the New Year, she wrote to Neave, inviting him and Diana to lunch at the family home in Flood Street, Chelsea. The lunch took place on 9 January and confirmed Neave's role as campaign manager. Her initial choice, the well-meaning but ineffectual MP Fergus Montgomery, was about to embark on an extended tour of apartheid South Africa, and would miss the first ballot. Her future was in Neave's hands. Five days later, Nigel Fisher told Neave that du Cann would definitely not be a candidate. Fisher also relinquished his role to Neave. The next day, 15 January, the 'du Cann group' held a meeting in Committee Room J in the Commons, chaired by Neave. He proposed that all twenty-five MPs present should turn themselves over to Thatcher en bloc. Fifteen immediately pledged themselves. Neave continued to entertain MPs over a glass of claret, often in the Westminster room of Robin Cooke, MP for Bristol West, when Thatcher would outline her general attitude to Tory policy. On Neave's advice, she avoided sharp definition but encouraged MPs to speak up on issues where they thought Heath was taking the party in the wrong direction. She was studiously ambivalent on Europe, which garnered an appreciable measure of support from MPs who were either anti-EEC in principle or felt that the party leader was too much of a Euro-enthusiast. She played down her pro-hanging, anti-U-turn policies, sticking to the theme of a 'listening leadership'. Neave's strategy has been described as 'a skilful ruse' to present Thatcher as something she essentially was not, but it worked. MPs became more comfortable with the idea of voting for a woman who could oust Heath.

The Home reforms were finally approved by the 1922 Committee on 16 January, and two days later Thatcher spoke in her Finchley constituency, explaining her decision to stand. The following day, Sunday 19 January, Neave, Shelton, Thatcher and Joseph met at Flood Street for the first of a series of weekly conferences. This 'gang of four' laid out the strategy. It would consist of a discreet but all-out assault on the parliamentary party. Every MP would be contacted and spoken to. There were no no-go areas. Neave's key contribution was his psy-ops style. Basically, he lied about the support building up for Thatcher in order to panic hesitant MPs into backing her. He would 'do the rounds' of Westminster, relaying black propaganda that Margaret was doing well, but nowhere near well enough to guarantee that Heath would fall, and that a second ballot would come about. His own canvass returns demonstrated that this was not true, but the device worked. Heath's biographer also speaks of 'Neave's role as the cunning master of undercover operations'.[12]

Events played into Thatcher's hands in her first week of campaigning. On 21 January, she addressed a lunch of the Parliamentary Press Gallery, and made an impressive showing with a set-piece speech on her political credo, followed up by questions and answers. Neave's canvass showed her pulling ahead, with sixty-nine committed votes to forty-three for Heath. The next day, she shone in the Commons chamber. In a debate on the Finance Bill, Chancellor Denis Healey savaged Thatcher as 'La Pasionaria of Privilege', and sat down thinking he had demolished her. It was a neat thrust, comparing her to the Communist heroine of the Spanish Civil War, and it cheered the government benches. But, winding up for the Opposition, Thatcher cut the old bully to pieces. She had hoped to have said he had done himself less than justice. On the contrary, he had done himself ample justice. 'Some Chancellors are micro-economic. Some Chancellors are fiscal. This one is just plain cheap.' This contemptuous sally delighted her own side and dismayed the government benches. Few, if any, Tory grandees had been able to take Healey down a peg or two, yet she had achieved it. The brilliance of her performance swiftly reflected in Neave's canvass returns. Thatcher was now leading by ninety-five to sixty-six. The following morning, BBC Radio 4's *Today* programme reported that Thatcher was in the lead. This was the last thing Neave wanted. His strategy was based on underplaying her promises of support to bring over the waverers.

However, a new contender emerged from the wings, or at any rate from the right wing: Hugh Fraser, MP for Stafford and Stone. Fraser, an aristocratic Scot, stood on a platform of 'traditional Tory values' and could have posed problems by taking right-wing votes from Thatcher. However, his candidature was seen as dotty rather than dangerous. Neave's headcount showed he had the support of only nine MPs. When nominations for the first ballot closed on 30 January, Heath, Thatcher and Fraser were the only candidates. Polling day was set for 4 February.

In a speech in Finchley on 31 January, Thatcher reaffirmed her political beliefs: concern for individual freedom; opposition to excessive state power; reward for the thrifty and hard-working, and the right to pass on those gains to their children; diversity of choice and defence of private property against the socialist state; and the right of a man to work without oppression by either employer or trade union boss. It was a litany to which Neave could say 'amen'. He had propounded it from the hustings for a quarter of a century. They thought alike. His own view of her later found its way into a collection of tributes put together by Tricia Murray, barrister wife of the broadcaster Pete Murray. Neave rated Thatcher as the most gifted politician in the Conservative Party and perhaps the most gifted politician for twenty-five years. 'She's the first real idealist politician for a long time,' he argued. 'Macmillan might have been the last in the Conservative Party – there may have been others on the other side of the House but Margaret is a philosopher as well as a politician.' He praised her approachability, compassion, patience, balance and her clear understanding of the opinions of men and women in the street. Thatcher was serious by nature and a great patriot, very concerned about the future of her country. But there was also a humorous side of her 'and off duty she can be very amusing and has the ability to laugh at herself'. Asked to single out one predominant characteristic, he replied, 'I would choose her great personal courage. It may be that she has many frightening experiences to come but the thing she will never lack is courage. That is her great quality. She is outspoken by nature and is essentially a fighter and nobody should be surprised if she tells the country a few home truths.'[13] That was the leader he was confident of surreptitiously giving the country. As she left Westminster to speak in Finchley, Neave gave her the latest canvass: she had forged even further ahead, with 120 promised votes, against eighty-four for Heath and Fraser still stuck on nine.

Heath was as good as finished but Neave and Shelton were not satisfied with crushing him in the first ballot. A second ballot would bring in other big-hitters – Willie Whitelaw, James Prior and Geoffrey Howe – who were initially backing Heath but ready to take advantage of the 'Cowards' Charter' and declare themselves as rightful heirs. If she was to beat them, Thatcher had to establish an unassailable lead in the first ballot, so that the other heavyweights would look like challengers to her. Here, Heath's campaign team came unwittingly to her aid. In conversations with the leader's head-counters, a number of MPs had pledged

themselves to support the leader while privately agreeing with
Neave to support Thatcher. Their actions inflated the Heath
camp's figures of support, in turn leading to overconfidence and
complacency. It was put about that Heath was well ahead and
would win easily in the first ballot. This smugness had the
unintended effect of persuading a considerable number of MPs
who did not like Thatcher but who calculated that a vote for her
would oust Heath and give them a chance to elect Whitelaw (or
another Heathite figure) to vote for her. 'In this way,' observed
John Campbell 'Heath's managers played into Neave's hands.'[14]

Neave began to step up his insidious campaign of disinformation, continuing to make his discreet rounds of the
Commons with the seductive message that Thatcher was doing
well, but not well enough to defeat Heath. Throughout the
campaign, he never disclosed his figures, but he used those of the
other side to support his case that conflicting canvass returns
made it imperative for all anti-Heath votes to be channelled in
support of Thatcher. Abstention would not suffice. This was far
from the truth. Not only was she well ahead, but the new
leadership rules put an extra premium on abstentions. Nonetheless, in the closing stages of the week, Heath staged a remarkable
rally. Buoyed by the support of Lord Home, an immensely popular
figure in the party, by a large majority in a write-in poll of Tory
peers, by a *Daily Express* poll that gave him the backing of 70 per
cent of Conservative voters and a strongly supportive canvass of
the Conservative National Union, on the eve of the election
Heath pulled back to level with Thatcher on 122 votes each, with
Fraser still trailing with nine. A further twenty-three said they
intended to abstain, or would not disclose their intentions. Neave
and Shelton took stock and agreed not to tell Thatcher how finely
things were balanced until the morning of the poll. Instead, Neave
engaged in a last-minute exercise of black propaganda. He went
on a final tour of the Commons, looking a worried man and
telling MPs that Thatcher could be sure of only seventy votes.
This blatant fib was designed to jolt the irresolute into action.

The true figure was 120 and he whispered to one Labour MP, 'I'd put your money on the filly, Tam, if I were you.' It was a high-risk strategy, as his confidant Patrick Cosgrave later recalled. 'Since pessimism is the most dangerous mood of all to project in a political struggle, this was Neave's most daring move so far,' he said. 'It was also his most successful.'[15] John Campbell further calculated: 'Neave's stratagem may have conned as many as forty Tory MPs into voting for a result they did not want.'[16] Critically, a group of around thirty centre-left MPs led by Sir John Rodgers and Sir Paul Bryan, who had intended to abstain, swung behind Thatcher at the eleventh hour so that Heath would not get the extra 15 per cent margin to stay in power. Another likely victim of Neave's ploy was no other than Michael Heseltine. Norman Tebbit has asserted that he and John Nott persuaded Heseltine to vote for Thatcher in order to boost the chances of his preferred candidate, Willie Whitelaw, in a second ballot. Heseltine, who became Thatcher's bitterest enemy, has always refused to admit for whom he voted, a signal in itself that he did not support Heath.

With the exception of the *Daily Mail*, the newspapers fell for Neave's deception. As MPs went to vote on the morning of 4 February, the London *Evening Standard* headline read: 'Ted Forges Ahead.' Most of the press, recorded Campbell, 'misled both by the overconfidence of the Heath camp on the one hand and Airey Neave's deliberate underplaying of the challenger's support on the other, still expected him to win.'[17] Even on the most pessimistic of assessments, Thatcher was in with a chance. Her adroit performance and Neave's machinations had ensured that Heath would be denied victory in the first round. Polling took place in Committee Room 14 at the Commons. Peter Walker had erroneously advised Heath that he would secure between 138 and 144 votes. One hundred and thirty-nine would be enough. Nicholas Fairbairn, the flamboyant MP for Kinross and West Perthshire, was the first to vote, emerging to trumpet his support for Thatcher. As the 3.30 p.m. deadline for voting neared,

Thatcher left the committee stage debate on the Finance Bill and went to Neave's room to await the outcome. Shelton attended the count but his face gave nothing away as he appeared in the noisy committee room corridor where MPs were waiting for the result. He told Neave the figures: Thatcher 130. Heath 119. Fraser 16. There were six abstentions and five spoilt papers. Neave went to his room and told her (as Thatcher herself later recollected, 'softly, but with a twinkle in his eye': 'It's good news. You're ahead in the poll. There will be a second ballot. You got 130 votes.' She was overjoyed. It was time for the champagne party, followed by a council of war in Neave's flat that evening. The defeated leader, closeted with his campaign managers and Lord Aldington, a close friend, prepared a resignation statement. 'So, we got it all wrong,' said Heath. Robert Carr, the former Employment Secretary with no ambitions to lead his party, took over as a caretaker, and the second ballot was fixed for 11 February.

Quite so, as the commentators observed. It was not over yet, however. Willie Whitelaw, a more acceptable Heathite figure, now entered the lists, as did Geoffrey Howe, the urbane former Solicitor General and Prices and Incomes Secretary in Heath's government, James Prior and John Peyton, ex-Transport Minister and Shadow Leader of the House. Neave's mixed bag of supporters, greatly enlarged by Thatcher's remarkable achievement, was prey to fresh fears: Whitelaw was hugely respected in the party and could genuinely offer himself as the unifying candidate, while Howe's right-wing views on economic affairs might take votes from Thatcher's natural constituency. Her support could haemorrhage away to both of them. Prior and Peyton were not regarded as a serious threat: in Prior's case, not even by the candidate himself. Neave calculated that as many as forty MPs had voted for Thatcher solely to ensure a second round in which they would switch to a more acceptable contender. Yet his initial canvass was encouraging. Thatcher had ninety-nine votes, against forty-one for Whitelaw with the others trailing far behind. By 6 February, the closing date for nominations, her headcount had gone up by seven, and Whitelaw's by five. The trend was good. Thatcher was now 'the man to beat'. Thanks in substantial measure to Neave's scheming in the first round, she was transformed from stalking horse to front-runner.

One issue worried Neave: Europe. Thatcher was struggling to wax even lukewarm about the EEC, British membership of which was the subject of a national referendum called by Harold Wilson. It was big news, and Neave, a pro-European himself, encouraged her to make a clear statement of policy that would reassure like-minded MPs who had backed Heath in the first ballot. She did so, paying tribute to Heath's pioneering sagacity in taking the UK into the EEC, and promising to pick up the torch he had laid down. 'The commitment to European partnership is one which I fully share,' she maintained. Neave further encouraged her to behave as if she was the leader in waiting, and Thatcher's rousing performance at the weekend conference of the Young Con-servatives won her headlines, while Whitelaw made a fool of himself by putting on a pinafore and washing dishes for the photographers. The distinction was clear. Maggie was 'the real man'. In the second round, Neave's dirty tricks proved un-necessary. By the eve of poll, his canvass now showed Thatcher on 137 – only two short of outright victory – and Whitelaw on seventy-eight. Howe had nineteen, Prior eleven and Peyton nine. Nine had not made up their minds, but could opt for her. Thirteen others would not disclose their intentions. It was all over bar the tears, of which there were many. On polling day, Thatcher again broke off from her work on the Finance Bill to await the result in Neave's room. He came in shortly after four o'clock to tell her: 'It's all right. You are now Leader of the Opposition.' His arithmetic had again been uncannily accurate. Thatcher took 146 votes, to Whitelaw's seventy-nine. Howe and Prior both secured seventeen votes, while Peyton got eleven. Two MPs either abstained or spoilt their papers. It was a remarkable achievement, substantially traceable to Airey Neave's skill, determination and black arts. The new leader staged a press conference in the Grand

Committee Room of historic Westminster Hall. 'To me it is like a dream that the next name in the lists after Harold Macmillan, Sir Alec Douglas-Home, Edward Heath is Margaret Thatcher. Each has brought his own style of leadership and stamp of greatness to his task. I shall take on the work with humility and dedication.'

Having played such a key role in Thatcher's victory, Neave could have had virtually any job in her Shadow Cabinet for the asking. To the surprise of many, he chose Northern Ireland, traditionally a graveyard for British politicians. He had not hitherto shown any public interest in the province, where an undeclared civil war had been raging for a decade, claiming hundreds of lives. At the age of fifty-nine, and not in the most robust of health, it was a striking choice. But Thatcher did not hesitate. 'His intelligence contacts, proven physical courage and shrewdness amply qualified him for this testing and largely thankless task,' she recorded later.[18] It is intriguing that she should single out, first and foremost, his intelligence contacts. Her remarks confirm that Neave was still in regular communication with the secret state. Thatcher also made him head of her private office, thus reinforcing his influence. He was now the gatekeeper to the leader, as well as the man to shape Conservative policy on Ulster. The taste of success was all the sweeter for the long years spent in the wilderness.

15

In the Shadows

Few politicians could more appropriately have been described as a 'shadow'. In parallel with his public life as an MP, Neave operated in the shadows for almost forty years. Sometimes his intelligence expertise came close to the surface, as in his role as midwife to Margaret Thatcher's ambitions, but there was a darker side to his activities. Despite his reputation as a vaguely progressive Conservative, Neave was now moving in very deep shadows on the hard right of British – and Irish – politics.

His emergence as a power broker in the Tory Party coincided with the appearance of a number of groups dedicated to 'saving' the nation from a perceived threat of breakdown of civil society, caused either by strikes or Communist subversion. These self-appointed groups, drawn from the ranks of former intelligence officers, the City, ex-army officers and the fanciful fringe of politics, had links with the security services. At their apogee, they organised a smear campaign to bring down Harold Wilson, who (absurdly) was believed to be a Communist, or to have Communist sympathies. As was subsequently disclosed by ex-MI5 officer Peter Wright in *Spycatcher*, a group of 'dissident' MI5 officers plotted the downfall of Wilson and his government from 1974 onwards. Other groups, often giving themselves quasi-military names like GB 75 and Civil Assistance, concentrated on the trade unions and the Labour left, particularly Tony Benn, who was a Cabinet minister in Wilson's government.

An investigation in 1987 by the respected anti-Fascist magazine

Searchlight found that the presence of Neave and an ally, George Kennedy Young, former deputy director of MI6, ran 'like a silken thread' through the various endeavours to discredit Labour, promote Thatcher and 'if necessary, organise unorthodox means of achieving their political goals'. *Searchlight*'s investigators asked whether 'a quiet coup' had taken place in Britain during the middle 1970s. In late 1974, the far right around the Conservative Party was 'deeply depressed and adrift'. Labour had won two elections, trade union influence in government was at an unprecedented level, and the alternative, a Tory government headed by Heath, promised 'only further betrayal' at the hands of a man who had backed down on immigration (the Ugandan Asians), sold out on sovereignty (joining the EEC) and caved in to the unions (the U-turn over Upper Clyde shipbuilders and his double defeat at the hands of the miners). Labour had to be discredited and Heath dumped. The unions had to be tackled, and contingencies set in train in case the unthinkable – a Labour victory over a new right-led Tory Party at the next election – happened.

Organisations and cabals were set up to deal with each of these problems, the *Searchlight* investigation established. These could be seen as unconnected efforts of right-wingers eager to save their country from the depredations of the left, but so many of the projects seemed to be linked to people who had been involved with MI5 or MI6 that a conspiracy theory did not seem to be far-fetched.

If it does strain credibility, however, it is worth considering the evidence. Neave had actually met Peter Wright before these events. Wright's original motive was to quiz Neave about one of his fellow Colditz inmates, Michael Burn, a journalist whose name had come to light as a possible contact of Soviet spy Anthony Blunt. Wright hoped to learn that Burn had shown Communist sympathies in Colditz but he drew a blank. However, 'Neave gave me a lot of valuable information on inmates who were either traitors or potential ones,' he later recorded.[1] The fact that Neave felt happy about informing on his fellow inmates some thirty years after their incarceration is unpalatable but a significant pointer to his real agenda.

Neave was closely connected with a number of the far right groups about whose existence much more is known now than at the time they were operating. After the Burn episode, Wright approached Neave again 'as one of the "suspect plotters" against Wilson'. On this occasion, he related that: 'The interview with Neave was whether he knew of any secret armies or proposed ones in the UK. He came out of the interview well, showing himself loyal to the Crown and to British democracy.' Astonishingly, Wright concluded that Neave 'was not a conspiratorial type of man'.[2]

Not by his own paranoid standards perhaps, but of course Neave was a natural plotter, as a glance at his history shows. Less well known is his role in setting up 'stay-behind' networks on Continental Europe, whose role was to gather intelligence after the war resistance in the event of a Soviet invasion.

Stephen Dorril observes: 'European accounts of the stay-behind networks are fairly consistent in their claims that, before hostilities had ceased, networks were already tentatively being planned. Central to these activities were personnel from SOE and in particular from IS9. It is interesting to note the postings of senior IS9 officers and the setting up of "fronts" as the war wound down. These fronts acted as intelligence gathering and recruitment centres and provided cover for MI9 and MI6 officers. It has been suggested that it is through these centres that the prototype stay-behind nets were recruited.'

Ken Livingstone, who made a particular study of Neave and the Irish problem, insists that 'Neave . . . kept his own friendships and contacts with the intelligence community throughout the post-war period.'[3] Who's Who records that Neave was Officer Commanding Intelligence School 9 (TA) from 1949 to 1951. Thereafter, he was in demand as a lecturer, particularly on escape and evasion, to the armed services including (on the admission of his daughter Marigold) the SAS. IS9 continued to operate through the Korean War before being transformed into the Joint Research Prisoner of War Intelligence Organisation (TA) and then the more anonymous Joint Reserve Reconnaissance Unit (TA). Its functions were taken over by the SAS in 1959. The decision was welcomed by Neave whose admiration for the regiment was 'unbounded'. According to the authors of *Smear! Wilson and the Secret State*, the Birmingham-based SAS unit had squadrons in the more important industrial centres and could provide a means of monitoring social unrest.[4] Neave also kept up his contacts in the security services, and it was only natural that when men like Colonel David Stirling, another fellow inmate at Colditz and founder of the SAS with whom he was still very friendly, began to harbour fears of a social collapse and a 'Communist takeover', they would turn to Neave for political support.

Within months of Thatcher's takeover of the Conservative leadership, and against a backdrop of a Labour government barely able to govern on a majority of three, the siren voices of the far right began to make themselves discreetly heard again. Retired General Walter Walker, formerly Commander-in-Chief of NATO's Northern Command, whose private quasi-army had a fantasy membership of 100,000, reported a conversation with Nicholas Ridley MP, later a Thatcher Cabinet minister. Ridley was (perhaps appropriately) talking in riddles, he complained: 'It seemed to me that what he was trying to convey, but hadn't the guts to say so openly, was that the only hope for the country would be a military coup.'[5] Talk of military action to forestall a Communist takeover filled the air. In 1974, a serving army officer wrote in *Monday World*, the journal of the Monday Club, of which Neave was a member, that some soldiers believed they would be 'called upon to act in England'. David Stirling said in July that year: 'Moving into installations owned by the government is a very delicate business, and that is one reason for the secrecy surrounding those people who have already made positive plans.'[6]

George Kennedy Young, author of the 'spies as leaders of

society' memorandum, joined in the fray. He invited General Walker to attend an informal reception on 30 April 1975 of a 'right-wing group' numbering twenty to thirty Tory MPs. The reception was given by Sir Frederic Bennett, Tory MP for Torbay 'along with Airey Neave, [a member] of Geoffrey Stewart Smith's Foreign Affairs Research Institute'.[7] It was probably through this group that in late 1974 or early 1975 Young and others, with the backing of Airey Neave, rapidly organised a network throughout the constituencies to support Margaret Thatcher. This network, called Tory Action, was formed when it became clear that Edward Heath would be challenged for the leadership.[8] According to *Searchlight*, Neave was in fact one of the original inspirations behind Tory Action, which sought not solely to oust Heath but to replace him with a leader and policies much further to the right.

Seditious talk of private armies and 'anti-chaos organisations' continued throughout the summer of 1975, while Neave worked his way into his new post as Shadow Northern Ireland Secretary. He appointed as his deputy John Biggs-Davidson, a right-wing Tory who was also a member of the Foreign Affairs Research Institute. The third member of the team, Sir William van Straubenzee, a former Northern Ireland minister, but no Thatcherite, completed the team. Writing in the *Irish Times*, Renagh Holohan explained that Neave brought 'considerable military and intelligence experience' to the task but his views on Ulster were a mystery. His appointment was seen by many as a concession to the right, she added.[9] In an interview with Desmond McCartan of the *Belfast Telegraph*, the province's leading newspaper, Neave denied that he represented a switch to the right. He signalled that the bipartisan approach on Ulster policy at Westminster would continue, but there would be occasions on which the Tories would differ. 'I also believe that the union should be maintained,' he asserted. Ulster Unionists welcomed the appointment of such a distinguished soldier and politician, while the SDLP preferred to keep an open mind. A spokesman from the Republican Clubs invited him to visit the Long Kesh internment centre 'and explain to the British people how it differed, not from Colditz but from Dachau and Buchenwald'.[10] Gerry Fitt, SDLP MP for West Belfast, observed that Neave's arrival 'would please the generals. It might persuade some that there could be a military solution, and such an attitude is doomed to failure.' Neave would find it more difficult to get out of Ulster than Colditz, Fitt joked. The pair, who were to become friends, exchanged banter in the television studios, with Neave pooh-poohing the concept of him as a walrus-moustachioed brigadier hell bent on a military solution. 'I am not particularly right wing,' he declared. On 20 February, he met Brian Faulkner, former leader of the Ulster Unionists, who was pleased that someone so close to Mrs Thatcher had been given the Northern Ireland portfolio. Early in March, he and Thatcher had talks in London with Garret FitzGerald, the Irish Foreign Minister. To the alarm of the Irish, Neave suggested that he might call for the abolition of incident centres set up in republican areas to monitor the current IRA ceasefire, but quickly dropped the idea when told that it might do more harm than good.

Neave admitted he was largely ignorant of the issues and had a lot of reading to do. In one interview, he argued in favour of making power-sharing work, but after meeting the Unionists he said: 'Power-sharing, by definition, means different things to different people.' Less than a year before, hard-line loyalists (with the tacit support of the security services) had brought down Ulster's first power-sharing administration by a political strike that brought the province to a halt. Their industrial action had not been viewed in the same subversive light as that of the coal miners. Labour was then setting up a seventy-eight-member elected Constitutional Convention to determine what form of government would be likely to command most widespread acceptance throughout the community. Neave promised to review Conservative policy on Ulster after the Convention elections, scheduled for 1 May.

In the spring of 1975 he made a number of visits to Northern

Ireland, talking to the Secretary of State Merlyn Rees, police and army chiefs and community leaders, including the Irish Congress of Trade Unions. His comments were guarded but a clear bias towards the Unionists, and hard-line Unionism at that, was becoming evident. Neave opposed the repatriation of IRA bombers Marion and Dolours Price from Durham gaol to Armagh prison, on the grounds that they might escape. He also expressed a conviction that the 'hard core' of internees in Long Kesh (subsequently rechristened the Maze in 1972 although the names remained interchangeable for a while) would never be released. Even the moderate Alliance Party was shocked, pointing out that no civilised country had indefinite internment. At Westminster, he argued for more MPs for Ulster, which would benefit the Unionists, and in a visit to Dublin on 5 May he told the Irish Foreign Minister that power-sharing could not be imposed on people who would not share power. The responsible thing to do was 'work for an accommodation'. When hard-line Unionists made considerable gains in the Convention elections, he pronounced power-sharing as good as dead. The Convention staggered on for another nine months before Merlyn Rees finally signed the death warrant.

Neave's first parliamentary foray came on 14 March, during a debate on Northern Ireland initiated by Merlyn Rees. The Ulster Secretary reported that a ceasefire announced by the Provisional IRA on 10 February was still holding, and there had been no major incidents between the security forces and republican terrorists. But violent feuds between the breakaway Irish Republican Socialist Party and the Official IRA were continuing. Fourteen people had died in inter- and intra-sectarian killing in the previous month, but the government was determined to press ahead with the phased release of internees. Eighty more would go by Easter, and more would follow if there was 'a genuine and sustained cessation of violence'. Rees rejected the notion of a 'ready-made textbook solution' of the kind propounded by some of Neave's dubious friends on the far right. Neave asked four questions, all seeking support for the RUC. Rees welcomed him to his Shadow post. It was not an effusive greeting. The two men never did get on. Garret FitzGerald subsequently noted Rees's 'dismissive attitude' towards Neave, whom he described as knowing nothing about Northern Ireland and showing no ability to learn about it quickly.

Later in the debate Neave asked more questions about the supervision of released internees. If it was not an impressive start to the handling of a highly charged political responsibility, it did set his style. On 26 March, he clashed with the Minister of State Stan Orme on the future of Belfast shipbuilders Harland and Wolff. The ailing company – builders of the *Titanic* – was brought into public ownership, with a measure of worker participation in management. The yard, employing almost 11,000 men (mostly Protestants), was the mainstay of employment in east Belfast and many other businesses depended on it. Neave asked a series of questions but raised no principled objections. A few weeks later, he complained that the release of internees was frustrating the work of the army, especially on the intelligence side. During Northern Ireland Questions on 15 May, he challenged the government's view that violence had genuinely ceased, since fifty people had been assassinated in less than six months.

That month, Neave announced a comprehensive review of Conservative policy on Northern Ireland. One of the options to be considered would be 'full integration' of the province within the United Kingdom, with more MPs at Westminster. Meanwhile, he demanded an end to internee releases, saying that the situation was 'too explosive'. The *Irish Times* exploded in a leading article that described Neave's tenure of the Ulster portfolio as 'undistinguished, ambiguous, ignorant and possibly dangerous' which could break up the bipartisan approach with Labour. 'It would be a mistake to exaggerate the personal importance of Mr Neave. He is, to be blunt, a lightweight whose appointment is owed to past favours for the party leader, Mrs Thatcher.'[11]

As the summer progressed, Neave became more confident with his brief. In June he handled the complex Criminal Jurisdiction Bill, which improved cross-border cooperation against terrorism. On 27 June, in a Commons debate on the Northern Ireland Bill, which made terrorism a specific offence, ended special category (political) status for convicted prisoners and introduced non-jury trials for terrorist offences, he spoke with composure and at length. He was also contemptuous of the IRA and their methods – 'we are talking about gangsterism, not "open and honourable warfare" ' – and supported a new power of detention as a legitimate weapon. Whatever the merits of his arguments, Neave must have realised that in making such statements he was raising his profile in the demonology of the republican movement and making himself a likely candidate for assassination. Moreover, the fragile IRA ceasefire was in the process of breaking down. In the second week of July, the Provisionals bombed the Crown Buildings in Londonderry and claimed responsibility. They also acknowledged that two bombings in April in Belfast were their work, as was the murder of a police constable in Londonderry in May. Neave put down a Private Notice Question, a device rarely granted by the Speaker, which compels the Secretary of State to make a statement to the Commons. Rees refused to halt the release of internees. Four days later, on 14 July, Neave spoke late in the evening on the Third Reading of the Northern Ireland (Emergency Provisions) Bill, which sought a gradual return to civilian policing in the province. Neave strongly objected to the Ulster Secretary's use of the term 'prisoners of war' in the context of IRA violence, however indirectly. He also called for the arrest of 'known terrorists' on criminal charges, such as membership of a proscribed organisation. Three days later, four British soldiers were killed by an IRA bomb at Forkhill, in the bandit country of south Armagh. The Crossmaglen Provisionals claimed responsibility. In the Commons, Neave condemned 'this contemptible ambush' and again demanded the arrest of 'known terrorist leaders'. He was at it again on 24 July, criticising Merlyn Rees's policy of releasing the last 200 internees (Neave invariably referred to them as terrorists) before Christmas.

Undeterred, Neave pressed ahead with his review. Irish newspapers noted that there had not been a major policy statement on Northern Ireland by the Conservatives since Mrs Thatcher had become leader and were scathing about the prospects for this fresh rethink. The *Irish Press* accused him of reverting to a 'pre-Carsonite stance'; John Hume's SDLP accused him of 'appalling ignorance'. In a speech in his constituency on 9 August, Neave made an interim statement, reiterating the Conservative Party's pledge to maintain the unity of the United Kingdom, with Northern Ireland a part of it; that the army should remain in Ulster to support the civil power until normal policing could be restored; and expressing further concern about the release of internees. He also opposed government actions which gave credibility or status to violent organisations or individuals, a reference to the covert contacts with Sinn Fein, the political arm of the IRA, which had first been initiated by Willie Whitelaw in 1972. His hostility to prisoner releases also went unheeded: the last detainees were released within months. Internment had proved a disaster, acting as a recruiting sergeant for the IRA and stepping up the violence.

There was, as yet, no sign of original thinking in Neave's enquiry. If anything, policy was reverting to a traditional pro-Unionist stance. This was the view of *The Times*, which said in a leading article: 'More by what he did not say than by what he said he appeared to move towards a position of simple constitutionalism, of natural alliance with Ulster Unionism.' That was where his party was before it was redirected by the events of 1969–72 and the leadership of Heath and Whitelaw. Neave deliberately left out the Heathite mantra that the exclusion of the Catholic minority must be rectified, that constitutional arrangements must take account of their nationalist aspirations and that no settlement could last which failed to win the support of the Irish people as a whole. The omission was not lost on the Irish people, of all persuasions.

That September, Neave accompanied Thatcher on a visit to the United States. According to an anonymous source close to the Conservative leadership, 'his [Neave's] job was to spread disinformation about the Wilson government in political and commercial circles. The story about Harold Wilson being a KGB agent first surfaced at that time.'[12] The informant was convinced that it was Neave's activities in the USA at that time that Thatcher was so keen to 'cover up'. Thatcher herself regarded the US trip as the most important of her years as Opposition leader, claiming that coverage in the British media 'transformed my political standing'. The informant who highlighted Neave's semi-clandestine role added: 'There was an amazing amount of knocking copy about the horrors of the welfare state and the Wilson government was described as something akin to Ukraine under the iron days of Stalin. This campaign was organised by Airey Neave and ——.'

While above-ground politics slipped further to the right, the secret politicking also gathered pace. Plans for the formation of the National Association for Freedom were laid in the summer of 1975, though it was not formally launched until December of that year. This body sprung from a lunch which took place with Michael Ivens, Director of Aims of Industry, and Lord De L'Isle, former Governor General of Australia. The talks had been organised by Colonel Juan Hobbs, a representative of British United Industrialists which acted as a conduit for business money into the Tory Party and right-wing political projects. Dorril and Ramsay characterise NAFF as a fusion of the anti-subversion tendency, middle protest groups and the right wing of the Tory Party. Chris Tame, who worked for NAFF in its early days, suggested that it was a successor to Ross McWhirter's organisation Self-Help, a second try after the original had been taken over by the racist Lady Birdwood. Ross McWhirter, an early convert to the anti-subversive tendency, was shot dead by the IRA on 27 November 1975 after offering a £50,000 reward for information leading to the arrest and conviction of a terrorist for murder.

NAFF's first director, John Gouriet, later said 'we felt that 1975 and the years that followed were really a watershed in British politics . . . down the slippery slope towards communo-socialism [sic] and a satellite state of the Soviet Union at its worst'. Neave, along with fellow Monday Club members Jill Knight and Rhodes Boyson, joined the Council of NAFF, as did Winston Churchill and Nicholas Ridley, both members of the Shadow Cabinet. Boyson, who blamed 'the virtual collapse of law and order in parts of our society' on the so-called liberal establishment, went on to found (with Margaret Thatcher) the Ross McWhirter Foundation. On 16 December, he attended a memorial service for McWhirter at St Paul's Cathedral. Sitting near him was Airey Neave. The address was given by Lord De L'Isle, progenitor of NAFF.

While it never achieved the grandiose aims set out in its Freedom Charter, NAFF did have an energising impact on the Tory right, particularly in the years of Opposition. In the months that followed its inauguration, the association launched legal actions against strikers, most notably and successfully in a *cause célèbre* dispute at Grunwick, the north London film processing factory. It also pushed the message of 'Marxist subversives' in the Labour Party, and social security 'scroungers', gaining valuable publicity in the press and arguably setting the agenda for Thatcher's war against 'the enemy within' during her first and second terms of office. In the view of Dorril and Ramsay, it would not be too far off the mark to say that Thatcherism 'grew out of a right-wing network with extensive links to the military-intelligence establishment'.[13] Her rise to power was the climax to a long campaign by this network which included a protracted destabilisation campaign against the Labour Party between 1974 and 1976, culminating in a right-wing Tory leader and then a right-wing government. NAFF finally won the blessing of Thatcher herself, who spoke at a fund-raising dinner in January 1977.

Long before then the lineaments of what her government would look like were clearly becoming visible. In mid-March 1976,

Harold Wilson shocked the nation by resigning as Prime Minister. He would be replaced by the Chancellor, James Callaghan, who as Home Secretary in the late sixties had a great deal more knowledge of the Irish problem than Neave, but by then Neave's above-ground political strategy was set in concrete. As detention drew to a close, he excoriated Labour for failing to give leadership in the fight against terrorism, prompting a rare charge from the Northern Ireland Minister of State Stan Orme that Neave was 'playing politics' when he should be upholding the bipartisan approach to Ulster that had underpinned consideration of the crisis from its inception. Rumours were already surfacing early in 1976 that Rees could be moved from the Northern Ireland office, and his departure could be marked by a tougher policy on IRA terror. Special category status for prisoners (which Neave had always opposed) was already on the way out.

On 6 January, Harold Wilson called in Thatcher and Neave for talks on the deteriorating security situation. Neave was in no doubt that the IRA had been 'dead for a long time'. The very next day, ten Protestant workers were shot dead in Kingmills. Wilson ordered in 600 extra troops, 150 of them from the SAS, who went into action in south Armagh. Neave welcomed the move as a signal that 'we mean business' in the campaign.

Even the Shadow Cabinet was critical of Neave's parliamentary and political performance on the crisis. Fellow front-benchers urged him to be more vocal in his criticisms of the government, though the best idea they could come up with was a suggestion that the Irish tricolour should be removed from Crossmaglen town hall. On a visit to south Armagh, he urged a more permanent British army presence. Four months' tour of duty was not enough to acclimatise the men to conditions, he insisted, brushing aside a media row over repeated incursions into the Republic in 'hot pursuit' of IRA suspects during which soldiers threatened to shoot Irish policemen. Neave kept up his ruthless harrying of Rees, accusing him of risking civil war by even discussing the phased withdrawal of the army in the event of a political settlement. The *Daily Mirror* had just become the first mainstream newspaper to ask whether troops should get out of Ulster. Events played into Neave's hands. Abolition of special category status from 1 March was accompanied by a predictable outbreak of violence, in which two people died and eleven were injured. In Belfast, buses were hijacked and set on fire and traffic disrupted. Neave promised Rees strong support, arguing that ending special category status was an essential step 'so that common thugs cannot be glamorised as political martyrs', but on 5 March he accused Rees of creating a political vacuum in the province by dissolving the moribund Constitutional Convention. He also demanded that talks should not take place with the political wings of paramilitary organisations. The papers were full of stories about secret contacts with Sinn Fein, all denied by the government but later proved to be true. Neave was not the only politician playing a clandestine game.

An adjournment debate in the Commons on 25 March opened up the fault lines between Neave and Rees. Neave had recently argued in a speech to the Young Conservatives that everything should take second place to the defeat of the terrorists. He wanted 'far more resolute military action'. With a clear eye on his opposite number, Rees argued that those who sought simplistic solutions to the security problem by 'war' on the terrorists displayed their own limited outlook. He rejected Neave's view that a political vacuum had opened up in Ulster. Neave evaded that issue, preferring to congratulate the SAS on driving the Provos out of south Armagh. An irritated Rees warned that it was 'dangerous to preen ourselves' prematurely. Neave brushed that aside, too, and attacked the government over reports of the talks with Sinn Fein. Stan Orme was compelled to reassure the House, as he did on 25 March, that there would be no negotiation. But there would. The IRA gave Neave their own answer a few days later, killing four British soldiers in Armagh over a thirty-six-hour period and bringing the total of such killings to forty-two in six years. Neave expressed his sorrow and called on ministers to strengthen military intelligence in the area.

He continued tacking towards Unionism, suggesting on a visit to Belfast in late March that Northern Ireland should have more MPs, and promising that a Tory government would seek to get rid of direct rule 'as soon as we could get agreement on the right course'. Generally speaking, he said, the Conservatives favoured the principle of devolved government. In fact, they discreetly proposed to Irish ministers an 'administrative council' for Northern Ireland. Given the disposition of the parties in the province, this hinted at a solution favourable to the Unionists. In Belfast on 9 April Rees once again accused Neave of never having understood the policy of ending internment. He was also 'fantastically interested' in his job and did not seek a move. However, on 5 April James Callaghan took over from Wilson and a switch in ministers – if not policy – was inevitable. Rees soldiered on, fending off fire from Neave on 'inadvertent' cross-border incursions into the Republic by the SAS. A weekend of killings in mid-May, which left five policemen and eight civilians dead with more than fifty injured, brought another Private Notice Question from Neave demanding 'tough and really quick decisions'. He proposed special anti-terrorist hit squads and again criticised a weary Rees for 'giving credibility' to Sinn Fein by holding exploratory talks. A similar exercise ensued after violence erupted again in the first weekend of June, claiming ten lives in Belfast.

The strong Tory in Neave could find few obvious outlets in a political situation where a Conservative Opposition and a Labour government were ostensibly engaged in a bipartisan approach to the great crisis of the day. But when, in mid-June, it came to industrial relations in Northern Ireland, Neave let rip. Heath's ill-fated 1971 Industrial Relations Act had never applied in the province, but the government was determined that its legislation repealing that measure and its own reforms of union law would. Neave was deeply hostile to this 'dose of socialist medicine'. However, his party did not oppose the change in principle and he was able only to score a few points before conceding. He was on more familiar ground on 14 June, accusing Rees of being half-hearted, world-weary and negative. He called on the government to 'go over to the offensive and declare war on terrorism'. In the border areas, he demanded identity cards and movement passes. To the faint hearts who raised difficulties, he had a simple message: 'That is not the way to win a war.' He also disclosed that his ideas for a new offence of terrorism, border-control zones, deployment of skilled marksmen and a specially trained anti-terrorist force of RUC and army experts had been 'informally made known in various quarters': presumably not just his formal contacts with the security forces, but with the secret state too.

The rancorous exchanges between Neave and Rees continued until early August with Neave indicting his rival as 'totally deluded' by the IRA, a charge rejected by a drained Rees, who predicted that history would ultimately vindicate him. So far it has judged Rees to have been in the right, but his successor came to the Northern Ireland Office with a very different agenda. On 2 September, the Defence Secretary Roy Mason, a short, pipe-smoking, ex-coal miner from Yorkshire, took over the exacting Ulster portfolio. An exceptionally pugnacious individual schooled in the cut-throat left–right politics of the National Union of Mineworkers, Mason was cut from different cloth from Rees, who was a former grammar school teacher. While still at the MoD, he had originally proposed sending in the SAS. He shared Neave's view that the first priority was security and he wanted constitu-tional change put on the back burner. At his first press conference, he offered no new security initiative but promised to punish terrorists 'as criminals, not politicals'. Within months, he could boast of doubling the activities of the SAS and 'harassing the IRA with as much vigour as was legally acceptable in a liberal democracy'.

Irish ministers adopted a wait and see policy on Mason but decided to raise their objections over Neave with Thatcher herself. The Dublin government was becoming increasingly concerned at the way the Conservatives were drifting away from support for power-sharing. It could not be denied that Neave was frequently scornful of the prospects of getting Unionists and Nationalists to cooperate on devolved self-rule. At the Tory Party Conference in early October, the hard-line Unionist MP the Reverend Martin Smyth had rejected power-sharing, and Neave not only failed to support the official party line but appeared to support his comments as being spoken 'not from theory but from practice and from the very heart'. These remarks prompted a fierce reaction from the SDLP, which threatened a boycott of political contacts with the Tories until they resumed the bipartisan approach. In the face of this pressure, Neave equivocated. It was also noticeable that at no time did Neave publicly condemn the army's apparently deliberate vacillation in the face of the 1974 loyalist strike that brought down Ulster's first power-sharing administration. It might be thought that he shared intelligence calculations that the experiment should be allowed to fail.

At any rate, Garret FitzGerald was detailed to raise the issue with Thatcher. He did so in London on 14 October 1976. Coincidentally, Neave was away that day on an official visit to Northern Ireland and was not present to take the flak. In the leader's Westminster office, Thatcher, Willie Whitelaw and Reginald Maudling listened with disbelief to Dublin's litany of complaints, reproduced in a short printed summary of Neave's speeches. FitzGerald later recorded: 'I went on to tell her and her colleagues that in my personal contacts with a Unionist leader during the previous year he had repeatedly insisted that he was confident that Conservative policy would change and that they would restore majority rule, and in my most recent encounter with him I felt that he believed what earlier he had merely hoped.'[14] Asked what should be done, FitzGerald suggested that Mrs Thatcher should make a major speech on Northern Ireland, unambiguously endorsing power-sharing. He conceded that this would involve overruling Neave on a high-profile political issue. FitzGerald left the meeting dismayed that, after eighteen months as party leader, Thatcher was still poorly briefed on Northern Ireland, but hopeful of reversing Neave's drift. He succeeded: soon afterwards, Neave wrote to Harry West, leader of the Official Unionists, reaffirming Tory support for power-sharing. He was angry nonetheless at being forced into a corner by Dublin.

For comfort, he turned to the heartening prospect of agreeing with his opposite number in parliament. In oral questions on 28 October, Neave welcomed Mason's 'difficult appointment' and asked if the government would put a stop to IRA 'godfathers' walking around scot-free and encouraging young people to commit murder. Mason replied: 'I am looking into the godfather law.' He conceded that it would be difficult to frame the right law, but offered hope that some means would be found to lock up these 'senior criminals'. That was music to Neave's ears – a virtually 180-degree turn on Rees's position – but Neave was also obliged to refer to his correspondence with the Unionists, and add: 'Our policy is for a devolved government within the province. Our policy has not changed.' Or if it had been going to, it had ceased to do so.

Meanwhile, the undercover operations had not ceased. Neave embroiled himself in what later became known as the Colin Wallace affair. Colin Wallace was the son of a Scottish Presbyterian father, born in 1943 in Randalstown, in staunchly Unionist County Antrim. Like Neave, he joined the Territorial Army in his late teens. Later he also entered the Ulster Special Constabulary – the B Specials, hated and feared by the Catholic nationalist community which saw them as the armed wing of Unionist ascendancy. He was a crack shot and a highly committed soldier. At the instigation of a senior officer, Wallace joined the regular army in May 1968 as an Assistant Command, Public Relations Officer, based in Lisburn barracks, HQ of the British army in Northern Ireland. It was a quiet period for the full-time soldier. The IRA was largely defunct and discredited, but the emergence of the civil rights movement, initially in Londonderry, changed everything. Brutally put down by the RUC and B

Specials, the protest swiftly turned to riot and spread across the province, most viciously in Belfast. James Callaghan, then Home Secretary, sent in the army to restore order and, initially at least, they were welcomed by Catholics being burned out of their homes by loyalist fanatics. But gratitude soon turned to hatred, as the soldiers were perceived to be on the side of the Unionist majority. The army public relations offensive became critical in the British government's efforts to restore order and the status quo. It also diversified into psychological warfare, working hand in glove with the intelligence services. Working for Army Information Policy, Wallace was drawn into these psychological operations. Strategic psy-war had 'long-term and mainly political objectives' designed to weaken the ability of enemies or hostile groups to wage war. 'It can be directed against the dominating political party, the government and/or against the population as a whole, or particular elements of it. It is planned and controlled by the highest political authority.'[15] It could have been more simply described as the secret state's lie machine.

In the first years of the Troubles, the Army propaganda drive enjoyed much success. Internment altered everything. The IRA, divided into Officials, the original organisation, and the more militant Provisionals who broke away to wage a more high-profile conflict against the security forces and the 'Orange statelet' of Northern Ireland, began to get the upper hand. The intelligence services and the Foreign Office therefore began to send in high-powered fixers to direct the information – and disinformation – effort. Army Information Policy also went in for deception operations, such as running a laundry in republican west Belfast from which clothes were tested for traces of explosives, and massage parlours to pick up operational information. In 1974, the year the Tories lost two general elections, Wallace also became intimately involved in Operation Clockwork Orange, a scheme to undermine terrorists in Northern Ireland with disinformation spread to media contacts. The operation swiftly extended and Wallace was fed 'facts' about the private lives of some, mainly

British, politicians. At first he was not alarmed: like many army officers in the field he felt that the actions of certain politicians, mainly Labour, were effectively aiding and abetting the enemies of the Crown by questioning the behaviour of the security services. However, the psy-ops campaign went way beyond events in Ulster, right to the top of the Conservative and Labour parties. Wallace's notes for the period include an analysis of the 'personality factor' in the first election of 1974, and suggest that 'every effort' be made to exploit character weaknesses, such as financial, sexual or political misbehaviour, in 'target subjects'. A list alongside mentions Edward Heath and a number of other leading Tories, together with Harold Wilson, Merlyn Rees ('suspicion') and the usual left-wing suspects: Benn, Foot, Eric Heffer, Barbara Castle and Tom Driberg. Wallace later insisted: 'The note did not express my personal view in any way. My handwritten notes were nothing more than extracts from documents passed to me in connection with Clockwork Orange.'[16] In the run-up to both elections, various alleged scandals involving most of these 'target subjects' were leaked to the press, without materially affecting the outcome, but the campaign continued long after Wilson won a tiny majority in October 1974. It is still today regarded by experienced commentators on security affairs as influential both in the downfall of Edward Health and Harold Wilson's decision to quit the premiership in 1976.

Before he was dismissed from Army Information Policy on trumped-up charges in 1975, a disillusioned man, Wallace wrote a paper for his superiors in Information Policy entitled 'Ulster – A State of Subversion'. It argued that the British government's effort in Northern Ireland was vitiated by a lack of moral courage, not simply lack of resources or will. Therefore there must be 'deep-rooted causes behind this sinister abdication of responsibility'. The Wallace paper further urged a major rethink of the handling of the situation in Northern Ireland, adding that 'that is most unlikely until the present government is defeated by public opinion'. Its solution was simple: 'Terrorism must not end; it must be defeated and seen to be defeated.'[17] Wallace later insisted again, that the paper was part of the Clockwork Orange operation and did not reflect his own opinion: he had acted as a sub-editor in drawing together the material which in his view had clearly *not* emanated from Northern Ireland.[18] Whatever its origin, the paper's analysis chimed well with Neave's assessment.

Wallace also subsequently linked the activities of the intelligence services in Northern Ireland with the general aims of the groups with which Neave found himself in sympathy during this period. MI5's increased role in the province, he said, coincided with growing industrial unrest throughout Britain; he continued that certain elements within the Security Services saw the situation as part of a worldwide Communist conspiracy. 'The intelligence community saw the Irish situation as the front line of the left's threat to the UK, and of a great conspiracy by the Communist bloc to undermine the whole of the UK.'[19] Evidence of Soviet involvement in Ulster has always been hard to find, but it does exist, most notably perhaps in the seizure at Schipol Airport by Dutch police in October 1971 of a consignment of Czech arms destined for the Provisional IRA. This was, according to Brian Crozier, the international expert on terrorism, 'another indication of clandestine [Soviet] support for revolutionary violence'. Crozier also logged Moscow Radio's report on 15 August that year represented the conflict in Northern Ireland as a conflict between Ulster workers defending their rights against an 'oppressive colonialist regime'. Russian journalists who wished to see the situation at first hand were treated with suspicion and followed if they were given permission to visit the province. Crozier insists to this day that the subversion threat was real. 'In the early 1970s, the USSR directly helped the IRA considerably, with arms and ammunition,' he claimed.[20] More to the point, he convinced Margaret Thatcher of his views. 'Broadly speaking, she did share my views. I saw her quite a lot before she came to power. It is almost as if I gave her a course in these things. She believed me about the IRA and the USSR. Of course, once she was in power, she had access to all the secret intelligence.'

At this point, Wallace comes into the Neave story. Out of work and his security clearance withdrawn, Wallace found it difficult to find a job in defence-related industry or public service, but he maintained contact with his old comrades in the information service. In late July 1976, he was approached by a former colleague asking if Neave had been in contact with him. He had not. The information officer, untraceable today, said Neave was anxious to get in touch. Wallace was pleased to hear that a Tory politician of such standing wanted to talk to him and offered a meeting immediately. Neave responded with equal celerity and they met in early August. Wallace fed his eager listener with material gathered in the Clockwork Orange operation, stressing the alleged Communist links of the Provisional IRA, particularly with Palestinian terrorists and Colonel Gaddafi. This was what Neave wanted to hear. Within days, he had given the material an excursion in a speech to the Young Conservatives in Brighton: 'Communist agitators are sowing seeds of despair and encouraging withdrawal of the army. They know such action would lead to civil war in Ireland, and delight in the Soviet Union.' His remarks were praised by the pro-Unionist *Daily Telegraph* as 'a new theme' and Neave pursued it with surprising vigour. He met Wallace twice more that month and on 31 August wrote to him saying: 'I enjoyed our talk last week, but I fear it was shorter than intended. I would like you to ring me on Thursday or Friday morning. I read your material with great interest and wonder if it could be updated to form the basis of a speech on September 10.'

Neave was clearly much taken with the analysis contained in 'Ulster – A State of Subversion', and Wallace put considerable effort into the 'update' required of him. Speaking in Seaton Delaval, Northumberland, Neave accused both wings of the IRA, but especially the Officials, of having 'increasingly Marxist aims', adding: 'The first is the creation of a socialist republic in Ireland for which Cuba is the model. They also work to end the links between the UK and Northern Ireland and the overthrow of the Irish government in Dublin.' He told his audience that the IRA was linked into a worldwide network of 'subversive organisations'. This was very much the global conspiracy so much in vogue on the far right of the Tory Party and its allies. Neave was thrilled with his new theme and continued to meet Wallace during the autumn. He also met Neave's assistant, Grattan de Courcey Wheeler, at the Turf Club. Neave proposed that Wallace should contribute an article on his analysis to the *Daily Telegraph*, edited by Neave's friend William Deedes, a former Tory minister himself. Wallace promptly obliged. The article, headlined 'Ulster's Two Basic Needs', based on Clockwork Orange material, appeared on 26 October. It restated the by now customary intelligence view, and condemned previous British governments for failing to come to grips with the Irish problem. He concluded: 'But it now appears that the present Conservative leadership is prepared to give the problem the time it requires to solve it.' This congratulatory note fits neatly with the view that Thatcher's election to the leadership was welcome to, if not part of the plans of, the intelligence community. Wallace was paid £70 for his article.

In the light of his enthusiasm for Wallace and his conspiracy theories, it might be asked if Neave had checked out his new-found intelligence contact, and if not why not. A few questions in the right place – and few were in a better position to ask them – would have shown him that Wallace was *persona non grata* to civil and military authorities alike. Indeed, Wallace had told him his side of the dismissal story in the hope of extracting a better deal from the Ministry of Defence. Neave listened sympathetically to his story but did nothing to help. There is no evidence to show that Neave, longing to believe what he was hearing, ever made enquiries, but it is unthinkable that he did not do so. More likely that he did and that the intelligence services were quite happy to allow Neave to float his Communist conspiracy theories. That, in fact, is Wallace's view: the intelligence services were a party to the great game. 'I suppose I was useful to them because I was no longer working officially for the government, and was what they would call "totally deniable" if anything went wrong. I am sure now that I was deliberately put in touch with Airey Neave so that the stuff which had been fed to me through Clockwork Orange would see the light of day without involving an active intelligence officer.'[21] Technically, of course, the pair of them were in breach of the Official Secrets Act, Wallace for giving the information and Neave for receiving it, but in the confines of the secret state this was a side issue. After Wallace moved to Arundel in Sussex, where he finally found employment as a press officer to Arun District Council, the contacts tailed off and finally ceased. In 1981, Wallace was sentenced to ten years' imprisonment for the manslaughter of a friend, Jonathan Lewis, whose battered body had been found in the River Arun in August the previous year. He served six years but the conviction was quashed by the Court of Appeal in 1996 and Wallace renewed his claims that the intelligence services had been behind the prosecution to shut him up.

Roy Mason's attempt to join the fight against terrorism met with Neave's approval. As 1976 closed, a debate on funding for Ulster found him lamenting the 'grave economic situation' in the province and promising not to create difficulties for the government. On 17 December, in a debate on the renewal of the Northern Ireland (Emergency Provisions) Act, the Christmas spirit extended to support for ministers' 'robust attitude' to security problems. However, Neave complained that after seven years of terrorism which had claimed 1,700 lives, little was understood about the central problem: the mind of the hard-core terrorist. On a visit to Belfast, two years earlier, the RUC told him the young people they were now arresting 'are among the hardest people they have ever seen', as witnessed by the cruel murders of young children and cripples. He welcomed the Peace Movement gathering momentum at the time and increased recruitment to the police, but argued that the terrorists' ultimate belief in their own success had to be destroyed. He continued to attack talks with Sinn Fein, insisting that there had to be a psy-ops programme against terrorism. There had indeed been a psychological campaign but it had been directed against British politicians through men like Colin Wallace and it had benefited his protégée, Margaret Thatcher. Instead of deadpan news reporting on death, injury, destruction and sorrow, Neave urged, there ought to be a concerted attack on 'these mindless barbarians' through the media. Newspapers and television should drop their 'lame attitudes to this terrible war' and give full support to the government, he added. Most newspapers already did so; it was clearly television he had in mind.

In 1976, 296 people died in the Troubles and 2,632 were injured. New Year 1977 brought an unexpected shift in policy by the Tories. Neave deplored the political no-man's-land in the province and promised to bring forward ideas for a Council of State. Evidently he had in mind a body that would act as a sounding board for opinion, 'a political forum that can discuss the subject of Ulster' rather than devolved government. He criticised Mason's failure to take a political initiative, and suggested a White Paper setting out the government's plans and the prospects for Northern Ireland over the ensuing five years. Mason flatly rejected his proposal as inopportune. Neave did not give up. In early February, he met John Hume's SDLP to reassure the nationalists that the Conservatives had not abandoned power-sharing. On 21 February, he visited Northern Ireland with Margaret Thatcher and in the Commons two days later envisaged the end of terrorism in 1977. But on 3 March, the day that Ulster Unionist leader Brian Faulkner died in a riding accident, he was back at the dispatch box asking a Private Notice Question on a series of assassinations in the province and requesting that more SAS troops be sent. Neave was keen to be seen to be 'doing something' on Ulster but his real political mission was more surreptitious. Behind the scenes, he was courting the Ulster Unionists under their new leader James Molyneaux. The small, disparate band of Northern Irish MPs was also being wooed by leading Labour figures, including

Merlyn Rees and Michael Foot, who saw them as a potential reserve force in the event of the failure of the Lib-Lab pact. The Dublin government got wind of these overtures and was alarmed. In these early days, Labour's efforts proved abortive, though they were later to bear fruit.

Neave offered the government full support from the Opposition when hard-line loyalists tried on 3 May to repeat the success of the 1974 workers' strike, this time in protest at security policy and in favour of a return to Stormont-style Unionist majority government. Mason insisted that the government would not be coerced, and Neave concurred that a repeat of the previous mayhem would ruin the Northern Ireland economy. In the event, the militants did not get their way. Some workers, particularly in the mainly Protestant engineering industries, stayed away and the port of Larne was closed, but most public services operated in near normal fashion. Neave paid a warm tribute to the courage and good sense of the Northern Ireland working people, and to the 'splendid calibre of the RUC and the way in which it has become an effective and impartial police force'. He was more than a little premature in the latter judgement: a quarter of a century later, the RUC was still not perceived as impartial.

In a volte-face later that month, and to rumbles of satisfaction in the Unionist camp, Callaghan announced the setting up of a Speaker's conference to consider more MPs at Westminster for Northern Ireland. This was one of the central demands of the Unionists in parliament. Not only would it strengthen their numbers, such a move would also copper-fasten Ulster into the United Kingdom, making the prospect of a united Ireland yet more remote. On a different political level, it would also make the Unionists beholden to Labour, and therefore less inclined to join with Neave in bringing down the precarious Lib-Lab coalition. Neave was obliged to welcome Mason's announcement of the initiative on 30 June, and the government's decision to restart discussions with the major political parties on constitutional arrangements in the province. Direct rule must be made 'more sensitive to public feeling', he urged, reiterating his call for a political forum. Few of Ulster's politicians shared his enthusiasm for such a body. It looked too much like a talking shop and Northern Ireland already produced more rhetoric than it could consume. Neave also proposed a Commons Select Committee on Northern Ireland, an idea which eventually did come to fruition, and the restoration of a Queen's representative in the province, which did not. The prospect of a cockaded plenipotentiary in regal uniform and a sword by his side evoked more mirth than serious consideration.

Meanwhile, the murders continued and Neave gave his standard rant about 'the hundred or so godfathers of crime' pitted against the vast majority of the population, who wished only for peace, order and reconciliation. 'The terrorists have no realistic political cause,' he contended. But they had, and the British army had privately told the politicians that they could not defeat the IRA militarily. They could not, in Neave's words, 'gain victory over the murder gangs of the IRA and the loyalist thugs at war with the state'. The terrorists on both sides were too deeply entrenched in their communities to allow such straightforward extirpation. Neave, however, remained convinced that, correctly deployed, the security forces could defeat terrorism.

A change of government in Dublin in the summer of 1977 slowed down the pace of political activity. Apart from a visit by the Queen to Ulster in August, when the royal progress was unimpeded by minor IRA bomb attacks, a season of inertia ensued. It was late September before the new Irish Prime Minister, Jack Lynch, met Callaghan in Downing Street. Two months later, Roy Mason floated a new political initiative. On 24 November, he told MPs his intention was to bridge the gulf between district councils in the province. He would devolve 'real powers' back to Northern Ireland, but not legislative authority. A new Assembly could be formed, elected by proportional representation, with a consultative role on legislation but devolved powers on issues such as transport, the environment and planning would be exercised through committees. The Unionists were sceptical, and Neave, while offering warm approval, was also dissatisfied, demanding a 'constitutional plan' and more democracy in local government. The vagueness of his proposals suggests that he was caught off guard, but this could scarcely have been the case as the Opposition was routinely informed of important government moves through 'the usual channels'. More likely, Neave did not want to open up too much ground between himself and the suspicious Unionists. The year ended with another debate on 8 December renewing the Emergency Provisions legislation. Neave had just returned from an 'inspiring' visit to Ulster, inspecting the security forces in action at Forkhill, Crossmaglen, Bessbrook and Newry. He also visited police stations where he was shocked by the 'fixed look of malevolence' in the photographs of the faces of wanted men. Those of young girls he found even more terrible. 'It is perfectly true that no military operation by itself will alter the existence of these hardened young monsters,' he admitted. Nonetheless, he suggested that terrorist killing should be redefined and made a capital offence – two decades after the abolition of hanging.

Whatever the Conservatives' formal position on Ulster's constitutional future, the Unionist in Neave could never be suppressed for long. So it was not surprising that the New Year (and his last full year in post) found him in trouble for saying that power-sharing in the province was 'no longer practical politics'. Fortunately, his unconventional ally, Roy Mason, was on hand to dig him out. During oral questions on Northern Ireland on 9 February, Clement Freud, the Liberal MP, raised Neave's remark, asking disingenuously how useful it had been to the security situation. Mason conceded that the comment had certainly upset some of the minority parties, but Neave insisted that bipartisanship was still alive because the government had no intention of reviving an executive on the lines of the 1974 Sunningdale model. Mason agreed that people in the province got hung up on words. 'That is why I have purposely never used the words "power-sharing".'

The Provisional IRA's horrific petrol bomb attack on the La

Mon restaurant in County Down on 17 February, which claimed twelve lives, prompted Neave to further expressions of disgust and a fresh call for increased activity by the SAS. It was his predictable response to every outrage, as was his demand that there should never be an amnesty for convicted terrorists. On this occasion, he also accused the government of miscalculation, drawing return fire from Mason who pointed out that only two months previously Neave had boasted about the army succeeding because it had adopted his military strategy. Neave was not to be diverted from his wrath. Specially trained troops, he urged, should 'pick off the gangsters' on their escape routes, at their arms caches and in their safe houses. 'There may be 100 or 200 really hard men, who are known to our intelligence services. It is these people whom we have to get, and only special services troops can do it.' This was the first time he had publicly advocated what came to be known as the 'shoot to kill' policy, the deliberate gunning down of suspected terrorists on sight. Tom Litterick, the left-wing Labour MP, immediately asked if he meant a 'shoot on sight' policy based on ID photographs handed to troops. Neave denied the charge but his intention was unmistakable. He also claimed that American M60 machine guns known to be in IRA hands had come through the subversive network of which he had spoken after collusion with Colin Wallace.

While Mason continued to talk to the Ulster parties about a 'partnership administration' in the province, Neave repeated his formula for giving more power to local government because power-sharing was not practical politics. On 13 April, an exasperated Gerry Fitt condemned Neave's 'very bellicose statements' which put him fairly and squarely on the side of intransigent Unionism to the exclusion of any consideration of minority views. Neave counter-accused Fitt of ritual inaccuracy, while admitting proudly: 'We on the Conservative side stand four-square for the Union of Great Britain and Northern Ireland.' Six days after this shameless pitch for the support of Unionist MPs, Callaghan announced that legislation would be introduced to increase the number of MPs to between sixteen and eighteen seats. Not to be upstaged, Neave urged early publication of the Bill.

The Emergency Powers were approved again in June, ten days after Neave took Margaret Thatcher on another visit to Ulster, where she met relations of the victims of the La Mon massacre. In the debate, Neave praised the army's covert operations but took a much more downbeat view about the future. 'Most of us were in a hopeful mood six months ago, but it is now certain that this struggle will be prolonged,' he told MPs, before reiterating his demand for a ban on Sinn Fein as a prelude to crushing the Provisional IRA. In a clear anticipation of the Conservatives forming the next government, he appealed to the minority parties in Ulster to support Thatcher's (i.e. essentially his and the Unionists') plan for greater powers for local councils. 'We cannot announce in Opposition a very detailed scheme,' he admitted, while promising to uphold the Union. In a rare show of unity, Neave and Mason issued simultaneous statements attacking calls in Britain for troops to be withdrawn. It was a testing time for the security services. Such was the impact of army and police presence in nationalist areas that on 4 November the SDLP's annual conference voted – with only two dissentients – that British withdrawal was 'desirable and inevitable'.

The heavy hand of soldiers and the RUC was also undermining one key element of support at Westminster. Gerry Fitt, a supportive mainstay of the minority Labour administration, was rethinking his position. If he withdrew his backing for Callaghan, and Neave could muster a clear majority of the Unionist MPs, then Labour was vulnerable to a parliamentary vote of confidence. The Unionists were natural bedfellows of the Conservatives, and their smouldering resentment over Edward Heath's abolition of 'their' parliament at Stormont had diminished. Recognising the danger, Callaghan pushed through the Bill giving Northern Ireland five extra MPs. The measure got a third reading on 17 January 1979. Neave reminded MPs that the Tories had promised just such a reform in their 1974 General Election manifesto. So both sides claimed parenthood.

As the election loomed, both government and Opposition became concerned about the 'dirty protest' in the Maze. Ministers were embarrassed at the bad publicity it was creating abroad for Britain and Neave asked for counter-measures against the IRA's skilful propaganda. During oral questions on Northern Ireland on 6 March 1979 his call for a locally elected forum in the province went unheeded once more. Both parties were essentially marking time. Callaghan's decision not to go to the country the previous autumn, followed by the 'winter of discontent', made Ulster something of a sideshow. The big question was: how long could the government last before it fell victim to a Tory ambush?

Neave asked his last Private Notice Question on 12 March, requiring a statement on allegations in the television programme *Weekend World* by Dr Robert Irwin, the official doctor of the RUC, that prisoners had been ill-treated by policemen. Neave thought the programme a calculated attack on justice and the security forces. Four days later, after reading an official report by Judge Bennett on the issue of maltreatment of prisoners, Neave backtracked. He conceded that 'a few' officers might have been involved in mistreatment, and invoked the provocation and danger to which the RUC was exposed in their favour. Nonetheless, the ex-POW and lawyer in him did surface. Any ill-treatment of suspects was totally indefensible, he insisted. It damaged the prestige and effectiveness of the police as a whole. That was the last the Commons ever heard from him. But not of him.

With only days to go before the fall of the Callaghan administration, Neave became involved in a fresh twist of the secret state dimension, bizarre even by the standards of previous plotting. A former MI6 electronics expert, Lee Tracey, was contacted by Neave and invited to a meeting at the Cumberland Hotel, in London's West End. Politically of the hard right, Tracey had never met Neave before but shared his strongly anti-Communist views and regarded him highly. At the meeting, held a week before the IRA struck so dramatically, Neave discussed his fears that Labour might be re-elected, and that premature retirement by James Callaghan could leave the way clear for Tony Benn to become Prime Minister. Tracey was asked to consider whether he would join a team, consisting of various intelligence and security specialists, which would 'make sure Benn was stopped'. It was a brief conversation but Tracey came away with the impression that violent means were a possibility. A second meeting was planned but Fate intervened. Tracey subsequently told his story to *Panorama*, which broadcast the allegations in late February 1982. The *New Statesman* also took up the case. Duncan Campbell was inclined to believe Tracey's story: 'He does not appear to be a mere fantasist,' he wrote. 'Furthermore, the fact that Mr Neave had conducted meetings of this sort just before his death was known to us in detail at the time, and has since been confirmed by another security agent.'[22]

In his diary for the period, Tony Benn recorded that on 17 February 1981 Campbell 'rang to tell me that two years ago he had heard from an intelligence agent that Airey Neave planned to have me assassinated if a Labour government was elected, Jim Callaghan resigned and there was any risk I might become leader'. Benn refused to comment, arguing that it would sound paranoid if he did. But he confided to his diary: 'It doesn't ring true in a way; it sounds like the dirty tricks department trying to frighten me by implying that a serious assassination attempt was being planned. No one will believe for a moment that Airey Neave would have done such a thing.'[23] Benn strongly objected to the *New Statesman* publishing the allegations, but the magazine went ahead anyway, believing that the evidence was sound. The matter was thereafter ignored.

Callaghan's minority government soldiered on despite the mounting pressures, with Neave intensifying his behind-the-scenes efforts to secure the key support of the Unionists. He appealed to their natural Tory instincts and was sympathetic to their views. But, according to Patrick Cosgrave, he remained 'flint-like, even going to the lengths of allowing the press to be informed that [Harry] West [Unionist MP] had been sent away empty-handed'.[24] Thatcher prepared the ground carefully for another vote of confidence in the government, her third in almost as many years. This time, the omens were better. David Steel, the Liberal leader, signalled his readiness to force an early General Election. The Scottish National Party, irate at the government's failure to deliver devolution north of the border, ranged its eleven MPs against Callaghan. Frank Maguire, the Independent Republican MP for Fermanagh and South Tyrone, announced his intention to make a rare appearance at Westminster 'to abstain in person'. Neave's discreet diplomacy alas appeared to pay off. On the night of the fatal vote, 28 March, all but two of the Unionist MPs went into the Conservative lobbies. Thatcher triumphed by a single vote – 311 to 310. It was the first time since 1924 that an incumbent Prime Minister had been driven from office and into a General Election by a parliamentary vote of no confidence. The next day, Callaghan had an audience with the Queen and announced a General Election for 3 May. A seat round the Cabinet table beckoned for Neave.

16

Plotting the Kill

Airey Neave prided himself on his clandestine skills. In the words of a former Tory minister, Jim Lester, 'he was always looking for a plot', but he regarded his own intrigues as essentially a continuation of his loyal service to Queen and Country during the war. As an honourable soldier he was doing good by stealth, and the secrecy was excused by the virtuous outcome of his deeds. His philosophy was a mirror image of the rationale of militant republicanism. They, too, believed that the ends justified the means, only their ends were diametrically opposed to his: the break-up of the Union with Britain and the expulsion of British troops. That had been their motivating force since the Easter Rising in 1916. The old militarist impulse was revived in late 1968 when the Unionist ascendancy made a brutal (and ultimately fatal) attempt to suppress the civil rights movement in Northern Ireland fighting for jobs, housing and votes, all denied in varying measure since partition. Furthermore, the nationalist, Catholic minority felt besieged by the RUC and the B Specials in their run-down terraced enclaves and many turned to the virtually defunct IRA for protection.

The split between the Official IRA and the Provisionals, which began in October 1969, has been well documented. Their numbers hugely inflated by an influx of young men after the introduction of internment in August 1971, the Provos went on to fight a fierce guerrilla war, informed in fluctuating degrees by emotional patriotism, Catholicism and occasional hazy talk of socialism. The Officials under chief of staff Cathal Goulding engaged in violence, both in Ulster and in Britain. They claimed responsibility for an explosion at the Aldershot headquarters of the Parachute Regiment, which killed seven, including five women canteen workers. But the Officials were also attracted to a political route to the achievement of their objectives: winning support in the minority community and putting candidates up for the parliaments in Dublin, Belfast and London. This uneasy ambiguity of purpose continued until May 1972, when they shot dead William Best, of the Royal Irish Rangers, a local boy home on leave in Londonderry. Driven from the Bogside and Creggan heartlands of the city by local protests over the murder, the Officials declared a ceasefire on 29 May. Military actions, except in self-defence and retaliation, were suspended. They talked instead of 'a new phase of civil struggle'.

The Provisionals appeared determined to emulate the Officials in the search for a political solution. Their chief objective was to win prisoner of war status for IRA inmates. In late June, they secured 'special category' status for their gaoled comrades from the Ulster Secretary William Whitelaw. He thought the concession was 'fairly innocuous', but it was to poison the political process for a decade and culminate in the hunger strikes of 1981. The Provisionals responded with a ceasefire from 26 June, and secret talks were arranged in London at the home of Northern Ireland minister Paul Channon. There, on 7 July, Whitelaw and other ministers met an IRA delegation that included Gerry Adams and Martin McGuinness. The talks swiftly foundered because the IRA called for British withdrawal from the province by 1975, an impossible demand that no Westminster government could have conceded. Whitelaw rejected their 'absurd ultimatum' and on 13 July hostilities were renewed by the Provisional IRA. However, 'special category' status was not withdrawn. As a genuine ex-POW, Neave was not happy with this categorisation: he did not regard the IRA as genuine soldiers.

The war was on again, but this time it was also an internecine war with the Officials. Some of Goulding's men in Belfast and Londonderry chafed at the order to halt offensive operations. Sporadic attacks on army and police strongholds continued and a new group opposed to the ceasefire began to coalesce around the Officials' most charismatic leader, Seamus Costello. Born in Bray in 1939, he had been active in the republican movement in his teens, and in local politics in his native County Wicklow. Costello, known as 'Volunteer Clancy' in the cryptic language of the Officials, was one of the movement's outstanding orators and thinkers. He was also a thorn in the side of the leadership, who finally ousted him at a rigged 'court martial' in the spring of 1974.

But Costello was one step ahead of his former comrades, having already formed the nucleus of what was to become the Irish National Liberation Army. A series of robberies and raids on gun shops put them in business, and, following his formal expulsion from the Official Sinn Fein, Costello gathered his eighty followers on 8 December 1974 at the Spa Hotel in County Lucan, near Dublin. His faction drew support from all parts of the country. In the morning, they formed a new party: the Irish Republican Socialist Party. Its prime objective was to revive the link between nationalism and revolutionary socialism. The title was a deliberate reworking of the Irish Socialist Republican Party, formed in 1896 by the Marxist soldier–revolutionary James Connolly, later shot by the British for his part in the Easter Rising. In the afternoon, 'those interested' were invited to a second session to explore 'other avenues', a euphemism for the armed struggle. Around fifty attended and from their number the INLA was born with Seamus Costello as the chief of staff.

The conference went virtually unnoticed until Costello called a press conference five days later. He identified 'British imperialist interference in Ireland' as the most immediate obstacle confronting the Irish people in their struggle for democracy, national liberation and socialism. The IRSP demanded Britain's immediate renunciation of any claim to sovereignty over any part of Ireland, and a pledge of an early date for total withdrawal of her military and political presence. In the interim, British troops were to return to barracks; all internees and convicted 'political prisoners' were to be freed by general amnesty; there was to be abolition of all 'repressive legislation' and a Bill of Rights giving complete political freedom and an end to discrimination. Britain must also compensate the Irish people for 'the exploitation which has already occurred'. The IRSP aimed to 'end British imperialist rule in Ireland and establish a thirty-two-county democratic socialist republic with the working class in control of the means of production, distribution and exchange'. From the outset, the party adopted an anti-EEC stance. Costello criticised the Provisionals for not being dedicated to a socialist republic. 'The primary emphasis should be on the mobilisation of the mass of the Irish people in the struggle for national liberation,' said the organisation's newspaper, the *Starry Plough*. 'We don't see Parliament as an institution likely to produce the results we want.' No political manifesto could have been more abhorrent to Airey Neave.

Costello claimed that the new party had 300 members, including 120 in Belfast. The most high-profile recruit was Bernadette McAliskey, née Devlin, who had won a famous by-election victory in Mid-Ulster to enter Parliament in 1969. To her admirers, the fiercely militant McAliskey was known as the Irish Joan of Arc. To the Unionists she appeared a 'mini-skirted Castro'. Her new party's stated intention to end British imperialist rule could have left few in doubt that, like Sinn Fein, the IRSP would have a military wing. This was confirmed a few days after the press conference when a group of previously Official IRA prisoners in Long Kesh announced that they had formed a branch of the IRSP in the gaol. A unit of the Officials in the Divis Flats on the Falls Road also deserted to join INLA, bringing their weapons with them. In the weeks that followed, rivalry between the Officials and INLA descended into intra-sectarian violence and the murderous fury intensified down the years.

Initially, the new organisation developed along lines that suited

Neave's intelligence-based analysis: a 'revolutionary socialist alternative' (in McAliskey's words) willing to 'organise the people's defence' (in Costello's words). But with the announcement of a Provisional ceasefire in February 1975, the violence turned inward on the republican movement, with shootings in bars and killings in disputed areas of Belfast. The existence of INLA could no longer be denied, though Costello attempted to do so in Belfast later that month. For public consumption, it was admitted only that the IRSP had people 'militantly sympathetic' to its aims. Not until April 1975 did black-clad members of the 'People's Liberation Army' appear in public at the funeral of one of their 'staff officers'. The IRSP registered itself as a political party in May, in Dublin, and claimed 400 members. At its annual conference, Costello praised the Communist insurgents in Vietnam whose war against the Americans was on the point of victory, and promised a 'broad front' of policy embracing small farmers, workers and the unemployed. But the party's armed wing was now openly in conflict with the RUC and the army, particularly in Londonderry where the INLA had a hundred members and a lethal armoury. In January 1976, INLA began claiming responsibility for its actions, by which time it had already killed at least twelve people, including soldiers and policemen, and injured dozens more. Its deadly intent was no longer in question. The *Starry Plough* published photographs of INLA men parading inside Long Kesh, and finally in December 1976 admitted the 'recent formation' of an armed wing whose aim was to end British imperialist rule and create an all-Ireland socialist republic.

Although INLA pledged to intensify operations against 'the enemy', it was at its least active in the following year. It murdered an army private in Belfast but a bid to kidnap the West German consul failed. The year 1977 also saw the assassination of Seamus Costello on 5 October in Dublin by the Provisional IRA. For a time, his murder threatened to bring about the collapse of the splinter military group and its political front. However, INLA's international contacts were now bearing fruit. They had always sought links with similar groups in Europe, and as early as 1975 the party toured Belgium, Germany, Austria and Switzerland on a five-week trip organised by the West German – Ireland Solidarity Committee. One member of this shadowy body, Rudolf Raab, also belonged to the anti-NATO paramilitary outfit, Revolutionary Cells. Historians of INLA say that Raab provided the IRA breakaway group with links to F18, the intelligence section of Yasser Arafat's al-Fatah wing of the Palestine Liberation Organisation.[1]

During 1977, this link-up yielded the first shipment of arms from the Palestinians. It brought rifles and Soviet- and Chinese-manufactured grenades, and for the next three years a steady stream of mainly Eastern bloc weaponry came overland by car and then by sea ferry to Northern Ireland. The great coup came in the summer of 1978, when two INLA members smuggled in a supply of Russian explosives behind the door panels of a van. Their lethal cargo comprised around eighty small batches of mixed penthrite and tolite, about the size of a bar of soap, pink in colour and packaged in Cellophane. The 8-ounce blocks were already fitted with holes for detonators. A further delivery brought two large blocks weighing about 5 lb. This destructive materiel, say INLA's historians, was extremely rare and hard to find in Western Europe. It was perfectly suited to the paramilitaries' favourite anti-personnel device, the under-car booby trap bomb. Its deadly impact could be directed upwards by newspaper packing, concentrating its force so that less explosive need be used. Furthermore, it was impossible to spot in the security scanners of the day, making it an extremely versatile weapon.

In May 1978, the *Starry Plough* published pictures of INLA 'volunteers' training in the hills, and again in September, with the headline 'Republicans, Socialists Launch OFFENSIVE'. An article on the same page accused the Israelis of creating a 'Jewish Ulster' for the Palestinians and sympathised with their struggle. It was also clear that Airey Neave was building himself into a hate figure for the IRSP. In the same edition of the *Starry Plough*, the party's chairperson, Miriam Daly, observed that Neave had 'built his career' on an escape from Colditz POW camp, whereas INLA member Jake McManus who escaped from Long Kesh 'concentration camp' in 1976 had been gaoled for a further two years and was on the blanket protest in H3 Block. By mid-1978, there were more than two hundred prisoners 'on the blanket' – wearing a blanket instead of prison clothes and smearing their excrement on the walls of their cells. Twenty-seven of them were INLA members and Miriam Daly insisted: 'Successful escape from a Special Category Compound is not a crime.' The IRSP–INLA were getting anxious about Neave, not only for his increasingly belligerent demands for tougher military action in Northern Ireland, but also because they feared that his understanding of POW mentality and escape and evasion gave him a unique insight into the minds and attitudes of republican inmates of the H Blocks. Their role in the development of the political and military struggle was massively underestimated outside the movement, and Neave's grasp of this undervalued dimension to republican terrorism marked him out even more as a target. Neave was also on the wanted list of the Provisional IRA. It became clear that the family home, the Old Vicarage in Ashbury, Oxfordshire, had been staked out by the Provisionals, a plan of the property having been found in the possession of the IRA Balcombe Street gang after they gave themselves up following a six-day siege in a London council flat in December 1975. Neave was forced to move. 'They [the IRA] had plans of various homes, and ours was one of them,' said his daughter Marigold. 'We were always moving, never in one place for very long. I think he found it quite difficult to be in one place.' The family lived at various times in Lockinge, Brightwell cum Sotwell, Grove, near Wantage, and Compton Beauchamp. They also moved from flat to flat in London, ending up at Westminster Gardens in Marsham Street.

With its new armoury of Palestinian weapons, INLA was ready to strike. It boasted that, whereas the Provos had five men for every gun, they had five guns for every man. But the group's technical capability was yet not matched by professional proficiency. They might call themselves an army of liberation but they were woefully ill-trained in the use of the sophisticated means at their disposal. Sniping attacks on the regular army in Belfast failed to claim lives. A plot to assassinate Sir Robin Haydon, British ambassador to Ireland, in St Patrick's Cathedral, Dublin, also misfired.

Frustrated INLA commanders in search of a 'spectacular' that would convince the authorities (and their own followers) that they were a force to be reckoned with opted for the most prominent target available, the Northern Ireland Secretary, Roy Mason. In January 1979, the *Starry Plough* carried a statement from INLA's Army Council, warning of a 'more active role' in the coming year. It accused the British authorities of imprisoning thousands of Irish men and women and added that during 1979 INLA's strategy would be geared to ensure that 'imperialism and its agents will see the futility of its policy of inflicting large-scale misery on the people'. In the same month, Miriam Daly singled out Mason as the politician trying to 'smash' the IRSP, and soon after the party leadership accused him of seeking to crush all political opposition in Ulster through the use of the Emergency Powers Act. Mason was frankly contemptuous of INLA, describing them as a 'pseudo-Marxist breakaway gang'. As a consequence, INLA volunteers were sent to Mason's home in his Barnsley constituency, where they staked out his house and the pub he frequented with his agent, Trevor Lindley. The plot was to stab Lindley and then shoot Mason at Lindley's funeral.

But political events undermined Mason more surely than a 'spectacular' assassination. With the Labour government limping to general election defeat, INLA turned their attention instead to Mason's Shadow, Airey Neave, for whom they felt equal fear and loathing. He was the obvious choice, not least because he supported Mason's tough policy on terrorism, and more. 'Neave was the only one, apart from Mayhew, who sought to be

Secretary of State,' a former INLA general headquarters member later disclosed. 'He was coming in on the heels of Mason – to settle the Northern Ireland question and make Mason look like a lamb. He wanted to bring in more SAS and take the war to the enemy.'[2]

Ronnie Bunting, director of intelligence for the organisation's GHQ and adjutant of the Belfast Brigade, is credited with ordering the murder of the man whose death would be 'a popular hit' in Ireland. Bunting was an unusual figure: a devout republican and socialist, but the son of a former army officer, Major Ronald Bunting, and hard-line loyalist supporter of the Reverend Ian Paisley. By profession a schoolteacher, he was denied employment by the Catholic Church and worked instead in the medical records department of the Royal Victoria Hospital in Belfast. He lived quietly in Turf Lodge, a militant republican neighbourhood in west Belfast, but he was well-known to the army and the RUC and had once been interned. In his turn, he too would become a target for assassination. Bunting 'chose the one man in British politics who was unequivocal in his denunciation of terrorism,' argues Martin Dillon, a security expert.[3]

INLA's historians insist that planning began only in March 1979, the month the Callaghan government fell. Jack Holland and Henry McDonald interviewed Ronnie Bunting only months after the operation and claim that unspecified 'important information' came from a 'political source' in England suggesting that Airey Neave was preparing a right-wing backlash with Thatcher as his chosen front. Thanks to this political source, it is alleged, INLA had the access and information necessary to launch a daring political assassination. This version sounds like revolutionary hyperbole. Neave's right-wing credentials were well known: they were on parade every month during Northern Ireland Questions at Westminster, and in his many speeches and interviews on Ulster. Nor were his intentions a mystery. He favoured the mother of all crackdowns on 'terrorist criminals', and as a former Officer Commanding in the Territorial SAS there could be no doubt about what form it would take. The situation did not require any 'important information' to justify a terror strike.

INLA volunteers travelled to London to carry out the operation. They knew where Neave lived – the address of his flat in Westminster Gardens was in *Who's Who*, and they were aware that he scorned personal security as much as Roy Mason revelled in it. The chosen weapon was a car bomb using the explosives smuggled in the previous year from Palestinian sources. It would be triggered by a mercury-tilt switch that completed an electrical circuit, activating a detonator plugged into the small, tightly packed explosive charge. Two experiments had already been successfully carried out on such a bomb. In December 1978, a prison officer was wounded when a charge exploded under his car, and in Portadown on 6 March 1979, Robert McAnally, an Ulster Defence Regiment serviceman, was fatally wounded by a similar bomb. He lost a leg and died six days later. The mercury-tilt detonator was invented by an INLA member from north Armagh who was fascinated with the technical side of bomb-making. He realised that the switch – freely available to the public in radio spares catalogues – could be adapted to detonate an explosive charge. When fixed to a vehicle moving up an incline, the water in the switch would come into contact with the mercury, triggering an electrical current that set off the detonator. More-over, the bomb did not require the use of radio signals which were susceptible to discovery by army scanning machines. Sometimes, they were also inadequate for the job (a failure of radio signalling had caused the intended assassination of Sir Robin Haydon to be aborted) but the new device, fixed by small magnets under the driver's side of the car, could be relied on to release a massive upward blast when the tiny tilt switch was activated.

Argument has raged as to whether the INLA men placed the bomb under Neave's car outside his flat on 30 March, or whether they penetrated the security of the Palace of Westminster and laid the charge in the Commons underground car park. Much is made by INLA's historians about inside information from within Westminster about the weakness of security around and within the Houses of Parliament. Jack Holland has argued that an unnamed 'left-wing sympathiser' gave them a layout of the place so they could gain entry to the car park posing as workmen. The weakness of this claim lies in the truth that security at Westminster *was* remarkably lax, and virtually anyone could walk in undetected to the bars (as the author did regularly) and other semi-public places like the car park if he could muster the self-confidence to walk past the policemen on duty at the St Stephen's entrance. A courteous and confident 'good afternoon' sufficed.

Police and security service sources have always claimed that the bomb was put in place outside Neave's flat a few hundred yards away. Of course the authorities would say that, to minimise embarrassment about their own incompetence. Dillon shares the view that the theory of bomb-placing in Westminster is 'incorrect'.[4]

Ronnie Bunting told INLA's historians that the assassins did infiltrate the car park and had no difficulty in locating Neave's powder-blue Vauxhall Cavalier. As they prepared to set the charge under the car, however, they realised that the timing device, set to explode the 16-ounce bomb, was faulty. The original timer was therefore replaced with a wristwatch, its hands scraped clean of any plastic that might otherwise interfere with the connection of the electrical circuit. Having armed the device and set it to go off within an hour, the unit calmly walked away, leaving Neave to his fate.

In the Commons, MPs were discussing the Credit Union Bill. Fewer than a dozen members were in the chamber. Most had either left to begin the battle to retain their constituencies or were packing up and dictating a last letter to their secretary. Enoch Powell MP was speaking when Neave left the building and walked down to the five-floor underground car park. Neave got into his Vauxhall, registration VYY 179, and set off home. At 2.58, as he drove up the cobbled ramp into New Palace Yard, the bomb exploded in the confined space of the steep exit. The force of the explosion blew out the doors, windows and bonnet and punched up the roof. Amid the debris, official papers and sheets of the familiar green and white Commons writing paper blew around. Police who rushed to the scene could not recognise the badly injured driver but guessed, from his attire, that he was a Tory MP. His identity was not verified until after he died in hospital an hour later.

INLA was jubilant. It was 'the operation of the decade' they told reporters. 'We blew him up inside the impregnable Palace of Westminster.' Initially, the murder was assumed to be the work of the Provisional IRA, and the Provos themselves claimed responsibility. INLA was held in such low regard that a member of the organisation calling Ulster Television from Dublin to claim responsibility was told to 'fuck off' and the phone was slammed down on him.[5] But in the tightly knit terrorist world, few questioned INLA's coup and within two hours of the explosion a caller with a strong Dublin accent had telephoned the *Irish Independent* to say it was the work of the INLA. He gave forensic details as proof of the claim. A second caller telephoned the newspaper at 8.00 p.m., saying he was from the Irish Republican Socialist Party. He read out a statement given to the IRSP's *Starry Plough* which gave further details of the assassination method.

The *Starry Plough* edition that followed carried a statement from the Army Council of INLA dated 31 March 1979. Under the headlines 'Break The Chains' and 'Airey Neave Executed' it said (sic):

THE IRISH NATIONAL LIBERATION ARMY re-iterate that one of it's active service units was responsible for the execution of Airey Neave, British Shadow Government Spokesman on Northern Ireland.

The INLA successfully breached intense security at the House of Commons to plant the device, consisting of one kilo of explosive. After taking stringent precautions to ensure that no civilians would be injured the ASU returned to base.

Airey Neave was specially selected for assassination. He was well known for his rabid militarist calls for more repression against the Irish people and for the strengthening of the SAS murder gang, a group which has no qualms about murdering Irish people.

The INLA took this action in pursuance of its aim to get British occupying forces out of Ireland. We recognise that this task is not going to be achieved in a short period of time. We are armed, trained militarily and politically, and able to sustain what is going to be a long struggle.

We are not associated with any other group as reported in the mass media; neither are we a cover group for the Irish Republican Army (Provisional). The Irish National Liberation Army is an independent military organisation whose primary aim is to secure a British military, political and economic withdrawal from Ireland and establish the right of Irish people to determine their own destiny.

As a republican socialist organisation we recognise that the cause of Ireland and the cause of Labour are linked; and in the words of James Connolly, we cannot envisage a free Ireland without a free working class. British imperialism is responsible for the sectarian divisions within the Irish working class and we pledge ourselves to rid Ireland of imperialism and all it's manifestations.

The statement was signed Seamus Clancy, the customary code-name for the Army Council spokesman. Alongside was a portrait of Neave, inset in a picture of the devastated car on the Commons ramp. That night in the IRSP's headquarters in the Falls Road, Belfast, there was an impromptu party. As the drink flowed, Ronnie Bunting exulted: 'We did it!' In their euphoria, INLA gave away more details of their organisation. A spokesman told the *Irish Times* that ninety of their number were in gaol, but in Belfast they had not lost a man on operations for over a year. He claimed responsibility for a number of bank robberies in Belfast and sniping at soldiers with Kalashnikov rifles. The organisation also gave intensive anti-lectures 'so they can stand up to what goes on in Castlereagh'.

An Phoblacht, the Provisional Sinn Fein newspaper, reported the murder with malicious glee, under the headline 'Election Campaign Gets Off To A Bang'. The front-page story described Neave as 'extremely right wing' and an advocate of immigrant papers for Irish people living or working in Britain. It heaped scorn on British leaders and the media for condemning the assassination, arguing: 'The hypocrites don't appreciate the charity between a discriminate political execution of an oppressor; was it as "cowardly" as dropping from half a mile up in the air thousands of tons of bombs on defenceless citizens?' This reference to British wartime bombing of Germany was followed by the revelation of a remarkable personal story. 'The eccentricity of the Neaves,' said *An Phoblacht*, 'was in evidence during a Radio 4 interview on *Good Morning Ulster*. His sister, who claimed to be clairvoyant, said she knew of his impending, violent death. Asked why she didn't inform him, she replied she didn't want to upset him and his wife as well!!!' (sic).

Reaction closer to home was one of shock and grief. The Queen sent her condolences to Neave's widow, praising his record in war and peace. Margaret Thatcher heard of the outrage from her aide Derek Howe as she was greeting well-wishers at a fund-raising event organised by Motability in her north London constituency of New Barnet. Initially, there were no details. Her first thought was, 'Please God, don't let it be Airey.' She went on to the BBC studios in Portland Place to record a Party Election Broadcast where her worst fears were confirmed. One of the producers took her into a private room: he told her it was Airey Neave and that he was critically injured. It was very unlikely that he would survive – indeed he might be dead already. 'There was no way I could bring myself to broadcast after that,' she recollected later. Cancelling her planned riposte to James Callaghan, she telephoned the Prime Minister to explain and then drove to the

Commons. 'I felt only stunned,' she remembered. 'The full grief would come later. With it also came the anger that this man – my friend – who had shrugged off so much danger in his life should be murdered by someone worse than a common criminal.'[6]

In her office, Thatcher sat down to compose a tribute to the man who had made her leader. She was, according to her biographer Patrick Cosgrave, 'utterly shattered and yet composed', completing a draft in twenty minutes. Her speechwriter, the playwright Ronnie Millar, took out only one word, 'hero', arguing that a soldier would not like to be called that. Her testimony scarcely did justice to the scale of Neave's contribution. 'The assassination of Airey Neave has left his friends and colleagues as stunned and grief-stricken as his family. He was one of freedom's warriors. Courageous, staunch, true, he lived for his beliefs and now he has died for them. A gentle, brave and unassuming man, he was a loyal and very dear friend. He had a wonderful family who supported him in everything he did. Now, there is a gap in our lives which cannot be filled.' In private, she was more positive. 'We must win now,' she insisted. 'We'll win for Airey.' Thatcher also urged Neave's widow Diana to keep up his political work, and she surprised friends by turning up at Central Office, volunteering for even the most menial tasks during the election campaign.

Parliament met again on 2 April, when tributes were paid by the Prime Minister and the Leader of the Opposition. Thatcher said feelingly: 'In peacetime Airey was a very gentle and unassuming man, but absolutely tenacious in pursuit of everything he believed in and strong to root out injustice. In wartime his valour and courage were unsurpassed. It was partly because of men like him that we meet to assemble in this place in free debate.'

The Speaker also announced his approval of recommendations by the Joint Committee on Security. Westminster Hall, the thousand-year-old edifice that had seen royal trials and the lying-in-state of kings and queens, was closed to the public. Public access was restricted to a single point, the St Stephen's entrance opposite the Abbey, and remains so more than thirty years later. Only MPs in their cars or cabs could use other gates. More security instructions for MPs would follow. The Home Secretary Merlyn Rees reminded MPs of reports that the IRA was planning an offensive campaign in mainland Britain to coincide with the general election, and announced new measures to protect 'those who may be particularly at risk'. He added that Neave had been in regular contact with the police over his own safety and had been satisfied with the steps they were taking for his protection. Rees further promised MPs that the General Election campaign would not be 'distorted' by terrorist threats.

The security authorities were closing Parliament's stable door rather belatedly. For the price of £5.12, the cost of the explosives smuggled into England via a third party in a chocolate box, the Tories had lost their Ulster strategist and Margaret Thatcher the man who had given her power and to whom she had given her trust. The assassination also left the Conservatives without a policy on Northern Ireland. Neave had kept his cards pretty close to his chest. Insofar as he had a political strategy, it was a twin-track approach continuing direct rule, with some devolution of powers to local councils, backed up by a ruthless suppression of the IRA. Thatcher supported his ideas, but without him there to put them into practice a political vacuum ensued. After the Tories' success in the May election, Humphrey Atkins, a genial ex-naval officer, was appointed Northern Ireland Secretary. His first act, on 2 July, was to ban the INLA.

17

Pursuit and Retribution

How could it have happened? How could a group of ruthless terrorists assassinate a leading political figure in the holy of holies, the Palace of Westminster? And would not there be the biggest manhunt in the history of policing to bring the perpetrators to book? James Callaghan promised within hours that 'no effort would be spared to bring his murderers to justice and to rid the United Kingdom of the scourge of terrorism'. The entire resources of Scotland Yard and the security services were mobilised to capture the gang and it was confidently expected that they would be swiftly arraigned.

Yet, in April 1987, more than eight years after the atrocity, Home Office minister Douglas Hogg told MPs: 'I very much regret to say that nobody has been charged with this matter, and I think it would be misleading for me to say that a charge is likely now, or in the immediate future.' Today, twenty-three years after the murder, not one of the INLA executioners has ever been brought before a court; nor is it now likely that they could be. Events in Northern Ireland have moved on so far that a prosecution would not only be legally difficult but politically divisive. Republican and loyalist terrorists found guilty of crimes even more heinous have been released as part of the peace process designed to end Ulster's nightmare.

At the time, however, Scotland Yard's Anti-Terrorist Squad were sure they would get their men. The hue and cry began before Neave's body was cold. Police flooded the area with enquiries, and initially it seemed that they would be successful. On 5 April, Scotland Yard said it was ready to publish a photofit of a suspect, based on interviews with people who were near the Commons at the time of the blast and close to Neave's flat in Westminster Gardens. The man was described by journalist Deric Henderson as 'a top republican bomber and master of disguise' who had been on the run in Ireland since being freed from his cell in a Dublin gaol by the IRA in 1976. He was in prison for running an IRA arms factory and had once worked as an electrician and later as a lab technician. The features of the Dublin escaper figured prominently in the photofit and 'according to police sources, he is *the* chief suspect'. Sources in the Gardai, the Irish police, who were cooperating closely in the enquiry, believed he had fled from England, having made the bomb in such a way as to leave him plenty of time to get out.[1] This wealth of substantial detail indicates that someone in the Gardai was talking off the record, while Scotland Yard played a more discreet game.

INLA's 'chief of staff' also appeared in semi-public briefly to tell the Dublin magazine *Magill* that Neave's murder was a one-off terror attack on British politicians. 'We felt it was time the Westminster armchair terrorists suffered directly the consequences of their policies,' he said, adding that it was INLA's intention to 'mark time on the British front'. There would be no more attacks on politicians before the 3 May General Election. No such inhibitions held back the Provisionals, who gave notice of a campaign to 'demonstrate capability' and remind politicians that Ireland was still a political issue. The IRA also claimed that they, too, had been stalking Neave and that INLA had beaten them to the target by a matter of hours. They further admitted killing Sir Christopher Sykes, British ambassador to The Hague, and a Belgian banker, shot dead in mistake for Sir John Killick, British ambassador to NATO.

On 10 April, Commander Peter Duffy, head of the Anti-Terrorist Squad, released mugshots of four men being sought for interview. They were artists' impressions, rather than photofit pictures. 'I think it likely that at least two of these men could have been involved,' Duffy told a press conference. The first man, aged around twenty-five, with long, unkempt hair and a pitiless face, had been seen in the Westminster Arms pub near to the Neave family flat, on the night before the murder. He was thought to be a stranger to the area and his actions had aroused suspicions. The second man was much older, aged between thirty-eight and forty-two. He was also long-haired and was pictured hunched into a high collar. He had been seen early on the day of the killing, in a service road beside the flats. The other two men were aged about twenty-four and twenty-nine. One had short, curly hair and a baby face; the other had long hair, eyes a little too far apart and thin lips. It would have been difficult to draw four more villainous-looking faces. Commander Duffy said it was possible that all four men had Irish accents. One of them could have been the bomber, or there could have been more than one. He appealed to hotel and guest-house owners in Victoria and Pimlico to rack their brains.

The evidence was not much to go on. It transpired that the first man had drawn attention to himself by drinking Guinness mixed with Coke in the Westminster Arms. The landlord remembered: 'We simply don't get many strangers here in the evening. This is mainly a lunchtime pub. People stand out.' The two men seen in the slip road had talked in Irish accents, according to a witness, but their conversation was innocuous. The last suspect had been seen on the slip road at 6.45 on the morning of the murder, and was thought to have driven away in a yellow Fiat, which may have been hired.

However, after detailed forensic tests, the Anti-Terrorist Squad were able to be more specific about the bomb. Commander Duffy said the explosive charge weighed about 1 lb. and it was of 'military' rather than industrial origin. It was a professional device and could not have been constructed in a backstreet workshop. Police speculated that it might have been supplied to INLA (now accepted as the perpetrators) by an agency or a country with access to such technology. Scotland Yard accurately identified it as a mercury-tilt bomb of the kind used to kill Robert McAnally just over three weeks earlier. Duffy said it was probably planted the night before Neave's death, when his car was parked in the service road. It would have gone off when the car went up a ramp or when the brakes were applied. These two statements do not tally. If the bomb had been planted the night before, and was susceptible to braking, it would have gone off before Neave got to the House. Even though it is a short distance, traffic is often heavy and it would have been impossible to drive to Westminster and then down an incline into the Commons car park without using the brakes.

On 14 April, the *Daily Mail* announced that the Neave hunt was closing in on a marked man. He was the familiar 'master of disguise', with one mark he could not hide – he was missing the little finger on his left hand, shot off in a gun battle with British troops in 1972. He had been identified by callers to Belfast police who claimed to have recognised him from the artist's impression. The suspect was from the republican stronghold of Ballymurphy, and he was wanted for questioning about bank raids, shootings and bombings north and south of the border.

Ten days later, the Yard swooped on a number of addresses in north London and arrested three men and a woman, all Irish, under the Prevention of Terrorism Act. They were taken to the top-security Paddington Green police station, the one normally used for interrogating terrorist suspects. By the evening, one man and the woman, together with another woman who had been arrested several days previously, were released without charge. By the next day, only one man remained in custody and a Scotland Yard spokesman said, somewhat sheepishly: 'It must be remembered that people will be detained from time to time in connection with this case.' An unnamed anti-terrorist detective was also quoted as saying: 'We believe we know how the killers got in and out of the country. What we now need to know is who they are.' The outcome of such intensive detective work still did not add up to very much. The last suspect, James Scanlon, a twenty-six-year-old labourer described as a founder member of the IRSP, was not released but served with an exclusion order from Britain. The London-based IRSP support group protested that it was subjected to 'systematic harassment and surveillance' by the police. Such close scrutiny would have been normal, despite INLA and the IRSP being thoroughly infiltrated by the RUC Special Branch and the security services, usually MI5. Seven of the support group's members had already been questioned, and four – the Paddington Green four – detained under the terrorism law. It looked very much a case of 'round up the usual suspects'. Police also detained a twenty-one-year-old man, Billy Dunlop, at Heathrow on his way from Ireland to a job in Germany, but he turned out to have no connections with the IRSP.

The search was going cold and getting more bizarre. In mid-May, *Paris Match* published an interview with two hooded men claiming to be the killers with connections with various liberation movements including the Palestinians This somehow gave rise to charges that Neave's assassins had been trained by the Russians in South Yemen, accusations that were promptly denied. In fact, the two 'men' were fakes: one was actually a woman and the other a French journalist persuaded to take part in the macabre mock-up.

In June the grim manhunt briefly took second place to more welcome news when Diana Neave was created a life peer in the Queen's Birthday Honours List on the personal recommendation of the new Prime Minister. As a tribute to her husband and his constituency, she took the title of Lady Airey Neave of Abingdon. She also disclosed that friends had urged her to take her husband's place as MP for the constituency. 'I did think about it very seriously,' she said. 'I think if there had been time to consider it more deeply I might have done so. I know Airey would have liked it. I realise now that would really have been too much to cope with so quickly.'[2] Lady Airey took up public life vigorously. The causes that he espoused, she also pursued, serving on the North

Atlantic Assembly and the Lords' Select Committee on the European Communities.

The speculation about her husband's killers continued, with the *Sun* repeating the false *Paris Match* claims in a splash story on 18 June. It was not until July that further leads turned up, unexpectedly in a television programme. BBC's *Tonight*, casting round for a story on Northern Ireland, was offered an interview with an INLA representative. A team headed by experienced reporter David Lomax went to Dublin, where a man calling himself Dr Gray gave telephone instructions to go to a series of hotels. The trail eventually led to a room on the outskirts of the city booked in Lomax's name. There, he met two men wearing wigs, dark glasses and false moustaches. They also wore surgical gloves and had 'strange bulges' in the pockets of their anoraks.

Outlandish as their garb might have appeared, it was clear in the interview that followed that they represented themselves as the real thing. Their authenticity is debatable. Asked by Lomax why they had murdered Neave, one of the men replied: 'Well, I murdered Airey Neave because he was a militarist. He was in fact Margaret Thatcher's principal adviser on security. He was an advocate of order and increased repression against a nationalist people in the six counties. And we find it a surprising question why people wonder why we executed Neave. The same questions weren't asked when ordinary British soldiers are shot.

'Neave was to be the head of the military apparatus in the north. We had done serious intelligence work on Roy Mason and obviously during the period of the Labour government, Roy Mason was also a prime target for the Irish National Liberation Army. We took the decision what to do, to switch our emphasis to Mr Neave when it became obvious that there would be a Tory government.'

Lomax asked how the act was carried out. The INLA man said it was an active cell of INLA, but would not say whether it was based in Britain or Ireland. 'That is a matter of security for us and it's up to the British intelligence agencies to puzzle out how, and who it was carried out by, for themselves.' In response to repeated questions, he insisted that the cell had breached security at Westminster, but would not say how. What, Lomax asked, had the murder achieved except widespread revulsion in Britain and a determination that force would not triumph over democracy? 'We didn't see any examples of that revulsion except from the ruling interests in Britain. We didn't see thousands of British workers marching in the streets mourning for Mr Neave, we saw no obvious reaction against Neave's assassination. Neave had a record of consistent anti-working-class attitudes towards the British people themselves,' said the INLA man.

Then what, Lomax pressed him, had the murder done for INLA? It was not a murder, but an assassination or execution, he replied, to be seen in the context of the overall struggle against British occupation forces 'because we have a war against the British military occupation forces. Neave had a responsibility for that.' Furthermore, 'Mr Neave was not a civilian, did not act, or never acted like a civilian in regard to the Irish people. Mr Neave was an advocate of torture in Ireland. Mr Neave was an advocate of capital punishment for Irish freedom fighters. The British establishment will have to know that it's not only their soldiers are at risk, but also the people who direct the actions of those soldiers, and it's up to the establishment to take responsibility for that position, not ours. Mr Neave was a legitimate target.' The INLA man also adduced evidence that the killing had had 'a visible effect' on the Tory Cabinet, particularly Mrs Thatcher, who relied very much on Neave. 'We don't think that just by assassinating Airey Neave that you are going to win the struggle,' he went on. 'We would see it more as a protracted struggle . . . that won't cease until Britain has granted the Irish people the right to self-determination.'

The INLA man parried questions on the size, composition, weaponry and activities of his organisation, and fell back on the customary IRSP rhetoric about building a democratic socialist republic in Ireland to describe the movement's political aims. 'We want power over the wealth that's created for the working people, and we would have a similar view for the people in Scotland, England and Wales. We think our politics has a relevance.' If Britain withdrew from Ireland, it would be to the benefit of working people everywhere. Some shadow-boxing over the future of the one million Protestants followed, before the INLA man offered: 'In a sense it's up to the British government to decide how long this conflict, this war, is going to last.' It could end 'tomorrow' if the British army specified a date to leave. Lomax finally asked if INLA intended to continue operations in Britain. 'It's our – it's our intention to continue military operations against the British military in the six counties. It is our intention to carry out those operations in England, or wherever the opportunity presents itself.'[3]

The twelve and a half minute interview created problems at the highest levels in the BBC. It was undoubtedly a scoop, but it also fell into the category of 'giving publicity to terrorists' that Neave had inveighed against throughout his time as Shadow Ulster Secretary. A decision went all the way up to Ian Trethowan, the director-general, before the interview was broadcast in the last edition of *Tonight* on 5 July 1979. The row that followed was slow to ignite. Northern Ireland Secretary Humphrey Atkins complained the next day but then silence descended. A week later, Lady Airey wrote to the *Daily Telegraph* arguing that the 'terrorist was given ample scope to besmirch the memory of my husband'. By muddle and mistake, Lady Airey had not been told of the programme before it went out and she was deeply aggrieved. She felt the decision to transmit the interview betrayed the traditional standards of British broadcasting. After her letter, the storm broke. The newspapers declared open season on the BBC and Mrs Thatcher angrily denounced the programme makers. Willie Whitelaw, the Home Secretary, later told *Tonight*'s editor Roger Bolton: 'She was desperately affected by Airey Neave's death, desperately. And in a way this affected her whole thoughts on broadcasting coverage of Northern Ireland. She had a mystical view of what he would do in Ireland, that he had actually been killed by the INLA because they thought he was going to do things in Ireland which would have been so successful it would have done a great deal of damage. I mean, this is much too sophisticated a view for me. The INLA killed Airey Neave because he was a good catch to kill.'[4]

Soon after the Prime Minister's outburst, Commander Peter Duffy interviewed Lomax and his team. They gave what information they could, having already warned the INLA interviewee that Special Branch would inevitably come looking for material to aid their enquiries. Their help did not take the search further forward. More weeks passed before Scotland Yard detectives turned up in Armagh to interview men detained in Gough Barracks over a number of killings. These were believed to include the prototype murder of Trooper McAnally. But by the end of August, as the inquest on Neave was delayed yet again, Scotland Yard admitted there had been 'no new developments' in the five-month-long enquiry. The stalemate was as exasperating as it was mystifying. In his *Sunday Express* column on 9 September, the editor John Junor wrote that Special Branch was said to know the names of the assassins. Then why not publish them, with a price of £100,000 on their heads – dead or alive – he asked.

The inquest was finally held in Horseferry Road, Westminster, on 15 October, almost seven months after Neave died. George Berryman, scientific officer at the Royal Arsenal, gave evidence about the 'highly sophisticated' bomb. His account of how the bomb exploded corroborated the by now generally accepted story. A very powerful explosive had indeed been used, but on the direction of the coroner he gave no further details, saying 'it would be wiser' to disclose no more. Neave's widow spoke quietly as she recalled the fateful day. He had phoned little more than an hour before his death to say he was going to his tailor's before they went down to the country. She had heard the explosion from Marsham Street but did not know where it had taken place.

Commander Michael Richards, of 'H' District of the Metropolitan Police and a member of the Anti-Terrorist Squad at the time of the killing, assured the court that the police enquiry was 'still very much in action'. The coroner returned a verdict of unlawful killing. After the thirty-minute hearing, Lady Airey said: 'I have great confidence in the police. I know they are doing their utmost, and the circumstances are not entirely easy.' It was almost two years before the story surfaced again, in a bizarre twist implicating a Roman Catholic priest, Father Vincent Ford, who had been sentenced to twelve years in gaol in March 1981 by a special criminal court in Dublin for leading a £56,000 bank raid in Ballina, County Mayo. Father Ford, a staunch republican from Sligo, had been ordained in 1968 and had been a priest in New York State before returning to Ireland where he became deeply involved in republican politics in late 1975. Irish and MI6 agents tracked him as he took up with the IRSP and its military wing, and he became a suspect in the Neave killing. One newspaper went so far as to suggest that British security chiefs believed he may have helped mastermind the assassination. Members of the Anti-Terrorist Squad were detailed to interview him but once more nothing came of it.

The trail went cold again until the late summer of 1982, when great excitement accompanied the arrest of three alleged members of INLA in Paris by French anti-terrorist police. In late August, a ten-strong squad of the elite Groupe d'Intervention de la Gendarmerie Nationale (GIGN) acting on a tip-off raided a flat at 82, Rue Diderot in the Vincennes area of Paris. They were looking for a burly Irishman who went under the pseudonym of James McCabe, and his comrades Stephen King and Mary Reid. McCabe was in fact Michael Plunkett, the heavily bearded founding member of the IRSP and the party's general secretary for four years. Aged thirty, he had been on the run from the Irish police since the summer of 1979, when he had jumped bail on a charge of possessing bomb-making equipment. He was one of the most important figures in the IRSP, a close associate of Seamus Costello and widely travelled in Europe where he had contacts with German revolutionaries. King, also thirty, from County Tyrone, was on the run too, having jumped bail on an arms possession charge. Mary Reid had joined the IRSP in 1977, moving swiftly on to become education officer and editor of the *Starry Plough*. All three were Irish citizens. King and Plunkett were arrested and both were so expertly bound, gagged and blindfolded that they imagined an SAS summary execution was at hand. Reid was picked up as she returned to the flat with her ten-year-old son. Police claimed that they found two handguns in the flat, plus a small quantity of pink-coloured explosives of a kind similar to that which had killed Airey Neave.

From here, the story goes back three months to May 1982, when British intelligence sent the French police a four-page advisory note about possible European terrorist links between the Irish, Basques and al-Fatah via a Belgian arms dealer. The note made special mention of two other 'dangerous terrorists' thought to be in Paris. It named Michael Plunkett as an INLA terrorist, a specialist in arms supplies for the organisation and the author of a series of attacks in West Germany. Two days after Plunkett's arrest, two senior Scotland Yard detectives went over to Paris to talk to Captain Paul Barril of GIGN. He showed them photographs found in the Rue Diderot flat. The arrests also caused a considerable diplomatic stir: a high-level member of the British embassy in Paris who enjoyed the confidence of Mrs Thatcher contacted the Elysée Palace to congratulate the authorities on the operation. Soon after came a further memorandum to the French police, in the form of a seven-page document from Commander John Wilson of the Special Branch, which was leaked to French journalists. The key part reads: 'Michael Oliver Plunkett, alias Mike, alias James McCabe, was born on 11 October 1951 in the Republic of Ireland ... was introduced to Irish extremism in 1969 when he entered the CP. Was a member of Official Sinn Fein from 1971 to 1974. Later he was a founding member of the IRSP and became a worldwide organiser. This position hides his activities within the INLA. He is the author of articles in the *Irish*

Times and the *Starry Plough*, official organ of the IRSP, protesting against allegations that the IRSP was responsible for killings and murder in Ulster. His name has been associated with those of confirmed terrorists, among whom — and Vincent Ford, two of the suspects in the Airey Neave murder in London on 30 March 1979, claimed by the INLA. He was also in Holland during the assassination of the British ambassador in 1979, for which he is still a suspect.'⁵ The blanked-out name is believed to be that of Brendan O'Sullivan, an IRSP member from Killorglin, County Kerry, who had once been questioned by Irish police investigating the kidnapping and ransom of an Irish bank manager in January 1980.

It was not long before news of the Paris arrests found its way into the British papers. On 5 September, the *Sunday Telegraph* reported that 'two members of the Irish National Liberation Army arrested by police in France nine days ago *were linked* [author's italics] with the murder of Mr Airey Neave, the Conservative MP'. The story, by the paper's crime correspondent Christopher House, was clearly written with inside information. It named Plunkett and King. It said that Special Branch officers had traced the movements of Plunkett 'and ten others' at addresses in north-west London and the Irish Republic before and after the killing. And it claimed that the arrests were 'potentially the first big breakthrough' in the continuing hunt for the bombers. The pair had information vital to the investigation. But how to get at them? Under French law, British officers could not demand to question the men. Since they were both Irish nationals, they could not ask for their extradition. Moreover, there was no extradition treaty between France and the Irish Republic, so they could not get them that way either. The only solution lay in a Commission Rogatoire, a diplomatic move involving an application by Scotland Yard to the Director of Public Prosecutions, who would then work through the Foreign Office. This complicated procedure would take at least six weeks and would require the approval of the French government. The *Sunday Telegraph* disclosed that, despite statements to the contrary, two Special Branch officers did go to Paris, but it was suggested that they were only there for twenty-four hours and that they left 'empty-handed'.

The 'Vincennes Three' were subsequently charged with illegal possession of explosives. Plunkett and King were held in the notorious La Santé prison for many months, but the case against them began to unravel almost immediately. It was suggested that the arms had been planted in the flat by police, and a gendarme in the raiding party later said in a sworn statement that he had been ordered to lie about the affair. Furthermore, contrary to French law, the trio had not been present when the evidence against them was detected. All three were finally released from prison in May 1983 and the charges against them were dropped.

The fact that they had been cleared of these charges did not prevent the *Mail on Sunday* from naming Plunkett in a story clearly inspired by Scotland Yard. On 24 July 1983, the paper said it had seen the secret Special Branch report prepared by Commander John Wilson which named Neave's killers as Vincent Ford and Brendan O'Sullivan. Ford was presumably the renegade Irish priest and O'Sullivan the IRSP member. But the paper went on to say that the Yard's real target was 'INLA terrorist' Michael Plunkett, now a free man again. O'Sullivan and Ford were merely 'persons of terrorist standing'. Scotland Yard described Plunkett as 'very dangerous' and the document further quoted Commander Wilson as saying: 'He is a central figure in Irish extremist affairs, with strong links with the Provisional IRA [sic] and extremists of the left in Germany and Holland.' However, no attempts were made by Scotland Yard to get their quarry into British jurisdiction. Information from the INLA to the author clears all three of the Rue Diderot suspects. Plunkett is admitted to be a member of the organisation, 'but more political than military'.[6]

In 1989, Plunkett, King and Reid successfully sued the French state for wrongful arrest and were awarded the princely sum of one franc. In June 1991, three gendarmes were charged with fabricating evidence to frame the trio and given light sentences that were quashed on appeal. Captain Barril, who was not among those charged, said in evidence to the court that they had raided the Rue Diderot flat after a tip-off from British intelligence that there would be a terrorist attack that weekend. Reid and King returned to live in Ireland. Plunkett fought for political asylum and was allowed to stay in France where in 1994 he was working as a plumber.

To this day, the Neave killing continues to spawn conspiracy theories. As the most high-profile operation of its kind during three decades of terrorism, it still exercises a powerful hold on the imagination. Enoch Powell, the maverick Tory MP who went over to the Ulster Unionists, brought his own unique style to bear on the 'whodunit' question. The MP for South Down, anxious about a perceived drift back to the Ulster power-sharing policies of Edward Heath, said in late 1981: 'I regret that I did not see it all earlier. I now think that the turning point was 1979, and that it came with Airey Neave's murder.' Neave's involvement with Ulster, he concluded, was not simply about a province (however important), 'but something central to the whole business of foreign policy, and directly related to the pattern of Western alliances'.[7] In the spring of that year, Geoffrey Sloane, a research student at Keele University, interviewed Clive Abbott, a senior official at the Northern Ireland Office. Abbott was dismissive of the Conservatives' pre-1979 policy, crafted by Neave, of returning powers to local government in the province. He suggested that the United States would have to play a discreet role in any final settlement, which could be 'a confederal Ireland' in which Dublin would have a say. This inflammatory material came into Powell's hands, and though ministers played down its significance Abbott did not lose his job: indeed, he was promoted.

Suspicion continued to burn in Powell's mind, and in January 1984 he claimed in an interview that the CIA had been responsible for a number of political assassinations, including those in 1979 of Airey Neave, Lord Mountbatten, the Queen's cousin, and the prominent Unionist politician Robert Bradford, a friend of

Neave, in November 1981. Powell elaborated on his theory in the *Guardian* on 12 March, claiming to have inside knowledge from members of the RUC to whom he had spoken. He alleged that the police were convinced of 'the effective existence of a policy and motivation outside and above the IRA and INLA' which had led to 'a series of assassinations which can be distinguished from the run-of-the-mill murders of persons connected with the security forces'. Powell traced the conspiracy to moves begun by Neave's successor, the elegant Humphrey Atkins, soon after becoming Ulster Secretary to bring together the US, UK and Irish governments for talks on the future of the province. The venue was to be New York. Powell, strongly opposed to the involvement of the USA, had been relieved when the plan was ditched.

On 18 October 1986, in a speech to Conservative students in Birmingham, Powell returned to his theme. He rejected INLA's claims to have murdered Neave and insisted that he had met his death at the hands of 'high contracting parties' made up of 'MI6 and their friends'. Neave had to be eliminated, he argued, because he (like Powell) was committed to a programme of integration of Northern Ireland within the United Kingdom. The killing of Neave was designed to shake the government into adopting a course more favourable to the United States, whose aim was to see a united Ireland firmly within the NATO military alliance. The plot to destabilise Ulster had begun twenty years previously, he said. It brought together the Foreign Office, British intelligence and the United States, especially the CIA. None of the Prime Ministers of recent years – Heath, Wilson or Callaghan – knew what was going on. America secured from Britain an undertaking to transfer Northern Ireland out of the United Kingdom into an 'all-Ireland, presumably confederal' state. The first objective in this grand plan was to get rid of the Unionist government at Stormont. 'MI6 and their friends proved equal to the job,' he asserted. But the Americans took fright ahead of the 1979 election, fearing that Thatcher and Neave would take the process of Northern Ireland integration into the UK so far that it could not be reversed. Washington was alarmed at 'evidence, or what they thought to be evidence' that the new leader Mrs Thatcher and aide Airey Neave had no intention of playing ball with the USA's long-term aims. Accordingly, 'the road block was cleared by eliminating Airey Neave on the verge of his taking office; and from then onwards events were moved ahead again along the timetabled path'. Powell refused to answer reporters' questions as to whether he was accusing the Americans of Neave's murder. Asked if it would have made any difference if the MP had not been killed, he replied, 'Perhaps not, but those who have assassinated him believed it would have done.'

Powell offered no supporting evidence for his theory, which outraged many of his fellow Conservatives. Dame Jill Knight, right-wing MP for Edgbaston, said: 'There was a time when Mr Powell's logic was respected. That day has long passed, and I must say that his latest outburst confirms the view a thousand per cent.'[8] The *Sunday Telegraph* took the unusual step of printing a brief opinion on its front page: 'The premise of Mr Powell's argument is that the Americans are desperate to secure defence facilities in Ireland, but there is absolutely no evidence for this – and absolutely no strategic reason why it should be so. Ireland could at most make a minimal contribution to NATO's security,' it read. 'From this premise, Mr Powell goes on to spin his tale of twenty years' murder and treachery by sections of the British government. It would make an interesting plot for a thriller; it is not what we expect from a Privy Councillor. Mr Powell thinks he has identified the enemies of Ulster: in fact, he is playing into their hands.' It was not until the following year that Powell pointed, in his usual Delphic manner, to CIA involvement in Central America and Iran, for which evidence only came to light much later.

The conviction that the security forces had a hand in Neave's assassination goes wider than Enoch Powell. The Irish writer and investigative reporter Kevin Cahill also believes that elements of the secret state were involved. He claims that Neave was on the brink of a massive overhaul of the security services, possibly involving a merger of MI5 and MI6 and arising from alleged corruption within the secret state. He links Neave's murder to that of Sir Richard Sykes and an attempt on the life of Christopher Tugendhat, former Tory MP and Commissioner, in December 1980. Neave would have been head of the new combined security services, Cahill believes, with Sykes and Tugendhat as his deputies, the former with responsibility for foreign operations and Tugendhat in charge of domestic activities.

Cahill's extraordinary story begins in March 1979, at the annual St Patrick's Day party at the Irish embassy in London, less than a fortnight before Neave died. Cahill was then working for Singer & Friedlander, the merchant bank. 'About eight in the evening, I came out into the downstairs foyer to get a taxi. None was available and I found myself in the company of an Englishman I recognised as Airey Neave. He was, as the Irish say, half-cut, but well in control of himself.' Cahill introduced himself as ex-army and an admirer of Neave's escape books. 'He said something to the effect of army, hmmm. And then, quite out of the blue and almost to himself, said words to the effect, "There are going to be changes here, big changes, soon. There is going to be cleaning of the stables, a cleaning of the Augean stables. There has been serious corruption." He then offered that the war was "all wrong. We have to change all that. No use playing games. We have to win. We have to make changes, big changes. We will win when the [corruption] is sorted out. Count on that."'[9]

Cahill found Neave's remarks 'quite incongruous' considering that his Shadow Cabinet responsibility lay in Northern Ireland. 'His preoccupations seemed to be internally oriented, towards the UK, with his Irish appointment almost a sideline.' Cahill assumed that the word 'corruption' referred to Soviet penetration of the security services – this was the period of Anthony Blunt and suspicions about Roger Hollis, the head of MI5. As it turned out the rogue elements in MI5 were right-wing dissidents, plotting the downfall of Harold Wilson and the Labour left.

Cahill, an engaging man with a Neavesque eye for a plot, moved into journalism and began investigating American interference in the UK computer industry. In late 1983 or early 1984, Paddy Ashdown, the Liberal Democrat leader, who also has an MI6 background, took up the issue. He also appointed Cahill his research assistant which gave him access to the House of Commons.

In this way, Cahill became friendly with Commons security staff, some of whom were ex-marines (like Ashdown). Slowly and elliptically, he began to ask about Neave. 'Of about six "chats" over the next few years, not one of the staff ever doubted that the bomb was planted while the car was in the House. Those who were technically interested usually stated the obvious, that the chances of the car making it to the House with the bomb on board were "slim to zero" but the more frequent line was that "everyone knew" what happened but no one could speak in detail as it was too dangerous. This was because not one of the six believed that the IRA did it. The average opinion was that it was an inside job.' Cahill also met Enoch Powell, who merely reiterated what he had told others: that he thought his source was reliable, that he had checked his source and that the facts were true. 'An MI6/CIA group had got rid of Neave because he posed a threat to them. This looked like a reasonable corroboration of all the informal material I had picked up,' Cahill concluded.

His overall view is that the scale of the operation, involving three 'hits' in three capitals had to be conducted by a large-scale organisation – which INLA was not – capable of collecting detailed intelligence on the movements of three very senior people in government, without being detected. Neave, he judged, was 'the conspirator's conspirator' but also 'a deeply unpleasant and flawed man, and arrogant'. Cahill concludes: 'He made a serious error by any standards, in that he threatened senior figures in the intelligence establishment, going so far as to threaten prosecution in the courts of certain individuals.' Ergo, Neave was murdered by the security services, probably by elements of MI6 working with the CIA.

Leaving aside the Hollywood dimension, this theory is difficult to swallow. In the first place, why would Neave, a lifelong covert operator well known for his secretive manner, suddenly decide to unburden himself to a complete stranger in the foyer of the Irish embassy after a St Patrick's Day party? Even if halfway drunk, as Neave sometimes was? People often drink too much at such parties and there tends to be loose talk, political bantering, among the high-level guests. But the idea of Neave disclosing his innermost intentions during a casual meeting is unlikely to say the least. Cahill's story does, however, illustrate the level of acceptance that Powell's ideas have gained. By his account, the 'inside job' theory is taken seriously by security professionals in Westminster. It would, of course, neatly explain why there has never been a single arrest, or a published report on the affair.

The MI6–CIA conspiracy theory also gets support from another source, superficially less likely but much closer to the heart of the secret state. Gerald James, former head of the ordnance firm Astra Holdings, was unsuccessfully prosecuted by the government over his role in the arms to Iraq affair. He had also been involved with Neave in the covert operations to prepare for 'civil breakdown' in the 1970s. James insists that Neave set himself the task of sorting out the intelligence services. Things could have been different for Astra if he had, but Neave made the mistake of saying these things publicly and was killed by a bomb. The crime was blamed on Irish terrorists, 'but bomb experts have since said that it couldn't have been an IRA bomb because it had a mercury fuse, tripped on the angle of the car, a type that was available only to the CIA at the time'.[10]

James told the author: 'Neave seemed to excite quite a lot of fear among certain sections, because one of the things he wanted to do was clean up the intelligence and security services. That's why a lot of people think he died. The man he was going to make head of MI6 [Sykes] got machine-gunned on his front doorstep.' There was also an attempt on the life of Christopher Tugendhat, Neave's putative head of MI5. 'Neave perceived it [the security service] as a problem. He felt they were abusing their position and the people in them were using it for their personal gain. They wanted to control things. It is a wonderful cover for corruption, national security.' MI6 was 'very inter-related' with the CIA, dissident elements of which were able to continue in business as a private organisation with money in secret bank accounts. The involvement of both organisations in Neave's murder was therefore 'highly likely', insists James. And because he was perceived as a dangerous person, they got rid of him.[11]

Another explanation has come from a self-confessed INLA member and police informer, Raymond Gilmour. Born and raised on the notorious Creggan estate in Londonderry, he joined INLA in 1978 and later switched to the Provisionals, but he maintains that throughout the decade of his terrorist activity, he worked as an undercover agent for the RUC Special Branch. In his book *Dead Ground*, published in 1998 after he had changed his identity to live incognito 'somewhere in Europe', Gilmour says that a unit was sent over to London to kill Neave after the successful trial run with the mercury-tilt bomb that mortally wounded Robert McAnally. The two men, allegedly Chris Bishop and Vincent O'Reilly, sailed for London on a coal boat from Londonderry. 'Chris Bishop' cannot be his real name, because Gilmour maintains that he has changed the names of all those connected with his narrative who are still alive (with the exception of Martin McGuinness). 'Bishop' has never been convicted of any terrorist offence. 'O'Reilly' must also be a false name, because while his whereabouts are not known he is not listed as dead. The two men were said to have reconnoitred Neave's movements for a number of days before fixing the bomb to the underside of his car with magnets. Two days after the killing, 'O'Reilly' and 'Bishop' returned to Londonderry. Nothing was said officially but the clear understanding among members of INLA in the city was that the pair had planted the bomb. 'When the police released a photofit picture of one of the suspects, it was an absolute ringer for O'Reilly,' writes Gilmour.[12] Republican sources in Londonderry and Belfast flatly contradict Gilmour's theory. In 1999, speculation surfaced that the bombers had been aided by left-wing sympathisers. Jack Holland alleged that information helping the two-man team to penetrate the House of Commons disguised as workmen came from 'leftist Labour Party activists' who told INLA that security around legitimate workmen engaged in renovations was slack. It is true that for much of the time, particularly during recess periods, Westminster resembles a giant building site. Holland claims the bomb was smuggled in in a workman's lunch box. But these 'left-wing activists' have never been identified and no other expert has suggested inside information from such a quarter. It is clear from the author's briefing with INLA sources, however, that the organisation did have an informer in London passing back security information about Neave and other high-ranking public figures.

On the available evidence, particularly the information given by INLA sources to the author, it seems clear that the assassins were virtually unknown adherents of the republican cause who melted back into civilian life after carrying out this operation. The masked INLA source insisted: 'They [the security forces] never came close at any point. These people were not around for them to get because their anonymity was such that they had safety in their professions and the lives that they were living. They were never up-front people; never arrested for INLA/IRSP activities. They had never come to the attention of the security services.' Rounding up the usual suspects would not have netted the unit, he added, because they had never been picked up, and their names were never on any list of volunteers potentially capable of such an action. 'They came out of professional lives they were in and went back, and no consequent change of activity or time lapse would suggest anything.'[13] They would erect such a smokescreen, it might be argued. But more than two decades of enquiry have failed to disprove this explanation.

In the years since the assassination, evidence has been pieced together to suggest that the British government, through the SAS and its proxy killers in the UDA, exacted a bloody revenge on the leadership of the IRSP and INLA. INLA's glorification in the murder of Neave was short-lived and its exultation in its success hid a parlous state of affairs in the IRSP. Miriam Daly had resigned six months earlier, weeks before the assassination. Mrs Daly, a lecturer at Queen's University, was an intelligent and well-respected republican. Her husband Jim was also active in the movement and shared her misgivings about the IRSP's lack of political direction and subordination to INLA. Her place was taken by Mick Plunkett, but he too disappeared in May, costing the party £5,000 in bail money. The party failed to contest local elections in the Republic, and the European elections in June 1979. Finally, after a particularly gruesome gun and grenade attack on women prison officers outside Armagh goal, in which a forty-year-old mother of six died, and the killing of an RUC constable outside the city's courthouse, on 2 July INLA was declared an illegal organisation throughout the United Kingdom. The party was virtually broke and could not even provide for its prisoners in the Maze, numbering about ninety at that time. The INLA Army Council was also deeply divided. John O'Doherty lost a vote of confidence but refused to accept the verdict, with the result that the Belfast fighters more or less went their own way under Ronnie Bunting.

The whole organisation was clearly vulnerable to outside attack, and with the investigation into Neave's killing going nowhere it came from a predictable quarter. In the view of Father Raymond Murray, historian of the SAS in Ireland, it took the form of Operation Ranc. This was a series of actions by British intelligence – an exercise in retribution – against the INLA following its admitted assassination of Neave. The campaign, over several months, used both official and unofficial personnel to carry out secret death sentences. 'Operation Ranc is believed to have cost the lives of Ronnie Bunting, a very senior INLA officer and his non-INLA colleague Noel Lyttle, Miriam Daly (former IRSP) and John Turnly,' wrote Father Murray. 'It was terminated prematurely following strong but private protests from the Irish government . . . Working through the SAS and picking up their old allies, the UDA once more, "Ranc" engineered three assassination operations. Since it lacked hard evidence for the Airey Neave killing, soft targets were chosen.'[14]

The Irish magazine *Hibernia* identified a special Cabinet sub-committee originally set up to deal with emergencies such as the 1974 miners' strike as the body responsible for Operation Ranc. It claimed that this committee gave *carte blanche*, including unlimited financial resources and promises of commendations, to members of the Anti-Terrorist Squad and the security forces who produced convictions for Neave's assassination. MI5, MI6, the shadowy security and intelligence group attached to the Territorial Army made up of SAS members, all made enquiries: 'as the months went by with little or no results, other more ominous noises began to emanate from the same agencies. If there were no convictions, the messages ran, then there would be satisfaction of another sort: even if it meant killing non-military members of the IRSP such as Miriam Daly.'[15] The involvement of a Cabinet sub-committee set up to deal with civil contingencies does not ring wholly true, and another theory put forward by one of *Hibernia*'s rivals, *Magill*, may be nearer the truth. This report in June 1979 claimed that an intelligence sub-committee was set up to hunt Neave's killers. It was headed by Angus Maude, the Paymaster-General with a strong right-wing track record. He liaised with Francis Brooks Richards, the Cabinet's Co-ordinator of Security and Intelligence. *Magill* reported that Maude, valued by Margaret Thatcher for his years of political experience, 'his sound views and his acid wit', had promised unlimited financial resources to capture Neave's murderers.

The first to die in this crusade of retribution was John Turnly, a forty-four-year-old former British army officer who came from a Unionist background. He was nonetheless a confirmed nationalist, a founding member of the Irish Independence Party and a councillor in Larne. He was not a member of the IRSP or INLA, but was closely associated with them on the National H-Blocks Committee. On the evening of 4 June 1980, he was gunned down while driving with his family to a public meeting in Carnlough. The gunmen rammed his car and shot him nine times with a sub-machine gun and a pistol. Four local men, members of the UDA, were charged with murder, including two brothers, Eric and Robert McConnell. The brothers received life sentences. During the trial RUC detectives admitted that notes from interviews with nineteen-year-old Eric McConnell had been destroyed on the instruction of a senior officer on the grounds that they contained 'sensitive information'. Robert McConnell told police he had been asked to keep Turnly's house under surveillance to find out if he was visited by INLA men. On the basis of his observations, the UDA decided that Turnly was a leading man in the INLA and McConnell's cell was given orders to shoot him.

But the most telling disclosures came at the end of the trial. In a statement from the dock after his conviction, Robert McConnell said he had been working for the SAS and named a sergeant and a corporal who had supplied him with army issue weapons. Moreover, they had discussed republicanism and its leaders, including Turnly, Mrs Daly and Bernadette McAliskey. In his statement, Robert McConnell said: 'They said they had information that over a two-year period the republicans had a plan to escalate tension in the province by civil disorder, large-scale importation of arms and explosives and by certain actions which would arouse the sympathy of the republican people with the objective of starting a political war. We realise now that this involved the hunger strikes.' The senior of the two SAS officers, Sergeant Tom Aiken, who had just returned from a tour of duty in Hong Kong, regarded Turnly as important because of his experience with imports and exports, and his links with Laos and Cambodia. McConnell said that Sergeant Aiken contacted him a number of times by telephone and arranged for him to pick up various items – weapons, uniforms and information on how to obtain intelligence-gathering equipment – on lonely roads at the dead of night. 'I am making this statement so that the court and the public will be aware that information on Turnly *and others* [author's italics] was fed through me by British intelligence . . .'[16] Robert McConnell was speaking after being given a life sentence for murder, and could not therefore expect any leniency to flow from his disclosures. It is more likely that the UDA man felt let down by his SAS minders, who deemed him expendable in the long war of attrition against militant republicanism.

The next victim was Miriam Daly. No longer active in the IRSP, she nonetheless remained an ardent republican who campaigned against conditions in the Maze. She had long been known to the security authorities, having worked with the Irish community in Camden Town in north London in the sixties, before returning to Belfast when the civil rights movement took off. Initially attracted to the politics of John Hume's SDLP, she soon turned to militant republicanism. She was 'a new breed of radical, ideally suited to INLA/IRSP politics. Like [Seamus] Costello, she dreamed of uniting all "anti-imperialist groupings in Ireland and was also prepared to sanction the use of terror".'[17] On the afternoon of 26 June, Mrs Daly went to the baker near her home in Andersonstown Road, Belfast, and bought a teatime treat for her ten-year-old adopted twins, Marie and Donal. Coming home from school later that afternoon, Marie found her mother, bound hand and foot, lying face down in a pool of blood. Nearby lay a bloodstained cushion with bullet holes. It had been used to deaden the sound of the six bullets fired into her head from a 9 mm semi-automatic pistol. The telephone lines had also been cut. It was a 'professional' job. A scene of crime officer commented: 'It seemed to me that an execution had taken place.' Her killers had evidently entered the house by the front door, evading the constant army and RUC patrols in this strongly Catholic area of Belfast. It was later suggested that the killers' original target was Jim Daly, but they tired of waiting for him to come home and settled on his wife as a high-profile 'political hit'. Nobody was ever charged with Mrs Daly's murder, though it was subsequently claimed by the UDA, whose 'strong connection' with British intelligence has been amply documented by Father Murray and others.

The third victim was Ronnie Bunting. A former internee hated by Protestant paramilitaries, he was arrested for the last time on 8 August 1980 and interrogated in Castlereagh for several days. During this inquisition, Bunting alleged that detectives said they could 'arrange' for him to get three slugs in the head. In the early hours of 15 October, Bunting was at home in bed with his wife Suzanne Fellow IRSP member Noel Lyttle was asleep in the front bedroom along with the Buntings' infant son Ronan. They were woken up by the sound of banging downstairs as masked men with sledgehammers broke down the front door of their home in Downfine Gardens, a quiet cul-de-sac in Andersonstown. Bunting and his wife leaped out of bed but the gunmen forced the door open and began firing. 'They wore those green, ribbed pullovers with suede patches on the shoulders and ski-type masks which covered their whole faces with only holes for the eyes,' Suzanne Bunting later recollected. 'They knew which room to find Ronnie and Noel in. They were cool and calm – like animals, without fear – they had no smell of fear.' Bunting fell dead on the landing. His wife was wounded in the shoulder and under her right arm, and as he left one of the gunmen shot her in the mouth. It was a miracle that she survived. Noel Lyttle had also been shot and lay dying on the bed, the baby screaming in his cot alongside.

No mainstream paramilitary organisation ever claimed responsibility for the double murder. And, unusually, the killers' car was never found. The obscure Protestant Task Force, heard of only once in 1974 and professing to be made up of former British soldiers, said it carried out the killings. But most expert opinion agrees that responsibility lies with the UDA, which used the same squad that murdered Miriam Daly and acted on 'intelligence provided'. Suzanne Bunting told the *Irish News* that RUC detectives suspected a loyalist gang. 'I told the police that I believe and know, with all my heart, that it was the SAS. The attack was too well planned by men who were cool and calm and knew what they were doing.' The layout of the house, which had five bedrooms, was well known to the police, who had raided it often. And Suzanne Bunting remembered that when Neave had been assassinated the previous year, Ronnie had warned, in a pointed reference to Margaret Thatcher, 'She'll want her pound of flesh.'

The attempt on Bernadette McAliskey's life followed three months later. In the early morning of 16 January 1981, three gunmen drove up to the remote family home in Derryloughan, Coalisland, and smashed in the front door with sledgehammers. Mrs McAliskey and her husband Michael were preparing breakfast for their three children. Mr McAliskey was shot four times as the would-be killers forced their way in and pursued his wife into the bedroom, where they shot her eight times. The gang leader, Andrew Watson, a twenty-five-year-old ex-member of the UDR and son of a former H-Block prison officer, stopped shooting only when the magazine of his 9 mm Browning pistol was exhausted. It seemed inconceivable that the McAliskeys could survive. However, unbeknown to the family, an undercover team of paratroopers was dug in around the house. They made no attempt to halt the break-in but arrested the gunmen as they left. For twenty minutes the McAliskeys were close to death. Their phone line had been cut by the would-be assassins, and the paratroopers – believed to be SAS – claimed that their radios were not working, before leaving the scene. Accounts of their conduct vary, one version suggesting that a member of the SAS team gave Mrs McAliskey medical help before the arrival of soldiers of the Argyll and Sutherland Highlanders stationed locally. Their prompt action saved the lives of the McAliskeys. The three gunmen were sentenced to terms ranging from fifteen years to life but the episode left many unanswered questions. Why did the undercover soldiers not act to avert the murder bid? Were they *in situ* because the security services had been tipped off that the McAliskeys were a target that day? It was later established that the murder attempt had been planned in a room above a pub in Lisburn owned by John McMichael, the UDA commander with links to the security services.

A clear pattern emerges from these assassinations and attempted killings. The murderers were skilled, perhaps professional killers, equipped with sophisticated intelligence knowledge about their quarry. They knew the layout of the houses they attacked, and the movements of their victims. They were not random sectarian shootings on the streets of Belfast. What motive links these events? It is unlikely to be proven – or, for that matter, disproved – in the lifetime of the combatants in Ireland's dirty war, but it is at least possible that, baulked of their main prize – Airey Neave's killers – the security services exacted retribution in the way they knew best. By killing the nearest thing the IRSP had to an intellectual leadership, and eliminating the important figure of Ronnie Bunting, the secret state badly disabled one dangerous arm of republicanism. And it is true that neither INLA nor the IRSP was ever the same again. The killings seriously weakened their ability to fight militarily or politically.

The intention was not lost on those who survived the whirlwind of death and it reverberates today. Paul Lyttle, spokesman for the IRSP, is unequivocal. 'We believe that Mrs Thatcher set about revenge for Airey Neave,' he insisted in an interview. 'They were very close friends. Four of the political leadership were assassinated, and there was an attempted assassination on Bernadette McAliskey. That type of operation was almost unheard of in Ireland prior to that. It signalled a change of strategy. These were political assassinations to make this organisation leaderless. We have been hit harder than any other republican organisation by the British. There has always been a vicious intent to crush this organisation. It has taken us ten years, even more, to sort out our act.'

The IRSP want an independent public enquiry, on the lines of the Savile Enquiry investigating the events on Bloody Sunday in Londonderry. 'We wish to see these executions investigated,' said Lyttle. 'We believe they were political assassinations.'[18]

His call was aired earlier by the independent intelligence magazine *Lobster*, which in 1985 pieced together the story of the secret state's retribution on the INLA and its supporters. Its investigation concluded that there was not enough evidence to sustain the idea that Thatcher called for a 'blood revenge'. 'Only an official enquiry could achieve that and we are not going to get one. In the end it comes down to our perception of Thatcher, sections of the British state and the intelligence empire. The question is: does the shoe fit?

INLA sources remain convinced that the killings were carried out by what they like to term 'the securocrats': the British intelligence and special armed services. 'We demand that there should be an enquiry,' insisted my masked informant. Citing the more recent deaths of lawyers Pat Finucane and Rosemary Nelson, he added: 'It is still [British] policy as far as we can see.'

18

The End of the Trail

The murder of Ian Gow by the Provisional IRA in July 1990 bore great similarities to the assassination of Airey Neave. Once again, a bomb was placed beneath an unsuspecting politician's car which exploded, killing him instantly. Gow had been very much Airey Neave Mark Two: a fervent supporter of Margaret Thatcher in her bid to unseat Edward Heath and an uncompromising Unionist who resigned ministerial office at the Treasury in protest at Thatcher's signing of the Anglo-Irish Agreement in late 1985. He felt it gave the Irish government undue influence in the affairs of the province. Gow continued to fight the Agreement, taking the campaign outside parliament with the creation, with his ally (and Neave's close colleague) Sir John Biggs-Davidson, of the organisation Friends of the Union. This body continued to propagate Neave's policies for a decade after his death.

Gow's murder was 'as brutal, and as shameful' as that of Airey Neave, said their mutual friend Patrick Cosgrave. Gow shared Neave's unyielding nature and would never give up in any fight he judged necessary. 'The Prime Minister was right when she said even if Ian knew what was going to happen to him he would never have counselled appeasement. He would want the fight against terrorists to continue unabated, and that would be his final testament,' Cosgrave wrote. 'Ian Gow would never give in.'[1] Gow's death also robbed Thatcher of the man she trusted most after Neave. Alan Clark confided to his diary on 30 July: 'Now they've got her two closest confidants, Airey and Ian.' After the second blow, Thatcher's grip on reality diminished. Republican terrorism may not have succeeded in killing her but it robbed her of the two people on whom she had most relied.

Another factor united the two in death: their killers were never found. There is something deeply suspicious about the failure of the authorities to track down the assassins. The security forces had informers working within the republican terror machine. INLA, in particular, was riddled with moles. Colin Wallace says: 'It was strange that INLA did it. Of all the terrorist groups, it was the one most heavily infiltrated. It was very small. Virtually everything they did was known about by Special Branch.' So why was there no arrest? 'There were very few terrorist incidents that we didn't know who did it. Certainly, by 1973 every morning we used to get intelligence over the last twenty-four hours. It would list every single incident, and most days you would have the names of the organisations and of the people. Sometimes forty-eight hours would elapse, but within a very short time you knew who was responsible. We had literally the whole of the IRA listed. In Belfast we had them all on one board. From an intelligence point of view, they were all informing on each other. The Provos gave information to people not knowing they were part of the British system.'[2]

Wallace finds it odd that nobody was detained, bearing in mind the significance of Neave, who was not just a British politician but very close to Thatcher. 'It could be argued that because INLA was so heavily infiltrated, the danger of having someone charged may well have brought about a confusion that *the system did not want*' (author's italics). Wallace raised the prospect of embarrassment for the security services, based on the fact that the identity of the loyalists who bombed Dublin in May 1974 and who killed the Miami Showband in July 1975 was 'extremely well known' to the authorities. Four of the key players were working for Special Branch and the intelligence services, he claims. 'They were never touched, and the great danger was that if they had been arrested and turned Queen's evidence, the security authorities would probably have found it very embarrassing.'

Wallace insists: 'I have no doubt that they know who did it. Why they didn't actually proceed with something I just don't know. That is the biggest question of the whole lot. There is no doubt that they – the security authorities – knew. The amount of detail known from 1974 onwards was enormous. That's why I don't accept that we didn't have chapter and verse about who did it and how it was done. I don't think it is credible. I think we do know. But for some reason – it may have been a very good reason – the system didn't move against them. It had to be a very powerful reason, because to say we have arrested and charged these people would have been a tremendous boost to the government at that time. Anybody who achieved that result, their career would have been made.'[3]

But no arrests were made. Nobody was charged. IRSP activists believe that the British government's thirst for revenge was slaked by the murders of the IRSP's top people. Wallace concedes that the security services could make a point by taking out prominent people in the organisation, but argues that in terms of psychological impact it would have been better for the British public to know who planted the bomb, and see them brought to justice. The official file is now closed.

Attempts to open the file since the government's announcement that no one would be prosecuted for Neave's murder have met with stiff official opposition. On 7 July 1987, Ken Livingstone, the new Labour MP for Brent East, broke with parliamentary tradition to make a controversial maiden speech in the Commons. He accused the Thatcher government of being 'ideal recruiting agents for the IRA' and demanded a united Ireland. He denounced the RUC's 'shoot to kill' policy and attacked the Prevention of Terrorism Act. Having thus established his political credentials, and speaking from the safe vantage point of parliamentary privilege, Livingstone unleashed a tirade on the activities of the security services, arraigning the British government for covering up 'acts of treason by MI5 officers' of which ministers were the beneficiaries. He accused the security services of working with the UDF in at least one cross-border raid to assassinate an active member of the IRA. He accused the SAS of acting in cahoots with loyalist terrorists in the killing of the Miami Showband, in order to end a ceasefire negotiated between the IRA and a Labour government because the secret state had rival objectives.

Finally, he turned to Neave. 'It looks increasingly likely that Mr Airey Neave was in touch with some of these officers, and it is certainly the case that Airey Neave delivered a speech that had been—' Here, he was interrupted by a furious Ian Gow, who described the references to Neave as 'deeply offensive'. Maiden speeches are traditionally heard in silence, and the Deputy Speaker, Harold Walker, ruled that Livingstone's remarks were in order. Livingstone continued: 'If Conservative Members are shocked that allegations are made about Airey Neave, they should join with me in demanding a full investigation so that Airey Neave's name can be cleared.' Needless to say, no investigation took place.

What, as Wallace hints, has the establishment got to hide? What is the 'powerful reason' for more than two decades of official silence? It cannot be argued that the trail had gone completely cold. The author was able to make contact with the killers, through intermediaries, with relative ease. There are those in the know still living and working for the republican cause in Ireland. If it is possible to gain, as the author did, fresh insight into the methodology and identity of Airey Neave's assassins, then why have the authorities refused to do so? It looks suspiciously like a cover-up. Colin Wallace believes this to be so. Neave's daughter Marigold is similarly convinced. The inescapable conclusion is that, for reasons of their own, the security services and their political allies do not want the full story of Airey Neave and his co-conspirators ever to become public knowledge. Even at this distance, it would be too damaging. Perhaps the truth about the retributive killings is the cause. More likely, the involvement of the security services in the plot against Wilson, and their continuing links with people like Neave for at least two years into the Thatcher government, constitute the real reason for closing down the key period of post-war history.

Following approaches in Belfast by the author over a protracted period, contact was made with the IRSP and the INLA which shows that the killers are alive and kicking, but their identity will never be voluntarily surrendered. There has been no amnesty for their crime.

It became clear from the authentic narrative of events from sources in the INLA to the author in March 2001 that Neave had been under close but discreet observation for some time before his assassination. A source described how 'a sympathiser, a professional man', not a member of an Irish republican terrorist cell, but an Englishman 'doing it out of his own resources', had stalked Neave for weeks in early 1979. The INLA, which had broken away from the Official IRA in late 1974, shortly before Neave took the Ulster portfolio, claimed that its operation was a mixture of preparation and opportunism. 'Neave was chosen because of his public pronouncements,' said the masked INLA operative involved in the assassination.[4] 'Our source perceived him as a very, very dangerous person who would inflict hurt and pain on the nationalists of the six counties. He would carry out what he threatened to do. He was deemed to be an ideal target for the INLA to assassinate, to establish itself as a force to be reckoned with.' The paramilitaries boasted that they 'knew everything about him': his pattern of behaviour, how often he went down to his constituency in Abingdon, his social life and his family background. This intelligence had come into their hands soon after the organisation had received considerable shipments of Soviet bloc guns and explosives from Middle East sources.

INLA simply describes the killing as 'an opportunity that came up', but more than events conspired to bring about the death. The INLA had a strategy of recruiting one-off 'volunteers'. They were often middle-class professional men, more mature than the run-of-the-mill foot soldiers who had been active in the Troubles since their early teens. They would not engage in street protests or risky operations, and therefore they would not come to the notice of the security forces. 'The tradition in the south has been that there was a significant minority of middle-class people who support a physical force campaign,' said INLA. 'They would enter and leave the struggle on different occasions. We are basically talking about people like that.'

Three of these 'sleepers' were approached to carry out the Neave action. 'They were only marginally involved at the time, and they have never been involved since,' said INLA. 'A conscious decision was made at the time that the people would never be involved in any other operation. They were only known to a few people in the organisation. They were not activists as such. They were different because they offered stability. It was always something that the organisation was looking for.' The trio was drawn from both north and south of the border. One of them was 'a college graduate', and they were in their thirties. 'From the normal lives they were living, they were in an ideal position to execute the operation, and were asked to do. They also had the ability to travel internationally, without attracting attention.' This was critical to the success of the operation. At the time, INLA did not have active service units *in situ* on the British mainland. The assassins would enter via a third country – presumed to be on the near Continent – with the explosives, carry out the operation and then melt back by the same route into anonymity in Ireland.

According to the INLA source, this is exactly what happened. In the days before the Neave operation, the trio journeyed to London through a third country. The explosives, cut from a larger chunk like a bar of soap, were carried in a perspex container. 'These devices are very straightforward,' INLA added. 'They are very simple things. They had access to more than one. They are a very easy thing to put together.' Prior surveillance had established where Neave's car was normally parked outside his block of flats in Westminster Gardens. A derring-do account of the operation, involving penetration of security at the MPs' underground car park at Westminster, originally put out by INLA, was dismissed to the author as 'a colourful story for the media'. The source continued: 'The device was fitted in the locality of the flat, yes. The car was easily identifiable and it was placed underneath the car on the driver's side with a magnet.' Inside the perspex box was a timer and a phial of mercury with two wires connected to the charge. When the timer expired, the bomb was live, but it would not detonate until the mercury surged down the tube and completed a circuit. 'When the car went up a ramp, it made contact and the explosive went off.'

Neave drove to the Commons as usual that Friday, though it was an unusual day. Parliament was on the point of being dissolved after the Labour government had lost a vote of confidence the night before. The timer was set to expire before Neave's normal time to leave Westminster for his constituency. It was live when he drove up the ramp from the car park; the result was fatal. By then, the bombers had gone. 'They would have been well gone, hours before that,' said INLA. Accounts of the trio returning to Dublin for a back-slapping, huggy party are also incorrect. 'They didn't come straight back to Ireland,' insisted INLA. Even had they done so, no one would have known who to congratulate. However, they did return to resume the conventional lives they had briefly quit. And that, says INLA, is what they are still doing, though they are now in their fifties. 'They had no choice, just to lead a normal life,' asserted the masked source. 'You can lose your life as a result of it [becoming known]. Anonymity was the only safety they had and that was the only reason they could live normal lives.'

But even today, though the prospect of a successful criminal trial is remote, the bombers are not safe from retribution, either at the hands of loyalist paramilitaries or (INLA fears) from covert action by the security services. 'The state would get very little out of it, but the military securocrat establishment would get a lot out of it,' the source continued. 'They would have had retribution for one of theirs being taken out. They have already got some of that but they would get the kudos for getting the people who actually did the operation because Airey Neave was one of them. For that reason, there is no contact any more.' This arrangement is not simply dictated by a desire for secrecy. 'Physical events' would almost certainly follow any disclosure of their identity or whereabouts. Given the passage of time and the very small number of people who know the killers, it is most unlikely that they will be brought to justice. Ministers in Margaret Thatcher's government publicly admitted there is no prospect of a successful prosecution, and Tony Blair's New Labour has not shown the slightest interest in reopening the case.

Yet the Neave affair continues to exercise a fascination, not solely because of the manner of his death but because he represents a bridge between the world of politics and the secret services whence he came. Perhaps the most revealing tribute to his life came from John Biggs-Davidson. 'The Nazis could not kill him,' he has said. 'The Nazis could not break him. The Nazis could not hold him. Now he has fallen to another tyranny, one of terror.' Like Neave, Biggs-Davidson identified militant republicanism with international Communism, in a dark global conspiracy to destroy the British way of life: a tyranny as despicable as Fascism, which manifested itself not only in Irish terrorism but in strikes and the perceived rise of left-wing Labour.

In June 1978, Neave made a speech in which he compared the return of a Labour government with the rise of the Nazis. Both Neave and Biggs-Davidson became involved in the right-wing movements of the 1970s, set up by people like themselves who feared a breakdown of civil order. They saw the authority of the Crown as superior to that of elected politicians like Harold Wilson and even Edward Heath, their own party leader. According to Northern Ireland security sources, Neave never severed his ties with MI6. And like most intelligence officers he saw his first loyalty as to the Crown. Conveniently, in such circles, this loyalty took whatever form the secret state wished it to take.

None of this double life featured in the obituaries to Neave. In the state of shock engendered by the first murder in the Palace of Westminster since 1812, the tributes were fulsome. The *Daily Telegraph* described him as 'that best type of public man who is inspired by duty rather than ambition to undertake the most difficult tasks' whose death was a tragic loss to his family, friends and country. Mistakenly blaming the Provisional IRA as his killers, the paper said he was murdered because they saw him as their most clear-sighted and formidable opponent.

Margaret Thatcher expressed her grief in her parliamentary tribute on 2 April. Still apparently stunned, she disclosed to the House that Neave had asked for the Northern Ireland portfolio: 'He loved it, felt that he was beginning to understand the sensitivities of the people, felt he had a contribution to make, and wanted to continue with it,' she insisted.

Neave visited Ulster regularly during his four years as Shadow Secretary of State, and occasionally on a social basis, as he did with his wife Diana in May 1976 to attend the wedding of Louise, daughter of Sir Robin and Lady Kinahan, at Templepatrick. He fitted naturally into the circles of the Unionist hegemony that had ruled the province since the partition of Ireland. Viewing Irish politics from that vantage point, it was not surprising that he took Conservative policy away from Edward Heath's cautious acceptance of power-sharing between nationalists and Unionists and towards closer integration of Ulster into the United Kingdom, underpinned by a militarist attitude towards republican terrorism. Equally unsurprisingly, this strategy brought him into direct conflict with successive Irish governments, who found his thinking on the great issue of the day shallow and badly informed. Relations between Dublin and Thatcher and her Shadow Ulster Secretary soured as time went by, culminating in Neave's outspoken remark in the Commons in January 1978 that 'the actions of a neighbouring state are becoming intolerable'.

Some commentators believed that Neave might not have been appointed Northern Ireland Secretary. His health had been weakened by his heart attack in 1959, and it was noted that he moved slowly and deliberately, as if wary of his condition. Neave was a quiet spoken, reserved man, who rarely shared his thoughts. The seasoned observer Conor O'Clery of the *Irish Times* commented: 'In the House of Commons, where attitudes towards Ireland do not form the basis for judgements of character, he was considered to have the dignity and manners – and the intellectual limitations – of an old-style Conservative.'[5] Neave was also sensitive, and felt deeply hurt by the sharp attacks on his policy towards Ulster, particularly from politicians in the south. But he was also steadfast, obstinate even, in the pursuit of what he believed to be right. In a policy arena where there was no shortage of stubbornness among the competing interests, obstinacy was not the quality most in demand. As much as the office he held, it marked him out as a potential target. Republican paramilitaries, particularly the INLA, whose active service unit killed him, also feared that, uniquely among British politicians ruling Northern Ireland, Neave understood the mentality of 'the men behind the wire' and their critical importance in the armed struggle.

Though he did not live to implement his twin-track approach of political integration and military defeat of the IRA, Neave's influence continued to be felt after his assassination. The failure of the authorities to find his assassins frustrated Thatcher, and her thwarted wrath has been identified as the moving force behind British intransigence in the face of the 1981 hunger strikes. Ironically, her attitude propelled militant republicanism into orthodox politics, with results that have undermined moderate Unionism and thrust Sinn Fein into the corridors of power. On a more controversial level, the establishment's determination to punish Neave's killers is widely held among nationalists to have prompted a campaign of secret service counter-assassinations of this operation still rankles today as the scandal of the 'forgotten victims' of the Troubles. Neave's guiding philosophy throughout his career informed his political views, and his policy towards Northern Ireland that eventually claimed his life. He saw the people of Eastern Europe as imprisoned in an evil Soviet Empire, and the British population of Ulster threatened with a similar regime. His was not an unusual view of the world. He grew up in a generation of boys who devoured John Buchan, whose characters, like the country doctor Tom Greenslade, a veteran of the First World War and Central Asian intrigue, could denounce the new generation of hard, untameable 'moral imbeciles' found among 'young Bolshevik Jews, among the young entry of the wilder Communist sects, and very notably among the sullen murderous hobbledehoys in Ireland.'[6]

Unlike Buchan, Neave lived out the boyhood fantasy. At Eton and Oxford he learned to fight for King and Country, when others preferred to wallow in what he saw as half-baked, self-indulgent Marxism. He experienced the vile, ruinous nature of Fascism at first hand, before the war, and fought it for six years across Occupied Europe and in the court room of Nuremberg. And when the struggle took a different, if long expected turn, against Communist expansionism, he was a ready volunteer. It may be argued that he valued his own liberty so much that he was prepared to take extreme measures to ensure the freedom of others.

But why did he imagine that he knew better than the rest? Neave was not a particularly gifted politician. It is difficult to believe that he would have risen to a post in a Conservative Cabinet. In the Commons of the late 1950s, Tory MPs with a good war behind them were still the norm, rather than the exception. Yet among that generation, he has left the greatest indelible mark on political history by riding an inner conviction that his grasp was somehow superior. Furthermore, he felt he understood human nature better than others, and should turn that comprehension to advantage. In short, he was a spook who knew, and acted on his beliefs and loyalties. He was not alone in this self-assurance. It is the stock in trade of the spy. Although he was not an orthodox MI6 officer, he remained close to the security services all his life. He may have been an elected politician in a democracy, but he shared the misgivings about the world around him that were expressed most clearly by George Kennedy Young, who talked of the spy as the 'main guardian of intellectual integrity' in a world threatened by lawlessness, disregard of international contract, cruelty and corruption.

Neave never fitted into any simple category. John Ranelagh thought him a 'very intelligent, hard-headed man' with a great deal of charm and capable of a high degree of personal loyalty. 'He was much tougher than he looked, and was often under-estimated.' He was in the party's mainstream, not involved in ideological battles. 'He was loved by many, and liked by most who met him. He had a reputation for operating secretly and put this trait to full use.'[7] This was most clearly evident in his campaign to supplant Edward Heath and ensure the succession of a right-minded leader in the shape of Margaret Thatcher. He could scarcely have foreseen that her impact on domestic and inter-national politics should be so far-reaching, or that she (despite being 'a Unionist at heart') would negotiate the 1985 Anglo-Irish Agreement that reopened the road to power-sharing in Ulster. Such a step would have been anathema to Neave, as it was to his friend Ian Gow.

However, it could also be argued that Neave's belief in the paramountcy of liberty did not extend to the fundamental freedoms of employment, housing and votes denied to many people in the minority Catholic community in Northern Ireland before the social upheavals of the late 1960s. Coming late to the crisis, six bloody years into a near civil war, he took a profoundly militarist view, one based on the inner conviction of a lifelong involvement with the security services and their self-appointed guardianship of the Crown's interests, that armed republicanism had to be crushed and the Union retained. INLA sources confirmed their fear that he might have succeeded in this enterprise, admitting: 'He would have been very successful at that job. He would have brought the armed struggle to its knees.'[8] But there are limits to the military containment of nationalism. The same sources pointed out: 'It has also been proved that there is a resilience to resist these things. If he did take draconian measures there would have been a reaction. If they [the security forces] had moved to close them [Provisional IRA and INLA] down in a military sense, they could do that.' It was never done, they argue, because of the political reaction at home and abroad. And today, power-sharing is broadly accepted as the key to Northern Ireland's future.

Therefore, did Neave's political career end in failure, in accordance with Enoch Powell's famous dictum? The province has enjoyed years of ceasefire by the Provos and, more reluctantly, by the INLA. In September 2001 the Provisional IRA began the process of decommissioning its armoury. This step was sufficient to revive the stalled peace process in Northern Ireland and restore the power-sharing executive at Stormont. However, Unionist opinion remained deeply divided about republican motives and an uneasy stand-off ensued. It is unclear what INLA intend to do with its weaponry, but unlikely that its much smaller arsenal will be 'put beyond use'.

But Neave's killers are still in the shadows. 'INLA has not gone away. It still exists and is still capable of carrying out operations like that [the Neave assassination] if it chooses. But obviously people will weigh up the consequences because of past experience,' said my INLA sources. The INLA 'believes that the circumstances for armed struggle no longer exist at the present moment. But things could change in the future.'

Does that ambivalent, and rather ominous, assessment negate Neave's career? Only on the most casual reading of Powell's oft-misunderstood axiom. Powell actually argued that 'all political lives, unless they are cut off in mid-stream at a happy juncture, end in failure because that is the nature of politics and human affairs'. Judged by that precept, Neave's life was a success. It was violently cut short, not in mid-stream and certainly not felicitously, but after an outstanding intervention that permanently changed the political landscape: the inauguration of Thatcherism. No final judgement can be reached on his Ulster strategy, for the obvious reason that he did not live to put it into effect. It is an index of his significance, however, that he had to be murdered to ensure that he did not. Less attractive is the 'spook' side to Neave's life. He loved the clandestine life and it tainted his politics. It also robbed him of a soldier's death.

Apart from his political legacy, Neave also bequeathed a compassionate endowment. Friends rushed to set up the Airey Neave Memorial Trust, which attracted wide, cross-party support. For more than twenty years, it has dispensed scholarships for the study of issues dear to his heart, including the problems of terrorism. Neave himself left only £55,000 in his will, published the month after his beloved Diana was made a life peer. Lady Airey died on 27 November 1992, aged seventy-three, almost forty years after her marriage to the quiet young officer whose life changed so many others. She had continued his work for more than a decade, evoking widespread admiration for her commitment. They are buried together beneath a modest headstone in the cemetery at Hinton Waldrist, bearing the Neave family motto: *Sola Proba Quae Honesta.*

References

Chapter 1

1. Interview with David Healy, 25 June 1996.
2. *Belfast Telegraph*, 31 March 1979.
3. Dedication in *Margaret Thatcher, Prime Minister*, Arrow Books, 1979.
4. Margaret Thatcher, *The Path to Power*, HarperCollins, 1995, p. 289.
5. Donald Hamilton-Hill, *SOE Assignment*, New English Library, 1975, pp. 13–14.
6. Interview with Stephen Dorril, 24 August 2000.
7. Ibid.
8. Interview with Roger Bolton, 27 October 1999.
9. George Kennedy Young, *No Other Choice: The Autobiography of George Blake*, Jonathan Cape, 1990, p. 168.
10. Richard Deacon, *'C': A Biography of Sir Maurice Oldfield*, Macdonald, 1984, p. 221.
11. *Irish Times*, 31 March 1979.
12. Interview with Marigold Webb, 12 January 2000.

Chapter 2

1. Interview with Julius Neave, 26 June 1999.
2. Interview with Marigold Webb, 22 January 2000.

3. *The Postmaster*, Merton College magazine, 1990.
4. Frank McLynn, *Fitzroy Maclean*, John Murray, 1992, p. 7.
5. Airey Neave, *Nuremberg*, Coronet Books, 1980, p. 19.
6. Ibid.
7. Ibid., p. 20.
8. Airey Neave, *They Have Their Exits*, Coronet Books, 1970, p. 19.

Chapter 3

1. *The Postmaster*, Merton College magazine, 1998.
2. Airey Neave, *They Have Their Exits*, Coronet Books, 1970, p. 18.
3. Michael Glover, *The Fight for the Channel Ports*, Leo Cooper, 1985.
4. Airey Neave, *They Have Their Exits*, p. 18.
5. Airey Neave, *The Flames of Calais*, Coronet Books, 1974, p. 106.
6. Michael Glover, p. 108.
7. Airey Neave, *The Flames of Calais*, p. 241.
8. Ibid., p. 243.
9. Michael Glover, p. 63.

Chapter 4

1. Airey Neave, *They Have Their Exits*, Coronet Books, 1970, p. 25.
2. Airey Neave, *Saturday at MI9*, Hodder & Stoughton, 1969, p. 27.
3. Ibid., p. 33n.
4. Airey Neave, *They Have Their Exits*, p. 43.
5. Ibid., p. 47.
6. Ibid., p. 52.

7. Airey Neave, *Saturday at MI9*, p. 31.
8. Airey Neave, *They Have Their Exits*, p. 60.
9. Ibid., p. 63.

Chapter 5

1. Reinhold Eggers, *Colditz: The German Story*, Robert Hale, 1991, p. 24.
2. Ibid., p. 19.
3. Airey Neave, *They Have Their Exits*, Coronet Books, 1970, p. 67.
4. Ibid., p. 71.
5. J. Ellison Platt, *A Padre in Colditz: The Diary of J. Ellison Platt*, Hodder & Stoughton, 1978, p. 109.
6. Interview with Lord Campbell of Alloway, 12 August 1999.
7. Interview with Ken Lockwood, 21 August 1999.
8. Reinhold Eggers, p. 64.
9. J. Ellison Platt, p. 134.
10. Airey Neave, *They Have Their Exits*, pp. 71–2.
11. Ibid., p. 87.
12. J. Ellison Platt, p. 134.
13. Airey Neave, *They Have Their Exits*, p. 89.
14. Reinhold Eggers, p. 48.

Chapter 6

1. Reinhold Eggers, *Colditz: The German Story*, Robert Hale, 1991, p. 69.
2. Interview with Toni Luteyn, 15 November 1999.
3. Airey Neave, *They Have Their Exits*, Coronet Books, 1970, p. 86.
4. J. Ellison Platt, *A Padre in Colditz: The Diary of J. Ellison Platt*,

Hodder & Stoughton, 1978, p. 151.

5. Airey Neave, *They Have Their Exits*, p. 78.
6. Interview with Toni Luteyn, 15 November 1999.
7. Ibid.
8. J. Ellison Platt, p. 163.
9. Interview with Toni Luteyn, 15 November 1999.
10. Airey Neave, *They Have Their Exits*, p. 95.
11. Interview with Toni Luteyn, 15 November 1999.
12. Ibid.
13. Ibid.
14. MOST SECRET, M19/S/PG (G) 676, War Office 208/3242, 173–75, Public Record Office.
15. Interview with Toni Luteyn, 15 November 1999.
16. Airey Neave, *They Have Their Exits*, p. 107.

Chapter 7

1. Interview with Toni Luteyn, 15 November 1999.
2. Airey Neave, *Saturday at MI9*, Hodder & Stoughton, 1969, p. 41.
3. Ibid., p. 47.
4. Airey Neave, *They Have Their Exits*, Coronet Books, 1970, p. 122.
5. Ibid., p. 141.

Chapter 8

1. Airey Neave, *They Have Their Exits*, Coronet Books, 1970, p. 141.
2. Ibid., p. 155.
3. *Observer*, 27 October 1974.
4. Ibid.

5. Airey Neave, *Saturday at MI9*, Hodder & Stoughton, 1969, p. 82.
6. Ibid., p. 127.
7. Ibid., p. 131.
8. Ibid., p. 138.
9. Ibid., p. 163.

Chapter 9

1. Airey Neave, *Saturday at MI9*, Hodder & Stoughton, 1969, p. 231.
2. Ibid., p. 264.
3. Peter Baker, *My Testament*, John Calder, 1955.
4. Ibid., p. 102.
5. Airey Neave, *Saturday at MI9*, p. 277.
6. Peter Baker, p. 107.
7. J.M. Langley, *Fight Another Day*, Collins, 1974, p. 219.
8. Airey Neave, *Saturday at MI9*, p. 279.
9. J.M. Langley, p. 230.
10. Peter Baker, p. 131.
11. Airey Neave, *Saturday at MI9*, p. 298.
12. Ibid., p. 316.
13. J.M. Langley, p. 245.

Chapter 10

1. Airey Neave, *Nuremberg*, Coronet Books, 1980, p. 46.
2. Sir John Wheeler-Bennett, *Friends, Enemies and Sovereigns*, Macmillan, 1976, p. 32.
3. Airey Neave, *Nuremberg*, p. 138.
4. Albert Speer, *Inside the Third Reich*, Macmillan, 1970, p. 510.
5. Airey Neave, *Nuremberg*, p. 199.

6.   Ibid., p. 250.
7.   Ibid., p. 254.
8.   Bonnie Kine Scott (ed.), *Selected Letters of Rebecca West*, Yale University Press, 2000.
9.   Victoria Glendinning, *Rebecca West: A Life*, Weidenfeld & Nicolson, 1987, p. 181.
10.   Airey Neave, *Nuremberg*, p. 258. Author's italics.
11.   Ibid., p. 314.

Chapter 11

1.   Interview with Lord Lawton, 2 August 1999.
2.   Interview with Sir Edward du Cann, 28 June 2000.
3.   *Middlesex County Times*, 27 May 1950.
4.   Ibid., 8 July 1950.
5.   *Middlesex County Times and Gazette*, 27 January 1951.
6.   *Middlesex Times*, 18 August 1951.
7.   Interview with Michael Elliott, 28 October 1999.
8.   *North Berkshire Herald and Advertiser*, 6 June 1952.

Chapter 12

1.   *Hansard*, 1 March 1954, cols 887–92.
2.   John Campbell, *Edward Heath: A Biography*, Jonathan Cape, 2000, p. 101.
3.   Morrison Halcrow, *Keith Joseph: A Single Mind*, Hodder & Stoughton, 1989, p. 88.
4.   Edward Heath, *The Course of My Life*, Hodder & Stoughton, 1998, p. 531.
5.   Interview with Sir Edward Heath, 3 October 1999.

Chapter 13

1. Interview with Brian Mares, 10 July 1999.
2. *Hansard*, 23 March 1962, col. 720.
3. Stephen Dorril and Robin Ramsay, *Smear! Wilson and the Secret State*, Fourth Estate, 1991, p. 35.
4. *Hansard*, 24 February 1964, col. 117.
5. Andrew Denham and Mark Garnett, *Keith Joseph*, Acument, 2001, p. 148.
6. *Hansard*, 27 April 1966, cols 873–4.
7. Ibid., 3 August 1966, cols 578–82.
8. Ibid., 16 February 1968, cols 107–70.
9. Ibid., oral answers, 2 February 1970, cols 27, 28.
10. Airey Neave, in Tricia Murray, *Margaret Thatcher*, W.H. Allen, 1978, p. 127.
11. *Hansard*, 16 November 1970, col. 860.
12. John Campbell, *Edward Heath: A Biography*, Jonathan Cape, 2000, p. 653.

Chapter 14

1. Interview with Sir Edward du Cann, 28 June 2000.
2. Ibid.
3. Morrison Halcrow, *Keith Joseph: A Single Mind*, Hodder & Stoughton, 1989, p. 88.
4. John Ranelagh, *Thatcher's People*, HarperCollins, 1991, p. 126.
5. Interview with Sir Edward du Cann, 28 June 2000.
6. Ibid.
7. John Ranelagh, p. 136.
8. Ibid., p. 140.
9. James Prior, *A Balance of Power*, Hamish Hamilton, 1986, p. 99.
10. Nicholas Wapshott and George Brock, *Thatcher*, Futura, 1983, p. 126.

11. Interview with Sir William Shelton, 18 July 1999.
12. John Campbell, *Edward Heath: A Biography*, Jonathan Cape, 2000, p. 666.
13. Tricia Murray, *Margaret Thatcher*, W.H. Allen, 1978, pp. 127–9.
14. John Campbell, p. 669.
15. Patrick Cosgrave, *Margaret Thatcher, Prime Minister*, Arrow Books, 1978, p. 71.
16. John Campbell, p. 673.
17. Ibid. p. 670.
18. Margaret Thatcher, *The Path to Power*, HarperCollins, 1995, p. 289.

Chapter 15

1. Peter Wright correspondence quoted in David Leigh, *The Wilson Plot*, Pantheon, 1988, p. 224.
2. Ibid.
3. Ken Livingstone, *Livingstone's Labour: A Programme for the Nineties*, Unwin, 1989, p. 59.
4. Stephen Dorril and Robin Ramsay, *Smear! Wilson and the Secret State*, Grafton Books, 1992, p. 379n.
5. Ibid., p. 283.
6. *The Times*, 29 July 1974.
7. Stephen Dorril and Robin Ramsay, p. 372.
8. Ibid., p. 283.
9. *Irish Times*, 19 February 1975.
10. *Belfast Telegraph*, 19 February 1975.
11. *Irish Times*, 13 May 1975.
12. Letter, 25 November 1988.
13. Stephen Dorril and Robin Ramsay, p. 288.
14. Garret FitzGerald, *All in a Life*, Macmillan, 1991, p. 286.
15. Quoted in Paul Foot, *Who Framed Colin Wallace?*, Macmillan, 1989, p. 11.

16. *Lobster*, 21, p. 17.
17. Quoted in Paul Foot, pp. 50–51.
18. *Lobster*, 21, p. 18.
19. Interview with Colin Wallace, *Red Pepper*, January 1997.
20. Interview with Brain Crozier, 14 March 2001.
21. Quoted in Paul Foot, p. 121.
22. *New Statesman*, 20 February 1981.
23. Tony Benn, *The End of an Era: Diaries 1980–90*, Hutchinson, 1992, p. 90.
24. Patrick Cosgrave, *Margaret Thatcher, Prime Minister*, Arrow Books, 1978, p. 225.

Chapter 16

1. Jack Holland and Henry McDonald, *INLA: Deadly Divisions*, Poulbeg, 1994, p. 130.
2. Quoted in ibid., p. 137.
3. Martin Dillon, *The Dirty War*, Hutchinson, 1990, p. 283.
4. Ibid., p. 287.
5. Ibid., p. 139.
6. Margaret Thatcher, *The Path to Power*, HarperCollins, 1995, p. 434.

Chapter 17

1. *Belfast Telegraph*, 7 April 1979.
2. Ibid., 16 June 1979.
3. Roger Bolton, *Death on the Rock*, W.H. Allen, 1990, pp. 307–13.
4. Ibid., p. 49.
5. Quoted in Jack Holland and Henry McDonald, *INLA: Deadly Divisions*, Poulbeg, 1994, p. 243.
6. Briefing, 24 March 2001.

7. Patrick Cosgrave, *The Lives of Enoch Powell*, Pan Books, 1990, p. 457.
8. *Observer*, 19 October 1986.
9. Kevin Cahill to author, 27 February 2000.
10. Gerald James, *In the Public Interest*, Warner Books, 1996, p. 47.
11. Interview with Gerald James, 27 October 1999.
12. Raymond Gilmour, *Dead Ground*, Warner Books, 1998, p. 105.
13. Briefing, 24 March 2001.
14. Raymond Murray, *The SAS in Ireland*, Mercier Press, 1990, p. 259.
15. Quoted in Martin Dillon, *The Dirty War*, Hutchinson, 1990, p. 291.
16. Ibid., pp. 305–6.
17. Ibid., p. 209.
18. Interview with Paul Lyttle, 17 November 2000.

Chapter 18

1. *Independent*, 31 July 1990.
2. Interview with Colin Wallace, 8 February 2001.
3. Ibid.
4. Briefing, 24 March 2001, see Preface.
5. *Irish Times*, 31 March 1979.
6. John Buchan, *The Three Hostages*, Wordsworth, 1995, p. 16.
7. John Ranelagh, *Thatcher's People*, HarperCollins, 1991, pp. 134–5.
8. Briefing, 24 March 2001.

Illustration Credits

Illustration of Neave's escape from Colditz prison: Miles Smith-Morris.

Photographs reproduced by kind permission of the following: Camera Press; Colditz Magazine; the Daily Mail; the Daily Express; the Daily Telegraph; The Estate of Airey Neave; Hulton Getty; Popperfoto; Press Association.

All reasonable efforts have been made by the author and the publisher to trace the copyright holders of the material quoted in this book. In the event that the author or the publisher are contacted by any of the untraceable copyright holders after the publication of this book, the author and the publisher will endeavour to rectify the position accordingly.

Index